The International Civil Service

Legal Aspects of International Organizations

VOLUME 64

The titles published in this series are listed at *brill.com/laio*

The International Civil Service

Redefining Its Independence

By

Alexandre Tavadian

BRILL | NIJHOFF

LEIDEN | BOSTON

Library of Congress Cataloging-in-Publication Data

Names: Tavadian, Alexandre, author.
Title: The international civil service : redefining its independence / by Alexandre Tavadian.
Description: Leiden ; Boston : Brill/Nijhoff, 2024. | Series: Legal aspects of international organizations, 0924-4883 ; volume 64 | Includes bibliographical references and index. | Summary: "This book explores the independence of international civil servants across various intergovernmental institutions. With rich historical insights and in-depth analysis, Tavadian uncovers the complex evolution of this independence, from its early days to contemporary challenges and practices"– Provided by publisher.
Identifiers: LCCN 2024026427 (print) | LCCN 2024026428 (ebook) | ISBN 9789004704589 (hardback) | ISBN 9789004704596 (ebook)
Subjects: LCSH: International officials and employees. | International officials and employees–Legal status, laws, etc. | International agencies–Privileges and immunities. | International organizations.
Classification: LCC KZ5270 .T38 2024 (print) | LCC KZ5270 (ebook) | DDC 331.7/95–dc23/eng/20240614
LC record available at https://lccn.loc.gov/2024026427
LC ebook record available at https://lccn.loc.gov/2024026428

Typeface for the Latin, Greek, and Cyrillic scripts: "Brill". See and download: brill.com/brill-typeface.

ISSN 0924-4883
ISBN 978-90-04-70458-9 (hardback)
ISBN 978-90-04-70459-6 (e-book)
DOI 10.1163/9789004704596

This book is printed on acid-free paper and produced in a sustainable manner.

To my wife, my greatest supporter and best friend,
To my children, who fill my heart with joy every day
To my parents and brother, who never stopped believing in me

Contents

Acknowledgements

This book would not have been possible without the support of Professors Niels Blokker and Brian McGarry. I felt privileged to have two exceptional legal minds by my side throughout this intellectually rewarding journey. Their wisdom and wealth of experience were inspirational. I was impressed by the breadth and depth of comments and recommendations they gracefully provided for each chapter. Please accept my sincere gratitude for your outstanding help.

I am indebted to my fellow international civil servants practising international institutional law in various intergovernmental organisations who kindly agreed to share with me the internal policies, practices, and, in some cases, challenges of their IGOs. More specifically, I would like to extend my thanks to Andres Munoz, Director of Legal Affairs of ACO-NATO; Felipe Rojas Ceballos, Principal Legal Advisor of the International Bureau of Weights and Measures; Jasmine Begum, Regional Director of Legal and Governance Affairs of ASEAN; Giuseppina De Marco, Assistant General Counsel at IDLO; Aleksandr Kuzmenko, Head of Legal Department of the Organisation for International Carriage by Rail; Teimuraz Antelava, Senior Legal Officer at IDLO and former Legal Advisor of Black Sea Economic Cooperation Organization; Nikolaj Gube, Deputy Head Legal and Institutional Affairs of the European Southern Observatory; Darius Campbell, Secretary of the North East Atlantic Fisheries Commission; and many others who expressly asked to remain anonymous.

Finally, my profound appreciation goes to my wife for her endless encouragement and wise counsel throughout this project. I would also like to thank my children for their understanding and patience. I would not have made it without my family's unwavering support over the past few years.

Tables and Diagrams

Tables

Diagrams

Biography

Alexandre Tavadian is a Canadian national. He holds an LL.B. from the University of Montreal, a master's degree in public international law from the University of Geneva, a master's degree in administrative law from the University of Montreal, and a Ph.D. in international law from Leiden Law School of Leiden University. Alexandre currently works as the Principal Legal Advisor of a large NATO agency headquartered in Luxembourg. Before joining NATO, he was a Senior Legal Officer at UNHCR in Thailand and Kenya. He also worked as a lawyer for the United Nations Secretariat in Lebanon and Kenya. Alexandre began his legal career as Legal Counsel in the Federal Department of Justice Canada. Alexandre is a seasoned litigator, having appeared before several national and international courts and tribunals. He is the Chair of the International Maritime Organization's (IMO) and World Customs Organization's (WCO) Staff Appeals Boards. He is also a Senior Lecturer at the United Nations Institute for Training and Research (UNITAR).

He is the author of articles and textbooks, the most recent of which is titled "United Nations Law, Politics, and Practice".

Disclaimer

While all care was taken, the responsibility for any errors or omissions and all views expressed herein remain with the author and cannot and should not be attributed to any organisation or institution I am affiliated with, including the United Nations and NATO.

Table of Cases

Jurisprudence of International and Arbitral Courts and Tribunal

Applicability of Article VI, Section 22, of the Convention on the Privileges and Immunities of the United Nations, Advisory Opinion, [1989] ICJ Rep 177

Beer and Regan v. Germany, [1995] Application no 28934/95 (ECHR)

Certain expenses of the United Nations (Article 17, paragraph 2, of the Charter), Advisory Opinion, [1962] ICJ Rep 151

Chapman v. Belgium, [2013] Application no 39619/06 (ECHR)

Competence of the ILO to Regulate Incidentally the Personal Work of the Employer, (1926) PCIJ (Ser B) No 13

Cristiani v. Italian Latin-American Institute, (November 25, 1985), [1992] 87 ILR 21 (ECHR)

Difference Relating to Immunity from Legal Process of a Special Rapporteur of the Commission on Human Rights, Advisory Opinion, [1999] ICJ Rep 62

Effect of awards of compensation made by the United Nations Administrative Tribunal, Advisory Opinion, [1954] ICJ Rep 47

European Molecular Biology Laboratory v. Federal Republic of Germany, Award of 29 June 1990, 105 ILR 1

Gasparini v. Italy and Belgium, [2003] Application No. 10750/03 (ECHR)

Interpretation of the Agreement of 25 March 1951 between the WHO and Egypt, Advisory Opinion, [1980] ICJ Rep 73

Judgment No. 2867 of the Administrative Tribunal of the International Labour Organization upon a Complaint Filed against the International Fund for Agricultural Development, Advisory Opinion, [2012] ICJ Rep 10

Jurisdictional Immunities of the State (Germany v. Italy: Greece intervening), Judgment, [2012] ICJ Rep 99

Jurisdiction of the European Commission of the Danube, (1927) PCIJ (Ser B) No 14

Klausecker v. Germany, [2015] Application No. 415/07 (Judgement on the Merits of 29 January 2015) (ECHR)

Legality of the Threat or Use by a State of Nuclear Weapons, Advisory Opinion, [1996] ICJ Rep 66

North Sea Continental Shelf, Separate Opinion of Judge Fouad Ammoun, [1969] ICJ Rep 3

Perez v. Germany, [2015] Application No. 15521/08 (ECHR)

Postal Administration of Turkey v. Postal Administration of Syria (1960) 23 *International Law Reports* 596 (arbitration by the International Postal Union)

Prince Hans-Adam II of Liechtenstein v. Germany, [2001] Application no 42527/98 (ECHR)
Reiniera Charlotte Brouerius van Nidek v. Inspecteur des Registratie en Successie, preliminary ruling of 3 July 1974, Case 7/74, ECR 1974, (Part II) ECLI:EU:C:1974:73
Reparation for injuries suffered in the service of the United Nations, Advisory Opinion, I.C.J. Rep. 1949, p. 174
Staatssecretaris van Financiën v. Velker International Oil Company Ltd NV, C-185/89 (CJEU) (1990)
Stichting Mothers of Srebrenica v. The Netherlands, Judgement of 11 June 2013, Application No. 65542/12 (ECHR)
Waite and Kennedy v. Germany, Judgement (Merits) of 18 February 1999, Application No. 26083/94 (ECHR)

Jurisprudence of International Administrative Tribunals

A. v. ICC, [2018] Judgment No. 4003 (ILOAT)
Abu Al Asal v. Secretary-General of the United Nations, UNDT/2020/123 (UNDT)
A.E. v FAO, [2016] Judgement No. 3593 (ILOAT)
AF v. Joint Force Training Centre, (2015) AT-J(2015)1044 (NATO AT)
A.J. v. IBRD, [2009] Judgement No. 389 (WBAT)
Adriantseheno v. Secretary-General of the United Nations, 2021-UNAT-1146/Corr.1 (UNAT)
Akello v. Secretary-General of the United Nations, 2013-UNAT-336 (UNAT)
Awoyemi (In re), [1998] Judgement No. 1756 (ILOAT)
Ballo (In re), [1972] Judgement No. 191 (ILOAT).
Banaj v. Secretary-General of the United Nations, UNDT/2022/060 (UNDT)
Bancroft v. Secretary-General of the United Nations, [1953] Judgment 35 (UNaT)
Basenko v. Secretary-General of the United Nations, UNDT/2010/145 (UNDT) affirmed by the United Nations Appeals Tribunal in 2011-UNAT-139
Bekele v. Secretary-General of the United Nations, UNDT/2010/175 (UNDT) affirmed by the United Nations Appeals Tribunal in 2012-UNAT-190
Bel Ghazi v WHO, [1996] Judgement No. 1475 (ILOAT)
Benamar v. Secretary-General of the United Nations, 2017-UNAT-797 (UNAT)
Bernstein (In re), [1955] Judgement No. 21 (ILOAT)
Bertucci v Secretary-General of the United Nations, 2010-UNAT-062 (UNAT)
Bissell v. Secretary-General of the UN, UNDT/2020/084 (UNDT)
B. K.-M. v WHO, [2011] Judgement No. 2973 (ILOAT)
C.C. v IAEA, [2014] Judgement No. 3412 (ILOAT)

C.E.S. v WHO, [2007] Judgement No. 2642 (ILOAT)
Chadsey (In re), [1968] Judgement No. 122 (ILOAT)
Clark & Gelbert v. Secretary-General of the United Nations, UNDT/2013/091 (UNDT)
Commission of the European Communities v. Édith Cresson, Case No. C-432/04, ECLI:EU:C:2006:455 (CJEU)
Connolly v Commission, [1999] ECR-SC I-A-87 and II-463, Court of First Instance of the European Communities (First Chamber) of 19 May 1999 in Joined Cases T-34/96 and T-163/96, affirmed in European Court Reports 2001 I-01611, ECLI:EU:C:2001:127
Conteh v. Secretary-General of the United Nations, 2021-UNAT 1171 (UNAT)
Dalgamouni v. Secretary-General of the United Nations, UNDT/2016/094 (UNDT)
Dauchy v. Secretary-General of the United Nations, [1990] Judgement No. 492 (UNaT)
Delaunay v. Registrar of the International Court of Justice, 2019-UNAT-939 (UNAT)
Diop v. Secretary-General of the United Nations, Judgment No. UNDT/2012/029 (UNDT)
Dispert and Hoe v. Secretary-General of the International Maritime Organization, 2019-UNAT-958 (UNAT)
Dodi (In re), [1991] Judgement No. 1061 (ILOAT)
Duberg (In re), [1955] Judgement No. 17 (ILOAT)
Eldridge v. Secretary-General of the United Nations, [1953] Judgment 32 (UNaT)
Elveson v. Secretary-General of the United Nations, Judgment 36 (UNaT)
Erefa v. Secretary-General of the United Nations, UNDT/2021/109 (UNDT)
F.Q. v. IFC, [2020] Judgement 638 (WBAT)
Fernandez v. Inter-American Development Bank, [2011] Judgement No. 74 (IDB AT)
Fichtner v. Commission of the European Communities, European Court Reports 2003 I-A-00007, Case T-75/00, ECLI:EU:T:2003:9
Froma (In re), [1955] Judgement No. 22 (ILOAT)
G.N. v. IBRD, [2022] Judgement No. 667 (WBAT)
Galbraith v. Secretary-General of the United Nations, UNDT/2013/102 (UNDT)
Gaskins v. Secretary-General of the United Nations, Judgment No. UNDT/2010/119 (UNDT)
Gisage v. Secretary-General of the United Nations, UNDT/2020/121 (UNDT)
Glaser v. Secretary-General of the United Nations, [1953] Judgment 38 (UNaT)
Glassman v. Secretary-General of the United Nations, [1953] Judgment 33 (UNaT)
Gordon v. Secretary-General of the United Nations, [1953] Judgment No. 29 (UNaT)

H. v. ITU, [2022] Judgement No. 4578 (ILOAT)
Harris v. Secretary-General of the United Nations, [1953] Judgment 31 (UNaT)
Hassouna v. Secretary-General of United Nations, UNDT/2014/094 (UNDT)
H.F. v IAEA, [2006] Judgement No. 2552 (ILOAT)
J. v. Asian Development Bank, [2018] Judgement No. 116 (ADB AT)
J.-D. v. ILO, [2018] Judgement No. 3982 (ILOAT)
J.M. v. NATO Communications and Information Agency, Judgment No. AT-J(2019)06 (NATO AT)
JMB v Organisation for the Prohibition of Chemical Weapons, [2003] Judgement No 2232 at para 16 (ILOAT)
Johnson v. Secretary-General of the United Nations, Judgment No. 2012-UNAT-240 (UNAT).
Jurado (In re), [1964] Judgment No. 70 (ILOAT)
K.E.G. v WHO, [2011] Judgement No. 2975 (ILOAT)
Kamara-Joyner v. Secretary-General of the United Nations, UNDT/2022/089 (UNDT)
Kazagic v. Secretary-General of the United Nations, UNDT/2016/086 (UNDT)
Khan v. Secretary-General of the United Nations, 2014-UNAT-486 (UNAT)
Kompass v. Secretary-General of the United Nations, Order No. 99 (GVA/2015) (UNDT)
Kozul-Wright v. Secretary-General of the United Nations, 2018-UNAT-843 (UNAT)
Krutzsch v OPCW, [2001] Judgement No. 2032 (ILOAT)
Kubwimana v. Secretary-General of the United Nations, Order No. 088 (NBI/2015) (UNDT)
Kuruc v. Secretary-General of the United Nations, UNDT/2015/008 (UNDT)
L.G. v CERN, [2007] Judgement No. 2569 (ILOAT)
Leff (In re), [1954] Judgements Nos. 15 and 18 (ILOAT)
Levcik v. Secretary-General of the United Nations, [1974] Judgement No. 192 (UNaT)
Loomba (In re), [1970] Judgement No. 169 (ILOAT)
Lubbad v. Secretary-General of the United Nations, UNDT/2013/132 (UNDT)
M. v. Global Fund, [2022] Judgment No. 4579 (ILOAT)
M. v. Asian Development Bank, [2019] Judgement No. 119 (ADB AT)
M.K. v. NATO Allied Air Command, (2017) Judgement No. AT-J(2017)023 (NATO AT)
Manirakiza v. Secretary-General of the United Nations, [1994] Judgement No. 663 (UNaT)
Mariki v. Secretary-General of the United Nations, UNDT/2014/138 (UNDT)
Megerditchian v. Secretary-General of the United Nations, UNDT/2010/035 (UNDT) affirmed by the United Nations Appeals Tribunal in 2010-UNAT-088

Mialeshka v. Secretary-General of the United Nations, UNDT/2011/055 (UNDT)
Milicevic v. Secretary-General of the United Nations, UNDT/2018/101 (UNDT)
Mutiso v. Secretary-General of the United Nations, UNDT/2015/059 (UNDT)
McCloskey v. Secretary-General of the United Nations, Judgment No. 2014-UNAT 424 (UNAT)
Moore (In re), [1995] Judgement No. 1405 (ILOAT)
Muteeganda v. Secretary-General of the United Nations, UNDT/2020/050 (UNDT)
Ndjadi v. Secretary-General of the United Nations, UNDT/2011/007 (UNDT), affirmed by the United Nations Appeals Tribunal in 2012-UNAT-197
Nsabimana v. IFAD, 2022-UNAT-1254 (UNAT)
O'Brian v. Secretary-General of the United Nations, UNDT/2021/166 (UNDT)
Older v. Secretary-General of the United Nations, [1953] Judgment 34 (UNaT)
Pankey (In re), [1955] Judgement No. 23 (ILOAT)
PD v. Headquarters Supreme Allied Command Transformation, (2021) AT-J(2021)0001 (NATO AT)
Porras v. Secretary-General of the United Nations, UNDT/2019/178 (UNDT) reversed in 2020-UNAT-1068 (United Nations Appeals Tribunal)
Qiu v. Secretary-General of the United Nations, [1990] Judgment 482 (UNaT)
R.D.A.G. v PAHO, [2014] Judgement No. 3295 (ILOAT)
Reed v. Secretary-General of the United Nations, [1953] Judgment 37 (UNaT)
Reznikov (In re), [1993] Judgement No. 1249 (ILOAT)
Roberts v. Secretary-General of the United Nations, UNDT/2010/142 (UNDT)
Rolli v. World Meteorological Organization, 2019-UNAT-952 (UNAT)
Rosescu (In re), [1980] Judgement No. 431 (ILOAT)
Rubio (In re), [1997] Judgment No. 1644 (ILOAT)
Sanchez Calero v. Secretary-General of the United Nations, UNDT/2015/074 (UNDT)
Sheffer v. Secretary-General of the International Maritime Organization, 2019-UNAT-949 (UNAT)
Souilah (In re), [1997] Judgement No. 1584 (ILOAT)
Spinardi v. Secretary-General of the International Maritime Organization, 2019-UNAT-957 (UNAT)
Stjernswärd (In re), [1998] Judgement No. 1732 (ILOAT)
Stepanenko v. Secretary-General of the United Nations, [1996] Judgment 763 (UNaT)
Sternfield (In re), [1972] Judgement No. 197 (ILOAT)
Stulz (In re), [1993] Judgement No. 1232 (ILOAT)
Svenchansky v. Secretary-General of the United Nations, [1953] Judgment 30 (UNaT)

Tal v. Secretary-General of the United Nations, UNDT Order No. 109 (NBI/2017) (UNDT)
Trudi v. Secretary-General of the United Nations, UNDT/2018/019 (UNDT)
Troncoso (In re), [1981] Judgement No. 448 (ILOAT)
Umar (In re), [1998] Judgement No. 1733 (ILOAT)
Van Gelder (In re), [1955] Judgement No. 24 (ILOAT)
Vedel v. Secretary-General of the United Nations, UNDT/2019/110 (UNDT)
Wallach v. Secretary-General of the United Nations, [1953] Judgment No. 28 (UNaT)
Wasserstrom v. Secretary-General of the United Nations, UNDT/2012/092 and UNDT/2013/053 (UNDT)
Webster v. Secretary-General of the International Seabed Authority, 2020-UNAT-983 (UNAT)
Wilcox (In re), [1954] Judgement No. 19 (ILOAT)
Williams v Court of Auditors of the European Communities, European Court Reports 1991 II-01293, ECLI:EU:T:1991:61

Jurisprudence of National Courts and Tribunals

Austria

NK v Austria, (Oberlandesgericht Wien) 77 IRL 470

Belgium

Ligue des États arabes c. T.M., No. S990103FV, 12 March 2001 (Cour de cassation of Belgium)
Secrétariat général du Groupe des États d'Afrique, des Caraïbes et du Pacifique c BD, No C070407F, 21 December 2009 (Cour de cassation of Belgium)
Secrétariat général du Groupe des États d'Afrique, des Caraïbes et du Pacifique c L M-A, C030328F, Cour de cassation of Belgium, 21 December 2009;
Western European Union v Siedler, S040129F, 21 December 2009 (Cour de cassation of Belgium)

Canada

Amaratunga v Northwest Atlantic Fisheries Organization, 2013 SCC 66 (Supreme Court of Canada)
Uber Technologies Inc v Heller, 2020 SCC 16 (Supreme Court of Canada)
Valente v The Queen, [1985] 2 SCR 673 (Supreme Court of Canada)
World Bank Group v Wallace, 2016 SCC 15 (Supreme Court of Canada)

France

Pourvoi n° 04-41.012, Chambre sociale, 25 January 2005 (Cour de cassation of France)

Pourvoi n° 07-44.240, Chambre sociale, 11 February 2009 (Cour de cassation of France)

Pourvoi n° 12-23.805, Chambre sociale, 13 May 2014 (Cour de cassation of France)

Italy

Drago v. International Plant Genetic Resources Institute (IPGRI), [2007] Final Appeal Judgment, Case No 3718, Giustizia Civile Massimario (Corte di cassazione of Italy)

Kenya

Tononoka Steels Limited v. Eastern and Southern Africa Trade and Development Bank [1999] K.L.R., Civil Appeal No. 255, 8 May 1998 (Court of Appeal, Nairobi district)

Switzerland

Groupement d'entreprises Fougerolle c. CERN, 21 December 1992, (Tribunal Fédéral suisse)

The Netherlands

Eckhardt v. Eurocontrol (No. 2), (1985) 16 NYIL 464 judgement of 12 January 1984 (Maastricht District Court)

Mothers of Srebrenica Association et al. v. The Netherlands, [2019] ECLI:NLLHR:2019:1223 (Supreme Court of the Netherlands)

Netherlands (Ministry of Defence and Ministry of Foreign Affairs) v. Nuhanović, [2013] ECLI/NL/HR/2013/BZ9225, ILDC 2061 (NL 2013), 12/03324, (Supreme Court of the Netherlands);

Spaans v. Iran-United States Claims Tribunal, [1985] ECLI:NL:HR:1985:AC9158 (Supreme Court of the Netherlands)

Stichting Mothers of Srebrenica v. The Netherlands, [2012] ECLI:NL:HR:2012:BW1999 (Supreme Court of the Netherlands)

Stichting Mothers of Srebrenica v. The Netherlands, [2019] ECLI:NL:HR:2019:1284 (Supreme Court of the Netherlands)

Supreme Site Services v. Supreme Headquarters Allied Powers Europe (SHAPE), [2021] ECLI:NL:HR:2021:1956 (Supreme Court of the Netherlands)

United Kingdom

R. v Secretary of State for Foreign and Commonwealth Affairs, [2018] UKSC 3 at para 69 (UK Supreme Court)
Attorney General v Nissan, [1969] UKHL 3 (United Kingdom House of Lords)
Trendex Trading Corporation Ltd v Central Bank of Nigeria [1977] 1 All ER 881 (Court of Appeal)

United States

Adair v. Commissioner, (1995) 70 T.C. 998 (U.S. Tax Court)
Amaral v. Commissioner, (1988) 90 T.C. 802 (U.S. Tax Court)
Askir v. Boutros Boutros Ghali, (1996) 933 F.Supp. 368, 95 Civ. 11008 (Southern District of New York)
Broadbent v. Organization of American States, (1980) 628 F. 2d 27, 35 (Court of Appeals District of Columbia)
Davis v. Passman (1979) 442 U.S. 228, 235 n. 11, 99 S. Ct. 2264, n. 11, 60 L. Ed. 2d 846 (United States Supreme Court)
De Luca v. United Nations Organization, (1994) 841 F. Supp. 531 (Southern District of New York)
Dombrowski v. Eastland 387 U.S. 82 (1967), 85, 87 S. Ct. 1425, 1427, 18 L. Ed. 2d 577 (United States Supreme Court)
Donald v. Orfila, (1986) 788 F.2d 36 at 37 (United States Court of Appeals, District of Columbia Circuit)
Donelly v. Ranollo, (1946) 187 Misc. 777, 67 N.Y.S.2d 31 (New York City Court)
Ex Parte Peru, 318 U.S. 573 (Supreme Court of the United States)
Georges v. United Nations, judgement of 18 August 2016, 834 F.3d (United States Court of Appeals 2d Cir.)
Jam v. International Finance Corporation, 2019 WL 938524 (United States Supreme Court)
Laventure v. United Nations, judgement of 28 December 2018, 17-2908-cv, 3 (United States Court of Appeals 2d Cir.)
Rendall-Speranza v. Nassim, (1996) 942 F. Supp. 621 and 932 F. Supp. 19 (United States District Court, District of Columbia).
Samantar v. Yousuf, (2010) 560 U.S. 305 (Supreme Court of the United States)

Table of Treaties and Agreements

Agreement between the Government of the Republic of Indonesia and the Association of Southeast Nations (ASEAN) *on Hosting and Granting Privileges and Immunities to the* ASEAN *Secretariat* (2012)

Agreement between the International Atomic Energy Agency ('IAEA') *and the Republic of Austria regarding the Headquarters of the* IAEA, (1957) 229 U.N.T.S. 110

Agreement between the United Nations and the United States of America regarding the Headquarters of the United Nations, UN Doc. A/RES/169(II)

Agreement between the United States and the North Atlantic Council, (1951) 5 U.S.T. 1098, T.I.A.S. 2992

Agreement concerning the Headquarters of the United Nations Economic and Social Commission for Western Asia, (1997) 1988 U.N.T.S. 339

Agreement Establishing the Inter-American Development Bank (1959) 389 U.N.T.S. 70

Agreement Establishing the World Trade Organization (1994) 1867 U.N.T.S. 154

Agreement for the Establishment of the International Development Law Organisation of February 5, 1988, as amended on June 30, 2002, November 30, 2002, March 28, 2008, December 13, 2012, and November 28, 2017

Agreement on the Privileges and Immunities of the International Criminal Court, (2002) 2271 U.N.T.S. 3

Agreement on the status of the North Atlantic Treaty Organization, National Representatives and International Staff (1951) 200 U.N.T.S. 3

Agreement on the Privileges and Immunities of the ITER *International Fusion Energy Organization for the Joint Implementation of the* ITER *Project* (2006) 2491 U.N.T.S. 317

Agreement regarding Headquarters of the Organisation of the Petroleum Exporting Countries ('OPEC'), (1974) 2098 U.N.T.S. 416

Amazon Cooperation Treaty establishing the Amazon Cooperation Treaty Organization (1978) 1202 U.N.T.S. 51

Arrangement relating to the International Office of Public Health (1907) signed at Rome

Articles of Agreement of the International Monetary Fund (1945) 2 U.N.T.S. 39

Articles of Agreement of the International Bank for Reconstruction and Development (1945) 2 U.N.T.S. 134

Charter of the United Nations (1945)

Charter of the Organization of American States (1948) 119 U.N.T.S. 3

Charter of the NATO *Support and Procurement Organisation*, C-M(2017)0048

Consolidated versions of the Treaty on European Union and the Treaty on the Functioning of the European Union (TFEU) [2016] OJ C202/47
Constitutive Act of the African Union (2000) 2158 U.N.T.S. 3
Convention concerning the formation of an International Union for the Publication of Customs Tariffs (1890)
Convention concerning the sugar regime (1902)
Convention establishing the International Institute of Agriculture (1905)
Convention for the Establishment of a European Space Agency (1975) 1297 U.N.T.S. 199
Convention internationale sur le transport de marchandises par chemins de fer (1890)
Convention on the Organisation for Economic Co-operation and Development (1960) 888 U.N.T.S. 179
Convention on the Privileges and Immunities of the United Nations (1946) 1 U.N.T.S. 15
Convention relating to the Establishment of the International Association of Seismology (1903)
Constitution of the Food and Agriculture Organization (1945)
Eurocontrol International Convention relating to Cooperation for the Safety of Air Navigation, (1960) 523 U.N.T.S. 117
General Convention on the Privileges and Immunities of the Organisation of African Unity (1965) 1000 U.N.T.S. 393
Headquarters Agreement between the Organization of American States and the Government of the United States of America (1992)
Headquarters Agreement between the Federal Republic of Germany and the European Molecular Biology Laboratory (1974)
Modus Vivendi (1926) LoN Doc. No. C.555/1926(V)
Protocol on Privileges and Immunities of the European Patent Organization (1973) 1065 U.N.T.S. 500
The Hague Convention on Pacific Settlement of International Disputes (1907)
The Meter Convention (1875)
Treaty constituting General Postal Union (1874)
Treaty on European Union (1992) 1759 U.N.T.S. 3
Treaty on Principles Governing the Activities of States in the Exploration and Use of Outer Space, Including the Moon and Other Celestial Bodies, annexed to the General Assembly Resolution 2222(XXI), UN Doc A/RES/2222(XXI) (19 December 1966)
United Nations Convention against Corruption (2003) 2349 U.N.T.S. 41
Vienna Convention on Diplomatic Relations (1961) 500 U.N.T.S. 95

Table of Resolutions

Committee of Ministers of the Council of Europe resolution, CM/Res (2014)

International Labour Conference resolution "*Statute of the Administrative Tribunal of the International Labour Organization*" (1946) as amended on 29 June 1949, 17 June 1986, 19 June 1992, 16 June 1998, 11 June 2008, 7 June 2016, 17 June 2019, and 18 June 2021

UNGA resolution "*Organization of the Secretariat*", (1946) UN Doc A/RES/13(I)

UNGA resolution "*Tax Equalization*", (1946) UN Doc A/RES/78(I)

UNGA resolution "*Establishment of an International Law Commission*", (1947) UN Doc A/RES/174(II)

UNGA declaration "*Universal Declaration of Human Rights*", (1948) UN Doc. A/RES/217A (III)

UNGA resolution "*Tax Equalization – Staff Assessment Plan*", (1948) UN Doc A/RES/239(III)

UNGA resolution "*Assistance to Palestine refugees*", (1949) UN Doc A/RES/302(IV)

UNGA resolution "*Statute of the Office of the United Nations High Commissioner for Refugees*", (1950) UN Doc A/RES/428(V)

UNGA resolution "*Question of the Peaceful Use of Outer* Space", (1958) UN Doc A/RES/1348(XIII)

UNGA resolutions "*International Cooperation in the Peaceful Use of Outer Space"*, (1959, 1961, 1962) UN Doc A/RES/1472(XIV), A/RES/1721(XVI), A/RES/1802(XVII)

UNGA resolution "*Declaration of Legal Principles Governing the Activities of States in the Exploration and Use of Outer Space"*, (1963) UN Doc A/RES/1962(XVIII)

UNGA resolution "*Establishment of the United Nations Conference on Trade and Development as an organ of the General Assembly*", (1964) UN Doc A/RES/1995(XIX)

UNGA resolution "*Institutional and financial arrangements for international environmental cooperation*", (1972) UN Doc A/RES/2997(XXVII)

UNGA resolution "*Review of the Role of the International Court of* Justice", (1974) UN Doc A/RES/3232(XXIX)

UNGA resolution "*United Nations Volunteers*", (1979) UN Doc A/RES/2659(XXV)

UNGA resolution "*Personnel Questions*", (1980) UN Doc A/RES/35/210

UNSC resolution "*Provisional Rules of Procedure of the Security Council*", (1982) UN Doc. S/96/Rev.7

UNGA resolution "*Revitalization of the United Nations Secretariat*", (1992) UN Doc A/RES/46/232

UNGA resolution "*Revitalization of the United Nations Secretariat*", (1992) UN Doc A/RES/46/232

UNGA resolution "*High Commissioner for the promotion and protection of all human rights*", (1993) UN Doc A/RES/48/141

UNGA resolution "*Review of the efficiency of the administrative and financial functioning of the United Nations*", (1994) UN Doc A/RES/48/218B

UNGA resolution "*Review of the procedure provided for under article 11 of the statute of the Administrative Tribunal of the United Nations*", (1995) UN Doc. A/RES/50/54

UNGA resolution "*Strengthening of the United Nations System*", (1997) UN Doc A/RES/51/241

UNGA resolution "*Human Resources Management*", (1997) UN Doc A/RES/55/226

UNGA resolution "*Human Resources Management*", UN Doc A/RES/55/226 (1997)

UNGA resolution "*Strengthening the mandate and status of the Commission on Human Settlements and the status, role and functions of the United Nations Centre for Human Settlements (Habitat)*", UN Doc A/RES/56/206 (2002)

UNGA resolution "*Human Rights Council*", (2006) UN Doc A/RES/60/251

UNGA resolution "*Administration of justice at the United Nations*", UN Doc. A/RES/61/261 (2007)

UNGA resolution "*Administration of justice at the United Nations*", UN Doc. A/RES/63/253 (2008).

UNGA resolution "*Statute of the United Nations Appeals Tribunal*", UN Doc A/RES/66/237 (2008)

UNGA resolution "*Safety and security of humanitarian personnel and protection of United Nations personnel*", (2013) UN Doc. A/RES/68/101

UNGA resolution "*United Nations Common System: report of the International Civil Service Commission*", (2014) UN Doc. A/RES/50/208 (1996)

UNGA resolution "*Rules of Procedure of the General Assembly*", (2021) UN Doc. A/520/Rev.19

UNGA resolution "*United Nations action on sexual exploitation and abuse*" (2022) UN Doc. A/RES/76/303

Table of Reports and Summary Records of Meetings

Conclusions of the Committee for whose appointment provision was made in the Council resolution of June 8th, 1925, relating to a claim submitted by M. Monod, (1925) 6:10 League of Nations O J 1409

Council Directive 2006/112/EC of 28 November 2006 on the common system of value-added tax, [2006] OJ L 347/1

Documents diplomatiques de la conférence de mètre, (1875)

International American Conference, Reports of Committees & Discussions Thereon, (1890)

Report submitted to the Fourth Committee of the Assembly by the Sub-Committee on the Administrative Tribunal, (1927) League of Nations OJ, Special Supplement 58

Report of Rapporteur (General) of Committee I/2 on Chapter X (Secretariat), UNCIO, Vol. VII, Commission I, Committee 2, Doc 1155, Ref. no. I/2/74 (2), (22 June 1945)

Verbatim Minutes of Third Meeting of Commission I, UNCIO, Vol. VI, Commission I: General Provisions, Doc 1167, Ref. No. I/10, (19 June 1945)

Fourth Report of the Administrative Committee on Co-ordination to the Economic and Social Council, (1948) UN Doc E/1076

Tenth Report of the Administrative Committee on Co-ordination to the Economic and Social Council, (1951) UN Doc. E/2161 and Corr.1

Report of the International Civil Service Advisory Board, "Standards of Conduct in the International Civil Service", (1954) UN Doc Coord/Civil Service/5

Report of the International Law Commission, "Draft articles on responsibility of international organizations, with commentaries", (2011) UN Doc A/66/10 and Add.1

Report of the Preparatory Commission of the United Nations, United Nations Conference on International Organization, Doc PC/20 (1945)

Report of the Secretary-General of the United Nations to the United Nations General Assembly, (1953) UN Doc A/2364

Report of the Secretary-General of the UN on Personnel Policy, (1953) UN Doc. A/2533

Report of the Secretary-General on the Work of the Organization 16 June 1960 – 15 June 1961, UN Doc A/4800/Add.1

Summary Record, Meeting of the Fifth Committee, (1977) UN Doc A/C.5/32/SR.6

Summary Record of the 39th meeting of the Fifth Committee, (1980) UN Doc A/C.5/35/SR.39

Report of the Secretary-General, "Model of Status-of-Forces Agreement for Peacekeeping Operations", (1990) UN Doc A/45/594

Report (Fifth) of the Special Rapporteur on Relations Between States and International Organizations, (1991) UN Doc A/CN.4/4/438

Report of the Secretary-General, "Review of the Procedure Provided for under Article 11 of the Statute of the Administrative Tribunal of the United Nations", (1994) UN Doc A/C.6/49/2

Report of the Secretary-General, "Financing of the United Nations Protection Force, the United Nations Confidence Restoration Operation in Croatia, the United Nations Preventive Deployment Force and the United Nations Peace Forces headquarters", (1996) UN Doc A/51/389

Report of the Secretary-General, "Administrative and budgetary aspects of the financing of the United Nations peacekeeping operations: financing of the United Nations peacekeeping operations", (1997) UN Doc A/51/903

Report of the Secretary-General, "Proposed United Nations Code of Conduct", (1997) UN Doc A/52/488

Report of the Redesign Panel on the United Nations system of administration of justice, (2006) UN Doc A/61/205

Report of the Redesign Panel on the United Nations system of administration of justice, (2007) UN Doc A/61/758

Report of the Joint Inspection Unit, "Procurement reforms in the United Nations system", (2011) UN Doc JIU/NOTE/2011/1

Report of the Joint Inspections Unit, "Transparency in the selection and appointment of senior managers in the United Nations Secretariat" (2011) UN Doc J/REP/2011/2

Report of the Advisory Committee on Administrative and Budgetary Questions, "Procurement activities in the United Nations Secretariat", (2017) UN Doc A/71/823

Report of the Secretary-General, "Composition of the Secretariat", (2020) UN Doc A/75/591

Report of the Secretary-General on the Administration of Justice of the United Nations, (2020) A/76/99

Report of the Secretary-General, Initial review of the jurisdictional set-up of the United Nations common system, (2021) UN Doc. A/75/690

Report of the Secretary-General, "Special measures for protection from sexual exploitation and abuse", (2022) UN Doc. A/76/702

Report of the Secretary-General on the Administration of Justice of the United Nations, (2022) UN Doc. A/77/156

Abbreviations and Acronyms

ADBAT	Asian Development Bank Administrative Tribunal
Am J Int'l L	American Journal of International Law
Art	Article
ASEAN	Association of Southeast Asian Nations
ASG	Assistant Secretary-General
AU	African Union
BIPM	International Bureau for Weights and Measures
CERN	European Council for Nuclear Research
CTBTO	Comprehensive Nuclear-Test-Ban Treaty Organization
DESA	Department for Economic and Social Affairs
EBRD	European Bank for Reconstruction and Development
ECA	Economic Commission for Africa
ECHR	European Court of Human Rights
ECOSOC	Economic and Social Council
ESA	European Space Agency
ESCWA	Economic and Social Commission for Western Asia
ESM	European Stability Mechanism
EU	European Union
FAO	Food and Agriculture Organization
HCCH	Hague Conference on Private International Law
IADBAT	Inter-American Development Bank Administrative Tribunal
IAEA	International Atomic Energy Agency
ICC	International Criminal Court
ICCO	International Cocoa Organization
ICJ	International Court of Justice
ICSAB	International Civil Service Advisory Board
IDLO	International Development Law Organisation
IFC	International Finance Corporation
IGO	Intergovernmental Organization
ILO	International Labour Organization
ILOAT	International Labour Organization Administrative Tribunal
IMF	International Monetary Fund
IMO	International Maritime Organization
Int or Int'l	International
IOIA	International Organizations Immunities Act
IOM	International Organization for Migration
ITER	International Fusion Energy Organization

ITTO	International Tropical Timber Organization
ITU	International Telecommunication Union
J.	Journal
L.	Law
LoN	League of Nations
NAFO	Northwest Atlantic Fisheries Organization
NATO	North Atlantic Treaty Organization
NCIA	NATO Communications and Information Agency
NSPA	NATO Support and Procurement Agency
NYU	New York University
OCHA	Office for the Coordination of Humanitarian Affairs
OECD	Organization for Economic Cooperation and Development
OIOS	Office of Internal Oversight Services
IOV	International Organisation of Vine and Wine
OAS	Organization of American States
O.J.	Official Journal
OHCHR	Office of the High Commissioner for Human Rights
OPCW	Organization for the Prohibition of Chemical Weapons
OSCE	Organization for Security Cooperation in Europe
PAHO	Pan American Health Organization
PCIJ	Permanent Court of International Justice
Rep.	Reports
Rev.	Review
Sess.	Session
UIA	Union of International Associations
UN	United Nations
UNaT	United Nations Administrative Tribunal
UNAT	United Nations Appeals Tribunal
UNCTAD	UN Conference on Trade and Development
UNDT	United Nations Dispute Tribunal
UNDP	UN Development Programme
UNEP	UN Environment Programme
UNESCO	United Nations Educational, Scientific and Cultural Organization
UNFCCC	United Nations Framework Convention on Climate Change
UNFPA	UN Population Fund
UNGA	United Nations General Assembly
UNGAOR	UN General Assembly Official Records
UNHCR	UN High Commissioner for Refugees
UNICEF	UN International Children's Emergency Fund
UNIDO	UN Industrial Development Organization

UNODC	UN Office on Drugs and Crime
UNON	UN Office at Nairobi
UNOPS	UN Office for Project Services
UNRWA	UN Relief and Works Agency for Palestine Refugees in the Near East
UNSC	United Nations Security Council
UNTS	UN Treaty Series
UPU	Universal Postal Union
USG	Under-Secretary-General
VAT	Value-added tax
VNC	Voluntary National Contribution
WBAT	World Bank Administrative Tribunal
WFP	World Food Programme
WHO	World Health Organization
WMO	World Meteorological Organization
WTO	World Trade Organization
YB	Yearbook

Introduction

I began writing this manuscript 12 years ago, not literally but figuratively, when I transitioned from the Canadian public service to the international civil service in the United Nations Secretariat. Soon after joining the United Nations Office of Administration of Justice as a Legal Officer, I became intrigued by why international organisations have a different understanding, interpretation, and application of the notion of independence of the international civil service. I found it perplexing that widespread practices of some organisations were not permissible in others because they were regarded as infringing on the independence of their secretariats and staff. I became even more interested in this question when I transferred from the UN Secretariat to UNHCR – a subsidiary body of the United Nations – and noticed that essential differences existed between international organisations and within the United Nations System itself. However, my curiosity peaked when I left the United Nations System to join NATO. I was surprised by how different these two major international organisations were and how differently they interpreted and applied the notion of independence of their secretariats and officials. My subsequent interactions with legal counsel from other international organisations, including the EU, OSCE, and OECD, reinforced my belief that independence means something different in each international organisation except for a few commonalities.

An element of independence common to all international organisations is the multinational composition of their secretariats placed under the authority of a governing body composed of several member states. Typically, intergovernmental organisations understand independence as a prohibition for international civil servants to seek or receive instructions from individual member states in performing their official functions and a prohibition for individual member states to influence international civil servants. International secretariats are expected to implement policy decisions made by the governing bodies of international organisations and refrain from complying with the wishes of a specific nation. The latter expectation stems from the principle of sovereign equality of states enshrined in Article 2.1 of the United Nations Charter. One is hard-pressed to find any other element of independence of international secretariats and staff that is common to all international organisations.

As a legal practitioner with extensive experience in international organisations, I regularly witness acts and omissions by various actors that harm the independence of international secretariats and their staff. Many intergovernmental institutions that condone seemingly problematic practices do not even recognise that these practices adversely affect their secretariat and

 | DOI:10.1163/9789004704596_002

staff. This is unfortunate principally because finding a solution requires one to acknowledge that there is a problem. An organisation unaware of practices that harm the independence of its secretariat and staff is not likely to remedy the situation.

Some IGOs, including most UN entities, are acutely aware of practices that impede the independence of their secretariats because, throughout their existence, they have faced hundreds of attempts by member states to influence the decisions and activities of their staff. Nevertheless, these IGOs are not always willing or able to foil such attempts. In many cases, the inability to change the status quo may be attributable to well-established, long-standing, and deep-rooted practices that have been followed for decades and have become part of the IGO's institutional culture.[1]

In other cases, IGOs may be unable to implement significant changes because their reliance on member states is so great that they might be fearful that any attempt to strengthen the autonomy and independence of the IGO's secretariat will lead to a loss of support. For instance, if a specific nation provides resources by seconding to the international secretariat national public servants, the IGO may be unable to refuse such support because it would deprive itself of an essential workforce. Similarly, suppose a member state makes its voluntary financial contributions contingent on fulfilling certain conditions that infringe on the independence of the secretariat (i.e. the requirement to recruit and employ its nationals). In that case, the IGO might not want to turn down the funds for fear of losing an opportunity to complete a project it views as crucial to its success.

Due to these factors, international organisations do not consistently interpret and apply independence as it relates to their secretariats and staff. Practices that some international institutions regard as highly problematic may be seen as tolerable by others. Faced with such profoundly divergent views and understanding of independence, I wondered whether the independence of international secretariats and civil servants is an entirely flexible concept that can be adapted to the needs or types of individual organisations or whether it is a relatively static notion composed of well-defined characteristics and elements. On the one hand, if independence is variable or entirely in the eye of the beholder, each international organisation may be justified in allowing practices that it

1 Institutional or organisational culture is "the pattern of beliefs, values and learned ways of coping with experience that have developed during the course of an organisation's history, and which tend to be manifested in its material arrangements and in the behaviours of its members." Andrew D Brown, Organizational Culture, 2d ed (London: FT Publishing International, 1998).

considers appropriate and avoiding or even prohibiting practices that it deems contrary to the independence of its secretariat and its staff. In such a case, independence would have as many meanings and definitions as intergovernmental organisations.

If, on the other hand, independence is a concept assessed objectively, then one must accept that independence either has only one meaning or at least certain essential and inherent characteristics. Consequently, problematic practices for one organisation must be equally problematic for all other organisations. In other words, practices that erode the independence of international secretariats and staff of some IGOs would be equally corrosive for all others.

The main question that animated this work is whether the independence of international secretariats is a flexible (dynamic) or unvarying (static) notion. A related question is whether defining or describing this independence is possible. Does independence in the context of international secretariats and civil servants have essential characteristics? If so, do these characteristics vary from one organisation to another? Suppose two international organisations interpret and apply the concept of independence differently. Does this necessarily imply that the secretariat and staff of one of these organisations are less independent than the secretariat and staff of the other?

The obvious starting point of this research is the history of international secretariats and civil servants. Chapter 1 traces the genesis of international secretariats and international civil servants back to multinational conferences. Examining the practice of international conferences helps to understand what preceded international secretariats. Chapter 1 then focuses on 100 years of evolution of international secretariats. The period from 1815 to 1919 is critical because it reveals tensions that made independence an essential consideration in establishing international secretariats. An in-depth review of diplomatic documents, including procès-verbaux and minutes of conference negotiations, shows when and why the concept of independence became a relevant factor in the eyes of member states.

How the independence of international civil service has evolved can be understood by comparing the institutional structure and composition of the first secretariats. A thorough analysis of various legal instruments establishing primitive forms of international organisations unveils the progression of secretariats from simple *protocolists* of international conferences composed almost exclusively of national public servants of the host nation to multinational bureaucracies of international public unions and bureaux placed under the authority of multinational governing bodies consisting of several or all member states. The progress from the most nascent form of secretariats to the most advanced configuration took time; it required several decades of experimenting with multinational institutions. Therefore, diplomatic documents and discussions that led to these gradual changes examined in Chapter 1 are essential.

Formal and explicit recognition of the independence of international civil service would have to wait until the establishment of the League of Nations. In May 1920, the Balfour report expressed the importance of recruiting staff members with a sense of 'international allegiance'.[2] In 1922, the League promulgated its first Staff Regulations, reiterating that the "officials of the Secretariat of the League of Nations are international officials, responsible in the execution of their duties to the Secretary-General alone" and that they were not permitted to "seek or receive instructions from any other authority." Chapter 1 describes the difficult negotiations that took place before the establishment of the League to equip the organisation with a truly international secretariat. It describes the instrumental role played by the first Secretary-General of the League of Nations – Sir Eric Drummond – in cementing the international nature of the League's secretariat. It then examines the erosion of the independence of the League's Secretariat under the leadership of the second Secretary-General of the League – Joseph Avenol.

In 1944 and 1945, the international community of states created several important organisations, including the United Nations and the Bretton Woods Institutions. For the first time, member states undertook in the UN Charter not to seek to influence the UN Secretary-General and his staff. However, the independence of international secretariats and civil servants remained ambiguous and vague. Soon after the establishment of the United Nations, other international organisations followed with diverse institutional structures, secretariats, and staff compositions. Whilst all international organisations recognised the importance of independence, they had different interpretations and applications of this idea.

Since the creation of the United Nations, the international community established dozens of new and significant intergovernmental institutions, such as the Organisation for the Prohibition of Chemical Weapons (OPCW) and the World Trade Organization (WTO). The rules applicable to these organisations refer to the independence of their international civil service. However, the concept of independence did not attract much attention or trigger much discussion. One would say there was no controversy at all surrounding this topic. Therefore, after a historical overview, I investigate whether independence is

2 AJ Balfour, "Procès-verbal of the Fifth Session of the Council of the League of Nations, Report relating to Staff of the Secretariat" (1920) 1:4 League of Nations *OJ* 115 at 137.

still relevant today and, if so, whether states are incentivised to safeguard the independence of international secretariats and civil servants. Chapter 2 begins by demonstrating that the independence of the international civil service is the foundation of the trust nations place in international institutions as neutral go-betweens or intermediaries. Without such trust, international cooperation cannot be optimal. This chapter is mainly definitional; it attempts to deconstruct the notion of independence by answering such questions as (a) what is independence? (b) whose independence does the concept regulate? (c) from what should independence be? (d) from whom should independence be? The answers to these foundational questions may seem obvious; however, there are no accepted definitions of who can be regarded as a member of a group commonly known as 'international civil service' or what can be called an 'international secretariat'. Chapter 2 then canvasses the essential characteristics of an independent secretariat and independent international civil servants. It also explores links between independence and the international organisation's legal personality, privileges, and immunities. It investigates the connection between the independence of international civil servants and their functional immunities, fiscal privileges, impartiality, neutrality, and anonymity. The same chapter identifies member states, international organisations, and international civil servants as the three actors responsible for maintaining and nurturing the independence of international civil service.

Chapters 3, 4, and 5 focus on practices that erode the independence of international secretariats and their staff. Chapter 3 addresses the practices of member states, whereas Chapters 4 and 5 deal with the practices of international organisations and civil servants, respectively. All three chapters establish a link between independence and its constitutive elements identified in Chapter 2 through real cases.

Chapter 3 consists of two sections. The first section lists practices of member states that adversely affect the independence of international secretariats, including failure to recognise the jurisdictional immunity of international organisations and to respect the inviolability of their premises, assets, archives, and fiscal privileges. The second section examines practices of member states that undermine the independence of international civil servants. Topics discussed in section two include functional immunities and fiscal privileges of international officials, as well as attempts by member states to influence decisions relating to personnel administration.

Chapter 4 discusses practices of international organisations that erode the independence of their secretariats and staff. It analyses acts and omissions that lead to breaches of their jurisdictional immunities, fiscal privileges, and inviolability of premises and archives. It then examines acts and omissions of international organisations that undermine the independence of their staff, such as failure to assert privileges and immunities and failure to investigate and sanction misconduct. The last section of Chapter 4 deals with the failures of international organisations to shield staff members from attempts by member states to intervene in decisions pertaining to selections, promotions, separations from service, and performance appraisals of staff members.

Chapter 5 surveys practices of international civil servants that erode their independence and the independence of their secretariats. The first question addressed in this chapter is to whom international civil servants owe the duty to preserve their independence. It then examines the constitutive elements of this duty by drawing inspiration from the Code of Conduct developed in the 1950s by the International Civil Service Advisory Board (present-day International Civil Service Commission). This document contains four fundamental standards of conduct or values. However, recognising that this Code of Conduct was developed for the United Nations System, Chapter 5 tests the hypothesis that these standards of conduct may have become universal.

The last part of this work draws conclusions on the current state of independence of international secretariats and civil servants. It provides recommendations to member states, international organisations, and international functionaries for strengthening the independence of the international civil service.

In addition to primary and secondary sources of information, I use my observations and knowledge acquired through many years of legal practice in the United Nations Secretariat, UNHCR, and NATO. I worked on various issues central to the independence of international secretariats and civil servants. More specifically, I provided legal advice and representation to international civil servants and international organisations. I advised and represented victims of misconduct and whistle-blowers. I prosecuted staff facing misconduct allegations, arguing over one hundred cases before international administrative and arbitral tribunals. I negotiated and prepared legal instruments regulating the privileges and immunities of IGOs and their staff and asserted privileges and immunities enjoyed by IGOs and their staff before domestic courts. I also advised member states through governing bodies of international organisations. During the last 14 years of experience in intergovernmental organisations, I have witnessed first-hand how suboptimal policy decisions affecting international organisations may have long-term repercussions on the independence of their secretariats and staff. I share this experience and knowledge with two objectives in mind.

My primary objective for pursuing this work is to contribute to the existing body of scholarship. A review of the literature reveals a significant gap in this field. Specifically, I could not find books or articles exploring the notion of independence in the context of international civil servants. The existing works focus on the institutional structures of international secretariats and the law applicable to the employment relationship between IGOs and their staff. Most books, book chapters, and articles explore the notion of independence through the prism of privileges and immunities. One scholarly work that provides a somewhat holistic overview of independence is Meron's piece in the *Recueil des Cours* of the Hague Academy of International Law.[3] However, besides being outdated, this article is intended to be more descriptive than analytical; it does not propose a framework for understanding the concept of independence.

A similar gap exists in the jurisprudence of national and international courts and tribunals. The International Court of Justice dealt with cases related to international civil service on nine occasions.[4] Although these ICJ pronouncements help to clarify a few fundamental characteristics of independence, none define or describe in detail what independence means or consists of. National courts and international administrative tribunals also occasionally consider cases where the independence of international secretariats and staff was a critical point. Nevertheless, they have stopped short of defining and describing the notion.

The jurisprudence of international administrative tribunals can also be very helpful in describing the notion of independence. The difficulty with this source of information is its episodical and anecdotal nature. International administrative tribunals are mandated to adjudicate specific employment disputes between IGOs and their staff. To the best of my knowledge, no scholar

3 Theodor Meron, "Status and Independence of the International Civil Service" (1980) 167 *Recueil des Cours de l'Académie de Droit International* 289.

4 *Difference Relating to Immunity from Legal Process of a Special Rapporteur of the Commission on Human Rights, Advisory Opinion*, [1999] I.C.J. Rep. 62; *Applicability of Article VI, Section 22, of the Convention on the Privileges and Immunities of the United Nations*, Advisory Opinion, [1989] I.C.J. Rep. 177; *Effect of awards of compensation made by the UN Administrative Tribunal*, Advisory Opinion, [1954] I.C.J. Rep. 47; *Reparation for injuries suffered in the service of the United Nations*, Advisory Opinion, [1949] I.C.J. Rep. 174; *Judgment No. 2867 of the Administrative Tribunal of the International Labour Organization upon a Complaint Filed against the International Fund for Agricultural Development*, Advisory Opinion, [2012] I.C.J. Rep. 10; *Application for Review of Judgement No. 333 of the United Nations Administrative Tribunal*, Advisory Opinion, [1987] I.C.J. Rep. 18; *Application for Review of Judgement No. 273 of the United Nations Administrative Tribunal*, Advisory Opinion, [1982] I.C.J. Rep. 325; *Application for Review of Judgement No. 158 of the United Nations Administrative Tribunal*, Advisory Opinion, [1973] I.C.J. Rep. 166; *Judgements of the Administrative Tribunal of the I.L.O. upon complaints made against the UNESCO*, Advisory Opinion, [1956] I.C. J. Rep. 77.

or practitioner has thus far attempted to compile and analyse all judgments of international administrative tribunals that pertain to the independence of international secretariats and civil servants.

The second purpose of this book is to demonstrate that it is in the best interest of states and IGOs to nurture and protect the independence of international secretariats and civil servants. Unlike national administrations, international bureaucracies are fragile, being legally and financially dependent on their member states. Therefore, they need a greater degree of protection.

This book is intended for a diverse audience. Scholars, researchers, delegates of member states, governmental officials dealing with international organisations, international civil servants, diplomats, and legal practitioners working with IGOs will likely find it helpful.

CHAPTER 1

The Genesis of International Civil Service and Its Independence

1 Period Preceding the League of Nations

Until the seventeenth century, international interactions consisted of individual and independent actions of states. No aspect of international relations had any institutional character. The community of states lacked integrated machinery representing the collective action of nations. Each state made its own arrangements with other states separately and cooperated only with those it was interested in. The Peace of Westphalia ending the Thirty Years' War in the middle of the seventeenth century is considered the beginning of internationalism. During this period, Europe had enough independent states to coordinate interstate action through general gatherings of diplomatic envoys.[1] The Congress of Westphalia of 1648 "marked the beginning of the European nation-state system."[2] It became the first modern conference to serve as an instrument of world affairs, setting a precedent for hundreds of gatherings of representatives of sovereign states in the following years.[3]

1.1 *International Conferences*

The year 1815 "marked the beginning of a mechanism that was to result in IGOs, based on the combination of conferences and follow-up conferences, first in 'high' then also in 'low' politics."[4] The Congress of Vienna helped to shape the core of international organisation by introducing new regulations for conducting multilateral conferences thereby facilitating the functioning of bilateral and multilateral diplomacy.[5] During the same period, the concept of

---

1 Norman L Hill, *The Public International Conference: Its Function, Organization and Procedure* (Stanford University: Stanford University Press, 1929) at 2.

2 James P Muldoon Jr et al, *Multilateral Diplomacy and the United Nations Today*, 2d ed (New York: Routledge, 2005) at 4.

3 Hill, *supra* note 1 at 2. Although several states attended the same meeting, the technique of multilateral treaty-making had not yet been mastered. States were signing several bilateral agreements instead of signing one multilateral agreement.

4 Bob Reinalda, *International Secretariats: Two Centuries of International Civil Servants and Secretariats* (London: Routledge, 2020) at 22.

5 *Ibid.*

 | DOI:10.1163/9789004704596_003

follow-up conferences appeared. The purpose of these follow-up conferences was to allow nations to monitor the implementation of their agreements or policies.[6] These follow-up conferences were a significant development for the formation of international organisations because they engendered a form of continuity and identified a need for institutional memory.

Although international and follow-up conferences were becoming increasingly frequent, no permanent machinery was set up for such a purpose. The organisation of each conference or congress was ad hoc and depended greatly on the host state. The procedure of diplomatic assemblies varied widely, and their degree of complexity depended mainly on the number of participating states.[7] Nevertheless, despite considerable diversity in the detailed arrangements accompanying specific international meetings, a few practices crystallised as customary norms.

For instance, concerning the executive leadership of congresses and conferences, it is important to recall that states met in international assemblies as equals. Therefore, no single state could claim superiority, and no national delegation could proclaim itself to be the leader of the conference without the express consent of other states. Naturally, the question that arose was who should chair international gatherings. Unlike national legislatures and parliaments, where the deliberations are led and directed by presidents or chairpersons, international assemblies lack a central authority or leadership. To fill this gap, a customary practice evolved; states tacitly agreed that the president of international conferences would be the principal delegate of the country where the international gathering is held.[8] Put differently, the highest-ranking delegate of the nation hosting the conference was elected by all participating nations as the chair of the conference. The existence of this customary rule was confirmed by the French Prime Minister – Georges Clemenceau – when he was elected President of the Paris Peace Conference of 1919:

> It is necessary, gentlemen, to point out that my election is due necessarily to lofty international tradition and to the time-honoured courtesy shown toward the country which has the honour to welcome the Peace Conference in its capital.[9]

---

6 *Ibid.* at 23.

7 Hill, *supra* note 1 at 61.

8 Ernest Satow, *International Congresses* (London: H.M. Stationary Office, 1920) at 15.

9 General Sessions [Paris Peace Conference] (1919) 6 *Int'l Conciliation* 805, at 816.

In most cases, one of the participating states had to propose that the principal delegate of the host state preside over the assembly.[10] The two Hague Conferences of 1899 and 1907 were notable exceptions to the custom of choosing the principal delegate of the inviting state as president. The highest-ranking delegates of Russia were elected as presidents on account of Russia's influence in the convocation of the meetings.[11] Nevertheless, "in both instances [...] some homage was paid to the practice of the past by the designation of the Ministers of Foreign Affairs from Holland as honorary presidents".[12]

The role of the president was primarily ceremonial and procedural. The ceremonial tasks required the president to open the assembly with an address broadly outlining the task which lay before the assembly, to refer to the program forming the basis of discussion, and to make a speech winding up the proceedings at the end of the conference.[13] The procedural functions of the president consisted of directing the sessions of the conference, bringing up for discussion in the correct order agenda items, giving the floor to the delegates in the order in which they asked it, deciding questions of order which arise in the discussions, and, when requested, calling for a vote and announcing to the conference the result of the vote. A president's ceremonial and procedural roles still exist during international conferences and permanent deliberative bodies of international organisations.[14]

Another customary practice accepted by states attending international conferences related to the secretariat. National delegates or plenipotentiaries of participating states needed to focus exclusively on intense negotiations and debates. They could not afford to be distracted by routine and procedural questions. Therefore, in addition to the national secretariats maintained by each participating state, conferences required secretarial support for all

10 Usually, the resolution for this election was moved by the principal delegate of the country that comes first in French alphabetical order (Satow, supra note 8 at 15). In many European conferences, Germany (Allemagne in French) or Austria (Autriche in French) were responsible for proposing the election of the host state's delegate as the president of the congress or conference.

11 Hill, *supra* note 1 at 65.

12 *Ibid.*

13 Satow, *supra* note 8 at 15.

14 For instance, in the United Nations General Assembly, the president is elected by a simple majority vote of the General Assembly for a non-renewable one-year term. The President cannot be a national of one of the five permanent members of the Security Council as this would give the permanent five a disproportionately high concentration of power. In the United Nations Security Council, each member holds the presidency for one calendar month in the English alphabetical order of their names (Rule 18 of the Provisional Rules of Procedure of the Security Council, UN Doc. S/96/Rev.7 (21 December 1982)).

participating nations acting collectively. The secretariats of international gatherings typically received and disseminated communications from participating states, translated documents, reports, and resolutions, recorded the speeches delivered during the meetings, drafted and circulated the minutes of the sessions, and performed any other tasks that the conference assigned to them. In addition to 'protocolists' in charge of the official documentation,[15] secretariats of some international gatherings also employed finance officers to handle the expenses of the conference, press reporters to deal with the public, and interpreters to interpret speeches and debates.[16] Similarly, since French was still the language of diplomacy until the early 1900s, it was customary to appoint at least one French official whose primary responsibility was to ensure that the written records of the conference were accurate and grammatically correct.[17]

In most cases, the members of the secretariat were nationals of the inviting state. For instance, during the Paris Conference of 1865, technical services were provided entirely by the French, and during the London Conferences in 1867 and 1871, by British diplomats.[18] The members of the secretariat were placed under the control of the inviting state, and the president was the official exercising this control on behalf of the host state. Exceptionally, the Hague Conferences of 1899 and 1907 had a Secretariat composed of diplomats of the participating countries.[19] In either scenario, all members of the secretariat were appointed only after informal consultations with the heads of delegations. The leading official of the secretariats was known as "principal secretary"[20] or "secretary-general",[21] a job title that was subsequently retained to designate the chief administrative officer of the League of Nations and the United Nations. In most cases, the secretary-general of international conferences was "a person holding an official position in the government of the inviting state."[22] They were often members of the diplomatic or foreign service staff. The main drawback resulting from the practice of having the secretariat in the state that hosted the conference was the loss of knowledge, expertise, and 'institutional memory' when the conference moved to another state.

15 For the use of this term, see Satow, *supra* note 8 at 16.

16 Hill, *supra* note 1 at 77.

17 Satow, *supra* note 8 at 16; Hill, *supra* note 1 at 77.

18 Dobromir Mihajlov, "The Origin and the Early Development of International Civil Service" (2004) 1 *Miskolc Journal of International Law* 79 at 80.

19 *Ibid.*

20 Satow, *supra* note 8 at 16.

21 Hill, *supra* note 1 at 76.

22 *Ibid.*

During the nineteenth century, international gatherings of states surged drastically. Between 1826 and 1907, sovereign nations held over three hundred conferences and congresses.[23] Organising so many conferences and congresses on an ad hoc basis became too burdensome and impractical. In addition, as participating states also increased in number, uniform and concerted action was becoming impossible. The desire to centralise the activities of states was the driving force behind the creation of the first 'multinational' organisations. The minutes of some international conferences that led to the establishment of permanent institutions leave no doubt that the need to achieve consistency through centralisation was the main motivation for creating multinational or international organisations.

Specifically, the plenipotentiary representing Prussia at the Congress of Vienna stated as early as 1815 that the regulation by various states of the navigation on the Rhine River required some centrality (*une centralité quelconque*). In his view, one way of attaining such centrality was to establish a central authority managed by a head (*chef*) chosen by all riparian states or by a panel composed of several members. He added that the autonomy of each riparian state would necessarily have to be subordinated to the collective will of all riparian states.[24]

On 4 August 1862, the Postmaster General of the United States dispatched a letter to all countries with which his government maintained diplomatic relations, pointing out that "many embarrassments to foreign correspondence exist" in all postal departments "that can be remedied only by international concert of action." He attributed constant mistakes made by various postal offices to the great diversity of routes, arrangements, and rates prevailing between the same points. He then affirmed that this causes severe delays and unnecessary expenses to correspondents. These considerations led to the establishment of the Universal Postal Union.[25]

Similarly, during the International Telegraphic Conference of Vienna in 1868, the Swiss delegate proposed to create permanent institutions after pointing out that European countries' national administrations unintentionally applied different tax rates to their common correspondence. Some applied rates

---

23 Simeon E Baldwin, "International Congresses and Conferences of the Last Century as Forces Working Toward the Solidarity of the World" (1907) 1:3 *Am J Int'l L* 565 at 808.

24 Congrès de Vienne: Recueil de pièces relatives à cette assemblée, des déclarations qu'elle a publiées, des protocoles de ses délibérations et des principaux mémoires qui lui ont été présentés, Tome III (Paris: Librairie Grecque Latine Allemande, 1816) at 280.

25 John F Sly, "The Genesis of the Universal Postal Union: A Study in the Beginnings of International Organization Document No. 233" (1926) 11 *International Conciliation* 395.

agreed on at one conference, while others used rates agreed on at another conference, and they did so in good faith. He then pointed out that these inconsistencies were bound to occur between national administrations far away from each other, which do not usually have direct communications between them and which both believe the circulars they received and understood. Even when some governments suspect that they do not apply the correct rates, they do not know from whom they should seek clarifications.[26]

After exposing the difficulties faced by participating nations, the Swiss delegate proposed the establishment of a permanent body whose task would be to centralise the activities of all participating states. The central role of the permanent body would consist of receiving the relevant information, processing it, and sending communications as often as required.[27]

Like Prussia's intervention during the Congress of Vienna in 1815, the Swiss proposal of 1868 to establish a permanent agency was also based on a need to centralise and standardise the activities of various nations in a specific non-political field.[28] The desire to centralise states' actions and standardise their practices seemed to be the main reason for the progressive institutionalisation of multilateral conferences, leading to the appearance of primitive forms of international organisations. The need to create permanent institutions so that they could play the role of independent or neutral intermediaries was not a consideration. Of course, the centralisation of activities was not the only reason for setting up permanent institutions. Other important reasons militated in favour of permanent structures. For instance, Georges Langrod attributes the appearance of first secretariats to the desire of states to avoid any gaps between two conferences, to ensure continuity in agreements reached during previous conferences, and to prevent prolonged interruptions between meetings from thwarting the benefits of cohesion achieved by contracting nations.[29] However, these considerations were incidental or secondary.

1.2 *River Commissions*

One of the first examples of states joining in international endeavours that required personnel and authority to some extent independent of the geographic and political sovereignty of the member states was the management of the Rhine and Danube rivers.[30] On 15 October 1804, the French Empire

26 Documents de la Conférence télégraphique internationale de Vienne (1868) at 383–385.

27 *Ibid.*

28 Jean Siotis, *Essai sur le Secrétariat International* (Geneva: Librairie Droz, 1963) at 32.

29 Georges Langrod, *La fonction publique internationale* (Leiden: Sythoff, 1963) at 31.

30 Maxwell Cohen, "The United States and the United Nations Secretariat: A Preliminary Appraisal" (1953) 1:3 *McGill Law J* 169 at 170–171.

and the Holy Roman Empire signed a treaty known as the Octroi Convention relating to the use of the Rhine River. The purpose of the agreement was to guarantee the unobstructed navigation of vessels on the Rhine, replacing a multitude of tolls in existence on the Rhine with consistent toll rates levied on ships using the river. To ensure compliance of both parties with the treaty, the two powers decided to put in place a bi-national administration headed by a jointly appointed Director General and an equal number of inspectors and toll agents in bureaux along the river.[31] This led to the creation of the Rhine River Commission, the first (and for a long time the only) transnational regime regulating free navigation on a river. Although in 1815, European states signed the Final Act of the Congress of Vienna and agreed in its articles 108–110 to guarantee free navigation of international rivers and a standardised toll system for the collection of duties, they took no action to carry out this agreement until 1856.[32] Hence, between 1804 and 1856, the Rhine was the only river with a legal framework and a multinational compliance monitoring mechanism. The European Commission of Danube, established by the Treaty of Paris of 1856 (which ended the Crimean War between Russia and the alliance of the Ottoman Empire, Great Britain, the Second French Empire, and the Kingdom of Sardinia), became the second river commission with a permanent administrative structure.

These two nascent international entities had a very basic structure and were established for a specific and limited purpose. They were composed of representatives of the treaty states,[33] and the composition of their workforce accurately reflected the balance of power in Europe.[34] Most importantly, their staff were not "internationalised", and "their work [was] international only in the sense that a crowd at the Gare du Nord may be international".[35] Staff members of the Commission took instructions from their governments and owed a degree of allegiance to their countries of citizenship.[36] For these reasons, literature on international organisations tends to neglect river commissions and authors who mention them do so only in passing. However, a closer look at the European Commission of Danube reveals that river commissions may

31 Reinalda, *supra* note 4 at 18.

32 Although administrations like the Rhine River Commission were set up for the rivers Elbe in 1821, Douro in 1835, and Po in 1849, they were not active.

33 Paul S Reinsch, "International Unions and Their Administration" (1907) 1:3 *Am J Int'l L* 579 at 619.

34 Siotis, *supra* note 28 at 38.

35 C Delisle Burns, "International Administration" (1926) 7 British Yearbook of International Law 54 at 58.

36 For a detailed description of their structure see Siotis, *supra* note 28 at 32–38.

have played a more critical role in shaping future international secretariats than initially believed. For instance, the Commission's powers were significantly expanded between 1856 and 1883 to include policing and adjudication powers.[37] Some authors called it "a supranational authority" or "a sovereign entity".[38] As of 1878, member states of the European Danube Commission recognised the international character of its staff members and delegated the authority to appoint them to the commission itself. The commission also enjoyed the status of neutrality in times of war.[39] Another very important aspect of the Danube Commission was the status of its personnel. Since the commission enjoyed the status of extraterritoriality, its staff had limited privileges and immunities, which varied in time and depended on their rank and seniority.

1.3 *International Public Unions*

During the second half of the 19th and early 20th century, the international community of states continued making significant progress by creating several bodies for international cooperation on technical issues and matters, namely transport, communication, weights and measures, and intellectual property.[40] They established a dozen administrative and technical bureaux and unions, including the International Telegraph Union in 1865, the Universal Postal Union in 1874,[41] the International Bureau of Weights and Measures in 1875, the International Union for the Protection of Industrial Property in 1883, the International Union for the Protection of Literary and Artistic Works in 1886, the International Union of Railway Freight Transportation in 1890, the International Institute of Agriculture in 1905, and the International Office of Public Health in 1907. These newly created institutions had an organisational structure reminiscent of contemporary intergovernmental organisations. Specifically, they had a legislative organ (governing body) and a distinct administrative organ (secretariat). States equipped these organisations with permanent administrative organs because they realised that secretariats, bureaux, and central offices would enable them to attain their goals more efficiently by facilitating cooperation through their technical expertise, through the specialised knowledge they would acquire over time, as well as through

37 *Ibid* at 35.
38 *Ibid.*
39 *Ibid.*
40 Jan Klabbers, *An Introduction to International Institutional Law*, 4th ed (New York: Cambridge University Press, 2022) at 16.
41 Clyde Eagleton, *International Government* (New York: Ronald Press, 1948) at 157–168.

ordinary secretariat functions that they would perform. These administrative organs were responsible for ensuring that member states received uninterrupted secretarial services such as the production of documents, recording of decisions, translation services and other housekeeping tasks during their multilateral conferences.[42] It is worth repeating that the primary consideration in setting up these embryonic secretariats was the desire to *centralise* the collective activities of member states.[43] Independence and neutrality had not yet become an important consideration since the mandate of these international entities was principally technical and, therefore, the functions of their secretariats were exclusively administrative and clerical.[44]

Permanent secretariats that preceded the League of Nations fell into two loose categories. The first and earliest generation of permanent secretariats were placed directly under the supervision of a participating state's government. For instance, the organisation and management of the International Bureau of Telegraphic Administrations (*Bureau international des Administrations télégraphiques*), established in 1868 during the International Telegraphic Conference held in Vienna, was entrusted to the Telegraphic Administration of the Swiss Confederation.[45] The issue of independence was not even raised during the telegraphic conference. The French delegate suggested only in passing that the newly created Bureau be based in a neutral city.[46]

Similarly, the Bureau of the Postal Union,[47] the International Bureaux for the Protection of Industrial Property and the Protection of Literary and

---

42 Leon Gordenker, *The UN Secretary-General and Secretariat*, 2nd ed (New York: Routledge, 2010) at 4.

43 Centralisation of collective activities was attained through a stable organisational structure and a supportive administrative apparatus that increased the efficiency of collective action and enhanced the organisation's ability to affect the understandings, environment, and interests of states.

44 See Henry G Schermers and Niels Blokker, *International Institutional Law*, 6th ed (Leiden: Nijhoff, 2018) at para 435.

45 Article 61 of the Convention on the International Telegraph Union as amended in Vienna in 1868 and Article 34 of the Regulations annexed to the Convention.

46 Documents diplomatiques de la Convention de Vienne de 1868, page 389: « Quant au siège de l'Agence générale, M. le Colonel de Chauvin proposerait de le placer dans une ville neutre. ».

47 Initially, Article 15 of the 1874 Treaty constituting General Postal Union established "the International Office of the General Postal Union, a central office, which shall be conducted under the surveillance of a Postal Administration to be chosen by the Congress". In 1878, the participating states signed the Convention and Final Protocol of Paris in which they agreed to rename the International Office to "International Bureau of the Universal Postal Union, a central office, which is conducted under the superintendence of the Swiss

Artistic Works,[48] and the Central Bureau of the International Union for Railway Transportation[49] were also placed under the supervision of the Swiss government. The fact that contracting states often agreed to establish the permanent seat of the International Bureaux in Switzerland could give the erroneous impression that Switzerland was chosen as the host nation due to its neutrality. However, it is unlikely that Swiss neutrality played a role in determining the location of permanent secretariats. For instance, the Bureau of the International Union for the Publication of Customs Tariffs was based in Brussels and the Bureau of the Metric Union was established in Paris.[50] Therefore, it is more likely that Switzerland was often chosen because of its experience and expertise acquired over time in administering and managing international secretariats. In any event, as pointed out above, the independence or neutrality of international secretariats had not yet become a significant concern or an important consideration during this period.

As a rule, the authority to appoint staff members of this first category (and more primitive form) of international secretariats was delegated to the host nation under whose control and supervision the *bureaux* were placed. For instance, the Ministry of Foreign Affairs of Belgium was given the power to appoint staff of the International Union for the Publication of Customs Tariffs and the Federal Council of Switzerland[51] was empowered to organise the central bureau of the International Union for Railway Transportation.[52]

Outside the European continent, the approach was similar. In March 1890, eighteen American States participated in the first International American Conference convened to deal with trade and arbitration. They approved the establishment of the International Union of American Republics headquartered in Washington, DC. An administrative body represented the Union called the Bureau of the American Republics,[53] which was placed under the

Postal Administration, and the expenses of which are borne by all the Administrations of the Union" (Article 16).

48 Paris Convention for the Protection of Industrial Property of 1883, Art. 13 and Berne Convention for the Protection of Literary and Artistic Works of 1886, Art. 16.

49 Convention internationale sur le transport de marchandises par chemins de fer of 1890, Art. 57 of and Règlement relative à l'institution d'un Office central of 1890, Art. 1. Reinsch, *supra* note 33 at 591.

50 Schermers and Blokker, *supra* note 44 at paras 434, footnote 157.

51 Convention concerning the formation of an International Union for the Publication of Customs Tariffs of 1890, Art. 5.

52 Reinsch, *supra* note 33 at 591.

53 Initially, the organ was called "Commercial Bureau of American Republics". However, it soon came to be known as the "International Bureau of American States". It was

supervision of the Secretary of State of the United States.[54] The Conference requested the Secretary of State to organise the Bureau but did not specify how the newly created entity would be staffed.[55]

The second generation or category of international secretariats, which appeared in 1875, was slightly different in that they were no longer under the control and authority of a single participating nation. The International Bureau of Weights and Measures, established in 1875, was the first secretariat to be placed under the authority of an international committee. This international committee was the Bureau's governing body and represented member states between general assemblies.[56]

The minutes of the 1875 Metre Conference held in Paris reveal that independence and neutrality gradually became important considerations when setting up international secretariats. More specifically, the German delegate declared that Germany would be prepared to participate in a joint endeavour relating to weights and measures only if their technical aspects were entrusted to an international body appointed by all participating states. He specified that Germany would accept that the headquarters of the new body be based in Paris, provided the requirements of neutrality and independence were met.[57] Consequently, the 1875 Metre Convention stated that the International Bureau would operate exclusively under the supervision and oversight of an international committee, which would be under the authority of the general conference on weights and measures composed of delegates of all contracting governments.[58] Another important element is that the authority to recruit and

designated by this title until the fourth International Conference of American States held in 1910 changed its name to Pan American Union.

54 Samuel Guy Inman, "Pan-American Conferences and Their Results" (1923) 4:3 *The Southwestern Political and Social Science Quarterly* 238 at 244.

55 International American Conference, Reports of Committees & Discussions Thereon (Revised under the Direction of the Executive Committee by Order of the Conference, Adopted March 7, 1890) (Washington, DC: Government Printing Office., 7) at 404.

56 Siotis, *supra* note 28 at 39.

57 *Documents diplomatiques de la conférence de mètre* (Paris: Imprimerie Nationale, 1875), p. 46: « M Foersteb (Allemagne) déclare que ses instructions portent comme condition de la participation ultérieure de l'Allemagne à toute entreprise commune au sujet des poids et mesures, la fondation d'un Bureau scientifique international et neutre, chargé de la vérification, de la conservation et de l'usage ultérieur des prototypes métriques, et placé sous la direction d'une commission internationale nommée par les Gouvernements qui participeront à la fondation de ce bureau; le siége du Bureau international des poids et mesures sera à Paris, si le Gouvernement français l'accepte dans des conditions de parfaite neutralité et indépendance. »

58 The Metre Convention of 1875, Art. 3: « Le Bureau international fonctionnera sous la direction et la surveillance exclusives d'un Comité international des poids et mesures,

appoint staff (except the deputies) was no longer delegated to the host nation but was instead given to the Director of the Bureau.[59] There was, however, one anomaly in the setup of the International Bureau of Weights and Measures; initially, the director of the Bureau was also a member of the governing body. This anomaly was subsequently corrected when directors were no longer allowed to be members of the international committee.[60]

The International Bureau of Weights and Measures marked a departure from the existing practice in two respects. First, the permanent secretariat was under the authority of an international governing body as opposed to the government of a specific participating state. Second, the appointment of staff was entrusted to the organisation's Director as opposed to one or several participating states. This approach gave rise to a new practice that placed the permanent secretariat under an international governing body. As of the 1900s, the configuration of the international secretariat of Weights and Measures became the norm. Specifically, the permanent bureau of the International Sugar Union,[61] the Central Office of the International Association of Seismology,[62] the permanent committee of the International Institute of Agriculture,[63] and

placé lui-même sous l'autorité d'une Conférence générale des poids et mesures, formée de délégués de tous les Gouvernements contractants. »

59 Regulations annexed to the Metre Convention of 1875, Art. 17: « Un règlement, établi par le Comité, fixera l'effectif maximum pour chaque catégorie du personnel du Bureau. Le directeur et ses adjoints seront nommés au scrutin secret par le Comité international. Leur nomination sera notifiée aux Gouvernements des Hautes Parties contractantes. Le directeur nommera les autres membres du personnel, dans les limites établies par le règlement mentionné au premier alinéa ci-dessus. »

60 Reinalda, *supra* note 4 at 28.

61 N Politis, "L'organisation de l'Union internationale des sucres" (1904) 2 *Revue de science et de législation financières* 1 at 3. During the 1902 Conference concerning the sugar regime held in Brussels, signatory states agreed to create a permanent commission composed of delegates of the different contracting States and a permanent bureau. The Convention did not specify the composition of the permanent bureau. However, nations agreed that the bureau would consist of technical and administrative staff appointed by the permanent commission.

62 Convention relating to the Establishment of the International Association of Seismology of 1903, Art. 5 and 12.

63 Convention establishing International Institute of Agriculture of 1905, Art. 2: "The institute shall be composed of a general assembly and a permanent committee, the composition and duties of which are defined in the subsequent articles." Art. 6: "The executive power of the institute is entrusted to the permanent committee, which, under the direction and control of the general assembly, shall carry out the latter's decisions and prepare propositions to submit to it." Art. 7: "The permanent committee shall be composed of members designated by the respective governments. Each adhering nation shall be represented in the permanent committee by one member."

the International Office of Public Health[64] were all placed under the authority and supervision of an international committee consisting of representatives of all contracting states.

Even the International Union of American Republics began changing its institutional structure to give the Bureau of the American Republics more independence. In 1896, the Bureau was placed under the supervision of a board called the Executive Committee, consisting of five representatives, including the US Secretary of State. In 1902, the independence of the Bureau was further strengthened when its supervision was transferred from the Executive Committee to a Governing Board composed of the chiefs of the Latin American diplomatic missions in Washington, DC, and chaired by the US secretary of state.[65]

Hence, *centralisation* was no longer the only consideration for creating permanent international secretariats; the dimension of *independence* of international secretariats was now gaining ground, albeit with many practical difficulties. For instance, although staff members of the International Institute of Agriculture established in 1905 were not permitted to take instructions from their governments,[66] they were made up not of agricultural technicians but of the diplomatic representatives of the member nations accredited to the Italian government, which was effectively controlling the policies, administration, and personnel of the Institute.[67] Furthermore, out of the 53 members of the personnel, 42 were Italian nationals. As a result of the disproportionate political influence of the Italian government, the Institute had effectively lost its international character.[68]

The table below traces the evolution of primitive forms of intergovernmental organisations and their secretariats, which paved the way for the League of Nations. It shows how the independence of international secretariats and civil servants was gradually strengthened.

64 Arrangement relating to International Office of Public Health signed at Rome, Art. 1: "The High Contracting Parties engage to found and maintain an International Office of Public Hygiene with headquarters at Paris." Art. 2: "The Office will perform its functions under the authority and supervision of a committee composed of delegates of the contracting Governments."

65 Reinalda, *supra* note 4 at 28.

66 Schermers and Blokker, *supra* note 44 at para 435.

67 See Asher Hobson, *The International Institute of Agriculture: An Historical and Critical Analysis of Its Organization, Activities and Policies of Administration* (Berkeley: University of California Press, 1931).

68 *Ibid.*

TABLE 1 Notable Unions and Bureaux created before the League of Nations

#	Name of entity	Year	Legal instrument	Article(s) or text dealing with secretariat or staff
1.	International Telegraph Union	1868	1868 International Telegraphic Conference in Vienna	Art. 61: Une Administration télégraphique, désignée par la Conférence, prendra les mesures propres à faciliter, dans un intéret commun, l'execution et l'application de la Convention. A cet effet elle organisera, sous le titre de « Bureau international des Administrations telegraphiques », un service special qui fonctionnera sous sa direction, dont les frais seront supportes par toutes les Administrations des États contractants […]
			Règlement de service international (destiné à compléter les dispositions de la Convention Télégraphique)	Art. 34: L'Administration télégraphique de la Confédération Suisse est désignée pour organiser le bureau international dans les conditions déterminées par l'article 61 de la Convention.
			Documents diplomatiques, page 389:	Quant au siege de l'Agence générale, M. le Colonel de Chauvin proposerait de le placer dans une ville neutre.
2.	General Postal Union	1874	Treaty constituting General Postal Union	Art. 15: There shall be organized, under the name of the International Office of the General Postal Union, a central office, which shall be conducted under the surveillance of a Postal Administration to be chosen by the Congress, and the expenses of which shall be borne by all the Administrations of the contracting States.
		1878	Convention and final protocol signed at Paris June 1, 1878	Art. 16: There is maintained, under the name of the International Bureau of the Universal Postal Union, a central office, which is conducted under the superintendence of the Swiss Postal Administration, and the expenses of which are borne by all the Administrations of the Union.

TABLE 1 Notable Unions and Bureaux created before the League of Nations (*cont.*)

#	Name of entity	Year	Legal instrument	Article(s) or text dealing with secretariat or staff
3.	International Bureau of Weights and Measures	1875	The Metre Convention	Article 3 : Le Bureau international fonctionnera sous la direction et la surveillance exclusives d'un Comité international des poids et mesures, placé lui-même sous l'autorité d'une Conférence générale des poids et mesures, formée de délégués de tous les Gouvernements contractants.
			Regulations	Article 17 : Un règlement, établi par le Comité, fixera l'effectif maximum pour chaque catégorie du personnel du Bureau. Le directeur et ses adjoints seront nommés au scrutin secret par le Comité international. Leur nomination sera notifiée aux Gouvernements des Hautes Parties contractantes. Le directeur nommera les autres membres du personnel, dans les limites établies par le règlement mentionné au premier alinéa ci-dessus.
			Documents diplomatiques de la conférence de mètre, (Paris : Imprimerie Nationale, 1875), p. 46 :	M. Foersteb (Allemagne) déclare que ses instructions portent comme condition de la participation ultérieure de l'Allemagne à toute entreprise commune au sujet des poids et mesures, la fondation d'un Bureau scientifique international et neutre, chargé de la vérification, de la conservation et de l'usage ultérieur des prototypes métriques, et placé sous la direction d'une commission internationale nommée par les Gouvernements qui participeront à la fondation de ce bureau; le siège du Bureau international des poids et mesures sera à Paris, si le Gouvernement français l'accepte dans des conditions de parfaite neutralité ct indépendance.

TABLE 1 Notable Unions and Bureaux created before the League of Nations (*cont.*)

#	Name of entity	Year	Legal instrument	Article(s) or text dealing with secretariat or staff
4.	International Union for the Protection of Industrial Property	1883	Paris Convention for the Protection of Industrial Property	Article 13: Un office international sera uissee sous le titre de Bureau international de l'Union pour la protection de la Propriété industrielle. Ce Bureau, don't les frais seront supportés par les Administrations de tous les États contractants, sera uiss sous la haute autorité de l'Administration supérieure de la Confédération uisse, et fonctionnera sous sa surveillance.
5.	International Union for the Protection of Literary and Artistic Works	1886	Berne Convention for the Protection of Literary and Artistic Works	Article 16: Un office international sera uissee sous le titre de Bureau de l'Union internationale pour la protection des œuvres littéraires et artistiques. Ce Bureau, don't les frais seront supportés par les Administrations de tous les États contractants, sera uiss sous la haute autorité de l'Administration supérieure de la Confédération uisse, et fonctionnera sous sa surveillance.
6.	International Union for the Publication of Custom Tariffs	1890	Convention concerning the formation of an International Union for the Publication of Custom Tariffs.	The persons composing the International Bureau shall be appointed through the agency of the Ministry of Foreign Affairs of Belgium, which shall advance the necessary funds and see that the institution is properly managed.
7.	International Bureau of the American Republics	1890	International American Conference	Paragraphs 15 of a resolution adopted on 29 March 1890 by the first International Conference of American Republics: 15: The Secretary of State of the United States is requested to organize and establish the Commercial Bureau as soon as practicable, after a majority of the countries here represented have officially signified their consent to join the International Union.

TABLE 1 Notable Unions and Bureaux created before the League of Nations (*cont.*)

#	Name of entity	Year	Legal instrument	Article(s) or text dealing with secretariat or staff
8.	International Sugar Union	1902	Convention concerning the sugar regime	The high contracting parties agree to create a permanent commission, having charge of the surveillance of the execution of the provisions of the present convention. This commission shall be composed of delegates of the different contracting States, and to it will be attached a permanent bureau. The commission elects its president; it will sit at Brussels.
9.	International Association of Seismology	1903	Convention relating to the Establishment of the International Association of Seismology	Art. 5: The organs of the Association shall be: a) the General Assembly. B) the Permanent Commission. C) the Central Office.
10.	International Institute of Agriculture	1905	1905 Convention establishing International Institute of Agriculture	Article 2: The institute shall be composed of a general assembly and a permanent committee, the composition and duties of which are defined in the ensuing articles. Article 6: The executive power of the institute is entrusted to the permanent committee, which, under the direction and control of the general assembly, shall carry out the decisions of the latter and prepare propositions to submit to it. Article 7: The permanent committee shall be composed of members designated by the respective governments. Each adhering nation shall be represented in the permanent committee by one member.
11.	International Office of Public Health	1907	Arrangement relating to International Office of Public Health signed at Rome	Art. 1: The High Contracting Parties engage to found and maintain an International Office of Public Hygiene with headquarters at Paris. Art. 2: The Office will perform its functions under the authority and supervision of a committee composed of delegates of the contracting Governments.

TABLE 1 Notable Unions and Bureaux created before the League of Nations (*cont.*)

#	Name of entity	Year	Legal instrument	Article(s) or text dealing with secretariat or staff
			Organic By-Laws of the International Office of Public Hygiene (Annex to Arrangement)	Article 2: [The Office] is independent of the authorities of the country in which it is placed. Article 6: The Office is placed under the authority and supervision of an International Committee consisting of technical representatives designated by the participating States in the proportion of one representative for each State.
				Article 8: The business of the office is conducted by a salaried staff, including a Director, a Secretary-General, and such force as may be necessary to perform the work of the Office. […] The Director and Secretary-General shall be appointed by the Committee. The Director shall attend the meetings of the Committee in an advisory capacity. The appointment and dismissal of employees of all classes appertain to the Director and shall be reported by him to the Committee.
12.	International Bureau of the Permanent Court of Arbitration	1907	The Hague Convention on Pacific Settlement of International Disputes	Article 49: The Permanent Administrative Council, composed of the diplomatic representatives of the Contracting Powers accredited to The Hague and of the Netherland Minister for Foreign Affairs, who will act as President, is charged with the direction and control of the International Bureau.

2 Period during the League of Nations

Permanent secretariats underwent a significant transformation with the establishment of the League of Nations. With its vast machinery of international cooperation, the League of Nations emerged as a mature international administration.[69] The League's Secretariat was the first attempt to establish a truly international staff.

The League's Secretary-General was appointed by the Treaty of Versailles. The Treaty not only established the Secretary-General's Office but expressly mentioned by name the individual who would be the post holder. The first occupant of the office became Sir Eric Drummond – an experienced civil servant of the British government. Drummond was recognised in the British Foreign Office for his diligence, precision, and effective communication.[70] Having served under Britain's top Liberal and Conservative leaders, Drummond had acquired valuable experience that had prepared him for the role of Secretary-General.[71] British Prime Minister Asquith, under whom Drummond worked as Private Secretary, described him as "a most intelligent, observant, delightful man".[72]

When Drummond accepted the appointment as the League's Secretary-General, he was asked to organise the Secretariat in the first days of an institution still in its infancy. The Treaty of Versailles was not ratified when the Secretary-General was asked to recruit personnel. Founding members hoped the treaty would be ratified within a few weeks of being signed. However, to their great disappointment, the Treaty of Versailles was signed on 28 June 1919 but was not ratified until 10 January 1920. During this period, the newly appointed Secretary-General had to begin the selection of the nucleus of his staff. The recruitment of personnel was a matter of pressing necessity. In an interview given to Manchester Guardian in May 1919, Eric Drummond explained the importance of recruiting staff before the Treaty of Versailles came into force. Specifically, the League had no legal existence or recognised officials until the Treaty of Paris was signed and ratified. Curiously, the terms of the treaty required that the League complete specific duties and tasks as soon as it came into effect. For instance, fifteen days after the coming into force of

69 Egon F Ranshofen-Wertheimer, "The International Civil Service of the Future" (1946) 24 *Int Concil* 60 at 62.

70 David Macfadyen et al., *Eric Drummond and his Legacies: The League of Nations and the Beginnings of Global Governance* (Cham: Palgrave Macmillan, 2019) at 8.

71 *Ibid.*

72 *Ibid.*

the treaty, a commission of five members, three of whom are to be appointed by the League, must be set to trace the exact frontier line of the Sarre Valley.

> It is, therefore, clearly necessary to make general provisions for the immediate and effective action of the League. To this purpose, I am selecting the personnel of the secretariat. Any scheme of organisation must be approved by the commission appointed by the Plenary Conference, and all appointments ratified by the Council. We are working out plans for a truly international secretariat. Its members will have an international character of mind. They must divest themselves of national preconceptions. Its members are not to be appointed by or to be regarded as the representatives of their respective nations.[73]

To assist him in developing a policy for personnel administration, the Peace Conference – acting in a plenary session – appointed a committee composed of nine member states to deal with the first stages of the organisation. Although the committee gave authority to the Secretary-General to make the necessary arrangements to appoint staff and fixed the amount of the Secretary-General's remuneration, it continued working on the nature of the secretariat that the League should have.

2.1 *Two Conflicting Theories and Proposals*

From the beginning, there was a difference of opinion at the Peace Conference on the nature and composition of the Secretariat.[74] Two competing and mutually exclusive approaches were proposed. The first approach advocated for a Secretariat composed of national delegations of League member states. The proponents of this approach argued that each delegation would be paid for by the country's government from which it came and be responsible to that government. This proposal was a continuation of the practice adopted at international conferences preceding the creation of the League. According to this theory, the role of the Secretary-General of the League would be limited to coordinating the services of the national delegations and to centralising administrative functions. Under this construct, the League's secretariat would be "nothing more and nothing else than a permanent conference of representatives of the powers members of the League".[75]

---

73 *Manchester Guardian*, 31 May 1919, p. 10, col. 3.

74 Eric Drummond, "The Secretariat of the League of Nations" (1931) 9:2 *Public Administration* 228 at 228–229.

75 *Ibid* at 228.

According to the second and more avant-garde theory, the secretariat of the League had to be independent of its member states. The proponents of this second approach argued in favour of an international civil service in which men and women of various nationalities would unite in preparing and presenting to the members of the League an impartial, objective, and common basis of discussion. According to this theory, the staff of the Secretariat would be responsible to the Secretary-General alone.[76]

Eric Drummond vigorously advocated for the second approach. He maintained that the old system had not given satisfactory results and urged the Committee set up by the Plenary Peace Conference to consider the matter of organisation that the second blueprint should be retained. Drummond recalled that, in the past, international conferences had often suffered from the lack of organised international preparatory work. Therefore, according to him, it would be of great value if an expert and impartial organisation existed which, before discussion by the national representatives took place, could draw up objective statements of the problems to be discussed and indicate those points on which the governments seemed to agree. He was adamant that the execution of decisions should be entrusted to people who, being the servants of all member states of the League, could be relied upon to carry them out with complete freedom from national bias.[77] The concept of an international secretariat independent of its multinational executive or legislative organs had grown partly out of the experience of inter-Allied commissions, committees and councils established during the war as coordination machinery for logistical support.[78] The structure devised for this purpose was a Council or Commission of Ministers of different nations with a permanent secretariat subordinated to this international body.[79] The fact that many individuals, including Monnet, transitioned from the network of 20 inter-allied committees to the League's Secretariat confirms that these committees inspired the League's institutional structure.[80]

It is believed that the idea of an international and independent secretariat was first proposed to Eric Drummond by his close friend Philip Kerr, a member of an influential group of British public servants and politicians known as the 'Round Table' or 'Round Table Movement'.[81] An article published by Kerr

---

76 Charles Howard Ellis, *The Origin, Structure and Working of the League of Nations* (London: George Allen and Unwin, 1928) at 172–173.

77 *Ibid* at 173.

78 Burns, *supra* note 35 at 61.

79 *Ibid.*

80 David Macfadyen et al., *supra* note 70 at 72.

81 *Ibid* at 74.

in March 1919 in the Round Table Journal gives credence to this theory. Kerr argued in this article that the League should have an international secretariat composed not of national ambassadors but civil servants under the authority of a non-national Chancellor.[82] Drummond's vision of the Secretariat was very similar, not to say identical, to that of Kerr.

In May 1920, the committee appointed by the Peace Conference to assist the League's Secretary-General in determining the nature of the Secretariat issued its report on the League's Secretariat. The Committee was presided over by the former British Foreign Secretary and Drummond's boss in the British public service, Arthur James Balfour,[83] who often backed Drummond's proposals and plans. Unsurprisingly, the Committee recommended the blueprint proposed by Eric Drummond to establish an independent secretariat composed of international public servants as opposed to national representatives. The relevant excerpt of Balfour's report reads as follows:

> I shall propose that no member of the Secretariat, during his or her term of office, shall accept any honour or decoration except for services rendered prior to the appointment. [...] The members of the staff carry out, as I have explained, not national but international duties. Nothing should be done to weaken the sense of their international allegiance; the acceptance of special marks of distinction or favour, either from their own or from any other country, militates in our view against the general spirit of the Covenant.[84]

The League Council adopted the Balfour Report, cementing the proposal that staff members were not civil servants of their country of citizenship but servants only of the League of Nations.[85] The Report also specified that the staff members should carry out not national but international duties.[86]

The following year, the Assembly of the League adopted the Noblemaire Report, which implicitly reiterated the support of the nations for the Secretary-General's concept of the international civil service.[87] The report recommended

82 Philip Kerr, "The Practical Organisation of Peace" (1919) 9:34 *The Round Table Journal* 217.

83 Arthur James Balfour was a prominent British statesman who was the British Prime Minister from 1902 to 1905 and Foreign Secretary from 1916 to 1919.

84 AJ Balfour, "Procès-verbal of the Fifth Session of the Council of the League of Nations, Report relating to Staff of the Secretariat" (1920) 1:4 *League of Nations OJ* 115 at 137.

85 SM Schwebel, "The International Character of the Secretariat of the United Nations" (1953) 30 *Brit YB Int'l L* 71 at 72.

86 Balfour, *supra* note 84 at 138–139.

87 Schwebel, *supra* note 85 at 72.

recruiting and promoting staff members based on competitive selection instead of national or political patronage. The report acknowledged that due to the exceptional circumstances under which the League of Nations was created, the Secretary-General was compelled to exercise absolute discretion in appointing a few individuals. However, it is also recommended that this discretionary and autocratic recruitment system be replaced by competitive selection and be departed from only in exceptional cases where the necessity for such departure can be established.[88]

The report also cautioned against recruiting personnel mainly from national public service. It explained that if staff members were drawn largely from national administrations, they would always think of the prospects of advancement in their own countries and be tempted to support a national rather than an international point of view.[89]

Another recommendation the Noblemaire Report made related to establishing a salary scale based on wages granted by various States to their highest-paid officials. This recommendation became known as the Noblemaire principle, which still governs how the United Nations determines salary scales for internationally recruited staff members.[90] The report stated the emoluments of staff should be calculated based on salaries granted to the highest paid officials in the various States Members of the League, "at the risk of seeing the Secretariat and the ILO deprived of the services of the aforesaid officials, which would have been out of the question."[91]

88 Report submitted by the Fourth Committee to the Assembly on the conclusions and proposals of the Commission of Experts appointed in accordance with the resolutions adopted by the Assembly of the League of Nations at its meeting of December 17th, 1920 (26 September 1921) at 6–7.

89 *Ibid* at 8.

90 See UNGAOR, 35th sess., Summary Record of the 39th meeting of the Fifth Committee held on 28 November 1980, UN Doc. A/C.5/35/SR.39 (8 December 1980). In its Judgement No. 825 – *In re Beattie and Sheeran* – the ILOAT summarised the Noblemaire principle as follows: "The Noblemaire principle, which dates back to the days of the League of Nations and which the United Nations took over, embodies two rules. One is that, to keep the international civil service as one, its employees shall get equal pay for work of equal value, whatever their nationality or the salaries earned in their own country. The other rule is that in recruiting staff from their full membership international organisations shall offer pay that will draw and keep citizens of countries where salaries are highest."

91 Report submitted by the Fourth Committee to the Assembly on the conclusions and proposals of the Commission of Experts appointed in accordance with the resolutions adopted by the Assembly of the League of Nations at its meeting of December 17th, 1920, supra note 88 at 5.

Beyond these rather general observations, the founders of the League left untended questions about the structure, form, and nature of the new international secretariat because they had had enough difficulty getting the Covenant negotiated without raising relatively unimportant matters.[92] Detailed rules regulating the rights and obligations of the League's personnel were promulgated through the Staff Regulations of the League in 1922. It is noteworthy that Article 1 of the Regulations reiterated that the officials of the Secretariat of the League of Nations are international officials responsible for the execution of their duties to the Secretary-General alone and that they were not permitted to seek or receive instructions from any other authority.

If the League's member states had opted for a Secretariat composed of national delegations, international organisations would have undoubtedly looked differently and been less effective in fulfilling their mandate. Following Drummond's recommendation and establishing an international civil service played a crucial role in forming and developing independent secretariats.

2.2 *The League's Secretariat under Sir Eric Drummond's Leadership*

Remarkably, no precedent or blueprint existed to guide the first Secretary-General of the League in setting up an entirely independent Secretariat.[93] Individual leadership matters in secretariat development from the outset, when the first executive head introduces national bureaucratic traditions like Eric Drummond introduced national and imperial traditions in the League of Nations Secretariat.[94] Having introduced a model similar to the Westminster system of public administration, Drummond became the architect of the first international and independent secretariat.[95] The first Secretary-General of the UN – Trygve Lie – observed in his memoirs that Eric Drummond's decision to create the first truly international Secretariat had such a profound significance that it was arguably "one of the most important and promising political developments of the twentieth century", securing him a place in history.[96]

Public servants were, for the first time, completely independent of the political apparatus of their national governments. Staff members of the League had to ensure that political considerations did not affect their actions and

92 Norman A Graham and Robert S Jordan, *The International Civil Service: Changing Role and Concepts* (New York: Pergamon Press, 1980) at 6.

93 Ranshofen-Wertheimer, *supra* note 69 at 70.

94 Reinalda, *supra* note 4 at 4.

95 Gordenker, *supra* note 42 at 5.

96 Trygve Lie, *In the Cause of Peace: Seven Years at the United Nations* (New York: Macmillan, 1954) at 41.

decisions. They received instructions from the League's Secretary-General and not from their national governments. In return, they had a career path that did not depend on political patronage but was based exclusively on merit. The delineation of the League's permanent secretariat from its deliberative bodies became the key feature of the institutional structure of contemporary international organisations.

To display the independence and neutrality of the League's Secretariat, Eric Drummond abstained from offering unsolicited advice to member states, advising them only if consulted.[97] He "had brought to his job all the traditions of faceless anonymity of the British Civil Service", making few personal initiatives.[98] He continuously emphasised to the staff of the Secretariat the strict necessity for impartiality.[99] Consequently, he always tried – and often succeeded – to shelter his staff from the political pressures of member states. However, Drummond's approach did not please everyone. Some critics questioned the value of showing absolute neutrality when Eric Drummond failed to condemn Japan during the 1931 Manchurian crisis.[100] Many view this unassertiveness as a sign of weakness.

While this unobtrusiveness may look like submissiveness, one must consider the relevant context. Initially, the post of the Secretary-General was called 'Chancellor'. In his memoirs, the British representative at the Peace Conference, Robert Cecil, writes that the Chancellor was supposed to be more than a permanent official. "He was to be the international representative of the League – its mouthpiece – its suggester, if not the director, of its policy. He would be at least as influential on the political side as Albert Thomas, the Director of ILO, was in industrial matters."[101] The League's founders had initially offered the position to the "charismatic and Anglophile Greek Prime Minister Eleftherios Venizelos."[102] However, Venizelos declined the offer. When no other suitable "statesman of European reputation" agreed to fill the newly created position, the title of the post was renamed and effectively downgraded to 'Secretary-General'.[103] This was the first signal from member states that the head of the Secretariat was primarily an administrative role.[104]

---

97 Evan Luard, *A History of the United Nations* (London: Palgrave Macmillan UK, 1982) at 12.

98 *Ibid.*

99 Macfadyen et al., *supra* note 70 at 15–16.

100 *Ibid* at 15.

101 Robert Cecil of Chelwood, *All the Way* (London: Hodder and Stoughton, 1949) at 150.

102 James Barros, "The Importance of Secretaries-General of the United Nations" in Robert S Jordan, ed, *Dag Hammarskjöld Revisited: United Nations Secretary-General as a Force in World Politics* (Durham: Carolina Academic Press, 1983) at 27–28.

103 Cecil of Chelwood, *supra* note 101 at 150–151.

104 Ellis, *supra* note 76 at 163 (footnote 2).

This signal was further reinforced after the establishment of the League. In 1921, the Noblemaire Report cautioned the secretariat of the League against showing any initiative, including making suggestions or interpreting decisions made by various organs. The influential committee of delegates stated that "the Secretariat should not extend the sphere of its activities [and] should confine itself to collating the relevant documents and the preparation of decisions without hazarding suggestions".[105] There was an expectation that once deliberative bodies made decisions, the Secretariat would confine itself to executing them in the letter and the spirit and should refrain even from interpreting them.[106]

Thus, to understand Drummond's reluctance to condemn the aggressive actions of some nations, one must be mindful of the political context, which restricted his freedom of action and defined the scope of his responsibilities. As one author aptly explains, the homogeneity of the system of international relations that gave rise to the League of Nations, combined with the diplomatic and administrative tradition of the Concert of Europe, shaped the administrative nature of its secretariat.[107] Therefore, if Eric Drummond and his staff had taken sides or condemned the actions of a member state, their intervention would have been regarded as an excess of power. Nevertheless, one must acknowledge that the administrative nature of the secretariat had some hidden benefits. Due to the Secretariat's primarily administrative nature, member states initially saw no interest in exerting political pressure on its staff. This, in turn, allowed the Secretary-General to establish a functionally independent structure and a robust secretariat without political interference from member states. The Swiss academic, former League official, and co-founder of the Graduate Institute of International Studies, William Rappard, attributes the lack of interest of member states in the League, especially during the first three or four years of its existence, to a widely held view that the new organisation was an insignificant instrument of international government. Consequently, member states were inclined to send to Geneva officials of minor importance who changed from time to time and for whom their intermittent League duties were never their main tasks. Rappard notes, however, that while the government of the League was weak, its civil service was correspondingly strong. Its

105 Report submitted by the Fourth Committee to the Assembly on the conclusions and proposals of the Commission of Experts appointed in accordance with the resolutions adopted by the Assembly of the League of Nations at its meeting of December 17th, 1920, supra note 88 at 3.

106 *Ibid.*

107 Siotis, *supra* note 28 at 50–51.

members were carefully chosen for their ability and devotion to the League's ideals. Rappard recollects that in all minor matters, and even in several important ones, the functions of the members of the Council and the Assembly consisted mainly of delivering speeches, reading reports, and voting resolutions that had been drafted for them by the League's Secretariat.[108]

Despite Eric Drummond's remarkable efforts, the independence of the League's secretariat still had critical shortcomings. The Covenant of the League had only two provisions dedicated to its Secretariat – Articles 6 and 7. Neither guaranteed its independence from the League's member states. These two provisions were not just silent on the question of independence; they explicitly undermined it. Specifically, Article 6(3) of the Covenant required the appointment of staff members of the League's Secretariat to be subjected to the Council's approval. Essentially, any member of the Council could object to the appointment of a specific staff member, which could have potentially exposed some candidates for a vacant post to undesired political pressures of certain member states. According to one author, "[t]he League had been vulnerable to national meddling – or even sabotage – because of its requirement that secretariat staff be approved by governments."[109] Although there is no evidence that Council members abused their power by blocking the appointment of undesired candidates, the League's Assembly attempted to curtail Drummond's authority to appoint staff members without their oversight and endorsement. At the 1920 Assembly, South African representative Sir Reginald Blankenberg proposed to set up a joint committee consisting of the Secretary-General and two Council members to approve all new appointments.[110] This proposal failed to gain traction. Nonetheless, there is ample evidence that in the late 1920s, governments of member states took a more active interest in the question of appointments and, in some cases, pressed the Secretary-General to appoint government officials, especially those belonging to their diplomatic services, whom they regarded as reliable. A League of Nations historian writes that "this pressure was not easy to withstand, the more so since Italy and Germany, who were particularly inclined to apply it, could claim with truth that they had fewer nationals in the Secretariat than France or Britain and ought therefore

108 William E Rappard, "The Evolution of the League of Nations" (1927) 21:4 *Am Polit Sci Rev* 792 at 811.

109 John Mathiason, *Invisible Governance: International Secretariats in Global Politics* (Bloomfield, CT: Kumarian Press, 2007) at 28.

110 Karen Gram-Skjoldager, "From the League of Nations to the United Nations: Milestones for the International Civil Service" in *100 Years of International Civil Service* (Dag Hammarskjöld Foundation), No. 3, at 4.

to be called onto fill such vacancies as might arise."[111] When the old team lost some of its brightest minds, including Monnet, Rappard, Madariaga, Nitobe, and Attolico, the vacant posts were gradually filled by officials seconded from the diplomatic services of Italy, Germany, Japan, and Spain.[112] A similar change occurred in the middle ranks as well.

A significant milestone in strengthening the independence of international secretariats and international civil servants was reached under Eric Drummond's leadership in 1926 when the provisional *modus vivendi* between Switzerland and the League of Nations was replaced with a formal agreement on the League's and the ILO's diplomatic presence in Geneva.[113] The agreement recognised, among other things, the League's legal personality, jurisdictional immunity, and fiscal and customs privileges in Switzerland. It also guaranteed the inviolability of the League's premises, archives, couriers, and correspondence. The Swiss government also accorded to senior officials (known as 'staff of the first category') and internationally recruited officials (known as 'extra-territorial staff') of the League and ILO immunity from civil and criminal jurisdiction in Switzerland unless such immunity was waived by the Secretary-General of the League or Director General of the ILO. Lower-ranking officials (known as 'staff of the second category') were granted functional immunities.[114]

Another significant milestone was reached in 1932 when, merely seven months before Eric Drummond's departure, two separate provisions dealing with loyalty were inserted in the League's Staff Regulations. The first provision dealt with the loyalty of the Secretary-General of the League, which strongly suggests that Eric Drummond had doubts about his successor's allegiances. The second provision addressed the loyalty of staff. In accordance with the new Article 3 of the League's Staff Regulations required officials of the League's Secretariat to make and sign a declaration that read as follows:

> I solemnly undertake to exercise in all loyalty, discretion and conscience the functions that have been entrusted to me as an official of the Secretariat of the League of Nations, to discharge my functions and to

111 FP Walters, *A History of the League of Nations* (New York: Oxford University Press, 1952) at 419.

112 *Ibid.*

113 "Details given to the 'Modus Vivendi' (1926) adopted by the Swiss Government and the organizations of the League of Nations with a view to the application of Article 7 of the Covenant" LoN Doc. No. C.555/1926(V).

114 Article VII of the Modus Vivendi.

> regulate my conduct with the interests of the League alone in view and not to seek or receive instructions from any Government or other authority external to the Secretariat of the League of Nations.[115]

The international civil service of the International Labour Organization was like that of the League in many respects. The difference between the two secretariats stemmed from the leadership and management styles of Eric Drummond and Albert Thomas. As a former British civil servant, Drummond encouraged a degree of delegation to lower management levels and general openness, leading to a devolved structure. In contrast, Thomas followed the French system of centralised control where, for example, all major documents passed through a Cabinet before and after being actioned at lower levels.[116]

2.3 *The League's Secretariat under Joseph Avenol's Leadership*

After 13 years in office, Drummond announced that he would retire in 1933. He handed over his functions to his successor on 30 June 1933.[117] Drummond was succeeded by his French deputy, Joseph Avenol – the one man Drummond had specifically tried to remove from consideration as his replacement.[118] In a letter addressed to the British Foreign Secretary – Sir John Simon – Drummond observed that "it may seem odd that I do not recommend the present Deputy Secretary-General M. Avenol, to take my place, but I do not think from a personal point of view the appointment would be altogether justified".[119] Eric Drummond went on to recommend "a well-known and much liked and respected in League circles" Dutch judge on the Permanent Court of International Justice at the Hague, Willem Jan Marie van Eysinga.[120] Drummond was probably unaware that an unwritten understanding had been reached in Paris in 1919 when the League's Covenant was being drafted that a Frenchman would replace him upon his departure as Secretary-General. Therefore, Eysinga was not even considered as a contender for the post. An event that made it even more inevitable for a French national to replace an Englishman as the League's Secretary-General was the death of Albert Thomas – the Director General

115 "Amendment in the Staff Regulations", Office Circular Nos. 75 and 76 (12 November 1932).

116 Macfadyen et al, *supra* note 70 at 210.

117 "Assumption of Office by M J Avenol, Secretary-General of the League of Nations Note" (1933) 14:8 *League of Nations OJ* 987.

118 James Barros, *Betrayal from Within – Joseph Avenol, Secretary-General of the League 1933–1940* (New Haven, Conn: Yale University Press, 1969) at 3; Macfadyen et al., *supra* note 70 at 49.

119 Barros, *supra* note 118 at 2.

120 Macfadyen et al., *supra* note 70 at 50.

of the International Labour Organisation (ILO) of French nationality – in May 1932. With France's support, Thomas was replaced by his British deputy, Harrold Butler, thereby making it extremely difficult for Britain not to support the appointment of Joseph Avenol.[121] Consequently, choosing Avenol to succeed a British citizen as Secretary-General of the League was "more a matter of satisfying national sensitivities than of choosing the best candidate".[122]

The second Secretary-General of the League was a financier "who showed more interest in figures and statistics than political issues".[123] Although he had been Deputy Secretary-General for over a decade, he lacked political awareness and was often more fascinated with form rather than substance.[124] Robert Cecil – a British politician who played a key role throughout the League's history – described Avenol as "wholly unsuited to the job" and "evidently out of his element".[125]

Unfortunately, Avenol lived up to his reputation and proved a disappointing leader. He discredited his office by "allowing the League's secretariat to become politicised as the geopolitical context deteriorated, to the extent that staff members of certain nationalities openly sided with their governments."[126] He undermined the trust of member states in the Secretariat, acting "as more a servant of his native France than of the League".[127] After the German occupation of Paris, he proposed to his colleagues from the leadership team of the League to "work hand in hand with Hitler in order to achieve the unity of Europe and expel England from Europe".[128] In June 1940, Avenol expulsed all officials of British nationality from the League[129] and "went so far as to pledge privately his allegiance to Marshal Petain, expressing willingness to demonstrate that allegiance by resigning if the Marshal so wished."[130]

---

121 *Ibid*; Barros, *supra* note 118 at 4.

122 Dorothy V Jones, "Seeking Balance: The Secretary-General as Normative Negotiator" in *The UN Secretary-General and Moral Authority* (Washington D.C.: Georgetown University Press, 2007).

123 Anique HM Van Ginneken, *Historical Dictionary of the League of Nations* (Lanham, Maryland: The Scarecrow Press, 2006) at 10.

124 Barros, *supra* note 118 at 50.

125 Cecil of Chelwood, *supra* note 101 at 151.

126 James OC Jonah and Amy S Hill, "The Secretariat: Independence and Reform" in *The Oxford Handbook on the United Nations*, 2nd ed (New York: Oxford University Press, 2018) at 213; Barros, *supra* note 117 at 2.

127 Jones, *supra* note 122 at 53.

128 Barros, *supra* note 118 at 219.

129 *Ibid* at 227.

130 Schwebel, *supra* note 85 at 73.

Avenol disgraced his office and the Secretariat also through his conduct as a private citizen when he invoked the privileges and immunities of the League's Secretary-General in legal proceedings instituted by his former spouse for family support.[131] As a consequence of his divorce proceedings, a French court ordered him to pay his ex-wife 12,500 francs per month[132] He appealed against this order, asserting that as Secretary-General of the League, he enjoyed diplomatic privileges and immunities under Article 7 of the Covenant of the League and enjoyed jurisdictional immunity before the courts of all member states of the League, including those of France. The French court rejected this argument as a "flagrant contradiction to the sacred and profound sentiment of justice".[133]

Under Avenol's leadership, the League's Secretariat had lost the confidence of the organisation's member states to the extent that one author partially attributed the failure of the League to Avenol.[134]

3 The Period Following the League of Nations

The international community of states learned much from the League's challenges. These lessons were instrumental when nations decided to create the United Nations. As an American diplomat observed:

> [W]e should abandon the notion, sometimes held, that in 1945, the United Nations sprang into being from nowhere, like Minerva from the brow of Zeus. The analogy, rather, should be the Phoenix arising from its own ashes. For while many felt it wise in 1945 to avoid dwelling on antecedents, those who laboured to create the United Nations would have had an extremely difficult time without the precedents of the League of Nations to guide them.[135]

3.1 *The Establishment of the United Nations Secretariat*

The founders of the United Nations knew from the League's experience that the Secretariat of an organisation with a principally political vocation would

131 Niels Blokker, "International Organizations: The Untouchables" (2014) 10:2 *Int'l Org L Rev* 259 at 263.

132 *Ibid.*

133 *Ibid.*

134 See Barros, *supra* note 118.

135 Francis O Wilcox, "The United Nations in the Mainstream of History" (1956) 50 Am Soc'y Int'l L Proc 187 at 187.

be constantly exposed to political pressures from various stakeholders. For this reason, they made impartiality and independence, referred to as "the Balfourian principles",[136] cornerstones of the UN Secretariat. The importance of guaranteeing the independence and impartiality of international public servants was formally acknowledged during the United Nations Conference on International Organization held in San Francisco. "In their consideration of provisions for the Secretariat of the Organization, the members of Committee I/2 quickly and unanimously agreed that because of its central importance to the work of the entire Organization, the Secretariat should be of the highest quality and should be organised on a truly international basis. There was no dissent from these principles, and such disagreement as did appear during the discussions was limited to the question of the extent to which specific detailed provision should be made in the Charter for the Secretariat."[137] Although some delegates argued that the Charter needed to set out the broad principles only and that more detailed provisions should be left for Staff Regulations, they did not take issue with the idea of a secretariat international in character and behaviour.

The Preparatory Commission of the United Nations – established to make practical arrangements for the transition from a proposal embodied in the Charter to a functioning organisation – pointed out that the "degree in which the objects of the Charter can be realised will be largely determined by how the Secretariat performs its task. The Secretariat cannot successfully perform its task unless it enjoys the confidence of all the Members of the United Nations."[138] Some delegations proposed that appointments of UN officials be subject to the consent of the member state's government of which the candidate was a national. The delegate of the sponsoring state explained that the purpose of this prior approval was to ensure that the newly recruited staff was acceptable to and had the confidence of their governments. The majority of the states rejected this proposal, arguing that this would give governments the ability to exert political pressures on the Secretary-General and his personnel. Indeed, the experience of the League of Nations, as manifested in the behaviour of Germany's and Italy's fascist governments, "underlined the desirability of including in the Charter itself an explicit obligation on officials and the Governments alike to respect fully the independence and the exclusively

136 Langrod, *supra* note 29 at 47.

137 UNCIO, Vol. VII, Commission I, Committee 2, Report of Rapporteur (General) of Committee I/2 on Chapter X (Secretariat), Doc. 1155, Ref. no. I/2/74 (2) (22 June 1945), at 386.

138 Report of the Preparatory Commission of the United Nations, UNCIO, 1945 at 81.

international character of the responsibilities of the Secretariat".[139] In the end, the requirements of independence and loyalty were elevated from an internal policy to a constitutional requirement. Consequently, three key provisions regulating the independence and impartiality of staff members were included in the Charter. Article 100 of the Charter guarantees the international character of the UN Secretariat:

> **Article 100**
> In the performance of their duties the Secretary-General and the staff shall not seek or receive instructions from any government or from any other authority external to the Organization. They shall refrain from any action which might reflect on their position as international officials responsible only to the Organization.[140]
>
> Each Member of the United Nations undertakes to respect the exclusively international character of the responsibilities of the Secretary-General and the staff and not to seek to influence them in the discharge of their responsibilities.

Article 100 of the Charter was not part of the Dumbarton Oaks proposals. Canada, New Zealand, and Uruguay proposed this addition at the San Francisco Conference.[141] Two other provisions of the Charter dealing with the Secretariat and staff are also relevant to their independence. Article 101 requires the Secretary-General to recruit staff who meet the highest standards of efficiency, competence, and integrity. Article 105 grants the UN such privileges and immunities as are necessary to fulfil its purposes. It also authorises the General Assembly to propose that conventions regulating the status, privileges, and immunities of the organisation and its staff be developed. Based on this provision, the General Assembly strengthened the independence of the Secretariat by adopting provisional Staff Regulations[142] and a Convention on the Privileges and Immunities of the United Nations.[143]

---

139 Dag Hammarskjöld, *The International Civil Servant in Law and in Fact: A Lecture Delivered to Congregation on 30 May 1961* (Uppsala: Dag Hammarskjöld Foundation, 2021) at 10.

140 The inspiration for this provision was the Staff Regulations of the League of Nations adopted in 1922. See Genowefa Grabowska, "Independence of the International Civil Servants" (1988) 17 *Polish YB Int'l L* 61 at 62.

141 Schwebel, *supra* note 85 at 76.

142 *Organization of the Secretariat*, GA Res 13 (I), UN Doc A/RES/13(I), Annex II (13 February 1946).

143 Convention on the Privileges and Immunities of the United Nations (3 February 1946), 1 UNTS 15 (entered into force 17 September 1946).

As to the UN Secretary-General, the founding states empowered him to bring to the attention of the Security Council any matter which, in his opinion, may threaten the maintenance of international peace and security.[144] While this power may seem like a tacit admission by governments that the Secretary-General is neither impartial nor neutral,[145] a more careful reading of Article 99 of the UN Charter reveals that member states never had the intention of giving the Secretary-General the authority to characterise the threat to the maintenance of peace and security as aggression or violation of international law. It merely authorises the Secretary-General to expose the relevant facts without taking sides. Indeed, in the *travaux préparatoires* of the negotiations for the drafting of the UN Charter, the delegates pointed out that the Secretary-General's power to bring to the attention of the Security Council any matter which, in his opinion, might threaten international peace and security manifests their deep trust in the Secretary-General to perform his tasks impartially and in the interests of the world at large.[146]

3.2 *The Proliferation of Intergovernmental Organisations and Erratic Development of International Civil Service Law*

While setting up the United Nations, the international community of states was concomitantly negotiating the creation of other universal organisations. The Bretton Woods institutions (1944–1945), including the International Trade Organization, which never saw the light of day, UNESCO (1945), FAO (1945), WHO (1946), WMO (1947), ICAO (1947), IMO (1948), the short-lived International Refugee Organization (1948), and the IOM (1952) were only a few universal institutions being envisaged. During the same period, regional organisations and alliances were established. The League of Arab States (1945), the European Coal Organisation (1945), Pan American Health Organization (1947), the Organisation for European Economic Cooperation (1948), NATO (1949), the Council of Europe (1949), and the Nordic Council (1952) were among the first ones created. These international organisations were diverse in their organic structure, vocation, membership, and geographic scope. Their secretariats were just as diverse. In fact, for some of these organisations, such as NATO, the founding treaties did not even expressly provide for an international

144 Charter of the United Nations, Art. 99.

145 Barros, *supra* note 102 at 27.

146 UNCIO, Vol. VI, Commission I: General Provisions, Verbatim Minutes of Third Meeting of Commission I, Doc. 1167, Ref. No. I/10 (19 June 1945) at 116 and 208.

secretariat as a separate organ. Some small international organisations continue to rely exclusively on national civil servants for secretariat functions.[147]

The proliferation of international organisations accelerated exponentially after decolonisation and peaked in the 1990s.[148] The exact number of international organisations is unknown and depends on how they are defined. Most authors estimate the number of intergovernmental organisations to be between 500 and 700.[149] By one estimate, there were approximately 300 traditional intergovernmental organisations in 2020.[150] Each organisation has a unique legal framework and institutional setup. Of course, a detailed description of all international secretariats is beyond the scope of this work. Nevertheless, there are five major systems of international civil service. They are the UN Common System, the World Bank Group, the EU civil service, the Coordinated Organisations, and other international organisations.[151] Although the law governing international officials of different organisations has many similarities,[152] major differences exist between international organisations, even in relation to basic principles. For instance, the Noblemaire[153] and Flemming[154] principles used by the United Nations to determine the salary scales of its staff members are not used by Coordinated Organisations such

147 See, for instance, Article XXII of the Amazon Cooperation Treaty establishing the Amazon Cooperation Treaty Organization 1202 UNTS 51, which provides that "*the functions of the Secretariat shall be performed pro-tempore by the Contracting Party in whose territory the next regular meeting of the Amazonian Cooperation Council is scheduled to be held.*"

148 Statistics published by the Union of International Associations in the Yearbook of International Organizations, Figure 6.1. Foundation dates of international organisations by type Edition 57, 2020/2021 (data collected in 2019).

149 Gerhard Ullrich, *The Law of the International Civil Service: Institutional Law and Practice in International Organisations* (Berlin: Duncker and Hublot, 2018) at 37.

150 Statistics published by the Union of International Associations (UIA) in the Yearbook of International Organizations, Number of IGOs by type.

151 Ullrich identifies four categories and does not assign a separate category to the World Bank Group: Ullrich, *supra* note 149 at 43–46.

152 Schermers and Blokker, *supra* note 44 at para 540.

153 Named after the French delegate, Georges Noblemaire, who chaired the committee established under the auspices of the League of Nations to set the salaries of the League's staff, the principle relates to the establishment of a salary scale for staff members in the professional category based on wages granted by various States to their highest paid officials.

154 While the emoluments of UN staff members in the professional and higher categories are determined in accordance with the Noblemaire principle, those of staff members in the General Services and related categories are determined in accordance with the Flemming principle. The Flemming principle requires that the salaries of locally recruited staff be established by the Secretary-General on the basis of the best prevailing conditions of employment in the locality where the specific United Nations office is situated.

as NATO or the Council of Europe. These organisations have different ways of establishing salary scales for their staff. Another important difference between IGOs is their acceptance and tolerance of secondments. Secondments are generally discouraged and frowned upon in the UN, whereas in NATO, OSCE and Interpol, they are ubiquitous. Similarly, some international organisations, including the OPCW, are non-career organisations with limited staff tenure. In contrast, most international organisations do not limit the number of years a person can serve as a staff member.

In conclusion, primitive forms of international organisations were initially created to centralise the actions of individual nations. To guarantee the trust of all participating states in these newly established institutions, states began granting intergovernmental organisations independence and demanded complete impartiality and neutrality of international civil servants. As intergovernmental institutions increased in number, mission, and diversity, so did their understanding, interpretation, and approach to issues common to all international organisations.

Since each international organisation is unique and is different in size, nature, mandate, and membership, it is only normal to have rules adapted to its specific needs. Unsurprisingly, staff regulations of the United Nations are significantly different from those of NATO or the EU. However, no differences should exist in relation to the core principles that define international civil service, namely its independence and impartiality. These essential attributes of any international civil service are sacrosanct and cannot be waived in the interests of efficacy, efficiency, or cost. Yet, there is no consistency in interpreting or implementing the notions of 'independence' and 'impartiality'. An act that is seen as violating the independence of a staff member in one organisation may be common practice in another. The main difficulty resides in the fact that no authoritative definition and common meaning exist for the terms 'independence' and 'impartiality'. Consequently, despite divergent – and often highly problematic – practices, each organisation may firmly believe that its secretariat and staff members are independent and impartial. Oddly, this firm belief is held in good faith.

CHAPTER 2

The Meaning of Independence and Essential Characteristics of an Independent International Civil Service

Chapter 1 traced the history of international cooperation and established that states initially began creating intergovernmental organisations to ensure the centralisation of their activities. This centralisation was achieved through concrete organisational structures and a supportive administrative apparatus. Through these structures, states increased the efficiency of collective action and enhanced the organisation's ability to provide services and support to its member states.[1] However, states eventually discovered that successful cooperation also required mutual trust because interstate cooperation entails a degree of competition or conflict.[2] Consequently, they needed to ensure that international institutions not only centralised their activities but also played the role of an impartial arbiter. To guarantee the impartiality and neutrality of these institutions, nations had to ascertain that no single state or a group of states could exert pressure on or influence the actions and decisions of international organisations. This is how the concept of independence appeared. Multilateral institutions began acquiring a truly international character when their independence from member states gradually increased and strengthened.

This chapter shifts the focus from a historical to a normative analysis. The first part of the chapter will explore the purpose and meaning of the term independence in the context of international secretariats and international civil servants. The second part will canvass the essential characteristics of an independent international secretariat and its staff.

1 The Purpose and Meaning of Independence

In its broadest sense, the term *independence* refers to the ability of an international organisation to act with a degree of autonomy within defined spheres

1 Kenneth W Abbott and Duncan Snidal, "Why States Act through Formal International Organizations" (1998) 42:1 *Conflict Resolution* 3 at 4–5.

2 Thomas Schelling, *The Strategy of Conflict* (Cambridge, MA: Harvard University Press, 1980) at 89.

 | DOI:10.1163/9789004704596_004

and to its capacity to operate as a *neutral* in preventing or managing interstate disputes and conflicts.[3] Yet, this broad description is insufficient to understand the concept of independence. The concept cannot have any useful analytical purpose without a proper definition or descriptive elements. If one agrees with the premise that the independence of international secretariats can vary significantly from one international organisation to another, then one necessarily accepts the idea that the independence of international secretariats and international civil servants is flexible at best; at worst, it is in the eye of the beholder. Put differently, if the notion of independence is not clearly defined or at least circumscribed, it is devoid of its meaning and purpose. Without identifying and understanding its constitutive elements, the concept of independence is too elusive and malleable; any international organisation could convincingly argue that its secretariat is sufficiently independent. Therefore, to assess whether an international bureaucracy is truly independent, one needs to agree on objective yardsticks for measuring independence.

The following pages attempt to deconstruct the notion of independence by exploring answers to the following four fundamental questions: (a) what is the purpose of independence; (b) whose independence does the concept regulate; (c) from whom should independence be; and (d) what type of behaviour does independence aim at preventing? We will then identify the principal characteristics and attributes that international secretariats must possess to be independent.

1.1 *What Is the Purpose of Independence?*

One of the most prominent questions in international relations theory is why states set up or cooperate through international organisations. Different schools of thought offer different explanations. Arguably, the most dominant approach – and the one that appears most convincing – is the theory known as 'realism' or 'neo-realism', which emphasises the competitive and adversarial side of international relations. According to the realist political theory, the well-known prisoner dilemma accurately describes the reason for international cooperation through permanent structures.

The prisoners' dilemma is based on the tale of two alleged offenders being questioned separately by the prosecutor. Each prisoner knows that if neither confesses, the prosecutor will only have sufficient evidence to convict them for a minor offence, leading to thirty-day prison terms for each. If both confess, however, they will be sentenced to a one-year prison term each. This seemingly

3 Abbott and Snidal, *supra* note 1 at 5.

simple situation is transformed into a dilemma when the prosecutor offers a deal that only one of the prisoners can get. Specifically, if either prisoner confesses, he will not be prosecuted, while his recalcitrant partner will get a five-year sentence. Faced with this difficult choice, each prisoner recognises that his interests would be served best if he confesses as soon as possible. In the best-case scenario, a confession will lead to the confessor's freedom, and in the worst-case scenario, it will result in a one-year prison term, saving the confessor from the punitive five-year sentence. The optimal outcome for both prisoners can be achieved if both remain silent and do not confess. However, since the prisoners have no reason to trust one another, they cannot count on each other's silence. If both prisoners are rational and self-interested (egoistic) individuals, they will both confess. They will receive prison sentences that they could have avoided if they had cooperated by remaining silent.[4]

The prisoner dilemma illustrates that when rational actors do not trust one another, they cannot reach an optimal solution even though they share many common interests. For this reason, states come together to build institutions to minimise distrust and facilitate cooperation. A slight variation of the prisoner dilemma story can assist in demonstrating the critical role that international organisations can play in strengthening trust among nations. Suppose our two prisoners belonged to the same community of criminals, such as a criminal syndicate. Under these conditions, defection would appear unrewarding because the short-term gains of avoiding a longer prison term will eventually be outweighed by the collective punishment over the long run. In other words, each prisoner would likely realise that a confession or betrayal would lead to much harsher consequences than a prison term.

According to the realist theory, international organisations represent this community of individual states that do not otherwise trust one another. States prefer cooperation but do not believe or cannot be sure that others will keep their end of a cooperative bargain and fear the costs of defection.[5] Hence, states create international institutions as neutral go-betweens. States trust international civil servants more than they trust each other in negotiations.[6] International organisations increase trust among states by transforming sequential transactions between states – where one party is vulnerable to

4 Robert O Keohane, *After hegemony: cooperation and discord in the world political economy* (Princeton, N.J.: Princeton University Press, 2005) at 68.

5 Brian C Rathbun, "Before Hegemony: Generalized Trust and the Creation and Design of International Security Organizations" (2011) 65:2 *Int Organ* 243 at 246.

6 Xu Yi-Chong and Patrick Weller, "To Be, But not To Be Seen: Exploring the Impact of International Civil Servants" (2008) 86:1 *Public Adm* 35 at 42.

defection – into a simultaneous and transparent exchange of benefits. Hence, trust is no longer the expectation of future reciprocity; it becomes part of the cooperation process through international institutions. International organisations also create a system where trustworthy partners are rewarded through low transaction costs, and unreliable partners are penalised through high transaction costs.

Nevertheless, the problem of distrust cannot be resolved if the go-between itself is not independent and impartial. That is why the independence and impartiality of international civil servants have often been linked to the proper functioning of the organisation itself. The International Court of Justice drew this link in its seminal advisory opinion, commonly known as the Reparation for Injuries case.[7] The General Assembly asked the Court whether the United Nations had the capacity to bring an international claim against the state responsible for the death of UN officials. The question arose as a result of the assassination in September 1948, in Jerusalem, of Count Folke Bernadotte, the United Nations Mediator in Palestine, and of other members of his team. The Court held that the ability of an international organisation to protect its agents is crucial to preserving their independence. The Court then added that the independence of its agents is vital for the proper functioning of the organisation itself:

> To ensure the independence of the agent, and, consequently, the independent action of the Organization itself, it is essential that in performing his duties he need not have to rely on any other protection than that of the Organization (save of course for the more direct and immediate protection due from the state in whose territory he may be). In particular, he should not have to rely on the protection of his own state. If he had to rely on that state, his independence might well be compromised, contrary to the principle applied by Article 100 of the Charter.[8]

In the advisory opinion *Immunity from Legal Process of a Special Rapporteur*, the International Court of Justice reiterated that the independence enjoyed by UN officials is not for their personal benefit but to ensure that they can successfully accomplish the mission entrusted to them by the organisation.[9]

---

7 *Reparation for injuries suffered in the services of the United Nations*, Advisory Opinion, [1949] ICJ Rep 174 [Reparation for Injuries].

8 *Ibid* at 183.

9 *Difference Relating to Immunity from Legal Process of a Special Rapporteur of the Commission on Human Rights*, Advisory Opinion, [1999] ICJ Rep 62 at para 51 [Immunity from Legal Process of a Special Rapporteur].

The jurisprudence of international administrative tribunals is to the same effect. For instance, in 2003, the Administrative Tribunal of the International Labour Organisation (ILOAT) reaffirmed that "in accordance with the established case law of all international administrative tribunals, [...] the independence of international civil servants is an essential guarantee, not only for the civil servants themselves but also for the proper functioning of international organisations."[10]

Similarly, in 2010, the UN Appeals Tribunal held that since "the United Nations is called upon to assume a peacekeeping role; to prevent world conflicts; to assist countries in need of assistance; to act diplomatically in influencing world politics; and, to work with the parties in conflict diplomatically through fact-finding and dispute resolution, all while remaining neutral" the "Secretary-General is obliged to maintain and to be seen to maintain, a degree of neutrality and independence from the member states so that he can be in a position to exercise 'quiet diplomacy' or act as mediator."[11]

Although the International Court of Justice and the administrative tribunals stopped short of defining the term 'independence' or explaining its main characteristics, they drew a close link between the independence of international civil servants and the proper functioning of international organisations. The intimate relationship between these two elements leads to the conclusion that the main idea behind the concept of independence is rather simple: it requires that international civil servants be placed in a position where they have nothing to lose by doing what is right and nothing to gain by doing what is wrong so that they can devote their best efforts to the conscientious performance of their duties.

1.2 *Whose Independence Does the Concept Regulate?*

The word independence is often used in relation to international organisations. Nevertheless, not all facets or parts of an international organisation are or can be independent. For instance, a deliberative body composed of all member states of an international organisation, such as the General Assembly of the United Nations, is not independent even if it adopts decisions on behalf of all member states. The academic literature distinguishes two facets or identities of an international organisation. Specifically, Inis Claude described the two distinct identities of an international organisation in the following manner.

---

10 *JMB v Organisation for the Prohibition of Chemical Weapons*, [2003] Judgement No 2232 at para 16 (ILOAT).

11 *Bertucci v Secretary-General of the United Nations*, 2010-UNAT-062 (United Nations Appeals Tribunal) at para 11 [*Bertucci*].

Europe[23] also include the totality of staff employed by these organisations.

However, in some international organisations, the use of the word secretariat may lead to confusion as it refers to a small portion of staff whose roles and responsibilities are limited exclusively to providing secretarial services to governing bodies. For instance, in NATO, the term secretariat designates a small team of internationally recruited staff members who receive and disseminate communications, record decisions, and organise meetings of deliberative and policy-making bodies such as the North Atlantic Council, various subsidiary committees and Agency Supervisory Boards.[24] In fact, neither the North Atlantic Treaty establishing NATO nor the agreement governing the status of the organisation and its personnel contain the word 'secretariat'. The Agreement on the Status of the North Atlantic Treaty Organization, National Representatives and International Staff signed in Ottawa in September 1951[25] uses the term 'International Staff' in the same sense as the UN Charter uses the term 'Secretariat'. Hence, NATO personnel who pledge allegiance to the organisation and whose functions are exclusively international are collectively referred to as 'International Staff'.

The Treaty on European Union uses secretariat in a similar manner. The institutional entity employing internationally recruited civil servants of the European Union is called 'the European Commission' or 'the Commission'.[26] The Treaty on European Union does not use the word secretariat as a synonym for Commission. On the contrary, it refers to the General Secretariat as the body of staff responsible for assisting the European Council and the Council of the EU.

Therefore, it is crucial to agree on the definition of the word secretariat before examining its independence. Georges Langrod provides the most appealing definition of the expression 'secretariat'. He defines it as an administrative mechanism external to national administrations and acting, by definition, in the interests of the entire organised community of member states

---

these developments, the OSCE Secretariat did not have a legal status recognised in any binding instrument until it signed the Headquarters Agreement with Austria and the Arrangement on the legal status of OSCE with Poland in June 2017.

23 Articles 10 and 36 of the Statute of the Council of Europe.

24 Agency Supervisory Boards refer to governing bodies of NATO's largest agencies, including the NATO Communication and Information Agency (NCIA) and the NATO Support and Procurement Agency (NSPA).

25 Agreement on the status of the North Atlantic Treaty Organization, National Representatives and International Staff signed in Ottawa, 20 September 1951, 200 U.N.T.S. 3.

26 Article 13 of the Treaty on European Union, 1759 U.N.T.S. 3.

of the given organisation, albeit under the control of the latter's deliberative bodies.[27] This work uses the term secretariat in this sense of the word.

1.2.2 Independence of International Civil Servants

International organisations employ a large variety of personnel to carry out their activities. The United Nations alone has at least six categories of personnel. They include internationally recruited staff,[28] locally recruited staff,[29] consultants,[30] individual contractors,[31] UN Volunteers,[32] Interns,[33] and Gratis Personnel.[34] NATO also employs different categories of civil servants, including international civilian personnel,[35] consultants,[36] temporary staff,[37] seconded staff,[38] and Voluntary National Contributions (VNCs).[39] The European Commission employs 'officials', temporary staff, contract staff, local staff, special advisors, and accredited parliamentary assistants.[40]

This diversity of international civil servants makes it very difficult to determine which categories of personnel are expected to be independent and which ones do not need to exhibit independence. This determination becomes even more difficult to make when one considers the fact that certain categories of personnel are unique to some international organisations. In particular, Voluntary National Contributions exist only in NATO, UN Volunteers exist only in the UN, and special advisors exist as a separate category of personnel only in the European Commission. Some categories of international civil servants exist in several international organisations but are fundamentally different. For instance, the rights and obligations of temporary staff and consultants

27 Georges Langrod, *La fonction publique internationale* (Leiden: Sythoff, 1963) at 43.
28 Staff Regulations and Rules of the United Nations, Staff Rule 4.5.
29 *Ibid.* Staff Rule 4.4.
30 Administrative Instruction on Consultants and Individual Contractors, UN Doc. ST/AI/2013/4.
31 *Ibid.*
32 General Assembly resolution 2659(XXV) "*United Nations Volunteers*", UN Doc. A/RES/2659(XXV) (7 December 1979).
33 Administrative Instruction on the United Nations Internship Programme, UN Doc. ST/AI/2020/1.
34 Administrative Instruction on Gratis Personnel, UN Doc. ST/AI/1996/6.
35 NATO Civilian Personnel Regulations, Preamble, para (v)(c).
36 *Ibid.* para (v)(d).
37 *Ibid.* para (v)(e).
38 *Ibid.* para (v)(f).
39 North Atlantic Policy on Voluntary National Contributions, NATO Doc. PO(2015)0202-AS1.
40 Regulation No 31 (EEC), 11 (EAEC), laying down the Staff Regulations of Officials and the Conditions of Employment of Other Servants of the European Economic Community and the European Atomic Energy Community.

in the United Nations System are markedly different from those of temporary staff and consultants in NATO. Similarly, the notion of 'contract staff' in the European Commission has little in common with the notion of 'Individual Contractor' in the United Nations.[41]

Consequently, the name or designation of the category of personnel is not always helpful when determining whether a specific category of officials needs to be independent. The most reliable way of determining whether a particular group of international officials needs to be independent is to examine their roles and responsibilities. As the International Court of Justice noted in 1989, the "essence of the matter lies not in their administrative position but in the nature of their mission".[42] This reasoning is consistent with a preliminary observation made by the Court in the *Reparation for Injuries* case – an Advisory Opinion issued four decades earlier – where it interpreted the word 'agent' of an organisation as "a paid official or not, and whether permanently employed or not, has been charged by an organ of the Organisation with carrying out, or helping to carry out, one of its functions – in short, any person through whom it acts."[43] Suzanne Bastid proposed a similar definition of international civil servant, being any individual entrusted by the representatives of several states or by a body acting on their behalf, following an inter-State agreement and under the control of one or the other, to exercise, subject to special legal rules, on a continuous and exclusive basis functions in the interest of all the states in question.[44] Alain Pellet and David Ruzié argue that the constitutive elements of the definition of international civil servants are (a) independent exercise of a public office in an international organisation, (b) exclusive and continuous exercise of functions, and (c) a specific legal regime of international character.[45] Bob Reinalda describes international civil servants as "persons employed by IGOs to fulfil international functions".[46] The United Nations Convention against Corruption defines an "official of a public international organisation"

41 See Gerhard Ullrich, *The Law of the International Civil Service: Institutional Law and Practice in International Organisations* (Berlin: Duncker and Hublot, 2018) at 260–261.

42 *Applicability of Article VI, Section 22, of the Convention on the Privileges and Immunities of the United Nations*, Advisory Opinion, [1989] ICJ Rep 177 at para 47 [Applicability of Article VI Case].

43 *Reparation for Injuries*, *supra* note 7 at 177.

44 Suzanne Bastid, *Les Fonctionnaires internationaux* (Paris: Gidel, 1931) at 53.

45 Alain Pellet and David Ruzié, *Les fonctionnaires internationaux* (Paris: Presses Universitaires de France, 1993) at 11–14.

46 Bob Reinalda, *International Secretariats: Two Centuries of International Civil Servants and Secretariats* (London: Routledge, 2020) at 8.

as "an international civil servant or any person who is authorised by such an organisation to act on behalf of that organisation."[47]

The approach of legal practitioners to the question of which officials of international organisations need to be independent is very similar to the ICJ's opinion as well. For instance, in 1998, the Representative of the United Nations Development Programme (UNDP) in a UN member state brought to the attention of the UN Legal Counsel several problems experienced by a category of UN personnel known as UN Volunteers in that country.[48] More specifically, the authorities of the concerned state required that UN Volunteers obtain a special visa and work permit and pass a medical exam before they arrive in the country. Under the Convention on the Privileges and Immunities of the United Nations,[49] UN officials are "immune, together with their spouses and relatives dependent on them, from immigration restrictions and alien registration".[50] However, the Convention does not specify to which categories of UN personnel it applies or whether UN Volunteers are also immune from immigration restrictions. Hence, the UN Legal Counsel was asked to determine whether the UN Charter and the Convention on the Privileges and Immunities of the United Nations also applied to UN Volunteers.

The main difficulty in answering this question stemmed from the fact that the Staff Regulations and Rules of the United Nations do not recognise UN Volunteers as a category of staff. This type of personnel was created by a General Assembly resolution in 1979[51] (over 30 years after the Convention on the Privileges and Immunities of the UN entered into force) and administered by the UNDP,[52] but never formally equated to international civil

47 United Nations Convention against Corruption adopted by the General Assembly in its resolution 58/4 of 31 October 2003, UN Doc. A/Res/58/4, 2349 U.N.T.S. 41.

48 United Nations Office of Legal Affairs, "Status of United Nations Volunteers – Article 105, Paragraph 1, of the Charter of the United Nations" *UN Juridical Yearbook* (New York: UN, 1998) at 474 (UN Volunteers are individuals with professional skills and academic qualifications or training, who contribute their time and expertise as international volunteers, outside their own countries, or where UN programs exist in their own countries, as national volunteers. Volunteers have proven specialised experience in their professional fields and serve in assignments with diverse UN agencies to support peace and development. United Nations Volunteers is also an entity that is headquartered in Bonn, Germany, and administered by the United Nations Development Programme (https://www.unv.org/volunteer-your-country-requirements)).

49 Convention on the Privileges and Immunities of the United Nations, 1 U.N.T.S. 15.

50 *Ibid.*, Art. V, Sec. 18(d).

51 General Assembly resolution 2659(XXV) "*United Nations Volunteers*", UN Doc. A/RES/2659(XXV) (7 December 1979).

52 Alexandre Tavadian, *United Nations Law, Politics, and Practice* (Toronto: Irwin Law, 2021) at 471–472.

servants. Despite this, the UN Legal Counsel concluded that "from the inception of the concept of volunteers, these individuals have been considered by the Organisation, and generally recognised by the member states, as international civil servants" and must, therefore, "be accorded the same privileges and immunities as enjoyed by United Nations officials under section 18 of the [1946] Convention" on the Privileges and Immunities of the United Nations.[53] To reach this conclusion, the Legal Counsel took into account the following three elements: (a) the status of UN Volunteers is characterised by impartiality and independence; (b) the assignment of United Nations volunteers is governed solely by the United Nations system and the scope of their activity is confined to projects assisted by the United Nations system; and (c) the activities of United Nations volunteers are not subject to the control and authority of national governments.

In another request for a legal opinion, the UN Legal Counsel was asked whether the Convention on the Privileges and Immunities of the United Nations applied to individuals serving on subsidiary bodies and expert panels established under the Kyoto Protocol.[54] The question consisted in determining whether these individuals could be considered "experts on mission for the UN" pursuant to Article VI of the General Convention. Relying on an internal statutory instrument issued by the UN Secretary-General,[55] the Legal Counsel recalled that only officials (a) appointed by the Secretary-General, (b) who perform missions for the UN, and (c) make a declaration of loyalty to the organisation can be regarded as experts on mission.

Read in conjunction, these two authoritative legal opinions confirm that the contractual link with the UN and the name of the category of personnel are not decisive factors in determining whether an individual should be considered an international civil servant and be independent of member states. The decisive questions are: (a) to whom does the individual owe loyalty; (b) does the individual perform exclusively international responsibilities; and (c) who appoints

53 United Nations Office of Legal Affairs, "Status of United Nations Volunteers – Article 105, Paragraph 1, of the Charter of the United Nations" *UN Juridical Yearbook* (New York: UN, 1998) at 474.

54 United Nations Office of Legal Affairs, "Interoffice memorandum to the Officer-in-Charge, United Nations Framework Convention on Climate Change (UNFCCC) Secretariat, regarding the privileges and immunities of individuals serving on constituted bodies established under the Kyoto Protocol to the UNFCCC" *UN Juridical Yearbook* (New York: UN, 2006) at 445.

55 Regulations Governing the Status, Basic Rights and Duties of Officials other than Secretariat Officials, and Experts on Missions, Secretary-General's Bulletin 2002/9, UN Doc. ST/SGB/2002/9.

or recruits the individual? Consequently, to be an international civil servant, an individual must:

(a) pledge allegiance to or take an oath of loyalty to the international organisation while performing their functions;
(b) be appointed by, report to, and take instructions from a chief administrative officer of the organisation, such as a Secretaries-General or Directors General;
(c) perform exclusively international responsibilities or missions.

1.3 *From Whom Should Independence Be?*

International secretariats and international civil servants must be independent to fulfil their role as neutral arbiters and reconcile the conflicting interests of member states. Secretariats do not normally adjudicate disputes like arbitration tribunals or judicial courts, even if, on a few occasions, they have been called upon to arbitrate disputes between member states.[56] Therefore, comparing the independence of international secretariats and their staff to the independence of judges or arbitrators is not apposite. Instead, secretariats and international civil servants act more like mediators. Mediation[57] and good offices[58] constitute a substantial part of an international secretariat's workload.[59] To enjoy the confidence of the disputants, a mediator should be independent of the parties.[60] Like mediators, international secretariats and civil servants must be independent of the parties that have or may have conflicting interests, namely the member states of the organisation.

Member states may attempt to influence international secretariats and their officials in various ways. The most obvious means of exerting pressure

56 In 1948, the postal administrations of Turkey and Syria signed a *compromis spécial* designating the UPU secretariat as an arbitrating authority: see Postal Administration of Turkey v. Postal Administration of Syria (1960) 23 *International Law Reports* 596. The SG of the UN adjudicated a dispute between France and New Zealand in the *Rainbow Warrior Incident*: see the ruling of the Secretary-General, 6 July 1986 (1987) 26 International Legal Materials 1346.

57 For a definition of mediation, see para. 123 of the *Handbook on the Peaceful Settlement of Disputes between States* (New York: United Nations Publication, 1992), UN Doc OLA/COD/2394.

58 Good offices are a third-party influence that facilitates one party's dealings with another. It generally implies that the third party uses his or her reputation or prestige (or those of his office) to convince the disputing parties to resolve their disagreement peacefully.

59 U Thant, *View from the UN* (London: David and Charles Publishing, 1978) at 49.

60 David Spencer and Michael Brogan, *Mediation Law and Practice* (Cambridge: Cambridge University Press, 2006) at 36.

is through permanent delegations or permanent representations of the member state to the organisation. Typically, this involves an 'office call' (a phone call or visit with no pre-determined agenda) from a senior official of the member state's permanent delegation to the executive head of the secretariat, during which the underhanded request is made. Political pressure can be exerted by or through other actors as well, including regional groups, multinational alliances, or governmental agencies. For this reason, constitutive instruments and staff regulations of many international organisations, including Article 100.1 of the UN Charter, prohibit staff members from seeking or receiving instructions from governments and "any other authority external to the organisation".

1.4 *What Type of Behaviour Does Independence Aim at Preventing?*

It has been pointed out above that the main idea behind the concept of independence of international civil servants is to ensure that they have nothing to lose by doing what is right and nothing to gain by doing what is wrong so that they can conscientiously carry out their official functions. Obviously, the lack of independence is not the only factor that can incite international civil servants to adopt wrongful conduct. Factors completely unrelated to their independence may lead officials of international organisations to breach their basic obligations. For instance, fraud, corruption, and theft are just a few examples of wrongful conduct that do not arise because of one's lack of independence. They occur owing to one's lack of integrity or questionable moral values. This type of conduct can occur in any public or private organisation. Thus, the real question is, what kind of problematic behaviour does the concept of independence of international civil servants aim to prevent?

The type of wrongful conduct that may occur when international civil servants lack independence is often more subtle but just as corrosive for international organisations as corruption and fraud are. It includes seeking instructions from parties external to the organisation, taking sides, looking after the interests of one or several member states at the expense of others, etc. Such conduct is corrosive because it undermines the mission and purpose of the international organisation, which is to be a neutral arbiter for all member states. It damages the trust and confidence of nations in international institutions and cooperation.

An autobiography by a former senior official of the United Nations – Arkady N. Shevchenko – entitled "Breaking with Moscow" is a telling illustration of how prejudicial the lack of independence of international civil servants can be.[61] Shevchenko served in the United Nations as the Under-Secretary-General for Political and Security Council Affairs between 1973 and 1978. In his autobiography, he describes how, before becoming the highest-ranking Soviet official to defect to the West, he used his office to appoint KGB agents to UN staff positions and to transmit information to the USSR. Brian Urquhart, a highly respected former UN official who served as the Under-Secretary-General for political affairs under several Secretaries-General, confirms this account in his autobiography in which he recollects that his Soviet assistant, Nikolai Fochin, and Arkady Shevchenko "seemed to be in a twenty-four-hour-a-day competition to be first to relay the output of [his] office to the Soviet delegation".[62] It was widely known that most UN staff from the USSR and its Eastern European allies had close links to their national governments.

A more recent example of highly questionable conduct attributable to a lack of independence occurred during the 2017 UN Indigenous Forum. Mr. Hongbo Wu, a Chinese diplomat appointed to the post of the Under-Secretary-General for the UN Department of Economic and Social Affairs (DESA), expelled from the forum Dolkun Isa, a Uighur activist, even though Mr. Isa was duly invited to the forum as a delegate representing a German NGO. after protests from American and German diplomats, Isa was eventually allowed to return. Wu, whose status as an international civil servant required him to be non-partisan, later boasted about his actions on Chinese state television CCTV, stating that he had to defend the 'motherland's interests'.[63]

2 Essential Characteristics of Independent International Secretariats and Their Staff

The independence of international secretariats can be examined from two complementary angles: collective and individual. First, a secretariat must be institutionally independent, and second, staff members must also be independent and impartial. The first type of independence relates to the body as a whole or to all staff members collectively. The second type of independence aims to safeguard the individual staff member's freedom from external influence.

61 Arkady N Shevchenko, *Breaking with Moscow* (New York: Ballantine Books, 1985).

62 Brian Urquhart, *A Life in Peace and War* (New York: Harper and Row Publishers, 1987) at 290.

63 "In the UN, China uses threats and cajolery to promote its worldview", *The Economist*, 7 December 2019 edition.

In distinguishing between collective and individual independence of judges, the Supreme Court of Canada explained that the relationship between these two aspects of independence is "that an individual judge may enjoy the essential conditions of judicial independence, but if the court over which he or she presides is not independent of the other branches of government [...] he or she cannot be said to be an independent tribunal."[64] This reasoning applies also to international secretariats. A staff member may be entirely neutral and impartial, but unless the secretariat is institutionally independent of member states and other stakeholders, the organisation cannot be said to have an independent civil service.

2.1 *Independence of the Secretariat as an Entity*

The strength of an international secretariat's institutional independence depends on its international and domestic legal personalities, privileges, and immunities. Section 2.1.1 shows the importance of international organisations having an international and domestic legal personality in the territory of states where they are required to operate. Section 2.1.2 draws a link between the organisations' privileges and immunities – including inviolability, jurisdictional immunity, and fiscal privileges – and the independence of their secretariats.

2.1.1 International and Domestic Legal Personality

Independence requires a sufficient degree of self-reliance. Therefore, to be independent, international organisations represented by their secretariats must be able to meet their needs autonomously without relying on member states. Any organisation with a permanent institutional structure needs, at minimum, a headquarters location for its staff, office supplies, utility and cleaning services, etc. For this reason, intergovernmental institutions must be able to acquire and dispose of property, sign contracts, and institute legal proceedings without the assistance or intervention of their member states. They can have such powers on the territory of a sovereign state only if that state grants the IGO legal personality in its national legal order.

In the *Reparation for Injuries* case, the International Court of Justice confirmed that international organisations, and by extension their secretariats, "exercise and enjoy [...] functions and rights which can only be explained on the basis of the possession of a large measure of international personality and the capacity to operate upon an international plane."[65] The Court also added

64 *Valente v The Queen*, [1985] 2 SCR 673 at para 20 (Supreme Court of Canada).

65 *Reparation for Injuries*, *supra* note 7 at 179.

that they "could not carry out the intentions of the founders if [they were] devoid of international personality".[66] In another advisory opinion of 1980, the ICJ reiterated this view by confirming that "[i]nternational organisations are subjects of international law and, as such, are bound by any obligations incumbent upon them under general rules of international law, under their constitutions or under international agreements to which they are parties."[67] The International Law Commission opined that in its advisory opinion on *Reparation for Injuries, the ICJ favoured the view that when the* legal personality of an organisation exists, it is an 'objective' personality. Therefore, it is not necessary to enquire whether a state has recognised the legal personality of an organisation.[68] For these reasons, it appears that it is now settled law that intergovernmental organisations possess an international juridical personality.

Nevertheless, the international legal personality of organisations, which enables them to operate on the international plane, is insufficient to enjoy the rights of a legal entity on the territory of nations. In many dualist states, legal capacity under domestic law can be conferred only pursuant to legislation authorising the granting of such capacity to organisations of which these states are members.[69]

The independence of the international secretariat requires the organisation to have an international legal personality and domestic legal capacity in the territory of its member states. Without a legal personality under domestic law, the organisation will be compelled to rely on its member states for routine matters, namely the signing of utility contracts or rental agreements, which could expose the organisation to political interference. It is not accidental that Article 104 of the UN Charter expressly recognises to the UN "such legal capacity as may be necessary for the exercise of its functions and the fulfilment of its purposes."[70] At the San Francisco Conference, it was proposed to insert into the

66 *Ibid.*

67 *Interpretation of the Agreement of 25 March 1951 between the WHO and Egypt*, Advisory Opinion, [1980] ICJ Rep 73 at para 37.

68 Draft articles on the responsibility of international organisations, with commentaries, adopted by the International Law Commission at its 63rd sess., in 2011, and submitted to the General Assembly as a part of the Commission's report covering the work of that session (UN Doc. A/66/10) at 76.

69 Andreas R Ziegler, "Article 104" in Bruno Simma et al, eds, *Charter of the United Nations: Commentary*, 3d ed (Oxford: Oxford University Press, 2012) at 2141.

70 Article 104 of the Charter of the United Nations. See also Article 47 of the Treaty on European Union; Article XV.1 of the Constitution of the Food and Agriculture Organization (1945); Article 9, Section 2 of Articles of Agreement of the International Monetary Fund (27 December 1945) 2 U.N.T.S. 39; Article VIII.1 of the Agreement Establishing the World Trade Organization (15 April 1994) 1867 U.N.T.S. 154; Article 133 of the Charter of the

Charter a provision on the status of the UN in domestic law "to overcome the administrative and legal difficulties, which had previously arisen around the League of Nations due to the absence of such rules in its founding treaty."[71] The only mention of the League's legal capacity could be found in an agreement with Switzerland, the League's host state, the so-called *modus vivendi*, which stipulated that the League possessed international personality and capacity and that it could not "in principle, according to the rules of international law, be sued before the Swiss Courts without its consent."[72]

Article 104 of the UN Charter should be read in conjunction with Article 1 of the *Convention on the Privileges and Immunities of the United Nations*, which sets out a non-exhaustive list of attributes of the UN's legal personality.[73] These attributes include the capacity to contract, acquire and dispose of property and institute legal proceedings. Inspired by the UN Charter and the 1946 General Convention, constitutive instruments of many international organisations contain a similar provision.[74]

An explicit recognition by member states of the organisation's legal personality in their internal legal order is critical to the international secretariat's independence from member states. Unfortunately, not all constitutive instruments of international organisations grant a juridical personality to the organisation under domestic law.[75] According to one author, even where the constituent instrument of an organisation does not expressly provide for legal personality in national law, member states of that organisation are probably under an implied obligation to recognise such personality in their national legal systems.[76] This author further argues that this obligation arises from the

---

Organization of American States (30 April 1948) 119 U.N.T.S. 3; Article 1 of the General Convention on the Privileges and Immunities of the Organisation of African Unity (25 October 1965) 1000 U.N.T.S. 393; Convention on the Organisation for Economic Co-operation and Development (with Supplementary Protocols Nos. 1 and 2), 14 December 1960, 888 U.N.T.S. 179.

71 Ziegler, *supra* note 69 at 2140.

72 Michael Wood, "Do International Organizations Enjoy Immunity under Customary International Law" (2014) 10:2 *Intl Organizations L Rev* 287 at 291.

73 Ziegler, *supra* note 69 at 2142.

74 See for instance Article IV of the *Agreement on the status of the North Atlantic Treaty Organization, National Representatives and International Staff*, supra note 25, which provides that NATO possesses juridical personality in all member states and shall have the capacity to conclude contracts, to acquire and dispose of property and institute legal proceedings.

75 Henry G Schermers and Niels Blokker, *International Institutional Law*, 6th ed (Leiden: Nijhoff, 2018) at para. 1565.

76 CF Amerasinghe, *Principles of the Institutional Law of International Organization*, 2nd ed (New York: Cambridge University Press, 2005) at 76.

relationship between the members and the organisation and the principle of good faith.

While this may be true, the absence of an explicit recognition of legal personality in a written instrument may give rise to practical difficulties. For instance, a problem arose when the International Commission for the Northwest Atlantic Fisheries, with headquarters in Canada, sought to introduce a superannuation plan for its staff. Canadian authorities informed the Commission that it did not have legal authority to enter into a contract.[77] Similarly, the Permanent Commission for the South Pacific, whose constitutive instrument is silent as to the Commission's legal capacity, considered it necessary to facilitate its administrative work and to ensure greater efficacity in the performance of its functions to pass a resolution urging its member states to adopt a convention designed to improve the Commission's legal status in their legal systems.[78] Such difficulties may still arise in many legal systems. Specifically, financial institutions in many European countries are required under their national anti-money laundering and tax evasion legislation to ascertain that the entity seeking to open a bank account possesses a legal personality in the country where it is headquartered. Banks regularly ask international organisations to provide evidence that they have a juridical personality. The international organisation whose constitution and other legal instruments are silent on this point would be unable to satisfy the financial institution that it has a juridical personality in the national legal order. The organisation will be compelled to seek the assistance of the host nation to complete a transaction as trivial as opening a bank account. Hence, it is irrelevant whether the host nation has an implied obligation to recognise legal personality; the organisation's reliance on the host nation to obtain a confirmation of its legal personality under that state's domestic law is undesirable because it undermines the organisation's independence from its host nation. Consequently, where an organisation's constitution does not expressly provide for legal personality under national law, it is imperative to conclude with the host nation a Seat Agreement (also known as Host Country Agreement or Supplementary Agreement) and include a provision recognising the legal personality of the organisation.

77 JE Carroz and AG Roche, "Proposed International Commission for the Conservation of Atlantic Tunas, The." (1967) *Am J Int'l L* 61:3 673 at 697–698.

78 *Ibid* at 698.

2.1.2 Privileges and Immunities

Privileges and immunities limit a country's absolute sovereignty over its territory.[79] Before World War II, the practice of the countries creating international organisations was to accord diplomatic privileges and immunities to the organisations' personnel and, by construction only, to the organisations themselves.[80] The most widely used formula for determining the extent of protection to be conferred continued to be that of diplomatic privileges and immunities.[81] Following World War II, the founding states considerably changed their approach and, for the first time in the history of international organisations, they began addressing the status, privileges and immunities of the organisations separately from those of the personnel.[82] The legal status, privileges and immunities accorded to international organisations were mostly determined based on functional need. This fundamental change in the approach is not surprising because the reasons behind granting immunity to international organisations differ from those underlying state immunity or diplomatic immunity.[83] The jurisdictional immunity of states is based on international comity and the principle of sovereign equality of states,[84] whereas "the attribution of privileges and immunities to international organisations is an essential means of ensuring the proper functioning of such organisations free from unilateral interference by individual governments."[85]

Their legal sources are also different. The prevailing view at present is that, unlike state or diplomatic immunity, no rule of customary international law confers immunity on international organisations,[86] even though the Supreme Court of the Netherlands has ruled at least twice that according to "unwritten international law", international organisations enjoy immunity

79 Pellet and Ruzié, *supra* note 45 at 85.

80 Josef L Kunz, "Privileges and Immunities of International Organizations" (1947) 41:4 *Am J Int L* 828; Edwin H Fedder, "The Functional Basis of International Privileges and Immunities: A New Concept in International Law and Organization" (1960) 9:1 *Am U Rev* 60.

81 Fedder, *supra* note 80 at 61.

82 *Ibid* at 62.

83 Eric De Brabandere, "Immunity of International Organizations in Post-Conflict International Administrations" (2010) 7:1 *Int'l Org L Rev* 79 at 82.

84 *Ibid* at 83.

85 *Waite and Kennedy v. Germany*, Judgement (Merits) of 18 February 1999, European Court of Human Rights (Grand Chamber), Application No. 26083/94 at para. 63; *Stichting Mothers of Srebrenica v. The Netherlands*, Judgement of 11 June 2013, European Court of Human Rights (Third Section), Application No. 65542/12 at para. 139(c).

86 *Amaratunga v Northwest Atlantic Fisheries Organization*, 2013 SCC 66, [2013] 3 SCR 866 at para 29 (Supreme Court of Canada); Wood, *supra* note 72.

from jurisdiction, at least in the State on whose territory the organisation is based, provided reasonable dispute resolution alternatives remain available.[87] Similarly, some courts have opined that no general principle of law within the meaning of Article 38.1(c) of the Statute of the ICJ recognises such privileges and immunities either.[88] International organisations derive their existence from treaties; the same holds true for their rights to privileges and immunities.[89] Unlike states, which have sovereignty over a well-defined territory and carry out activities on the territory of other states only by exception, international organisations operate as a matter of course on the territory of states. Moreover, they must operate through individuals who have the nationality of their member states and are, therefore, vulnerable to interference, making their "immunity essential to the efficient and independent functioning of international organisations."[90] This vulnerability requires that international organisations be granted privileges and immunities to maintain their independence vis-à-vis their member states, particularly their host states.[91]

Privileges and immunities of international organisations, and by extension of their secretariats, fall into three distinct categories. The first category is known as 'inviolability'. The second category is immunity from jurisdiction.

87 *Spaans v. Iran-United States Claims Tribunal*, Judgement of 20 December 1985, ECLI:NL:HR:1985:AC9158, at para. 3.3.4; *Supreme Site Services v. Supreme Headquarters Allied Powers Europe (SHAPE)*, Judgement of 24 December 2021 ECLI:NL:HR:2021:1956, at para. 3.1.2. See also *Cristiani v. Italian Latin-American Institute* (November 25, 1985), [1992] 87 ILR 21, where the Italian Court of Cassation held that "Once it has been ascertained that the IILA does indeed have legal personality, there is no doubt that it is also entitled to jurisdictional immunity (irrespective of the presence or absence of treaty provisions explicitly granting that right) pursuant to the rule of customary international law *par in parent non habet jurisdictionem*." On the requirement to have a reasonable alternative avenue for a fair trial, see *Klausecker v. Germany*, Judgement (Merits) of 29 January 2015, European Court of Human Rights (Fifth Section), Application No. 415/07 at para. 69 and *Perez. v. Germany*, [2015] Application No. 15521/08 (European Court of Human Rights, Fifth Section), at para. 93.

88 *Ligue des États arabes c. T.M.*, 12 March 2001 (Cour de cassation of Belgium) p. 390–395; *Groupement d'entreprises Fougerolle c. CERN*, 21 December 1992 (Tribunal Fédéral suisse): « Les raisons de cette différence doivent, notamment, être recherchées dans le fondement juridique même de l'immunité octroyée aux organisations internationales, à savoir une convention internationale et non pas une règle de droit international général [...] ».

89 *Amaratunga v Northwest Atlantic Fisheries Organization*, *supra* note 86 at para 29 (Supreme Court of Canada).

90 *Ibid.*

91 Isabelle Pingel, "Article 105" in Jean-Pierre Cot, Alain Pellet and Mathias Forteau, eds, *Charte des Nations Unies : Commentaire Article par Article*, 3d ed (Paris: Economica, 2005) at 2159.

The third category consists of fiscal privileges, including exemptions from all direct taxes and most forms of indirect taxes.

2.1.2.1 *Inviolability*

The International Congo Commission was probably the first non-diplomatic entity to be granted 'inviolability'.[92] Article 18 of the *Berlin Congo Act* of 1885 provided that the International Commission's offices, archives, members, and appointed agents are invested with the privilege of inviolability in the exercise of their functions.

A similar protection could be found in Article 7 of the Covenant of the League of Nations which stated that the "buildings and other property occupied by the League or its officials or by Representatives attending its meetings shall be inviolable". The Host Country agreement, commonly known as *modus vivendi* of 1921 (as amended in 1926), concluded between the League and Switzerland provided that 'inviolable' meant 'no agent of the public authority may enter' without the consent of the League.[93]

Inviolability may relate to premises, vehicles, documents, official correspondence, personnel, and personal property. Although the term 'inviolable' is a protean word whose "meaning is necessarily sensitive to its context and purpose",[94] it generally "entails freedom from any form of unilateral interference on the part of a state".[95] In a resolution that dealt with the safety and security of UN personnel, the UN General Assembly urged all member states to respect and ensure respect for the inviolability of United Nations premises, recalling that such inviolability is "essential to the continuation and successful implementation of United Nations operations".[96]

Inviolability prohibits the host state and its governmental entities, including law-enforcement agencies, from entering the organisation's premises without its explicit consent, impounding its aircraft,[97] searching, seizing, or

---

92 Kunz, *supra* note 80 at 829.

93 "Communications from the Swiss Federal Council Concerning the Diplomatic Immunities to be Accorded to the Staff of the League of Nations and of the International Labour Office" (1926), 7 *League of Nations O.J.* 1422, at 1423.

94 *R. v Secretary of State for Foreign and Commonwealth Affairs*, [2018] UKSC 3 at para 69 (UK Supreme Court).

95 *World Bank Group v Wallace*, 2016 SCC 15, [2016] 1 SCR 207 at para 78 (Supreme Court of Canada).

96 UN General Assembly resolution 68/101 on *Safety and security of humanitarian personnel and protection of United Nations personnel*, UN Doc. A/RES/68/101 (13 December 2014) at para 3.

97 See Yearbook of the International Law Commission [1967] Vol. II, at para. 125.

confiscating vehicles[98] and other assets owned or rented[99] by the organisation, forcibly opening or intercepting the pouch with official documents[100] or telecommunication signals, etc. Without guarantees of such inviolability, international secretariats would be too vulnerable to interference in their affairs by the host nation.

An unusual case dealing with the inviolability of archives of an international organisation reached the Supreme Court of Canada in 2016. The facts of the case can be summarised as follows. The World Bank investigated allegations that representatives of SNC-Lavalin (a major construction company based in Montreal) were planning to bribe officials of the government of Bangladesh to obtain a contract related to the construction of a bridge valued at US$2.9 billion. The World Bank Group shared some information from its investigation with the Royal Canadian Mounted Police (RCMP). The RCMP obtained wiretap authorisations, collected incriminating evidence, and pressed charges for corruption against four alleged offenders. The accused individuals challenged the wiretap authorisations and applied for a third-party production order to compel senior investigators of the World Bank Group to appear before a Canadian court and produce documents. Although the World Bank asserted its inviolability and immunity from all forms of legal process, the trial judge granted the applications. This order resulted in successive appeals to the Court of Appeal and the Supreme Court. The Supreme Court of Canada ruled that the World Bank's inviolability of archives prevents any search, seizure or compelled production of documents stored by it. In the same judgement, the Court linked the organisation's inviolability to its independence:

> Shielding an organisation's entire collection of stored documents, including official records and correspondences, is integral to ensuring its proper, independent functioning.[101]

2.1.2.2 *Immunity from Jurisdiction and Enforcement Measures*

It became apparent during the early years of the League of Nations that immunity from jurisdiction was indispensable to preserve the independence of

98 See United Nations Office of Legal Affairs, "Illegal seizure of UNICEF property to satisfy court order", *UN Juridical Yearbook* (New York: UN, 2000) at 346.

99 See Yearbook of the International Law Commission [1967] Vol. II, at para. 91.

100 See United Nations Office of Legal Affairs, "Status of United Nations Correspondence Dispatched in Bags", *UN Juridical Yearbook* (New York: UN, 1987) at 208.

101 *World Bank Group v Wallace*, 2016 SCC 15, [2016] 1 SCR 207 at para 71.

international secretariats as it allowed them, among other things, to prevent interference by national courts in employment disputes between international organisations and their staff.[102]

Immunity rules are primarily procedural. They do not exempt their beneficiaries from the substantive applicability of the local laws. Jurisdictional immunity does not grant immunity from liability;. it merely exempts their beneficiaries from local jurisdiction.

The immunity of international organisations, also called immunity from legal process, is a generic term composed of two elements. The first element is the entity's immunity from the adjudicatory process of national courts. This type of immunity is also known as 'immunity from suit' and 'immunity from jurisdiction'. The second element is the institution's immunity from measures aimed at enforcing claims already adjudicated.[103] This second category of immunity is also known as 'immunity from enforcement', 'immunity from execution', or 'immunity from measures of execution'.[104] The immunity from legal process is often contained either in the constitutive instruments of international organisations or in multilateral or bilateral treaties between states or between states and international organisations.

Although today, immunity from jurisdiction occasionally arises in tort cases or commercial disputes,[105] in most cases, it becomes a relevant issue before national courts in labour disputes. Typically, an international organisation asserts its immunity from jurisdiction when its staff members institute legal proceedings against it before national courts. Staff members may decide to seize domestic courts either because the international organisation does not

---

102 Alain Plantey and François Loriot, *Fonction Publique Internationales*, 2d ed (Paris: CNRS Éditions, 2005) at 52.

103 August Reinisch, *The Privileges and Immunities of International Organizations in Domestic Courts* (Oxford: Oxford University Press, 2013) at 64–65.

104 *Ibid.* at 65.

105 *Jam v. International Finance Corporation*, 2019 WL 938524 (United States Supreme Court); *Supreme Site Services v. Supreme Headquarters Allied Powers Europe (SHAPE)*, *supra* note 87; *Mothers of Srebrenica Association et al. v. The Netherlands*, judgement of 19 July 2019, ECLI:NLLHR:2019:1223 (Supreme Court of the Netherlands); *Netherlands (Ministry of Defence and Ministry of Foreign Affairs) v. Nuhanović*, judgement of 6 September 2013, ECLI/NL/HR/2013/BZ9225, ILDC 2061 (NL 2013), 12/03324 (Supreme Court of the Netherlands); *Georges v. United Nations*, judgement of 18 August 2016, 834 F.3d (US Court of Appeals 2d Cir.); *Laventure v. United Nations*, judgement of 28 December 2018, 17–2908-cv, 3 (US Court of Appeals 2d Cir.); see also United Nations Office of Legal Affairs, "Note to the Ministry of Foreign Affairs of [State], concerning the privileges and immunities of a [United Nations entity] and its officials from legal process initiated against it by a former service contractor" *UN Juridical Yearbook* (New York: United Nations, 2013) 377.

offer them any dispute resolution mechanism or because the aggrieved staff member is dissatisfied with the decision made by the organisation's internal dispute settlement body, namely an international administrative tribunal, and decides to seek recourse before domestic courts.

Properly invoked jurisdictional immunity "shields a defendant not only from the consequences of litigation's results but also from the burden of defending themselves".[106] Whether the organisation acted in bad faith or with improper motives is irrelevant. If domestic courts determine that the organisation enjoys jurisdictional immunity, they are obligated to decline jurisdiction without examining the merits of the case and without turning their minds to such considerations as intentional infliction of emotional distress or bad faith. In a case opposing the Organisation of American States to one of its staff members, a D.C. Circuit court explained that if it were to determine whether the international organisation acted in bad faith before deciding whether the jurisdictional immunity applies, "the immunity shield [...] would be evanescent".[107] The United Kingdom Employment Appeal Tribunal adopted a similar reasoning when adjudicating a complaint for discrimination submitted by a candidate against the European Bank for Reconstruction and Development. The Tribunal cautioned against reviewing the merits of the case for the sole purpose of determining whether the jurisdictional immunity applies. It recalled that the purpose of conferring immunity is to protect the relevant organisation from having legal proceedings brought against it for alleged wrongs, whether the organisation has actually committed those wrongs or not.[108]

Whereas state immunity is based on the principle of sovereign equality,[109] the immunity from legal process of international organisations normally derives from legal instruments and not from their international legal personality,[110] even though some courts, particularly in the Netherlands, have opined

106 *De Luca v. United Nations Organization*, 841 F. Supp. 531 (S.D.N.Y. 1994) (United States District Court) at 533 quoting *Davis v. Passman* 442 U.S. 228 (1979), 235 n. 11, 99 S. Ct. 2264, n. 11, 60 L. Ed. 2d 846 and *Dombrowski v. Eastland* (1967) 387 U.S. 82, 85, 87 S. Ct. 1425, 1427, 18 L. Ed. 2d 577.

107 *Donald v. Orfila* (1986) 788 F.2d 36 at 37 (United States Court of Appeals, District of Columbia Circuit).

108 *Mukoro v. European Bank for Reconstruction and Development*, [1994] UKEAT 813_92_2303 (United Kingdom Employment Appeal Tribunal).

109 *Jurisdictional Immunities of the State (Germany v Italy: Greece intervening)*, Judgment, [2012] ICJ Rep 99 at para 57.

110 Lucius Caflisch, "La Pratique Suisse en Matiere de Droit International Public 1992" (1993) 3:5 *Swiss Rev Int'l & Eur L* 669 at 692. See also United Nations Office of Legal Affairs, "Note to the Ministry of Foreign Affairs of [State], concerning the privileges and immunities of a [United Nations entity] and its officials from legal process initiated against it by a former

that the immunity from legal process of international organisations may also derive from 'unwritten international law' or customary international law.[111]

Another important distinction between state immunity and the immunity of international organisations relates to their scope. Most national courts interpret sovereign immunity restrictively. More specifically, they recognise that foreign states enjoy immunity in relation to *juri imperii* or sovereign acts but not in relation to commercial acts.[112] On the other hand, the immunity of international organisations needs to be broader.

In one case, a US Supreme Court judge noted in his dissenting opinion that "international organisations, unlike foreign nations, are multilateral, with members from many different nations. [...] That multilateralism is threatened if one nation alone, by applying its own liability rules, can shape the policy choices or actions an international organisation believes it must take or refrain from taking."[113] In a case dealing with immunity from jurisdiction in labour disputes, the Court of Appeal of the District of Columbia observed that "[d]enial of immunity [to international organisations] opens the door to divided decisions of the courts of different member states" thereby exposing the international organisation to an untenable position.[114] The following additional reasons justify a broader immunity from jurisdiction for international organisations:

- Sovereignty entails the ability to carry out a wide range of activities, including activities normally reserved for private persons. Thus, it is logical to deny states immunity from jurisdiction when they act in

---

service contractor" (New York: United Nations, 2013) 377 at 379: "While the immunity of States derives from their respective sovereignty and depends on the nature of the activity in question (commercial or in exercise of governmental functions) as well as the possibility of invoking reciprocity, the immunity of intergovernmental organizations is designed to protect their ability to function independently of any government."

111 *Spaans v. Iran-United States Claims Tribunal*, Judgement of 20 December 1985, ECLI:NL:HR:1985:AC9158 at para. 3.3.4; *Eckhardt v. Eurocontrol (No. 2)* (1985) 16 NYIL 464 judgement of 12 January 1984 (Maastricht District Court); *Supreme Site Services v. Supreme Headquarters Allied Powers Europe* (SHAPE), *supra* note 87, at para. 3.1.2. See on this point Michael Wood, "Do International Organizations Enjoy Immunity under Customary International Law?" in Niels Blokker and Nico Schrijver, ed., *Immunity of International Organizations* (Leiden: Brill Nijhoff, 2015) at 40–41.

112 Hazel Fox and Philippa Webb, *The Law of State Immunity*, 3d ed (Oxford: Oxford University Press, 2013) at 673–674.

113 *Jam v. International Finance Corporation*, 2019 WL 938524 (United States Supreme Court) per Bryer J (dissenting).

114 *Broadbent v. Organization of American States* (1980) 628 F. 2d 27, 35 (Court of Appeals District of Columbia).

an entirely private as opposed to public or governmental capacity. International organisations, on the other hand, can only perform activities that do not exceed their vocation and are necessary for the fulfilment of their mandate.[115] Therefore, to allow international organisations to carry out their mission without undue restriction, it is logical to grant them absolute jurisdictional immunity as opposed to a restricted one.

- The jurisdictional immunity of states is *de facto* better protected because states can retaliate against one another. Each state has an incentive not to encroach excessively or unreasonably on the jurisdictional immunity of other states because it understands that other states may reciprocate such treatment. International organisations cannot retaliate against their member states. Therefore, their immunity is more vulnerable and needs to be unconditional.
- International organisations have an incentive to enjoy their jurisdictional immunity sparingly and not to abuse it because member states always have the possibility to limit it by imposing specific restrictions through treaties.[116]

Consequently, a secretariat cannot be institutionally independent of its member states unless it is accorded absolute immunity from jurisdiction.

International organisations are also immune from enforcement measures that may follow an unfavourable court order or judgement. In particular, the organisation's assets, funds, and other types of property cannot be garnished, seized, or confiscated.

2.1.2.3 *Fiscal Privileges*

Many believe that the reason for exempting international organisations from taxation is based on sovereignty and sovereign equality of states. Specifically, funds contributed by member states to the international organisation in question should not be diverted into the treasuries of host states using national taxes levied on the organisation because this would amount to taxation of states by other states.[117] While this is an important consideration, it is not the main reason, much less the only one.

---

115 *Legality of the Threat or Use by a State of Nuclear Weapons*, Advisory Opinion, [1996] ICJ Rep 66 at para 25.

116 Éric David, *Droit des Organisations Internationales* (Bruxelles: Bruylant, 2016) at 645–646.

117 Sam Muller, "International Organizations and Their Officials: To Tax or Not to Tax?" (1993) 6:1 *Leiden J Int'l L* 47 at 49.

The primary purpose of exempting international organisations from taxes is not to minimise the cost of their operations; it is to ensure that individual member states do not interfere with the independent functioning of international organisations. The international community of states highlighted the importance of exempting international organisations from taxation when setting up the United Nations. The founders of the UN acknowledged that to guarantee the functional independence of the United Nations, no state should be permitted to hinder in any way the working of the organisation by taking measures, the effect of which could increase the financial burdens of the organisation.[118] If an intergovernmental organisation were subjected to the fiscal jurisdiction of its member states, the taxing authorities of those member states would have the means of exerting pressure and controlling, at least indirectly, the activities of the organisation.

The very nature of an international organisation as a means by which a collective undertaking of the member countries is carried out and through which their relations with each other in a particular sphere of common interest are regulated bears with it that any attempt by one of the member countries to tax an international organisation would allow such country to exercise undue control over the organisation.[119]

Another argument in favour of granting international organisations tax exemption relates to their autonomy. To be truly independent, international secretariats are normally enabled to administer their personnel without external interference. The autonomy to administer personnel entails the power to establish salary scales that apply to all staff without distinction as to their nationality. However, this power cannot be exercised effectively if the emoluments are not exempt from national taxation and vary from one nation to another.[120]

In sum, the institutional independence of international secretariats requires member states to recognise the juridical personality of international organisations, respect the inviolability of their premises, assets, and information, assert

118 United Nations Conference on International Organization, 1945, vol. XIII at 780.

119 Rutsel Silvestre Martha, "Exemptions from Taxes, Customs Duties, and Prohibitions on Imports and Exports" in August Reinisch, ed, *Convention on the Privileges and Immunities of the United Nations and Its Specialized Agencies* (Oxford: Oxford University Press, 2016) at 220.

120 See arguments raised by the European Commission in *Reiniera Charlotte Brouerius van Nidek v. Inspecteur des Registratie en Successie*, preliminary ruling of 3 July 1974, Case 7/74, ECR 1974 (Part II) ECLI:EU:C:1974:73 at 762.

the jurisdictional immunity of IGOs before their courts, and grant them broad fiscal privileges.

2.2 *Individual Independence of Staff*

In addition to their institutional independence, international secretariats must also be staffed by functionaries and agents who are themselves independent. To be independent, international civil servants must (a) enjoy privileges and immunities, (b) be impartial and neutral, and (c) remain anonymous.

2.2.1 Privileges and Immunities of International Officials

It would be meaningless to grant international organisations privileges and immunities without providing similar protection to their staff because international secretariats carry out their activities through the intermediary of international civil servants. The privileges and immunities that international civil servants enjoy are normally more limited than those granted to international organisations. More specifically, the jurisdictional immunity granted to international staff is not absolute but functional. Similarly, unlike international organisations, international civil servants are not exempt from all forms of direct and most indirect taxes. Their fiscal privileges are much more limited.

The privileges and immunities of most international civil servants are also less broad than those diplomats enjoy. Diplomatic privileges and immunities are based on the principle of sovereign equality of states and reciprocity. Since international organisations are not sovereign states and do not have a territory of their own, they are neither equal to states nor can reciprocate in exchange for obtaining more generous privileges and immunities for their staff. Most importantly, international civil servants do not need broader privileges and immunities to remain independent. All they need is an assurance that the Chief Administrative Officer of their organisation has the ultimate authority to decide whether their privileges and immunities should be asserted or lifted. Nevertheless, a finite number of senior officials of many international organisations are granted privileges and immunities equivalent to those enjoyed by diplomats.

2.2.1.1 *Functional Immunity*

When acting in their official capacity, the acts of international civil servants are in effect the acts of the international organisation itself. In a Note to a permanent mission of a UN member state, the Legal Counsel of the United Nations explained the rationale for such immunity as allowing organisations and their staff to carry out their official functions impartially and free from interference. He noted that without immunity, individuals employed by the organisation could find themselves vulnerable to criminal prosecution and civil suits in local courts and tribunals worldwide for claims arising from their official acts. For this reason, this immunity is vital for the organisation to function as it secures not only its independence as an institution but also the independence of its officials from regulation under national law.[121]

While it is true that functional immunity primarily protects international personnel against suits and prosecutions for acts performed in their official capacity, it also indirectly protects the organisation, its documents, archives, and information. Indeed, without adequate jurisdictional immunity, officials could be compelled to appear as witnesses in court to give evidence on official matters. They could be subject to arbitrary arrests and interrogations by state authorities on issues arising out of their official duties. The subjection of international officials to these forms of legal process could easily lead to the disclosure of matters which, within any civil service, are regarded as internal matters of a confidential nature.[122]

For these reasons, international officials must be (and normally are) immune from legal process in respect of words spoken or written and all acts performed by them in their official capacity and from national service obligations. To take any action against an international civil servant covered by functional immunity, national authorities should first seek a waiver of the staff member's immunity from the head of the organisation (or another official with the required authority). National courts are often unable to appreciate fully the mandate and the needs of international organisations; therefore, they should not have the authority to determine whether the alleged acts were committed as part of an international official's functions. As one author argues, if the grant of immunity is made dependent upon the trial of the issue of fact whether at the time that the offence charged was committed, the official was discharging such functions as were necessary for the efficient functioning of the organisation itself, nothing will remain of functional immunity. Any requirement of that

121 United Nations Office of Legal Affairs, "Note to the Permanent Mission of [State] concerning the privileges and immunities of United Nations officials performing functions in [State] and who are [State] nationals or permanent residents", *United Nations Juridical Yearbook* (New York: UN, 2015) 303 at 305.

122 United Nations Office of Legal Affairs, "Scope and effect of the privileges and immunities required under the 1946 Convention on the privileges and immunities of the United Nation for locally recruited staff", *United Nations Juridical Yearbook* (New York: UN, 1968) 212 at 213.

nature would make a mockery of the whole principle of immunity from suit.[123] This is why the International Court of Justice held that since the chief administrative officer of the international organisation has the primary responsibility to safeguard the interests of the organisation, it is up to that official to assess whether the organisation's agents acted within the scope of their functions.[124]

As the privileges and immunities enjoyed by international officials are conferred in the interests of the organisation and not for the personal benefit of the individuals themselves, they do not provide an excuse to the staff members who are covered by them to fail to observe laws and regulations of the state in which they are located.[125] Staff of international organisations must comply not only with the local laws of their host nation but also with their private obligations such as child support payments, alimonies, and bank loans. When the international organisation determines that its staff is abusing their immunity, it must waive such immunity so as not to impede the course of justice.[126]

2.2.1.2 *Fiscal Privileges*

Fiscal privileges that play an essential role in preserving the independence of international civil servants are exemptions from national taxation of salaries and emoluments paid by international organisations. Fiscal exemptions are not designed to create a privileged class of civil servants. Although international officials do not pay national income taxes on their emoluments, their salaries are generally fixed by reference to the wages of governmental officials holding comparable posts after tax deductions. Furthermore, many international organisations, including the United Nations, levy from their staff amounts "comparable to national income taxes".[127] The funds collected from staff assessment are distributed among member states in proportion to their

123 Kuljit Ahluwalia, *The Legal Status, Privileges and Immunities of the Specialized Agencies of the United Nations and Certain Other International Organizations* (The Hague: Martinus Nijhoff, 1964) at 111.

124 *Immunity from Legal Process of a Special Rapporteur*, supra note 9 at para 60.

125 United Nations Office of Legal Affairs, "Note to the Permanent Mission of [State] concerning the privileges and immunities of United Nations officials performing functions in [State] and who are [State] nationals or permanent residents", *United Nations Juridical Yearbook* (New York: UN, 2015) 303 at 305.

126 *Ibid.*

127 UN General Assembly resolution 239(III), "Tax Equalization – Staff Assessment Plan", UN Doc. A/RES/239(III) (18 November 1948).

contributions to the organisation's budget. In the UN, this distribution serves as an offset against amounts otherwise owed by the member states involved.[128]

Courts, practitioners, and scholars often focus on three reasons for exempting staff members from national income taxes. First, to achieve equality in salary treatment for officials of equal rank, the organisation must be able to fix comparable salary levels for comparable posts throughout the entire area of its operations without the need for continuous adjustment, which would be necessary if changes and variations in national tax legislation had to be taken into account.[129] This reason can also be found in the UN General Assembly resolution 78(I) of 7 December 1946, in which nations were requested to take action "[i]n order to achieve full application of the principles of equality among Members and equality among personnel of the United Nations" by exempting from taxation, salaries and allowances paid out of the budget of the organisation. If a state could tax its nationals employed by international organisations, there would be a disparity in treatment because some staff would inevitably earn less than their colleagues of equal rank and seniority.[130] This would also deprive the organisation of its ability to establish salary scales that apply fairly and equally to all staff.

Second, the exemption is said to ensure that the funds contributed by member states and private organisations for the support of the organisation are not diverted into the coffers of host states by taxing salaries funded by all nations. In other words, the operations of an international organisation should not become a source of revenue for one of its member states.[131]

Third, personnel employed by intergovernmental organisations should only be taxed once. As mentioned above, many international organisations already levy some form of income taxes. If staff were to pay national income taxes, they would be taxed twice on the same income.

---

128 *McCloskey v. Secretary-General of the United Nations*, Judgment No. 2014-UNAT 424 (United Nations Appeals Tribunal); *Johnson v. Secretary-General of the United Nations*, Judgment No. 2012-UNAT-240 (United Nations Appeals Tribunal).

129 *Reiniera Charlotte Brouerius van Nidek v. Inspecteur des Registratie en Successie*, preliminary ruling of 3 July 1974, Case 7/74, ECR 1974 (Part II) at 764.; United Nations Office of Legal Affairs, "Note to the Ministry of Foreign Affairs of [State], concerning privileges and immunities enjoyed by certain categories of United Nations personnel in [State]" *United Nations Juridical Yearbook* (New York: UN, 2013) 371 at 375.

130 Muller, *supra* note 117 at 49.

131 United Nations Office of Legal Affairs, "Scope and effect of the privileges and immunities required under the 1946 Convention on the privileges and immunities of the United Nation for locally recruited staff", *United Nations Juridical Yearbook* (New York: UN, 1968) 212 at 214.

However, the main reason for exempting international civil servants from national income taxes is their independence. Anyone subjected to national fiscal legislation is necessarily exposed to that nation's taxation laws and the jurisdiction of its tax courts. Specifically, in case of disputes between staff members and their national tax authorities, the matter would be resolved by national courts competent to hear tax law cases. As soon as international civil servants are exposed to national courts and authorities on issues related to their official functions, including income taxes due on their salary for performing their official functions, they become vulnerable to political pressure and harassment by national authorities. The ILO Administrative Tribunal recognised the nexus between fiscal privileges and the independence of international civil servants when it ruled that "exemption from national taxes is an essential condition of employment in the international civil service and is an important guarantee of independence and objectivity."[132]

The notorious case of *Dumitrescu* illustrates the risk of subjecting international officials to national fiscal legislation. Dumitrescu, a Romanian national serving with UNESCO, was accused of violating a fiscal decree which provided that Romanian citizens employed in international organisations transmit to Romania a portion of their net income in accordance with a detailed schedule.[133] Romania was not the only country imposing such obligations on its nationals. Many Eastern European governments used to require their nationals serving in international organisations to transfer to their governments a sizeable portion of their salaries, failing which their secondment to the international organisation was terminated, and they were repatriated to face criminal charges. This practice, which was discontinued after the fall of communism in Eastern Europe, was just another form of taxation.

For these reasons, staff members should be exempt from national income taxes on their salaries and emoluments. This does not mean that they should not pay any form of taxes. It merely means that national authorities should not be involved in taxing international civil servants. This power should be delegated to and exercised by international organisations on behalf of nations.

2.2.2 Impartiality and Neutrality

Independence, impartiality, and neutrality have often been confounded. While they are similar and related, they are distinguishable notions. Independence

---

132 *Krutzsch v. Organisation for the Prohibition of Chemical Weapons*, [2001] Judgement 2032 at para 17 (ILOAT).

133 Theodor Meron, "Status and Independence of the International Civil Service" (1980) 167 *Recueil des Cours de l'Académie de Droit International* 289 at 326–327.

is a question of relationships between the international civil service and others. It refers to the ability to act and decide in opposition to political power. Independence is usually "associated with certain institutional guarantees or safeguards that allow adjudicators to free themselves to some extent from external pressures when making their decisions."[134]

Impartiality, on the other hand, is a question of a state of mind.[135] It is the absence of bias or preconceived ideas about people, groups, cultures, races, and even politics. In 1954, the International Civil Service Advisory Board stated, "[i]mpartiality implies objectivity, lack of bias, tolerance, restraint – particularly when political or religious disputes or differences arise." Acknowledging that staff members' personal views and convictions remain inviolate, the Advisory Board noted that international officials do not have the freedom of a private person to 'take sides', to enter a dispute as a partisan, or publicly express their convictions on matters of a controversial nature. The Advisory Board added, "just as the practice of impartiality will strengthen the Secretariat, repeated instances of partiality, or bias, will do serious harm to the organisation."[136]

Neutrality is the expression or manifestation of impartiality; it is how international civil servants exhibit their impartiality through actions and inactions. In a famous lecture on the neutrality of international civil servants delivered at the University of Oxford in May 1961, Dag Hammarskjöld stated that international staff must keep themselves under the strictest observation. They are not requested to be neuters in the sense that they can have no sympathies or antipathies or have no ideas or ideals that matter to them. Instead, they are expected to be aware of these human reactions and meticulously check themselves so that these reactions are not permitted to influence their actions.[137]

In August 1961 – three months after this speech at Oxford – the Secretary-General produced an annual report to the General Assembly in which he equated neutrality to integrity, implying that someone neutral may be in complete disagreement with the actions that they take in the organisation's interests:

134 Diego M Papayannis, "Independence, Impartiality and Neutrality in Legal Adjudication" (2016) 28 *Revus: J Const Theory & Phil Law* 33 at 35.

135 United Nations, International Civil Service Advisory Board, Report on Standards of Conduct in the International Civil Service (COORD/CIVIL SERVICE/5) (New York, 1954) at 5.

136 *Ibid.* at 5.

137 Dag Hammarskjöld, *The International Civil Servant in Law and in Fact: A Lecture Delivered to Congregation on 30 May 1961* (Uppsala: Dag Hammarskjöld Foundation, 2021).

> While it may be said that no man is neutral in the sense that he is without opinions or ideals, it is just as true that, in spite of this, a neutral Secretariat is possible. Anyone of integrity, not subjected to undue pressures, can, regardless of his own views, readily act in an 'exclusively international' spirit and can be guided in his actions on behalf of the Organization solely by its interests and principles, and by the instructions of its organs.[138]

Impartiality and neutrality are both prerequisites of independence.[139] Without impartiality and neutrality, an international civil service is nothing more than a multinational bureaucracy. In the context of international civil service, the notions of impartiality and neutrality are often used together or interchangeably. Essentially, the concept of impartiality and neutrality means that international civil servants must adopt an attitude of impartiality toward the conflicting positions and interests of member states. This attitude, termed the doctrine of political neutrality of the public service, implies two propositions. First, public servants must abstain from participation in national politics while retaining the right to private discussion of political issues and voting freely. Second, public servants are ethically bound to administer the policy decisions of legislative and executive bodies with equal zeal, irrespective of which country or region will benefit more from their work.[140]

2.2.2.1 *Code of Conduct*

Typically, international organisations impose several obligations and restrictions on their staff to ensure their compliance with their obligation to be neutral and impartial. For instance, internal rules and regulations of many international organisations require their staff members to ensure that their personal views, political convictions, and religious beliefs do not adversely affect their neutrality and impartiality and are not incompatible with the proper discharge of their official functions.[141] Most international organisations prohibit their staff from becoming candidates for or holding a public office of a

---

138 UNGAOR, 16th Sess., Supp. 1A, Annual Report of the Secretary-General on the Work of the Organization 16 June 1960 – 15 June 1961, UN Doc. A/4800/Add.1 at 6.

139 Papayannis, *supra* note 134 at 42.

140 David M Levitan, "The Neutrality of the Public Service" (1942) 2:4 *Public Administration Review* 317 at 317.

141 See Staff Regulations and Rules of the United Nations, UN Doc. ST/SGB/2018/1/Rev.1, Regulation 1.2(f).

political character.[142] Similarly, staff members are not permitted to accept any honour, decoration, favour, or gift from any government.[143] These restrictions play a significant role in maintaining the impartiality and neutrality of international civil service.[144]

International secretariats aspiring to be independent must 'set the tone' by developing and promulgating codes of conduct with basic obligations for their officials. Obligations aimed at ensuring the neutrality and impartiality of staff must be at the centre of such codes of conduct. Of course, a mere adoption of a code of conduct is insufficient to achieve the impartiality of international officials. No statutory text can guarantee compliance with the legal norms contained therein. To ensure compliance with these obligations, international secretariats must also equip themselves with credible investigative capabilities. For instance, the Office of Internal Oversight Services (OIOS) of the United Nations is an independent department within the UN Secretariat employing experienced investigators specialised in investigating allegations of misconduct. In contrast, until recently, NATO had no internal investigative capability. It relied primarily on its security services, which had little or no investigative expertise. In 2023, various NATO bodies began establishing investigation posts.

In addition to establishing investigative mechanisms and bodies, international secretariats must also have fair disciplinary procedures to sanction conduct found to be inconsistent with the basic obligations of impartiality and neutrality. Without fair disciplinary procedures, neither member states nor staff members will trust the organisation's ability to detect and sanction bias and partiality.

2.2.2.2 *Meritocracy*

Over a century ago in Britain, it has been proven that the abolition of recruitment by patronage in the civil service significantly contributed to the neutrality of the civil service since it severed personal allegiances between the hiring minister and civil servants.[145] Civil servants recruited through competitive selection processes have the assurance that they were appointed because they

142 NATO Civilian Personnel Regulations, Art. 12.2.1(a); Staff Regulations and Rules of the United Nations, UN Doc. ST/SGB/2018/1/Rev.1, Regulation 1.2(h).

143 Staff Regulations and Rules of the United Nations, *supra* note 142, Regulation 1.2(j); NATO Civilian Personnel Regulations, Art. 12.2.4; Staff Regulations of Officials of European Union, Art. 11.

144 Proposed United Nations Code of Conduct, Report of the Secretary-General, UN Doc. A/52/488 (17 October 1997) at 35.

145 SE Finer, "The Individual Responsibility of Ministers" (1956) 34:4 *Public Adm* 377 at 380.

demonstrated during the selection process that they were the most suitable candidates for the vacant post. Conversely, officials recruited through nepotism or patronage know they would not have been selected had their sponsor not intervened. Naturally, they feel indebted to the person who helped them be recruited, and their loyalty to the organisation and its mission may not be absolute. Therefore, Article 13 of the League of Nations Staff Regulations of 1922 provided that "[a]ppointments on the Secretariat are made by the method of competitive selection", including examinations or tests.

The United Nations has introduced several measures for eliminating nepotism, including the prohibition of offering employment to interns, consultants, and temporary staff until after a certain cool-off period. Since these categories of staff can be recruited more efficiently and less competitively, the UN wanted to avoid recruiting staff through the back door. Another measure that NATO, the UN and a few other IGOs opted for was to prohibit the employment of a serving staff member's close relatives.[146]

Constitutive documents or staff regulations of the largest IGOs recognise in varying forms that the paramount consideration in recruiting staff is the necessity of securing the most qualified candidates. While having such broad principles expressly recognised is important, they do not suffice. Any international secretariat must establish a selection and recruitment system that objectivises the decision-making process and leaves no room for arbitrary or discretionary decisions. Selection and recruitment policies requiring anonymised written assessments, interviews by two or more differently constituted panels, and

146 Rule 4.7 of the Staff Regulations and Rules of the United Nations provides that "an appointment shall not be granted to a person who is the father, mother, son, daughter, brother or sister of a staff member." Article 3(f) of the NATO Civilian Personnel Regulations reads as follows: "Staff members are appointed to and hold posts on the establishment of a NATO body only on condition that: (f) they are not closely related to a member of the staff". Rule 104.14(a) of the Staff Rules of the General Secretariat of the Organization of American States is even more restrictive: "No appointment to the staff of the General Secretariat shall be granted to the following relatives of a staff member: spouse, son or daughter, stepson or stepdaughter, father or mother, stepfather or stepmother, brother or sister, half-brother or half-sister, stepbrother or stepsister, uncle or aunt, nephew or niece, first cousin, father- or mother-in-law, son- or daughter-in-law, or brother- or sister-in-law." Rule 1.03/1 of Staff Rules of the Asian Infrastructure Development Bank also contains a similar provision. Still, the basis of the restriction is not to prevent nepotism but to ensure the highest standards of efficiency: "In order to ensure that the highest standards of efficiency are not compromised by familial relationships between Staff Members, the Partner or Close Relative of a Staff Member of the Bank shall not be appointed to the staff of the Bank, other than in exceptional circumstances as provided in this Staff Rule."

extensive reference checks have proven to be an effective method for objectivising decisions in some IGOs.

2.2.2.2.1 Seeking or Receiving Support from Member States in Recruitment and Promotion Decisions

International civil servants and the governments of member states play an important role in preserving the meritocracy of the international civil service. As tempting as it can be, staff members should never seek support from member states in recruitment and promotion decisions.[147] Similarly, governments of member states should never interfere in personnel management.[148]

Unfortunately, member states of many international organisations, particularly the UN and its complex web of agencies, routinely exert pressure on chief administrative officers of the secretariat to recruit their nationals for key positions.[149] Some senior posts in the UN System are still earmarked for certain nations even though the General Assembly passed several resolutions requesting that "the principle that there should be no monopoly on senior posts by nationals of any state or group of states should be strictly observed and implemented."[150]

A recent example of improper influence was an unsuccessful attempt made by France in 2020 to persuade the UN Secretary-General Guterres to appoint a French national to head the UN's nascent political mission in Khartoum. Despite strong pushback from other Security Council members, particularly from Russia and China, the French vigorously lobbied on behalf of this candidate, who happened to be married to a Sudanese national with ties to one political faction in Khartoum.[151] Had the Secretary-General yielded to the

147 *Bel Ghazi v World Health Organization*, [1996] Judgement 1475 (ILOAT): "It is inadmissible that a staff member should involve government officials in questioning the Organization's internal workings."

148 *Reznikov v World Health Organization*, [1993] Judgement 1249 (ILOAT); *Stulz v UNESCO*, [1993] Judgement 1232 (ILOAT).

149 Jeffrey Feltman, "Restoring (some) impartiality to UN senior appointments" (2020) Cairo Rev Glob Aff.

150 *Strengthening of the United Nations System*, GA Res 51/241, UNGAOR, 51st Sess., UN Doc A/Res/51/241 (1997) 1 at para 66 [*Strengthening of the United Nations System*]; *Revitalization of the United Nations Secretariat*, GA Res 46/232, UNGAOR, 46th Sess, UN Doc A/RES/46/232 (1992) 3 at para 3(e) [*Revitalizing of the UN Secretariat*]; *Personnel Questions*, GA Res 35/210, UNGAOR, 35th Sess, UN Doc A/RES/35/210 (1980) at para I.3. See also *Dauchy v. Secretary-General of the United Nations*, Judgement No. 492 (1990) (United Nations Administrative Tribunal).

151 Feltman, *supra* note 149.

pressure, the UN would not have been seen as an impartial and neutral actor in Sudan.

2.2.2.2.2 Interference in Decisions to Appoint and Separate from Service Staff Members

The opposite scenario – when nations oppose certain candidates rather than advocate for them – is equally problematic. Nations often block the appointment of candidates based on considerations unrelated to the candidates' qualifications or suitability. For instance, in 2017, when the UN Secretary-General announced that he intended to name Salam Fayyad, a respected former Prime Minister of Palestine, to lead the UN support mission in Libya and help broker talks on a faltering political deal, the United States objected merely because of Fayyad's Palestinian nationality.[152] Occasionally, member states go as far as insisting that the appointment of international officials be terminated or not renewed.[153]

In most cases, such interferences by member states are case-specific. However, in some cases, they are institutionalised. For instance, in some international organisations, internal policies require that senior officials secure the 'sponsorship' of their country of nationality before they can be appointed – a practice that was held to be *ultra vires* by the ILO Administrative Tribunal as it was inconsistent with the requirement not to seek or receive instructions from states.[154] The former Administrative Tribunal of the United Nations also

---

152 "Trump envoy blocks ex-Palestinian PM from UN job 'to support Israel'", *The Guardian* (11 February 2017).

153 See *Troncoso v. World Health Organization*, [1981] Judgement No. 448 (ILOAT): "The organization cannot bow to governments' wishes not to extend the appointment before making sure that they are compatible with its own interests."; *Rosescu v. International Atomic Energy Agency*, [1980] Judgement No. 431 (ILOAT): "The head of the organization cannot forgo taking a decision not to renew the contract of a government official of a member state in the organization's interest for the sole purpose of satisfying a member state."; *Diop v. Secretary-General of the United Nations*, Judgment No. UNDT/2012/029 (United Nations Dispute Tribunal): "The staff of the United Nations enjoys independence in the exercise of their duties and this would be seriously compromised if the views of a Member State were taken into account when considering whether or not to renew a contract."; *Gaskins v. Secretary-General of the United Nations*, Judgment No. UNDT/2010/119 (United Nations Dispute Tribunal).

154 *Umar v. International Atomic Energy Agency*, [1998] Judgement No. 1733 (ILOAT): "The IAEA Administrative Manual and staff notice provide that applicants for posts subject to geographical distribution must have the sponsorship of the government of their country. [...] The sole reason for rejecting his application was the failure to secure government sponsorship. The requirement of government sponsorship in those two provisions is ultra vires. The provisions must comply with the requirements of Articles VII.D and F of the

cautioned the Secretary-General against making decisions pertaining to his staff in order to please member nations. The tribunal pointed out that while the Secretary-General has the right to consult member states when exercising his power of appointment or renewal of contract, such consultations should not contravene the principles of independence and neutrality referred to in Article 100 of the *UN Charter*.[155] In other words, the purpose of the consultative process must be analogous to a reference check rather than an endorsement of his choice by a member state.

Unfortunately, this pervasive practice still exists in many IGOs. In particular, in accordance with the constitutive instruments of at least two large NATO agencies[156] (employing over 4000 staff members), candidates for senior ranking posts cannot be appointed without the endorsement by consensus of their candidacy by all 30 nations. In a recent case, the Financial Controller of a NATO agency whose performance was seemingly satisfactory was separated from service because the governing body composed of all member nations of NATO did not endorse the recommendation made by the Executive Head of the NATO body to renew his contract. The Financial Controller challenged the decision not to renew his contract before the NATO Administrative Tribunal, arguing *inter alia* that the governing body inappropriately interfered with the renewal process. Although the NATO Administrative Tribunal noted that the only reason for not renewing the staff member's contract was the absence of a consensus in the governing body, it refused to set aside the impugned decision.[157]

2.2.2.3 *Permanence or Career Service*

The Preparatory Commission of the United Nations, convened in London shortly after the San Francisco Conference to envisage the future organisation and composition of the UN Secretariat, recognised that unless members of the staff can be offered some assurance of being able to make their careers in the Secretariat, they cannot be expected to subordinate the special interests of their

Statute. In the performance of their duties the Director General and staff may not seek or receive instructions from any source external to the Agency. For the Director General to allow a member State a veto on the appointment of a staff member is to 'receive instructions' from an external source and an interference with the paramount consideration of securing staff of the right calibre."

155 *Qiu v Secretary-General of the United Nations*, [1990] Judgment 482 (United Nations Administrative Tribunal).

156 NATO Support and Procurement Agency and NATO Communication and Information Agency.

157 *PD v. Headquarters Supreme Allied Command Transformation*, AT-J(2021)0001 (NATO Administrative Tribunal).

countries to the international interest if they are merely detached temporarily from national administrations and remain dependent upon them for their future.[158] This recommendation was a marked departure from the League's approach. Under Article 6(a) of Staff Regulations of the League of Nations, senior officials could be offered appointments of up to seven years only.

The United Nations Secretariat began operating under Trygve Lie's leadership as an organisation that granted its staff permanent appointments. The second Secretary-General of the UN, Dag Hammarskjöld, was a strong proponent of permanent appointments and career service of international civil servants. He realised that a "risk of national pressure on the international official may [...] be introduced, in a somewhat more subtle way, by the terms and duration of his appointment".[159] A national bureaucrat seconded by his government for a year or two to serve in an international organisation would be in a different position psychologically and politically from the permanent international civil servant who does not contemplate a subsequent career with his national government.[160] Therefore, Hammarskjöld resisted proposals from some member states to switch from a system that makes career service a rule to a system of fixed-term appointments granted to seconded officials. He viewed the latter approach as inconsistent with Articles 100 and 101 of the UN Charter.[161]

However, subsequent Secretaries-General of the UN felt less strongly about this issue. The contractual arrangements of the UN Secretariat faced considerable political scrutiny in the 1970s. Although UN member states had initially opted for a permanent international secretariat with a career civil service symbolised by permanent contracts to ensure independence, the Soviet Union and its allies rejected that concept. They instructed their nationals to accept only two- to five-year, fixed-term contracts to ensure their loyalties remained with their governments.[162] In 1974, only one of the 153 Soviet nationals employed by the UN Secretariat had a permanent contract. Of the 45 appointments of individuals from Eastern Europe (including the U.S.S.R.) in 1977, none were permanent.[163]

158 Report of the Preparatory Commission of the United Nations, UNCIO, 1945 at para 59.

159 Hammarskjöld, *supra* note 137 at 20.

160 *Ibid.*

161 *Ibid.* at 21.

162 James OC Jonah and Amy S Hill, "The Secretariat: Independence and Reform" in *The Oxford Handbook on the United Nations*, 2nd ed (New York: Oxford University Press, 2018) at 213.

163 Norman A Graham and Robert S Jordan, *The International Civil Service: Changing Role and Concepts* (New York: Pergamon Press, 1980) at 17.

Initially, the Western group of UN member states strongly supported the career concept.[164] For instance, in 1974, the United Kingdom delegate to the Fifth Committee of the General Assembly noted that "an international civil service should be composed predominantly of men and women who wish to dedicate their working lives to international service, thus providing continuity of knowledge, esprit de corps, and dedication to the ideals of the United Nations."[165] However, this support began waning after the Cold War when Western nations saw a drastic increase in IGO's expenses related to staff. Under Kofi Annan's two terms, permanent contracts were increasingly phased out against resistance from the Staff Union.[166]

Consequently, over the years, the notion of career service gradually lost its importance in international secretariats. Some nations claimed that permanent contracts resulted in a complacent workforce within the organisation, even though contractual modalities are not as relevant to poor performance as effective performance appraisal systems can be. Some international organisations, including the Organisation for the Prohibition of Chemical Weapons (OPWC) and the Preparatory Commission for the Comprehensive Nuclear-Test-Ban Treaty Organization (CTBTO), instituted a system with employment contracts of limited duration with no possibility of renewal after a certain period of service.

A career service does not necessarily entail granting permanent appointments. Secretariats may still issue fixed-term contracts provided their renewal is not arbitrary or subject to external pressures. Similarly, career service does not mean that staff members cannot be separated from service. Instead, career service requires that the termination of contracts be based on very specific pre-established grounds and be made by the organisation's chief administrative officer without any external influence.

2.2.2.4 *Wide Geographical Representation*

If international civil servants owe allegiance and loyalty to the international organisation only, their nationality is irrelevant. If we push this reasoning one step further, we can argue that the geographical composition of international secretariats can have no impact on the neutrality and impartiality of international civil servants since they "must develop a distinct identity and

---

164 *Ibid.*

165 Summary Record, Meeting of the Fifth Committee UN Doc. A/C.5/32/SR.6 (30 September 1977).

166 Jonah and Hill, *supra* note 162 at 7.

esprit de corps so that the interests of the international body can be adequately served."[167]

Yet, member states continuously monitor how they are represented in the international civil service and strive to have more of their nationals recruited as international staff. At the sixtieth session of the General Assembly in 2005, several delegations from the G77 & China coalition voiced concerns at the apparent dominance of nationals from Europe and North America, particularly at the most senior levels in the Secretariat, arguing that this imbalance could lead to political bias, thus lack of neutrality.[168]

How can this apparent contradiction be explained? If international civil servants are expected to exhibit an international *esprit de corps*, why does it matter which parts of the world they come from? The answer to this question is not legal but sociological. Humans view others through their own cultural lens.[169] International secretariats composed of individuals from similar cultures would be unable to form an international *esprit de corps*. Homogeneous groups have an unconscious bias and cannot always be impartial despite their best efforts. To ensure an internationally diverse workplace, Article 15 of the League of Nations Staff Regulations specified that to maintain and develop "the international character of the organisation", "preference shall be given to a candidate whose nationality is not already adequately represented in the staff".

To the detriment of principles of neutrality and impartiality, in some international organisations, including the United Nations, the desirability of having a geographically diverse secretariat has been perverted. The UN produces detailed statistics on the representation of each country in the Secretariat. Complex formulas allow it to determine the number of individuals the UN should ideally employ from each member state. However, the founding fathers did not intend the 'geographical basis' to mean a national representation.[170] They especially did not consider a system of 'desirable ranges for the geographical distribution of staff'[171] based on member states' membership, geography, and level of financial contributions.[172] They simply wanted to ensure the widest possible 'representation' of nationalities in the Secretariat. The Preparatory

167 Graham and Jordan, *supra* note 163 at 2.

168 Jonah and Hill, *supra* note 162 at 7.

169 Erin Meyer, *The Culture Map: Decoding How People Think, Lead, and Get Things Done Across Cultures* (New York: Public Affairs, 2014) at 13.

170 Theodor Meron, "Status and Independence of the International Civil Service" (1980) 167 *Recueil des Cours de l'Académie de Droit International* 289 at 299.

171 Report of the Secretary-General, "Composition of the Secretariat", UN Doc A/75/591 (9 November 2020).

172 Meron, *supra* note 170 at 299.

Commission of the United Nations observed that to enjoy the confidence of the organisation's members, the Secretariat must be truly international. Therefore, the Commission spoke of adequately represented geographical regions rather than adequately represented states.[173] By putting an emphasis on nationality and citizenship, international organisations do more harm than good to the concept of geographical diversity.

2.2.3 Anonymity of International Civil Service

There is consensus in the literature that strong similarities exist between the concept of the international civil service and the British secretariat tradition of administration,[174] known as the 'Westminster model'. The Westminster model of civil service began shaping after the Crimean War, which exposed the inefficiencies of the British civil service and led to the formation of the Administrative Reform Association.[175] The Association demanded, among other things, that patronage be replaced by a test of practical skills in the appointment of officials.[176] In 1854, the British government instructed a panel of experts to carry out a detailed analysis of its civil service. The Northcote-Trevelyan Report,[177] issued in 1854, marked the beginning of Britain's modern civil service system.[178] The broad recommendations in a 23-page report gradually led to a civil service appointed on merit through open competition rather than patronage.[179] Although the British civil service has undergone several major reforms since the Northcote-Trevelyan report, its fundamental features of anonymity and neutrality remained intact.

The literature invariably mentions these two features when comparing the international and British civil services.[180] In the Westminster system, civil servants should remain anonymous because anonymity promotes neutrality. Public

173 Report of the Preparatory Commission of the United Nations, UNCIO, 1945 at para 61.

174 Graham and Jordan, *supra* note 163 at 5.

175 G Kitson Clark, "'Statesmen in Disguise': Reflexions on the History of the Neutrality of the Civil Service" (1959) 2:1 *Hist J* 19 at 22.

176 Rodney Lowe, *The Official History of the British Civil Service: Reforming the Civil Service*, Vol. 1: The Fulton Years, 1966–81 (London: Routledge, 2011), s 1.2.1.

177 Staffort H Northcote and C E Trevelyan, Report on the Organisation of the Permanent Civil Service (presented to both Houses of Parliament) (London: 1854).

178 Andrew Massey, *International Handbook on Civil Service Systems* (Cheltenham: Edward Elgar, 2011) at 34.

179 Lowe, *supra* note 176, s 1.4.1 The Northcote-Travelyan report remained largely silent on anonymity and neutrality. These two conventions evolved over time.

180 Evan Luard, *A History of the United Nations* (London: Palgrave Macmillan UK, 1982); Dobromir Mihajlov, "The Origin and the Early Development of International Civil Service" (2004) 1 *Miskolc Journal of International Law* 79 at 81.

servants should neither be blamed nor praised publicly.[181] This anonymity is necessary to protect public officers from all forms of pressure when acting on behalf of the government. It allows public servants to remain non-political and loyal to the administration of the day[182] and to perform their functions conscientiously. Ministers in charge of their departments are supposed to defend and shield public officers by accepting responsibility for their actions or omissions. Ministers alone are answerable to Parliament for every act or omission of their civil servants. In the Westminster tradition, civil servants do not have a 'constitutional personality' separate from their minister's. In an international context, the chief administrative officer of an international organisation must take credit and responsibility for the secretariat's successes and failures.

The corollary of the anonymity rule requires civil servants to refrain from taking a stance on controversial issues or releasing statements and publications without first seeking authorisation from their employer. The earliest reference to this kind of behaviour can be found in the second edition of the book Parliamentary Government, published in 1864 by the 3rd Earl Grey. The author cautioned civil servants against engaging in public controversy, noting "with great alarm some few examples, which have of late years occurred, of persons who hold permanent offices under the government meddling in political contests by being concerned in party newspapers, or writing in the newspapers on the disputed political questions of the day."[183] He then added that it is irrelevant whether the views expressed by civil servants were to support or oppose the Administration of the time; this is a matter of neutrality and anonymity.

In 1875, after a few embarrassing incidents of deliberate leaks to the press, British civil servants were forbidden to publish or give public statements without prior ministerial consent.[184] It is not a coincidence that Staff Regulations of the League of Nations contained a similar prohibition. Article 3 of the Regulations stated that "no official of the Secretariat may, during the term of his appointment, publish or cause to be published or assist in the publication of any book, pamphlet, article, letter or other document, or deliver any lecture or speech, describing, discussing, or in any way directly related to any activity of the League of Nations". Staff regulations and rules of many contemporary

181 Lowe, *supra* note 176, s 1.4.1: Noting that civil servants are not authorised to respond to unwarranted criticisms or personal attacks for performing their official duties, a well-known senior British official quite inappropriately equated attacking civil servants by Parliamentarians to hitting a woman.

182 Massey, *supra* note 178 at 34.

183 Earl Grey, *Parliamentary Government*, 2d ed (London: John Murray, 1864) at 331.

184 Lowe, *supra* note 176.

international organisations still prohibit international civil servants from giving interviews or writing articles without prior authorisation of their organisation.[185] Regulation 1.2(f) of the United Nations Staff Regulations and Rules expressly draws a link between the independence and impartiality of UN staff and their anonymity, leaving no doubt that anonymity is a crucial ingredient of independence:

> [Staff members] shall avoid any action and, in particular, any kind of public pronouncement that may adversely reflect on their status, or on the integrity, independence and impartiality that are required by that status.[186]

Member states play an important role in preserving the anonymity of international civil servants. They should not engage directly with staff members except in the normal course of official duties and transparently. If they wish to criticise the actions or omissions of some officials, they shall express their dissatisfaction to the head of the organisation and let him or her address the shortcoming.

Similarly, when allegations arise that some international civil servants have breached their basic obligations, member states should allow the head of the organisation to investigate the allegations and, if necessary, to prescribe disciplinary measures. Demanding from the head of the organisation further disciplinary action or that a specific type of disciplinary measure be imposed on the alleged offender would be a direct form of political interference with the international civil service. This would be a breach of the principle of anonymity.

185 See Art. 12.2.5 (b) of NATO Civilian Personnel Regulations: "make or release for publication through the press, radio, television or other agencies of public information statements on matters in any way related to the aims and activities of the Organization"; UN Staff Rule 1.2(t); OECD Staff Regulation 4(d) and (e): "Officials shall … (d) refrain from publicly doing, stating or publishing anything incompatible with their duties or obligations or liable to involve the responsibility of the Organisation; (e) make public statements concerning the Organisation or its activities only with permission from the Organisation."; Staff Rule 101.4(e) of Staff Rules of the General Secretariat of the Organization of American States: "Except in the normal course of their duties, or with prior authorisation by the Secretary-General, staff members shall not engage in any of the following acts, if the purposes, activities, or interests of the Organization are involved: (i) Issue statements to the press, radio, or other public information media; (ii) Deliver addresses or lectures; (iii) Take part in film, theatre, radio, or television productions; or (iv) Publish articles, books, or other material."

186 Staff Regulations and Rules of the United Nations, UN Doc. ST/SGB/2018/1/Rev.1, Staff Regulations 1.2(f).

To conclude, the independence of international organisations, and by extension of their secretariats, is a core element of international cooperation. Without such independence, states cannot have trust in the institutional structures they set up to facilitate cooperation. If states do not trust international institutions, they can have no incentive to participate in their creation and establishment. Yet, international organisations are prominent actors in many critical episodes in international politics and reality. NATO's role in containing Russia's aggressive stance and imperialist aspirations, WHO's role in fighting against the COVID-19 pandemic and UNEP's role in galvanising global action to preserve the environment are only a few recent examples of indispensable functions international institutions have. Consequently, it is in the interests of all nations to protect the independence of intergovernmental institutions, particularly the independence of their secretariats and international civil servants. The concept of independence of the international civil service is so prevalent and important that it may have become a general principle of law (a point that will be explored further in the last Chapter). Regrettably, member states often act against their own interests by undermining the independence of international organisations, their secretariats, and their staff. This will be the subject of Chapter 3.

CHAPTER 3

Practices of Member States That Erode the Independence of International Secretariats and Their Staff

Three actors have an important role in preserving the independence of international secretariats and international civil servants. They are the member states, international organisations, and international civil servants. This chapter canvasses the actions or omissions of one of these three actors. Specifically, it explores practices of states and their governments that erode or undermine the independence of international secretariats and their personnel. The practices of international organisations and their personnel that can be prejudicial to the independence of international secretariats will be examined in the subsequent two chapters, Chapters 4 and 5.

This chapter consists of three sections. Section 1 deals with breaches by member states of privileges and immunities of international organisations and, by extension, of their secretariats. Although breaches of this nature can be diverse, in the interests of brevity, this work focuses on three types of most frequently encountered violations of privileges and immunities. These three categories of infringements are (a) breaches of IGOs' inviolability, (b) refusal to recognise the jurisdictional immunity of IGOs, and (c) violations of fiscal privileges of IGOs.

Section 2 covers violations by member states of privileges and immunities enjoyed by international civil servants, namely (a) their functional immunities, (b) their right to be exempt from immigration restrictions, and (c) their exemption from income taxes.

Section 3 explores actions that affect the neutrality and impartiality of international civil servants. Once again, this Section does not purport to be a comprehensive list of inappropriate state practices; it is merely a survey of situations that international organisations confront most. They relate to (a) interference by governments in decisions on the selection, appointment, and separation from service of international civil servants and (b) secondments.

 | DOI:10.1163/9789004704596_005

1 Breaches by States of IGOs Privileges and Immunities

Recall that Section 2.1.2 of Chapter 2 classified privileges and immunities of international organisations, and by extension of their secretariats, into three distinct categories. The first category is known as 'inviolability.' The second one is immunity from jurisdiction. The third category consists of fiscal privileges, including exemptions from all direct taxes and most forms of indirect taxes.

1.1 *Breaches of IGOs' Inviolability of Premises, Documents, Archives, Communications, and Vehicles*

Inviolability refers to "freedom from any form of unilateral interference on the part of a state."[1] International organisations regularly communicate with member states, with each other, with public and private institutions, and with private individuals. They keep files on their staff, on projects, on studies, and on any other action in which they may be involved with a view to achieving the aims for which they were created.[2] To fulfil their mission, all international organisations are entitled to a degree of secrecy. As Reuter explains,

> chacune de ces institutions est tenue elle-même de faire dans ses conditions de fonctionnement une certaine place au secret, pour mieux assurer son indépendance et pour donner aux États les garanties de discrétion qu'ils désirent.[3]

Intergovernmental organisations must enjoy the inviolability of their documents and archives to safeguard the confidentiality of their information and protect not only their safety and their right to privacy and private property but also the safety and privacy of documentation addressed or entrusted to them by member states.[4] In fact, Reuter draws a close nexus between an organisation's right to secrecy and confidentiality and its autonomy and independence:

> [U]n certain droit à l'intimité sanctionne également l'autonomie du groupe : sans intimité point de liberté, sans liberté point d'autonomie.[5]

1 *World Bank Group v Wallace*, 2016 SCC 15, [2016] 1 SCR 207 at para 78 (Supreme Court of Canada).

2 Leonardo Diaz-Gonzalez, Fifth Report of the Special Rapporteur on Relations Between States and International Organizations, UN Doc. A/CN.4/4/438 (7 May 1991) at para. 6.

3 Paul Reuter, "Le droit au secret et les institutions internationales" (1956) 2 *Annuaire français de droit international* 46 at 47.

4 Leonardo Diaz-Gonzalez, *supra* note 2 at paras. 6–7.

5 Reuter, *supra* note 3 at 61.

To keep the secrecy of its documents and archives, the organisation must also be able to protect the place where the secret is kept. That is why the inviolability of documents and archives of international organisations is closely linked to the inviolability of the premises occupied by those organisations.[6] Although archives are often in the organisation's offices, they can sometimes be in official vehicles or diplomatic pouches. The inviolability of the premises, vehicles, and pouches means that authorities of a state, particularly of the host state, may not enter or inspect the premises, vehicles, or diplomatic bags without the permission of the administrative head, even for the purpose of arresting or serving a writ on an individual.[7] Inviolability must be secured against all persons and not merely the authorities of the host state, which implies that the host state has a duty to protect the premises.[8]

Unfortunately, member states frequently fail to comply with their obligation to ascertain that international organisations' premises, assets, and archives remain inviolable. The United Nations Juridical Yearbooks describe a range of such violations. For instance, the Juridical Yearbook for the year 2000 refers to the seizure by national authorities of UNICEF property to satisfy a court order.[9] The 2004 volume reproduces an objection from the UN to an unidentified member state for freezing the bank accounts of the World Food Programme.[10] The 2006 Yearbook contains a legal opinion sought from the UN Legal Counsel relating to searches of UN-owned laptops.[11] In most cases, violations of this nature are unintentional and result primarily from a lack of understanding by law enforcement officials and customs officers of IGOs' right to inviolability. However, not all breaches of IGOs' inviolability are innocuous.

More egregious and intentional violations come to light accidentally, particularly during renovations of premises. For instance, workers renovating parts of the United Nations Headquarters buildings in Geneva and New York

6 Leonardo Diaz-Gonzalez, *supra* note 2 at para. 7.

7 CF Amerasinghe, *Principles of the Institutional Law of International Organization*, 2nd ed (New York: Cambridge University Press, 2005) at 330–331.

8 *Ibid.* at 330.

9 United Nations Office of Legal Affairs, "Note verbale to the Permanent Representative of [Member State] to the United Nations", *UN Juridical Yearbook* (New York: UN, 2000) at 346.

10 United Nations Office of Legal Affairs, "Note verbale to a Permanent Representative of a Member State to the United Nations regarding the freezing of bank accounts of the World Food Programme", *UN Juridical Yearbook* (New York: UN, 2004) at 326.

11 United Nations Office of Legal Affairs, "Interoffice memorandum to the Deputy of the Under-Secretary-General for Safety and Security on the search of United Nations laptop computers by Host Country customs", *UN Juridical Yearbook* (New York: UN, 2006) at p. 455.

found sophisticated bugging devices behind decorative panels and other semi-permanent structures in various rooms of UN premises.[12] Similarly, credible allegations arose that Australia, Canada, New Zealand, the United Kingdom, and the United States had intercepted sensitive UN communications and had bugged the office of Secretary-General Kofi Annan in the lead-up to the invasion of Iraq in 2003.[13] Further, in 2012, Edward Snowden disclosed internal communications of the United States National Security Agency, corroborating the suspicion that the United States government had bugged the headquarters of the United Nations and of the International Atomic Energy Agency.[14] In June 2022, the security service of the Netherlands revealed that a deep-cover Russian spy tried to infiltrate the International Criminal Court as an intern by pretending to be Brazilian.[15]

Such practices undermine international cooperation, create an environment of mistrust among nations, and affect the degree of trust nations place in international organisations. When nations realise that a few states have had access to information that other countries were not privy to, they suspect that international civil servants are the source of information and favour some nations over others, which weakens the credibility of intergovernmental institutions and their staff. Section 1.1 of Chapter 2 illustrated through the prisoners' dilemma that when rational actors do not trust one another, they cannot reach an optimal solution even when they share many common interests. For this reason, states unite to build institutions to minimise distrust and facilitate cooperation. This cooperation can succeed only if international organisations remain neutral. Nations disengage from international organisations whose secretariats and staff they lose trust in. This disengagement need not be express or formal. It may consist of unilateralism or reluctance to cooperate with other states. It may also entail a refusal to pay their dues or to honour their budgetary commitments to international organisations. Essentially, a nation that loses trust in an international organisation is a 'prisoner' facing a dilemma.

---

12 See Brian Whitaker, "Bugging device found at UN offices", *The Guardian* (18 December 2004).

13 Mark Forbes, "Australia 'party' to bugging of UN", *The Age* (19 June 2004) available online at www.theage.com.au/national/australia-party-to-bugging-of-un-20040619-gdy2jv.html (accessed on 20 April 2022).

14 Madeline Chambers, "U.S. spy agency bugged U.N. headquarters: Germany's Spiegel", *Reuters* (25 August 2013) available online at https://www.reuters.com/article/us-usa-security-nsa-un-idUSBRE97O0DD20130825 (accessed on 21 April 2022).

15 Gordon Corera, "Russian GRU spy tried to infiltrate International Criminal Court", *BBC* (16 June 2022) available online at https://www.bbc.com/news/world-europe-61831961.

1.2 *Refusal to Recognise Jurisdictional Immunity*

Reinisch writes, "international organisations need to enjoy privileges and immunities, in particular immunity from the jurisdiction of domestic courts, to remain independent and unimpeded in the fulfilment of their functions and duties."[16] Jurisdictional immunity prevents any member state from exercising undue influence on an international organisation and thwarting the majority's will through its courts.[17] For example, adjudication by the courts of one country declaring the activities of an international organisation illegal or a multimillion-dollar judgment from the host country's courts where the organisation's accounts are maintained could incapacitate an organisation if it is not shielded by immunity.[18] In addition, jurisdictional immunity ensures that in disputes between a member state and an international organisation, the member state does not become both judge and party by having the dispute adjudicated in its judicial system.[19]

There are three scenarios where domestic courts may decide to restrict the jurisdictional immunity of international organisations. First, some treaties establishing international organisations or governing their legal status, privileges, and immunities expressly limit their jurisdictional immunity.[20] Second, domestic courts in many jurisdictions disregard the jurisdictional immunity of international organisations when such immunity is seen to breach an individual's right to access a court. Third, some states refuse to recognise jurisdictional immunity to international organisations for actions regarded as *jure gestiones* acts.[21] These three scenarios will be examined below under separate headings.

1.2.1 Jurisdictional Immunity Limited by Treaty

International and regional development banks often allow private creditors to sue the organisation in loan transactions.[22] For instance, the Articles of

16 August Reinisch, "To What Extent Can and Should National Courts Fill the Accountability Gap" (2014) 10:2 *Int'l Org L Rev* 572 at 573.

17 William M Berenson, "Squaring the Concept of Immunity with the Fundamental Right to a Fair Trial" (2012) 3 *World Bank Legal Review* 133 at 134.

18 *Ibid.*

19 *Ibid.*

20 August Reinisch and Ulf Andreas Weber, "In the Shadow of Waite and Kennedy – The Jurisdictional Immunity of International Organizations, the Individual's Right of Access to the Courts and Administrative Tribunals as Alternative Means of Dispute Settlement" (2004) 1 *Int'l Org L Rev* 59 at 61.

21 Luca Pasquet, "Litigating the Immunities of International Organizations in Europe: The 'Alternative-Remedy' Approach and its 'Humanizing' Function" (2021) 36:2 *Utrecht J Int Eur Law* 192 at 193.

22 Reinisch and Weber, *supra* note 20 at 61–62.

Agreement of the International Bank for Reconstruction and the Agreement Establishing the Inter-American Development Bank provide that claims "may be brought against the Bank only in a court of competent jurisdiction in the territories of a member in which the Bank has an office, has appointed an agent for the purpose of accepting service or notice of process, or has issued or guaranteed securities."[23] Purists may argue that such limitations expose intergovernmental institutions to abusive lawsuits aimed at curtailing their independence from the state where the legal action is instituted. Nevertheless, the risk is mitigated by the fact that the right to sue is granted to non-governmental actors in relation to very specific claims related to loans. Hence, in principle, lawsuits are inadmissible unless a loan exists and the claim is related to the loan.

Some legal instruments regulating international organisations' status, privileges and immunities exclude immunity for specific tort actions, namely car accidents. For instance, the Protocol on Privileges and Immunities of the European Patent Organisation and Annex 1 on Privileges and Immunities of the European Space Agency provide that the organisations have immunity in relation to their official activities except "in the case of a civil action brought by a third party for damage resulting from an accident caused by a motor vehicle belonging to, or operated on behalf of, the Organisation, or in respect of a motor traffic offence involving such a vehicle."[24] While this type of surgical restriction of jurisdictional immunity is not advisable either, it has not led to any serious issues, probably because international organisations normally insure their vehicles, and insurance companies are required to handle third-party claims.

The two scenarios below pose a much greater risk to the independence of international organisations, including their secretariats and personnel.

1.2.2 The Right to Have Access to Court

Access to a fair trial by an independent and impartial tribunal is a fundamental human right explicitly recognised in many international legal instruments[25]

23 Articles of Agreement of the International Bank for Reconstruction and Development, 27 December 1945, 2 U.N.T.S. 134; Art. VII.3; Agreement Establishing the Inter-American Development Bank, 8 April 1959, 389 U.N.T.S. 70, Art. XI.3, para. 1.

24 See for instance Agreement on the Privileges and Immunities of the ITER International Fusion Energy Organization for the Joint Implementation of the ITER Project, 21 November 2006, 2491 U.N.T.S. 317, Art. 4(1)(b); Protocol on Privileges and Immunities of the European Patent Organization, 5 October 1973, 1065 U.N.T.S. 500, Art. 3(1)(b); Convention for the Establishment of a European Space Agency, 30 May 1975, 1297 U.N.T.S. 199, Art. IV(1)(b).

25 Reinisch and Weber, *supra* note 20 at 66.

and national constitutions or other legislative acts.[26] At the same time, international organisations' immunity from national jurisdiction pursues the legitimate aim of incentivising interstate cooperation.[27] These two interests often collide, and national courts have struggled to reconcile them. Typically, in such cases, domestic courts erroneously believe that these two competing interests cannot coexist and are mutually exclusive. They see a choice between disregarding the jurisdictional immunity of the international organisation, on the one hand, and denying plaintiffs their right of access to a court, on the other. Attempts to accommodate an individual's right to access a court without unduly denying international organisations jurisdictional immunity have led to erratic approaches.

The trend to disregard the jurisdictional immunity of international organisations began in the field of employment law. Staff members of international organisations filed before national courts legal challenges against decisions made by their employers. To determine whether the jurisdictional immunity of an international organisation should be recognised, courts assessed the effect it would produce on the aggrieved individual. If recognising jurisdictional immunity led to a denial of the individual's right to a court of law, national courts would be inclined to lift the immunity and adjudicate the dispute.

In deciding when an IGO's jurisdictional immunity overrides an individual's right of access to a court, the European Court of Human Rights (ECHR) considers "as a material factor whether there were reasonable alternative means to protect effectively the rights" of the individual.[28] Specifically, the jurisdictional immunity would be upheld if (1) the limitations applied do not restrict or reduce the access left to the individual in such a way or to such an extent that the very essence of the right is impaired; (2) the immunity pursues a legitimate aim; and (3) the means employed were reasonably proportional to the aim sought to be achieved.[29] The ECHR has already ruled that an

---

26 See for instance: Universal Declaration of Human Rights, UN Doc. A/RES/217A (III) Art. 10; European Convention on Human Rights (Convention for the Protection of Human Rights and Fundamental Freedoms), 213 UNTS 221, Art. 6.1; American Convention on Human Rights, 1144 UNTS 123, Art. 8.1; African Charter on Human and Peoples' Rights, 1520 UNTS 217, Art. 7.1.

27 *Waite and Kennedy v Germany*, [1999] Application no 26083/94 (European Court of Human Rights, Grand Chamber) at para 63.

28 *Prince Hans-Adam II of Liechtenstein v Germany*, [2001] Application no 42527/98 (European Court of Human Rights, Grand Chamber); *ibid* at para 68; see also *Beer and Regan v Germany*, [1995] Application no 28934/95 (European Court of Human Rights, Grand Chamber) at para 58.

29 *Waite and Kennedy v. Germany, supra* note 27 at para. 59.

IGO's jurisdictional immunity does not disproportionately affect individuals if internal dispute settlement mechanisms are available.[30] Conversely, if no alternative avenues for settling disputes are available, national courts in many jurisdictions set aside the immunity of international organisations and entertain the case.

In France, courts consider that depriving individuals of their right to a court of law violates "*la conception française de l'ordre public international*."[31] For this reason, the French *Cour de Cassation* ruled that national courts have jurisdiction over labour disputes between an IGO and its personnel where the aggrieved staff member is a French national and has no access to internal dispute resolution procedures.[32] Consequently, in 2005, the *Cour de Cassation* of France disregarded the jurisdictional immunity of the African Development Bank and entertained an appeal submitted by one of its staff members.[33] The Belgian *Cour de Cassation* adopted a similar approach by setting aside the jurisdictional immunity of the General Secretariat of the African, Caribbean, and Pacific States Group after observing that it offered no internal dispute resolution mechanism to its staff.[34]

In 2007, the Italian *Corte di cassazione* refused to grant immunity to the International Plant Genetic Resources Institute because the organisation had failed to provide an independent and impartial judicial remedy for resolving employment-related disputes, which was incompatible with Article 24 of the Italian Constitution.[35]

In some cases, courts go a step further and engage in a far-reaching substantive review of the internal dispute settlement mechanism for the purposes of determining whether the alternative was reasonable and adequate.[36] In 2009, the *Cour de Cassation* of Belgium concluded that the internal dispute resolution

30 *Chapman v. Belgium*, [2013] Application no 39619/06 (European Court of Human Rights, Fifth Sec).

31 See *Pourvoi n° 07-44.240*, Cour de cassation, civile, Chambre sociale, 11 February 2009; *Pourvoi n° 12-23.805*, Cour de cassation of France, civile, Chambre sociale, 13 May 2014.

32 *Pourvoi n° 04-41.012*, 2005 Cour de cassation of France, civile, Chambre sociale, 25 January 2005. See also *pourvoi n° 12-23.805*, Cour de cassation, civile, Chambre sociale, 13 May 2014.

33 *Ibid.*

34 *Secrétariat général du Groupe des États d'Afrique, des Caraïbes et du Pacifique c BD*, No C070407F (21 December 2009); *Secrétariat général du Groupe des États d'Afrique, des Caraïbes et du Pacifique c. L M-A*, C030328F (21 December 2009).

35 Rosalyn Higgins et al., *Oppenheim's International Law: United Nations* (Oxford: Oxford University Press, 2017) at 566, footnote 80. *Drago v. International Plant Genetic Resources Institute* (*IPGRI*), [2007] Final Appeal Judgment, Case No 3718, Giustizia Civile Massimario.

36 *Western European Union v. Siedler*, [2009] S040129F, Cour de cassation of Belgium, 21 December 2009.

mechanism of the Western European Union (dissolved in 2010) was not independent enough to be 'reasonable and adequate.' As a result, the Court refused to recognise the IGO's jurisdictional immunity.[37] In 2014, the *Cour de Cassation* of France carried out a similar review of the dispute settlement mechanism of the Pacific Community and concluded that it was not independent enough to be called "*recours de nature juridictionelle.*"[38]

These are dangerous precedents. National courts should not subject international organisations and their organs and bodies to any form of review and control, as this gives rise to legal unpredictability and undermines their independence by exposing them to political interference. The legal framework of most international organisations requires them to seek the approval of their member states before creating or establishing an internal dispute settlement mechanism. For instance, the internal justice system of the United Nations was set up with the approval of the UN General Assembly and the creation of the NATO Administrative Tribunal was endorsed by the North Atlantic Treaty. International organisations do not have the authority to establish internal justice systems without the express approval of their governing bodies.

The proposal by international organisations to their governing bodies to set up an internal dispute resolution mechanism is an opportunity for each member state to voice its concerns about the satisfactoriness of the mechanism. Once they agree to the proposed mechanism, their domestic courts can no longer rule on their adequacy. Even if a member state unknowingly or inadvertently approves the creation of an internal dispute resolution mechanism but subsequently realises that the mechanism is flawed, it can always propose changes to it through the IGOs governing body. However, the member state's courts are not the appropriate forum to address systemic deficiencies in dispute settlement mechanisms of intergovernmental organisations.

In any event, as noted by the International Court of Justice in the *Jurisdictional Immunities* case, there is no basis in the State practice from which customary international law is derived that international law makes the entitlement of immunity dependent upon the existence of effective alternative means of securing redress.[39] While this judgement dealt with state immunity, the reasoning also applies to international organisations. International law does not view the absence of effective alternative means of securing redress as a valid basis for lifting or disregarding the jurisdictional immunity of IGOs.

37 *Ibid.*

38 *Pourvoi n° 12-23.805*, Cour de cassation, civile, Chambre sociale, 13 May 2014.

39 *Jurisdictional Immunities of the State (Germany v Italy: Greece intervening)*, Judgment, [2012] ICJ Rep 99 at para. 101.

Many scholars and human rights advocates applaud judgements that reject an IGOs jurisdictional immunity to entertain a labour dispute. They typically argue that this approach promotes human rights. They are correct in pointing out that international civil servants should not be deprived of their human rights for the sake of preserving the independence of international organisations. Nevertheless, disregarding the jurisdictional immunity of international organisations is not the only way to protect the rights of individuals who seek an effective and reasonable remedy. An IGO's jurisdictional immunity is a self-imposed limitation of a state's sovereignty. When a state chooses to limit its sovereignty by accepting international obligations, it effectively exercises its sovereignty. By granting international organisations jurisdictional immunity, states voluntarily relinquish an essential part of their sovereignty, namely the jurisdiction of their courts over an entity operating on their territory. This relinquishment is a public act that must be subject to review by domestic courts. In a functional democracy, courts are empowered to review a government's actions. Suppose citizens of a specific state are of the view that their government deprived them of their right of access to a court by granting international organisations jurisdictional immunity without first ascertaining that internal dispute settlement mechanisms existed. In that case, they should turn against their government and seek redress. This would be akin to lifting the corporate veil of the international organisation to hold its member states responsible for not equipping the IGO with the required dispute resolution procedures. A state is not absolved of its responsibility vis-à-vis its citizens by transferring some of its powers and prerogatives to international organisations.[40] In the *Gasparini* case, the European Court of Human Rights pointed out that when transferring a part of their sovereign powers to an international organisation of which they are a member, states have an obligation to ensure that the organisation provides adequate guarantees to its staff:

> les États membres ont l'obligation, au moment où ils transfèrent une partie de leurs pouvoirs souverains à une organisation internationale à laquelle ils adhèrent, de veiller à ce que les droits garantis par la Convention reçoivent au sein de cette organisation une « protection équivalente » à celle assurée par le mécanisme de la Convention. En effet, la responsabilité d'un Etat partie à la Convention pourrait être mise en jeu au regard de celle-ci s'il s'avérait ultérieurement que la protection des

40 *Waite and Kennedy v. Germany*, *supra* note 27 at 67; *Chapman v. Belgium*, *supra* note 30 at 50.

droits fondamentaux offerte par l'organisation internationale concernée était entachée d'une insuffisance manifeste.[41]

The *Conseil d'État* of France held in 2011 that the French government could be held liable for serious prejudice to one of its citizens resulting from the jurisdictional immunity of another state, which is 'received' in the French legal order through customary law.[42] The *Conseil d'État* did not find that the French government had committed a fault or was negligent in granting jurisdictional immunity to another state. It simply noted that the absence of an effective recourse against another state due to jurisdictional immunity could trigger the liability of the French government. This reasoning is even more convincing in relation to jurisdictional immunities of international organisations because whereas the source of state immunity is customary law (where no explicit consent of the host nations is required), the source of IGO immunity is treaty law. A state must explicitly articulate its consent so that IGO can be granted jurisdictional immunity on its territory. If domestic courts do not already have jurisdiction to review decisions by their governments to relinquish a part of the state's sovereignty, they should be empowered to do so.

Hence, instead of focusing on the adequacy or reasonableness of internal dispute resolution mechanisms of an IGO, national courts should hold their governments responsible for setting up IGOs without ensuring that the organisation can adequately deal with claims and grievances. This is particularly true since international organisations often recommend certain improvements to their internal dispute settlement mechanisms but cannot implement the required changes because their member states decide not to follow them. For example, the formal dispute settlement mechanism of the UN is open only to its staff members.[43] Consultants, workers on a service contract,[44] and interns[45] do not have standing before the UN Dispute Tribunal and the UN

41 *Gasparini v. Italy and Belgium*, [2003] Application No. 10750/03 (European Court of Human Rights) at 6. See also *Klausecker v. Germany*, [2015] Application No. 415/07 (European Court of Human Rights) at para. 63.

42 No. 329788, Conseil d'État, Section du Contentieux, 14/10/2011 (recueil Lebon).

43 *Ndjadi v. Secretary-General of the United Nations*, UNDT/2011/007 (United Nations Dispute Tribunal) affirmed by the United Nations Appeals Tribunal in 2012-UNAT-197.

44 *Megerditchian v. Secretary-General of the United Nations*, UNDT/2010/035 (United Nations Dispute Tribunal) affirmed by the United. Nations Appeals Tribunal in 2010-UNAT-088; *Mialeshka v. Secretary-General of the United Nations*, UNDT/2011/055 (United Nations Dispute Tribunal).

45 *Basenko v. Secretary-General of the United Nations*, UNDT/2010/145 (United Nations Dispute Tribunal), affirmed by the United Nations Appeals Tribunal in 2011-UNAT-139;

Appeals Tribunal. This jurisdictional limitation excludes approximately 35,000 individuals engaged by the UN Secretariat and the UN Funds and Programmes as individual consultants, service contractors, or UN Volunteers.[46] Some of these members of UN personnel have no meaningful recourse and cannot seek justice either before the domestic courts or the UN's internal tribunals. Arbitral proceedings before the Permanent Court of Arbitration may be available to consultants and contractors if their contracts contain a dispute resolution clause. Nonetheless, such proceedings are prohibitively expensive, which dissuades most individuals from instituting legal proceedings against the UN. In 2007, the UN Secretary-General recommended that the General Assembly open the internal justice system to all individuals performing work for the organisation by way of personal services,[47] but member states voted against this recommendation mainly due to financial considerations. Hence, the absence of a reasonable alternative for settling employment disputes of some UN members of personnel is not attributable to the UN but to its member states. Therefore, it would be illogical to hold the UN liable for not having an adequate dispute settlement mechanism when the responsibility for this flaw can be laid at the door of its member states.

Of course, in many countries, holding governments liable is not possible under national laws due to constitutional constraints or other insurmountable obstacles. In such cases, Reinisch is correct in pointing out that "the decision to exercise jurisdiction by national courts should be the measure of last resort only as opposed to a matter of course."[48] National courts should incentivise their governments to equip international organisations with adequate alternative dispute settlement mechanisms. They can also play a role in incentivising international organisations to set up functioning internal dispute resolution systems. For instance, national courts can postpone the proceedings for a reasonable period and allow the IGO to remedy the absence of an adequate dispute resolution mechanism by setting up a permanent or at least an ad hoc mechanism for that specific dispute. If the IGO does not take this opportunity and refuses to rectify the situation by offering the claimant a reasonable

---

Roberts v. Secretary-General of the United Nations, UNDT/2010/142 (United Nations Dispute Tribunal).

46 *Report of the Redesign Panel on the United Nations system of administration of justice*, UNGAOR, 61st Sess, UN Doc A/61/758 (2007) at footnote 2 [*Report of the Redesign Panel 2007*].

47 *Report of the Redesign Panel on the United Nations system of administration of justice*, UNGAOR, 61st Sess, UN Doc A/61/205 (2006) at paras 19–20; *Report of the Redesign Panel 2007*, above note 264 at paras 10–12.

48 Reinisch, *supra* note 16 at 587.

alternative dispute resolution mechanism, it would not be acting in good faith. In such cases, national courts would be justified in intervening by rejecting the organisation's jurisdictional immunity and adjudicating the dispute.

However, it is noteworthy that national courts are inconsistent in their approach.[49] They set aside immunities in some cases but not in others without any apparent justification. When domestic courts are seized of tortious claims, particularly claims for compensation resulting from peacekeeping activities, they uphold the jurisdictional immunity of international organisations, perhaps because they realise that this would be infinitely more intrusive and problematic.

Peace operations frequently cause losses and injury to third parties. The most commonly encountered loss and injury in the practice of peacekeeping activities include non-consensual use and occupancy of premises,[50] personal injury,[51] property loss arising from the ordinary operation of the force, and injury and damage stemming from combat operations.[52] According to a well-established general principle of law, damage caused in breach of an international obligation that can be attributed to an international organisation entails the international responsibility of that organisation and triggers an obligation to compensate.[53] Some international instruments, namely paragraph 51 of the model status-of-forces agreement,[54] require IGOs to have a mechanism in place to settle claims resulting from damage caused by members of the force

49 August Reinisch, *The Privileges and Immunities of International Organizations in Domestic Courts* (Oxford: Oxford University Press, 2013).

50 See, for instance, *Attorney General v. Nissan*, [1969] UKHL 3 at page 646 [*Nissan*]; *NK v. Austria* (Oberlandesgericht Wien) 77 IRL 470 [*NK*]; *Askir v. Boutros Boutros Ghali*, 933 F.Supp. 368 (S.D.N.Y. 1996), 95 Civ. 11008.

51 *Georges v. United Nations*, 834 F.3d 88 (2nd Cir Ct App 2016) [*Georges*] for actions of the United Nations Stabilization Mission in Haiti (MINUSTAH); *Mothers of Srebrenica et al v. State of The Netherlands and the United Nations*, C-10/4437, [2012] 160 ILR 58 [*Mothers of Srebrencia*].

52 *Administrative and budgetary aspects of the financing of the United Nations peacekeeping operations: financing of the United Nations peacekeeping operations*, Report of the Secretary-General to the General Assembly, UNGAOR, 51st Sess, UN Doc A/51/903 (1997) at para 2.

53 Draft articles on responsibility of international organizations, with commentaries, Report of the International Law Commission, UNGAOR, 63rd Sess, UN Doc A/66/10 and Add.1 (2011) at Chapter V; Financing of the United Nations Protection Force, the United Nations Confidence Restoration Operation in Croatia, the United Nations Preventive Deployment Force and the United Nations Peace Forces headquarters, Report of the Secretary-General to the General Assembly, UNGAOR, 51st Sess., UN Doc A/51/389 (1996) para 6.

54 *Model of Status-of-Forces Agreement for Peacekeeping Operations*, Report of the Secretary-General, UNGAOR, 45th Sess, UN Doc A/45/594 (1990).

in the performance of their official duties and, which, for reasons of immunity of the organisation and its members, could not have been submitted to local courts. UN boards of inquiry set up to settle claims are not judicial or quasi-judicial bodies; they are composed of members of the mission.[55] Therefore, they do not offer a "*recours de nature juridictionnelle*" to use the expression of the French *Cour de Cassation*. Yet, national courts do not view this lack of effective and independent mechanism as a basis for lifting the UN's jurisdictional immunity. In fact, in all cases where claimants sought the intervention of national courts to obtain compensation for damages caused by peacekeeping activities, domestic courts have declined jurisdiction even after the defendant organisation failed to demonstrate the existence of an alternative mechanism for settling such claims.

In the case of *Mothers of Srebrenica*, the Supreme Court of the Netherlands held that the UN enjoys absolute immunity and that the unavailability or inexistence of alternative routes of access to justice did not justify the lifting of the UN's jurisdictional immunities.[56] ECHR also confirmed that the UN had absolute jurisdiction, acknowledging that its jurisprudence does not stand for the proposition that in the absence of an alternative remedy, the recognition of immunity of an international organisation is *ipso facto* a violation of the right of access to a court.[57]

Luckily for the plaintiffs, the Supreme Court of the Netherlands found the Dutch government liable for damages.[58] However, not all victims of wrongful acts by peacekeepers obtain compensation, and many are left without recourse because they cannot sue either the troop-contributing nation or the UN. Take, for example, the cholera outbreak in Haiti. The Nepalese peacekeeping troops stationed in the Artibonite Valley as part of the United Nations Stabilization Mission in Haiti caused a cholera outbreak in the country by discharging human waste from their military base into a river. Approximately 750,000 people around the military base became seriously ill, and almost 9,000 died. The victims sued the UN before New York courts, but due to the UN's immunity from every form of legal process, their lawsuit was dismissed as

55 Office of Internal Oversight Services (OIOS) of the United Nations, Audit Report on Inspection of Boards of Inquiry in peacekeeping operations, 2 June 2020 at para. 14.

56 *Stichting Mothers of Srebrenica v. The Netherlands*, [2012] ECLI:NL:HR:2012:BW1999.

57 *Stichting Mothers of Srebrenica and Others v. The Netherlands*, [2013] Application no 65542/12 (European Court of Human Rights, Third Sec) at para 164.

58 *Stichting Mothers of Srebrenica v. The Netherlands*, [2019] ECLI:NL:HR:2019:1284.

not receivable.[59] While this outcome was unfortunate, as the Supreme Court of Canada pointed out, it is the purpose of jurisdictional immunity:

> The fact that the appellant has no forum in which to air his grievances and seek a remedy is unfortunate. However, it is the nature of an immunity to shield certain matters from the jurisdiction of the host state's courts. [...] it is an inevitable result of a grant of immunity that certain parties will be left without legal recourse, and this is a policy choice implicit in the legislation.[60]

It is unclear why national courts in some jurisdictions treat labour law cases differently from tortious cases. From a practical viewpoint, jurisdictional immunities apply with equal force to all claims, be they in tort or contract, including employment contracts. There is no justification for rejecting an IGO's jurisdictional immunity in employment law claims while declining jurisdiction in civil liability claims when there is no reasonable alternative to settle disputes for either type of case. Unless domestic courts and tribunals can provide a sensible rationale for treating differently claims in tort and claims in contract, they should recognise the jurisdictional immunity of international organisations in all cases.

1.2.3 Absolute versus Restrictive Jurisdictional Immunities

Historically, the privileges and immunities of international organisations originated by analogy to diplomatic or State privileges and immunities.[61] However, as explained in Section 2.1.2 of the previous chapter, while state immunity is based on the principle of sovereign equality,[62] the immunity from legal process

---

59 See for instance the cases of *Georges*, above note 144, for actions of the United Nations Stabilization Mission in Haiti (MINUSTAH); *Mothers of Srebrenica*, above note 144, for actions of Dutch peacekeeping troops in Bosnia and Herzegovina. After several years of refusing to compensate the victims, the UN carried out an investigation that concluded beyond any doubt that the Nepalese peacekeepers were directly responsible for the outbreak. The UN finally admitted liability and decided to make reparations, but this was done voluntarily as opposed to forced by national courts (see Jonathan M Katz, "UN Admits Role in Cholera Epidemic in Haiti" *New York Times* (18 August 2016) A1).

60 *Amaratunga v. Northwest Atlantic Fisheries Organization*, 2013 SCC 66, [2013] 3 SCR 866 at para 29 (Supreme Court of Canada).

61 Edward Chukwuemeke Okeke, *Jurisdictional Immunities of States and International Organizations* (Oxford: Oxford University Press, 2018) at 348; Josef L Kunz, "Privileges and Immunities of International Organizations" (1947) 41:4 *Am J Int Law* 82.

62 *Jurisdictional Immunities of the State (Germany v. Italy: Greece intervening)*, Judgment, supra note 39 at para. 57. Most customary rules on jurisdictional immunity of states

of international organisations derives from legal instruments and not from their international legal personality.[63] Although some courts, particularly in the Netherlands and Italy, have opined that the immunity from legal process of international organisations may also derive from customary international law, this viewpoint remains uncommon.[64] It has already been shown above that national courts interpret sovereign immunity restrictively and recognise foreign states' immunity in relation to *juri imperii* or sovereign acts only. States do not enjoy jurisdictional immunity for commercial acts.[65] This approach is consistent with customary international law.[66] The practice is erratic concerning the jurisdictional immunity of international organisations. In some countries, international organisations enjoy absolute jurisdictional immunity; in others, namely the United States, Canada, Brazil, and Russia, they enjoy restrictive immunity.

This issue took centre stage in the *Jam* case, where the United States Supreme Court refused to recognise jurisdictional immunity to the International Finance Corporation (IFC).[67] This judgement resulted from a lawsuit introduced by a group of farmers and fishermen from a small village in India before the United States District Court for the District of Columbia against the IFC.

---

have been codified in the United Nations Convention on Jurisdictional Immunities of States and Their Property (not yet in force) adopted by the UN General Assembly on 2 December 2004, UN Doc. A/RES/59/38, annex, Official Records of the General Assembly, Fifty-ninth Session, Supplement No. 49 (A/59/49).

63 Lucius Caflisch, "La Pratique Suisse en Matière de Droit International Public 1992" (1993) 3:5 *Swiss Rev Int'l & Eur L* 669 at 692. See also United Nations Office of Legal Affairs, "Note to the Ministry of Foreign Affairs of [State], concerning the privileges and immunities of a [United Nations entity] and its officials from legal process initiated against it by a former service contractor" (New York: United Nations, 2013) 377 at 379.

64 *Spaans v. Iran-United States Claims Tribunal*, Judgement of 20 December 1985, ECLI:NL:HR:1985:AC9158 at para. 3.3.4; *Eckhardt v. Eurocontrol (No. 2)* (1985) 16 NYIL 464 judgement of 12 January 1984 (Maastricht District Court); *Supreme Site Services v. Supreme Headquarters Allied Powers Europe (SHAPE)*, Judgement of 24 December 2021, at para. 3.1.2. See on this point Michael Wood, "Do International Organizations Enjoy Immunity under Customary International Law?" in Niels Blokker and Nico Schrijver, ed., *Immunity of International Organizations* (Leiden: Brill Nijhoff, 2015) at 40–41.

65 Hazel Fox and Philippa Webb, *The Law of State Immunity*, 3d ed (Oxford: Oxford University Press, 2013) at 673–674.

66 Cedric Ryngaert, "The Immunity of International Organizations before Domestic Courts: Recent Trends" (2010) 7:1 *Int'l Org L Rev* 121 at 123.

67 The IFC is an international development bank headquartered in Washington, D.C., whose mission is to supplement the activities of the World Bank by furthering economic development in the less developed areas of member countries and financing private-sector development projects around the world.

These petitioners alleged that the IFC financed a power plant project that polluted the surrounding area's air, land, and water. Based on IFC's audit report, they argued that the organisation failed to supervise the project adequately. The District Court concluded that the IFC was immune from suit and declined jurisdiction. The US Court of Appeals for the District of Columbia affirmed the judgement, and the matter then proceeded to the United States Supreme Court.

The outcome of this case depended mainly on the statutory interpretation of the International Organizations Immunities Act (IOIA) of 1945, which granted intergovernmental institutions based in the United States the "same immunity from suit […] as is enjoyed by foreign governments". In 1945, when Congress passed the Act, foreign governments enjoyed absolute immunity from suit. American courts "looked to the views of the Department of State in deciding whether a given foreign government should be granted immunity from a particular suit."[68] If the Department of State submitted a recommendation to recognise jurisdictional immunity, courts deferred to the recommendation,[69] but if it did not do so, the courts decided themselves. With time, the jurisdictional immunity of states evolved and became more limited. Foreign governments continued to enjoy immunity from public acts only, but they had no jurisdictional immunity in relation to actions deriving from commercial activities in which they engaged. The newer restrictive theory of foreign sovereign immunity was adopted in 1952 because governments were increasingly involved in commercial activities.[70] Nevertheless, it was unclear what effect the decision of the State Department to restrict the immunity enjoyed by foreign governments had on the jurisdictional immunity of IGOs. On the one hand, the jurisdictional immunity of IGOs was initially conceived to be absolute. On the other hand, the IOIA was never amended to decouple state immunity from IGO immunity; it still provides that international organisations have the same immunity from suit as foreign governments enjoy. Hence, the Supreme Court of the United States concluded that the jurisdictional immunity of international organisations which was still tied to the immunity of foreign governments also shrank over time.[71] In other words, the Court extended the doctrine of restrictive jurisdictional immunity to IGOs.[72]

68 *Jam v. International Finance Corporation*, 139 S Ct 759 (2019), s I.B.

69 See *Samantar v. Yousuf* (2010) 560 U.S. 305, 310–312; *Ex Parte Peru*, 318 U.S. 573, 581.

70 Chukwuemeke Okeke, *supra* note 61.

71 *Jam v. International Finance Corporation, supra* note 68.

72 See Clemens Treichl and August Reinisch, "Domestic Jurisdiction over International Financial Institutions for Injuries to Project-Affected Individuals: The Case of Jam v International Finance Corporation" (2019) 16:1 *Int'l Org L Rev* 105.

This approach was not entirely new. In at least three older cases, US courts had refused to decline jurisdiction and adjudicated disputes between private parties and international organisations.

In the *Dupree Associates Inc.* case,[73] a construction company sued OAS for breach of contract arising from the construction of a building. OAS asserted its jurisdictional immunity and moved to strike the suit. Noting that the action concerned the construction of a building which is a commercial activity, the District Court denied OAS's motion to dismiss. The Court concluded that the scope of IGOs' jurisdictional immunity is the same as that of states; therefore, they were entitled to restrictive immunity only.[74]

In the *Rendall-Speranza* case,[75] the plaintiff sued her supervisor and her employer – the IFC – for sexual harassment and assault. IFC moved to strike the suit based on its jurisdictional immunity. The Court denied the motion and ruled that the IOIA grants international organisations the same immunity that foreign governments enjoy. Although the court acknowledged that Congress had enacted the IOIA in 1945, when foreign governments enjoyed broad immunity, Congress chose not to revise the IOIA when the immunity of foreign governments shrank with the passage of the Foreign Sovereign Immunities Act (FSIA). Therefore, the Court was of the view that inaction on the part of Congress implied that Congress felt that the more restrictive immunity afforded foreign governments under the FSIA was to apply in like fashion to international organisations.[76] However, this was insufficient to reject IFC's jurisdictional immunity because sexual harassment is not a commercial activity. The Court pursued its analysis and held that the actions of the plaintiff's supervisor which consisted of grabbing her wrists, twisting her arm behind her back, and kicking her shin, cannot be said to be a 'discretionary function' within the meaning of the FSIA or an official act.

In the *OSS Nokalva Inc.* case,[77] a software solutions and services supplier initiated legal proceedings before United States Courts against one of its customers – the European Space Agency (ESA), an international organisation headquartered in Germany. ESA asserted absolute immunity from suit based on its status as an international organisation and filed a motion to dismiss OSS

73 *Dupree Associates Inc. v. the Organization of American States* (1982) 63 I.L.R. 92; see also United Nations Office of Legal Affairs, *UN Juridical Yearbook* (New York: UN, 1977) at 260.

74 Reinisch, *supra* note 49 at 200.

75 *Rendall-Speranza v. Nassim* (1996) 942 F. Supp. 621 and 932 F. Supp. 19 (United States District Court, District of Columbia).

76 *Rendall-Speranza v. Nassim*, 932 F. Supp. 19 (D.D.C. 1996).

77 *Oss Nokalva Inc. v. European Space Agency*, U.S.C.A., Third Circ., 617 F.3d 756 (3d Cir. 2010).

Nokalva's claims. The District Court held that ESA is generally entitled to absolute immunity but that it had waived such immunity by accepting the jurisdiction of US courts. ESA appealed the conclusion that it waived immunity and the OSSN cross-appealed the finding that ESA was entitled to absolute immunity in the first place. The Court of Appeal ruled that granting absolute immunity to ESA would lead to an anomalous result because individual member states of international organisations enjoyed no immunity in respect of their commercial activities:

> We find no compelling reason why a group of states acting through an international organization is entitled to broader immunity than its member states enjoy when acting alone. Indeed, such a policy may create an incentive for foreign governments to evade legal obligations by acting through international organizations.

Canadian courts adopt a similar approach to the jurisdictional immunity of IGOs. The Supreme Court of Canada articulated Canada's position in the *Amaratunga* case.[78] Amaratunga was a senior official of the Northwest Atlantic Fisheries Organization (NAFO) – an international organisation founded in 1979 and headquartered in the province of Nova Scotia in Canada – which was responsible for the management of fishery resources in the Northwest Atlantic.[79] He sued NAFO for breach of his contract of employment before the Canadian courts, but NAFO claimed immunity from his action. Under the bilateral host country agreement between the organisation and the government of Canada, NAFO enjoyed immunity "as may be required for the performance of its functions, [...] the privileges and immunities set forth in Articles II and III of the Convention for the United Nations" whereas its officials enjoyed such privileges and immunities "as may be required for the performance of their functions, [...] the privileges and immunities set forth in Article V of the Convention for officials of the United Nations".[80] The main issue before the Supreme Court of Canada was to determine what kind of immunity the organisation had in Canada. Unfortunately, like the Supreme Court of the United States in the *Jam v. IFC* case, the Supreme Court of Canada approached this matter almost entirely from a domestic perspective. The Court began its

78 *Amaratunga v. Northwest Atlantic Fisheries Organization*, 2013 SCC 66, [2013] 3 SCR 866 (Supreme Court of Canada).

79 Convention on Future Multilateral Cooperation in the Northwest Atlantic Fisheries, 20 April 1979, 1135 U.N.T.S. 369.

80 Northwest Atlantic Fisheries Organization Privileges and Immunities Order, SOR/8064.

analysis by pointing out that privileges and immunities are granted to intergovernmental organisations to shield them from "undue interference in [their] operations"[81] and that "[w]ithout immunity, an international organisation would be vulnerable to intrusions into its operations and agenda by the host state and that state's courts".[82] It went on to construe the phrase "as may be required for the performance of their functions" to have the same meaning in determining the scope of the IGO's jurisdictional immunity as it does in determining the functional immunity of its officials. Consequently, the Court ruled, "in limiting these immunities and privileges to the extent required for NAFO to perform its functions, the [government of Canada] did not grant NAFO the absolute immunity conferred on the United Nations in the Convention on the Privileges and Immunities of the United Nations."[83] It concluded that the Canadian government granted NAFO a functional immunity, which according to the Court meant "the immunity required to enable NAFO to perform its functions without undue interference."[84]

This conclusion is not well-founded for two reasons. First, the United Nations Organisation was only given absolute jurisdictional immunity because nations realised that only absolute jurisdictional immunity could shield it from political interference. If 'functional immunity' had been sufficient to attain the same objective, no nation would have agreed to grant the UN broader immunity. After all, the recognition of jurisdictional immunity to an international organisation is a renunciation of a part of a state's sovereignty. No state would have surrendered more sovereignty than required to achieve the desired objective. Second, an international organisation enjoys legal personality only to the extent necessary to perform its functions.[85] It is legally unable to act beyond its functional personality because any act not permitted by its constitutive document is *ultra vires*. In other words, any activity of an international organisation is either official or ultra vires.[86]

The Brazilian approach to jurisdictional immunities of IGOs is also flawed. In 2017, the Supreme Court of Brazil adjudicated a dispute between Paes de Castro, a Brazilian national hired as an independent contractor and his employer – the United Nations Development Programme (UNDP). After the

81 *Amaratunga v. Northwest Atlantic Fisheries Organization, supra* note 78 at para. 1.
82 *Ibid.* at para. 45.
83 *Ibid.* at para. 49.
84 *Ibid.*
85 *Legality of the Threat or Use by a State of Nuclear Weapons*, Advisory Opinion, [1996] ICJ Rep 66 at para. 25.
86 Reinisch, *supra* note 49 at 9.

expiration of his contract, Paes de Castro sought judicial recognition of his status as a permanent employee and the payment of benefits deriving from such a status. The government of Brazil was the Respondent party because, under the 1964 Revised Standard Agreement with the United Nations, it had an obligation to defend all UN Funds and Programmes against claims brought against them by third parties. The Supreme Court of Brazil held that immunity from jurisdiction and execution is not a necessary attribute of international organisations.[87] The Court recognised that UNDP was immune from suit because the 1946 Convention on the Privileges and Immunities of the United Nations provided for absolute immunity, which was subsequently transposed into Brazilian legislation. Although the court did not address the applicability of the doctrine of restrictive State immunity to IGOs, it implicitly confirmed that an international organisation does not enjoy such immunity unless a treaty provides for jurisdictional immunity.

The Court of Appeal at Nairobi in Kenya also held that the government of Kenya could not have possibly granted an international organisation absolute immunity from suits and legal process even in purely commercial transactions, as this would have been contrary to international law.[88] In support of this conclusion, the Court of Appeal erroneously relied on a decision of the Court of Appeal in England which dealt with state immunity, where the court stated that "over the last half century there has been a shift from the concept of absolute immunity to a narrower principle which excludes ordinary mercantile transactions from the ambit of sovereign immunity notwithstanding the sovereign status of a party to those transactions."[89] The misguided premise that jurisdictional immunity of IGOs is akin to state immunity led the court to restrict the immunity of IGOs based in Kenya. As Kenya is the largest UN hub in the southern hemisphere, hosting the United Nations Environment Programme (UNEP), the United Nations Human Settlement Programme (UN-Habitat), and the UN Office at Nairobi (UNON), the impact this decision may have on UN entities based in Kenya cannot be underestimated.

A Court of Appeal in Greece decided it had jurisdiction over an employment dispute with the International Centre for Superior Mediterranean Agricultural

87 Tuyama Sollero, Barbara, "The Jurisdictional Immunity of International Organizations before the Brazilian Supreme Federal Court" (2021) 18:1 *Braz J Int'l L* 45 at 46. In a partially dissenting opinion, Justice Edson Fachin expressed the view that jurisdictional immunity was a logical outcome of the recognition of international personality.

88 *Tononoka Steels Limited v. Eastern and Southern Africa Trade and Development Bank* [1999] KLR, Civil Appeal No. 255 of 1998 (8 May 1998).

89 *Trendex Trading Corporation Ltd v Central Bank of Nigeria* [1977] 1 All ER 881.

Studies, even though an agreement had expressly granted the defendant organisation absolute immunity. The Court erroneously concluded that labour relations were not the result of exercising sovereignty but were concerned with the organisation's private activity. Hence, the Court of Appeal interpreted the organisation's unqualified jurisdictional immunity as incorporating restrictive immunity like the one granted to states.[90] Courts in many national jurisdictions, including Russia,[91] adopt a similar approach.

The doctrine of restrictive immunity is not well suited to international organisations for at least two reasons. First, applying the restrictive approach to IGOs requires invasively scrutinising their activities and interfering in their functioning. For instance, if a vendor sues NATO in relation to a purchase of pharmaceutical products and medical equipment, national courts will need to determine the end user of these products and the place of their delivery so that they can understand whether they were purchased for military or civilian use. Such inquiry would be very invasive and objectionable.

Second, the line separating IGOs' public acts from their commercial acts is often blurred. It is more difficult to draw such a distinction between public and private acts for international organisations than it is for states. For instance, characterising UNHCR's procurement of tents for refugee camps or UNICEF's rental of warehouses for storing medication as exclusively commercial acts or as acts required to fulfil their mandate is subjective. One can present strong arguments in support of both positions.

The national courts in some countries adopt a more legally sound approach. For instance, "the Supreme Court of Argentina has confirmed the acceptance of a clear distinction between state immunity and the immunity of international organisations" and rejected "the analogous application of sovereign immunity exceptions to legal claims against international organisations."[92] Similarly, the Supreme Court of Austria ruled that "international organisations enjoyed more far-reaching immunities than states, which had immunity for *acta iure imperii* but not *acta iure gestionis*" and that "the immunities of international organisations [...] must be understood as 'absolute'."[93] This reasoning

---

90 CF Amerasinghe, *Principles of the Institutional Law of International Organization*, 2nd ed (New York: Cambridge University Press, 2005) at 327; Reinisch, *supra* note 42 at 191.

91 Ryngaert, *supra* note 66 at 129 footnote 27; Higgins et al, *supra* note 35 at 565 footnote 80.

92 Raùl E Vinuesa, "Argentina" in August Reinisch, ed, *The Privileges and Immunities of International Organisations in Domestic Courts* (Oxford: Oxford University Press, 2013) at 29.

93 Gregor Novak and August Reinisch, "Austria" in August Reinisch, ed, *The Privileges and Immunities of International Organizations in Domestic Courts* (Oxford: Oxford University Press, 2013) at 43.

is consistent with the position of the UN Legal Counsel, who opined that the "immunity accorded [to] international organisations under this system of law is an absolute immunity and must be distinguished from sovereign immunity which in some contemporary manifestations, at least, is more restrictive."[94] For these reasons, domestic courts should avoid likening the jurisdictional immunity of IGOs to state immunity. They should also avoid applying the restrictive doctrine when dealing with cases involving international organisations.

Section 2.1.2.2 of Chapter 2 identified some risks of denying international organisations jurisdictional immunity. The main risk is the threat to multilateralism through the erosion of IGOs' independence. As Justice Bryer of the United States Supreme Court observed in his dissenting opinion in the *Jam* case, "multilateralism is threatened if one nation alone, through application of its own liability rules can shape the policy choices or actions that an international organisation believes it must take or refrain from taking."[95] Denying jurisdictional immunity to international organisations may also expose documents and information that several member states share with it on a confidential basis to disclosure before the national courts of one member state. The mere possibility of such disclosure could dissuade other states from cooperating through IGOs.

State sovereignty entails the ability to carry out a wide range of activities, including those normally reserved for private persons. International organisations do not enjoy such freedom; they can only perform activities authorised by their constitutive instruments.[96] An activity of an international organisation is either *intra vires* or *ultra vires*. Activities that are intra vires are by default equivalent to *acta iure imperii*. By scrutinising the acts of international organisations to determine whether they were necessary for the fulfilment of their mandate, national courts expose international organisations to improper interference and undermine their independence.

1.3 *Taxing IGOs*

Most legal advisors of large international organisations have faced, at some point in their careers, attempts by states to tax the activities or transactions

94 United Nations Office of Legal Affairs, "Memorandum to the Legal Adviser, United Nations Relief and Works Agency for Palestine Refugees in the Near East", *UN Juridical Yearbook* (New York: UN, 1984) p. 188.

95 *Jam v. International Finance Corporation*, 2019 WL 938524 (United States Supreme Court) per Bryer J (dissenting).

96 *Legality of the Threat or Use by a State of Nuclear Weapons, Advisory Opinion*, *supra* note 85 at para. 25.

of their organisation. The UN Juridical Yearbook alone provides an impressive number of such examples. For instance, the 2014 Juridical Yearbook reproduces a Note sent by the United Nations to the Ministry of Foreign Affairs of an unidentified member state of the UN, objecting to the imposition of certain taxes in respect of fuel purchases for a UN peacekeeping mission.[97] The 2011 Juridical Yearbook refers to an incident where a state refused to reimburse certain amounts of value-added tax paid by the United Nations Development Programme.[98] In earlier Juridical Yearbooks, there are examples of the UN being charged disguised taxes as fees for aircraft parking,[99] circulation fees in relation to UN official vehicles,[100] or taxes on UNICEF publications.

While unfortunate and undesirable, these incidents appear to be isolated instances that can be normally resolved through diplomatic correspondence. The refusal to recognise fiscal exemptions to international organisations is infinitely more perilous when it becomes part of a nation's fiscal policy. A case in point is the EU legislation on value-added tax, which is a form of indirect tax.[101]

The legislative act governing the value-added tax in the European Union is the EU Directive on the Common System of Value Added Tax ('VAT Directive').[102] Unlike EU Regulations, Directives do not have a binding legal force in EU member states of the European Union; they lay down the desired outcome to be achieved while allowing each EU member state some freedom to decide how the broad principles should be transposed into their national laws

97 United Nations Office of Legal Affairs, "Note to the Ministry of Foreign Affairs of [State] concerning the imposition of certain taxes in respect of fuel purchases on [a United Nations Mission]", *UN Juridical Yearbook* (New York: UN, 2014) at 329.

98 United Nations Office of Legal Affairs, "Note to the Permanent Representative of [State] concerning the non-reimbursement of certain amounts of Value-Added Tax paid by the United Nations Development Programme (UNDP)", *UN Juridical Yearbook* (New York: UN, 2011) at 487.

99 United Nations Office of Legal Affairs, "Letter to the Minister of Foreign Affairs and International Cooperation of a Member State", *UN Juridical Yearbook* (New York: UN, 1994) at 452.

100 United Nations Office of Legal Affairs, "Letter to the Minister of Foreign Affairs and International Cooperation of a Member State", *UN Juridical Yearbook* (New York: UN, 1964) at 221.

101 United Nations Office of Legal Affairs, "Interoffice memorandum to the Secretary to the Commission and Officer-in-Charge of the General Services Section, Economic Commission for Africa (ECA), regarding new Directive on Value Added Tax in Member State", *UN Juridical Yearbook* (New York: UN, 2008) 408, at 409.

102 Council Directive 2006/112/EC of 28 November 2006 on the common system of value-added tax [2006] OJ L 347/1.

to achieve the desired outcome.[103] However, the VAT Directive is very detailed, leaving little room for flexibility in transposing the expected outcomes into national legislation. As a result, the VAT substantive rules in all member states of the European Union are generally well harmonised. The only variations in EU member states that can be observed are mainly in VAT rates, procedures, or administrative aspects.

One powerful tool for harmonising the rules on value-added tax is the Value Added Tax Committee established under Article 398 of the VAT Directive to promote the uniform application of the provisions of the Directive. It consists of representatives of EU member states and the EU Commission. This advisory committee interprets and provides guidance on the application of various provisions of the VAT Directive. Although the guidance is theoretically not binding, in practice, it bears tremendous weight; the fiscal authorities of EU member states usually comply with it. The guidance takes the form of 'Working Papers'.

Working Paper No. 897 of 10 February 2016 dealt with, among other things, fiscal exemptions on acquisitions made by 'international bodies'. Although Article 151(1)(b) of the VAT Directive grants to recognised international bodies a general exemption for the supply of goods or services, it does not define the term 'international bodies' and does not specify which transactions are exempt and which attract taxes. One of the questions explored by the VAT Committee in its Working Paper 897 was whether all acquisitions of goods and services by eligible international bodies could benefit from exemption or only acquisitions made for certain activities of these entities.

The Committee begins by recognising that the term 'international bodies' refers to intergovernmental organisations. It then provides a peculiar description of entities that it believes qualify as international organisations under the VAT Directive:

> It was concluded that to qualify as such, an international organisation would have to be set up by at least two states recognised by the European Union or by an existing international organisation (possibly acting jointly with other international organisations or states) and have legitimate objectives that are jointly pursued and essentially non-economic in nature. The fact that the organisation has legal personality or constitutes

---

103 Article 288 of the Consolidated versions of the Treaty on European Union and the Treaty on the Functioning of the European Union (TFEU) [2016] OJ C202/47.

an organisation within the meaning of international law was not found decisive in this regard.[104]

An entity does not need to be recognised by the European Union as an international organisation. The European Union does not have a process for recognising international organisations. Recognition of an entity by the European Union is irrelevant for the purposes of fiscal exemptions. Any member state of the European Union may independently recognise such status to an organisation and grant it broad fiscal privileges.

The Committee then acknowledges that international organisations are governed by public international law and are not usually involved in economic activities; therefore, they would, as a starting point, be regarded as 'non-taxable persons'. The Committee then goes on to suggest that "when carrying out an activity or transaction, they would also be treated as a non-taxable person whenever they carry them out as a public authority [...] However, when the treatment as non-taxable persons would lead to significant distortions of competition, the international body should be regarded as a taxable person."[105] Essentially, if transactions of a specific IGO distort competition, they become taxable transactions. The IGOs privileges and immunities recognised in international agreements to which EU member states are parties become secondary, if not irrelevant.

The criterion of 'distortions of competition' is so ambiguous that it is arbitrary. The Committee neither defines this term nor specifies who is competent to determine that treating IGOs as non-taxable persons would lead to significant distortions of competition. In any event, although distortions of competition are harmful, they should not be a relevant consideration in deciding whether an IGO is exempt from indirect taxes. The only relevant factor should be the intention of member states and the text of the agreement granting fiscal privileges. Moreover, distortions of competition are preferable to distortions of international cooperation because of interference by one member state in the financial affairs of an IGO.

The VAT Committee then draws another flawed conclusion, stating that an international body cannot be regarded as acting as a public authority when it acts under the same legal conditions as those applicable to corporations. In essence, the VAT Committee implies that the IGO is a taxable person in

104 Value Added Tax Committee, Working Paper No. 897 of 10 February 2016, *VAT exemptions on acquisitions made under diplomatic and consular arrangements, by the European Institutions, by international organisations and by armed forces* at 6.

105 *Ibid.* at 24.

relation to *jure gestiones* acts. This conclusion once again conflates state immunity and jurisdictional immunity of IGOs. In addition, as mentioned previously, international organisations do not have the authority to carry out activities not explicitly or implicitly permitted under their constitutive instruments; therefore, all activities of international organisations are deemed necessary in fulfilling their mandate unless one is prepared to assume that IGOs regularly exceed their mandate and mission. If constitutive instruments of IGOs allow them to trade or conduct business for the common good of their member states, such transactions must be exempt from indirect taxes, even if they occasionally distort competition. On the other hand, if a specific international organisation engages in activities that fall outside its mandate, its member states should demand an explanation and request its chief administrative officer to ensure that such activities cease immediately. Further, to determine which transaction of an international organisation was carried out as an act of a public authority, national fiscal authorities would need to have full visibility of all transactions. This would expose the IGO to undue interference by one member state in its internal affairs.

Most importantly, however, treating international organisations as taxable entities under the EU VAT Directive will inevitably trigger a panoply of additional encroachments on their independence. For instance, any taxable person under the VAT Directive has an obligation to register for a VAT number and submit detailed monthly and annual statements with aggregated amounts for each taxable transaction to national fiscal authorities.[106] This would automatically give the governmental authorities of one specific state an unlimited amount of information on the activities of the organisation. If the organisation refuses to comply with this obligation, the concerned state may fine and prosecute the IGO under its fiscal legislation, which would constitute a breach of the organisation's immunity from every form of legal process. Furthermore, imposing onerous administrative procedures on IGOs to seek and obtain a refund or remission of VAT may also constitute a breach of their fiscal privileges.[107]

---

106 Commission implementing Regulation (EU) 2020/194 of 12 February 2020 laying down detailed rules for the application of Council Regulation (EU) No 904/2010 as regards the special schemes for taxable persons supplying services to non-taxable persons, making distance sales of goods and certain domestic supplies of goods [2020] OJ L40/114.

107 United Nations Office of Legal Affairs, "Interoffice memorandum to the Secretary to the Commission and Officer-in-Charge of the General Services Section, Economic Commission for Africa (ECA), regarding new Directive on Value Added Tax in Member State", *UN Juridical Yearbook* (New York: UN, 2008) at 408.

The VAT Committee's blanket statement is not entirely consistent with the EU internal law either, which recognises that the rights and obligations arising from international "agreements concluded before 1 January 1958 or, for acceding states, before the date of their accession, between one or more EU member states on the one hand, and one or more third countries on the other, shall not be affected by the provisions of the EU treaties".[108] Many treaties granting privileges and immunities to international organisations of which most EU member states are signatory parties, including the Convention on Privileges and Immunities of the United Nations[109] and the Ottawa Agreement,[110] were concluded before 1 January 1958. Certain practices have developed over decades in international organisations. These practices reflect the interpretation of the agreements containing fiscal exemptions. These practices and corresponding interpretations should not be affected by subsequent EU legislation. Therefore, the VAT Committee erred in recommending an approach that would fundamentally change the fiscal privileges of international organisations established before 1 January 1958. The Committee proposed no alternative steps to eliminate any incompatibilities that could arise from its interpretation of Article 151(1)(b) of the VAT Directive and the fiscal privileges that an organisation may have been granted before 1 January 1958.

While it is true that exceptions to any general regime must be interpreted restrictively,[111] fiscal privileges from indirect taxes have often been granted to IGOs before the value-added tax even existed.[112] Domestic legislation relating to VAT was a new restriction imposed on an existing broad exemption that major international organisations had already been enjoying for some time. Hence, the argument of interpreting exceptions restrictively cuts both ways: the VAT Directive is as much of an exception to fiscal privileges of

108 Article 351 of the Consolidated versions of the Treaty on European Union and the Treaty on the Functioning of the European Union (TFEU) [2016] OJ C202/47.

109 Convention on Privileges and Immunities of the United Nations, 13 February 1946, 1 U.N.T.S. 15.

110 Agreement on the status of the North Atlantic Treaty Organization, National Representatives and International Staff signed in Ottawa, 20 September 1951, 200 U.N.T.S. 3.

111 CJEU, judgment of 26 June 1990 in case C-185/89 Velker International Oil Company.

112 Donald W Parker, "The Value-Added Tax in the European Economic Community" (1988) 11 *B C Int'l & Comp L Rev* 155 (Although VAT was initially conceived by economic theorists in the United States in the early part of the twentieth century, France was among the first countries to adopt it. It is only in 1967 that the EEC adopted a VAT system with the First Directive, which instructed the member states of the EEC to replace their present system of taxation with a VAT).

international organisations as tax exemptions of international organisations are an exception to the VAT Directive.

Nations should endeavour to grant international organisations broad fiscal privileges to preserve their independence. The amount of VAT collected from international organisations is so negligible that it is not worth jeopardising their independence from their member states by subjecting them to national fiscal laws. There is no evidence supporting the VAT Committee's assertion that the activities of IGOs are so considerable that they can significantly distort competition.

Those who support taxing the economic activities of international organisations also argue that this approach helps prevent abuses of fiscal privileges. However, abuses of fiscal privileges by international organisations represent a negligible risk because member states can always collectively address such abuses through the organisation's governing body. Consequently, the risk of eroding the independence of international organisations by taxing some of their activities outweighs the risk of abuses of IGO's fiscal privileges.

Based on this EU VAT Directive, tax authorities of some member states of the European Union argued that NATO must register with their fiscal authorities and obtain a VAT number like any other entity performing economic activities on the territory of the EU. However, registering with national fiscal authorities and obtaining a VAT number would subject the organisation to the fiscal legislation of these member states and allow their tax authorities to seek information that non-EU member nations of NATO would not want to disclose. This could potentially give EU fiscal authorities a certain leverage over NATO. This example illustrates the way fiscal policies of individual member nations may potentially affect an organisation's ability to carry out its activities, undermine its independence vis-à-vis the authorities of some member states, and prejudice other member states.

2 Breaches by States of Privileges and Immunities of International Civil Servants

The previous Section described state practices that erode the independence of international secretariats by breaching the privileges and immunities of international organisations. This Section will examine state practices that weaken the independence of international civil servants by infringing on their privileges and immunities.

2.1 *Violations of Functional Immunity*

It is believed that the first time a national court interpreted the notion of functional immunities of an international civil servant was in 1946 when the driver of the UN Secretary-General Trygve Lie was charged with exceeding the speed limit while transporting the Secretary-General to a conference in a UN-owned vehicle. The UN Counsel asked the court to decline jurisdiction on the grounds that all staff members of the United Nations are immune from prosecution for any violation of law while acting in an official capacity. The presiding judge refused to decline jurisdiction, ruling that the immunity of the United Nations does not extend to employees who merely contribute to the personal convenience and comfort of officials of the United Nations, but only to employees whose functions are necessary for the actual operations of the United Nations.[113] Essentially, the judge unilaterally determined that some staff members are essential to the organisation while others are not:

> To recognize the existence of a general and unrestricted immunity from suit or prosecution on the part of the personnel of the United Nations, so long as the individual be performing in his official capacity, even though the individual's function has no relation to the importance or the success of the organization's deliberations, is carrying the principle of immunity completely out of bounds. […] such immunity should be available only when it is truly necessary to assure the proper deliberations of the organisation.[114]

The opinion in this case, delivered in November 1946 by a city court judge, also contained the first judicial construction of the International Organization Immunities Act of the United States enacted in December 1945 to implement the provisions of Articles 104 and 105 of the Charter of the United Nations.[115] The Secretary-General chose not to appeal this ruling. He waived his driver's immunity and paid the fine.

A cursory reading of the City judge's reasoning is sufficient to conclude that the rationale for his refusal to decline jurisdiction was unsound. First, if national courts are allowed to determine whose functions are important for the success of the organisation, functional immunities would not serve their basic objective, which is to prevent abusive interferences by national authorities. Second,

113 Lawrence Preuss, "Immunity of Officers and Employees of the United Nations for Official Acts: The Ranallo Case" (1947) 41:3 *Am J Int'l L* 555 at 556–557.

114 *Donelly v. Ranollo*, 187 Misc. 777 (N.Y. City Ct. 1946), 67 N.Y.S.2d 31.

115 Preuss, *supra* note 113.

no objective criteria exist to assess the importance of a staff member's functions. Consequently, drawing a distinction between essential and unessential functions is arbitrary. Third, the judge confounded functional immunity with impunity. In particular, he assumed that recognising functional immunities to UN staff members prevents the host State from prosecuting them. However, there has never been any doubt that the host State can request that the organisation waive privileges and immunities enjoyed by its personnel.

Functional immunities of international officials or of persons performing functions for international organisations continued to come under attack since then. They even became the subject of two advisory opinions of the International Court of Justice. Both cases revolved around immunities of Special Rapporteurs of the former Commission on Human Rights.[116]

The first dispute related to Dumitru Mazilu, a Romanian national, appointed as a Rapporteur of the Sub-Commission on the Prevention of Discrimination and Protection of Minorities of the former Commission on Human Rights. Mazilu had been entrusted with the task of writing a report on human rights and youth in Romania. Displeased with the contents of Mazilu's report, the Romanian authorities used different means to prevent Mazilu from submitting his report. Mazilu informed the United Nations that his government was denying him a travel permit and preventing him from attending the session of the Sub-Committee where he was expected to present his findings. When the United Nations sought clarifications from Romania, its authorities asserted *inter alia* that functional immunities and privileges granted by the Convention on the privileges and immunities of the UN applied only when Mazilu left on a journey connected with the performance of his mission. Romanian authorities argued that in Romania, Mazilu enjoyed privileges and immunities only with respect to actual activities relating to his mission. In 1989, the Economic and Social Council (ECOSOC) of the UN sought an advisory opinion from the International Court of Justice on the scope of privileges and immunities enjoyed by Mazilu. The Court opined that persons to whom the organisation entrusted a mission were entitled to the privileges and immunities necessary to perform their functions independently. The Court also clarified that during the whole period of such missions, these persons enjoyed functional privileges and immunities irrespective of whether they travelled and that those

116 In 2006, the General Assembly replaced the Human Rights Commission with the Human Rights Council and placed the newly created subsidiary body under its authority, removing it from ECOSOC's purview: *Human Rights Council*, GA Res 60/251, UNGAOR, 60th Sess, UN Doc A/Res/60/251 (2006) 1.

privileges and immunities may be invoked against the State of nationality or of residence.[117]

The second issue arose when the Special Rapporteur of Malaysian nationality faced several lawsuits filed in Malaysian courts by plaintiffs who asserted that he had used defamatory language in an interview published in a specialist journal and who sought damages of US$30 million. The UN Secretary-General informed the Malaysian authorities that the Special Rapporteur had been speaking in his official capacity and was thus immune from legal process by virtue of the UN Convention on the Privileges and Immunities. The disagreement between the United Nations and Malaysia had originated in the government of Malaysia not having informed the Malaysian courts of the Secretary-General's finding that the UN Special Rapporteur had spoken the words at issue while carrying out his mission and was, therefore, entitled to immunity from legal process. The ICJ held that the Secretary-General, as the organisation's chief administrative officer, has the primary responsibility to safeguard the organisation's interests. Therefore, "it is up to him to assess whether its agents acted within the scope of their functions and, where he so concludes, to protect these agents, including experts on mission, by asserting their immunity."[118] This means that the Secretary-General has the authority and responsibility to inform the government of a member state of his finding and to request it to bring his finding to the knowledge of the local courts if acts of an agent have given or may give rise to court proceedings.[119] The ICJ clarified that when national courts are seized of a case in which the immunity of an international official is in issue, they should immediately be notified of any finding by the organisation's chief administrative officer concerning that immunity. "That finding, and its documentary expression, creates a presumption which can only be set aside for the most compelling reasons and is thus to be given the greatest weight by national courts."[120]

Unfortunately, this Advisory Opinion did not deter some member states from arresting or detaining officials of international organisations after a

---

117 *Applicability of Article VI, Section 22, of the Convention on the Privileges and Immunities of the United Nations*, Advisory Opinion, [1989] ICJ Rep 177 at para. 47 [Applicability of Article VI Case].

118 *Difference Relating to Immunity from Legal Process of a Special Rapporteur of the Commission on Human Rights*, Advisory Opinion, [1999] ICJ Rep 62 at para. 60 [Immunity from Legal Process of a Special Rapporteur].

119 United Nations Office of Legal Affairs, "Note Verbale to the Permanent Representative of [State] concerning the privileges and immunities of [a United Nations entity]", *UN Juridical Yearbook* (New York: UN, 2010) at 501.

120 *Immunity from Legal Process of a Special Rapporteur*, *supra* note 118 at para 61.

unilateral determination by their law enforcement authorities that the alleged wrongdoing was not related to the performance of the official's functions.[121] Therefore, the immunity from legal process was inapplicable. The administrative tribunals of international organisations regularly adjudicate employment law disputes where staff members take issue with their employers' failure to assert their privileges and immunities or at least examine whether the alleged wrongdoing occurred during the performance of their functions.[122] These cases reveal that national authorities usurp the power of the organisation's chief administrative officer by unilaterally determining that functional immunities do not cover a specific act of the official.

A high-profile case that illustrates how states ignore or disregard the chief administrative officer's role in assessing whether its agents acted within the scope of their functions was Turkey's arrest, trial, and sentencing to a term of almost eight years of imprisonment of Judge Aydin Sefa Akay. Akay is a Turkish citizen and worked during the relevant period as a judge in the United Nations Mechanism for International Criminal Tribunals.[123] A few months after the attempted *coup d'état* in Turkey in July 2016, the Turkish authorities arrested Judge Akay for his alleged links to the Gülenist movement blamed for the failed revolution against the current Erdogan regime. The United Nations Secretary-General protested by reminding Turkish authorities that Judge Akay enjoyed privileges and immunities accorded to diplomatic envoys. Turkey responded that the arrest was unrelated to his functions. Therefore, Judge Akay did not enjoy UN privileges and immunities.[124]

2.2 *Restrictions and Conditions for Recruiting Personnel*

Member nations of international organisations often oppose the appointment or the continuous employment of specific staff members. In some cases, governments of member states try to retain control over the identity

121 On this point, see Teresa F Mayr, "Where Do We Stand and Where Do We Go: The Fine Balance between Independence and Accountability of United Nations Experts on a Mission" (2018) 15:1 *Int'l Org L Rev* 130.

122 See *Bekele v. Secretary-General of the United Nations*, UNDT/2010/175 (UN Dispute Tribunal) and *Mutiso v. Secretary-General of the United Nations*, UNDT/2015/059 (UN Dispute Tribunal).

123 "Letter dated 5 October 2016 from the President of the International Residual Mechanism for Criminal Tribunals addressed to the President of the Security Council", UN Doc. S/2016/841 (5 October 2016).

124 International Residual Mechanism for Criminal Tribunals, Press Release, Statement of the President on the Non-Reappointment of Judge Akay (July 3, 2018), www.unmict.org/en/news/statement-president-non-reappointment-judge-akay.

of their citizens being recruited or employed by international organisations. For instance, in 2016, after the unsuccessful coup d'état in Turkey, the Turkish government initiated a purge of not only national but also international civil servants whom it suspected of having links to the exiled billionaire Fethullah Gülen.[125] As a result, several NATO officials of Turkish nationality and alleged sympathisers of Gülen saw their security clearances revoked by Turkey. This action compelled NATO to terminate the employment contracts of these staff and separate them from service. It is noteworthy that Article 9.1(iv) of the NATO *Civilian Personnel Regulations* allows but does not mandate NATO to terminate contracts of staff members whose countries of nationality withdraw or do not renew their security clearance. Nevertheless, in 2015, the NATO Administrative Tribunal ruled that when NATO is informed of national authorities' decision to withdraw a staff member's security clearance, it is obliged to terminate the staff member's contract with immediate effect without assessing the merits of the withdrawal.[126]

The government of another country issued a decree regarding the recruitment and management of its nationals working for international organisations. Under this decree, international organisations could recruit nationals of this state only through recruitment agencies designated or authorised by the state's Ministry of Foreign Affairs. These recruitment agencies were given the responsibility to select and introduce candidates to international organisations. IGOs were required to appoint one of the pre-selected candidates and could not select a candidate not endorsed by a designated recruitment agency.[127]

Member states often oppose the appointment of international civil servants who hold critical views of their governments or are nationals of a state that they consider unfriendly. The most frequent ways of opposing appointments or

---

125 Robin Emmott, "Turkey's purged NATO staff not coup plotters: alliance commander", *Reuters* (7 December 2016); Teri Schultz, "Purged by Turkey, An Ex-NATO Officer Speaks Out about Detention under Erdogan", *NPR* (15 August 2018); Patrick Kingsley, "Turkey sacks 15000 education workers in purge after failed coup", *The Guardian* (20 July 2016); Joseph Hincks, "Here is a Time Line of the Insane Number of People Turkey's President Has Fired Since July 15", *Time* (23 November 2016); "Turkey's failed coup attempt: All you need to know", *Aljazeera* (15 July 2017).

126 *AF v. Joint Force Training Centre*, Case No. 2015/1044 (21 December 2015) (NATO Administrative Tribunal).

127 United Nations Office of Legal Affairs, "Note to [State] concerning privileges and immunities of United Nations staff members regarding the recruitment of nationals of [State] by the United Nations, its Funds and Programmes and other subsidiary bodies in [State]", *UN Juridical Yearbook* (New York: UN, 2016) at 337.

employment of such individuals by international organisations are (a) refusal to grant credentials or *agrément*, (b) declarations of *persona non grata*, or (c) refusal to issue immigration papers. However, recourse to these three tactics is legally untenable and constitutes a serious breach of an international civil servant's independence.

2.2.1 Refusal to Grant Agrément

In accordance with Article 4 of the Vienna Convention on Diplomatic Relations, "the sending State must make certain that the *agrément* of the receiving State has been given for the person it proposes to accredit as head of the mission to that State. The receiving State is not obliged to give reasons to the sending State for a refusal of *agrément*."[128] This provision applies to bilateral relations between states. It does not apply to international organisations and their officials as staff members[129] "are not accredited to a government but must serve as independent and impartial international officers responsible to the [international organisation]".[130] Nevertheless, for obscure historical reasons, the UN and many of its agencies have sought an *agrément* from their member states before appointing their highest-ranking officials to a specific country. This vetting procedure gives host nations an ideal opportunity to veto the appointment and exert pressure on the UN Secretary-General to appoint citizens of friendly nations or specific individuals. In recent years, some African countries have occasionally withheld an *agrément* when the Secretary-General proposed a candidate who was not a national of a friendly African state.

2.2.2 Declarations of *persona non grata*

Under the Vienna Convention on Diplomatic Relations, a sovereign state "may at any time and without having to explain its decision, notify the sending State that the head of the mission or any member of the diplomatic staff of the mission is *persona non grata* or that any other member of the staff of the mission is not acceptable."[131] In any such case, the sending State must either recall the person concerned or terminate his functions with the mission. This rule applies only to bilateral relations between States. The Convention on the

---

128 Vienna Convention on Diplomatic Relations, 18 April 1961, 500 U.N.T.S. 95, Articles 4.1 and 4.2.

129 United Nations Office of Legal Affairs, "Memorandum to the Chief of Protocol, Executive Office of the Secretary-General" *UN Juridical Yearbook* (New York: UN, 1995), at p. 403.

130 United Nations Office of Legal Affairs, "Aide-Mémoire to the Permanent Representatives of various Member States" *UN Juridical Yearbook* (New York: UN, 1964), at p. 261.

131 Vienna Convention on Diplomatic Relations, *supra* note 128.

Privileges and Immunities of the United Nations and other similar agreements neither provide nor envision any right for member states hosting international organisations or their operations to declare international civil servants *persona non grata* or to take equivalent action.[132]

Nevertheless, some member states regularly compel international organisations to remove from their territory staff members whom they do not favour by declaring these staff *persona non grata*. For instance, in the *Porras*,[133] *Hassouna*,[134] *Milicevic*,[135] and *Tal*[136] cases, the Sudanese government declared UN staff members *persona non grata* and demanded their immediate removal from its territory. Each time, the United Nations protested against such measures through a Note Verbale.[137] The governments of several member states continue to use this tactic whenever UN staff members act in a way contrary to their interests or wishes.

2.2.3 Refusal to Issue Immigration Papers

In some cases, member states refuse to issue or renew the visas of international civil servants to prevent their appointment or the renewal of their employment contract. In 2015, a member state of the United Nations declined to renew the visa of a UN Country Director because its government did not approve of the Secretary-General's decision to extend the individual's appointment. As a result, when the UN staff member's visa expired, he was required to leave the country. A similar situation had already occurred with other UN officials assigned to the same country. The Secretary-General of the UN addressed

132 United Nations Office of Legal Affairs, "Note to [State] concerning privileges and immunities of United Nations staff members regarding a declaration of a United Nations country representative as persona non grata", UN Juridical Yearbook (New York: UN, 2016) at 347.

133 *Porras v. Secretary-General of the United Nations*, UNDT/2019/178 (United Nations Dispute Tribunal) reversed in 2020-UNAT-1068 (United Nations Appeals Tribunal).

134 *Hassouna v. Secretary-General of United Nations*, UNDT/2014/094 (United Nations Dispute Tribunal).

135 *Milicevic v. Secretary-General of the United Nations*, UNDT/2018/101 (United Nations Dispute Tribunal).

136 *Tal v. Secretary-General of the United Nations*, UNDT Order No. 109 (NBI/2017) (United Nations Dispute Tribunal).

137 United Nations Office of Legal Affairs, "Note to the Ministry of Foreign Affairs of [State A] concerning a request to [State B] staff members of the United Nations to leave the country or face possible detention", *UN Juridical Yearbook* (New York: UN, 2012) at 457; United Nations Office of Legal Affairs, "*Note to [State] concerning privileges and immunities of United Nations staff members regarding a declaration of a United Nations country representative as persona non grata*", *UN Juridical Yearbook* (New York: UN, 2016) at 347.

a written protest to the authorities of the member state[138] but to no avail. As a result of these practices, the United Nations often finds itself in an untenable position where it is compelled to choose between two equally bad solutions. Specifically, it can withdraw a conditional offer of appointment made to candidates selected for vacant posts when the immigration authorities of the receiving state delay the issuance of visas. In such cases, the UN does not have any guarantee that a different candidate will obtain a visa easier. Alternatively, the UN can persist at the risk of prolonging indefinitely the appointment of a candidate. Whenever the organisation opted for the first solution by withdrawing an offer of appointment due to difficulties in obtaining visas, it faced legal challenges before the UN Dispute Tribunal and was ordered to pay compensation to candidates who had been offered vacant positions but never appointed.[139]

2.3 *Attempts to Tax International Civil Servants*

Many multilateral agreements that regulate the status, privileges and immunities of international organisations contain provisions that exempt officials of these institutions from income taxes. For instance, Article V, Section 18, paragraph (b) of the Convention on the Privileges and Immunities of the United Nations provides that officials of the United Nations shall be exempt from taxation on the salaries and emoluments paid to them by the United Nations. Article 19 of the Agreement on the Status of the North Atlantic Treaty Organisation, National Representatives and International Staff (Ottawa Agreement) contains a similar text. In some cases, fiscal privileges of international civil servants can be found in bilateral agreements between the Host Nation and the IGO.[140]

138 United Nations Office of Legal Affairs, "Note to the Ministry of Foreign Affairs of [State] concerning privileges and immunities of United Nations officials to be granted visas, and other travel documents, necessary to enter [State] on official United Nations business" *UN Juridical Yearbook* (New York: UN, 2015) at 308.

139 *Abu Al Asal v. Secretary-General of the United Nations*, UNDT/2020/123 (United Nations Dispute Tribunal); *Trudi v. Secretary-General of the United Nations*, UNDT/2018/019 (United Nations Dispute Tribunal).

140 See Article XIII, Section 1(b) of the Headquarters Agreement between the Organization of American States and the Government of the United States of America (1992): "Except as provided in Section 3 of this Article, officials of the Organization shall [...] be exempt from taxation, whether by local, state, or federal authorities of the United States, which has been or may hereafter be imposed on monies paid to them by the Organization that constitute salaries, emoluments, or other compensation under the Internal Law of the Organization." See also Article 141(ii) of the Agreement between the Government of the Republic of Indonesia and the Association of Southeast Nations (ASEAN) on Hosting and Granting Privileges and Immunities to the ASEAN Secretariat (2012): "The Secretary-General, the Deputy Secretaries-General and Staff of the Secretariat referred to in

As pointed out in Chapter 2, the rationale for exempting international civil servants from income taxes is twofold. First, it ensures equality of treatment for all officials, irrespective of their nationality.[141] Specifically, to achieve equality in salary treatment for officials of equal rank, the organisation must be able to fix comparable salary levels for comparable posts throughout the entire area of its operations without the need for continuous adjustment, which would be necessary if changes and variations in national tax legislation had to be taken into account.[142]

Second, the exemption ensures that the organisation's operations do not become a source of revenue for one of its member states at the expense of others.[143]

Not all countries agree to exempt their nationals from income taxes. For instance, Canada, Laos, Mexico, and Turkey made reservations to Article V, Section 18(b) of the General Convention with regard to their nationals or permanent residents working for the UN on their territory. The United States went one step further and made a reservation to the provision in relation to its citizens and permanent residents irrespective of where they work. As a result, UN staff members who are permanent residents or citizens of the United States

Paragraph 3 of Article 13, to the extent that they are not Indonesian nationals within and with respect to the territory of the Host Country, shall, while in the performance of and for the independent exercises of their respective duties, functions and responsibilities, be granted privileges and immunities as stipulated in the Vienna Convention on Diplomatic Relations 1961 and [...] be exempt from taxation on the salary and emoluments paid to him or her by ASEAN through the Secretariat".

141 United Nations Office of Legal Affairs, "Privileges and immunities of locally recruited staff members of the United Nations – Obligation of Member States under Article 105 of the Charter to accord all staff members whether internationally or locally recruited such privileges and immunities as are necessary for the independent exercise of their functions" *UN Juridical Yearbook* (New York: UN, 1972) at 191, and UN General Assembly, *Tax Equalization*, 7 December 1946, A/RES/78(I).

142 *Reiniera Charlotte Brouerius van Nidek v. Inspecteur des Registratie en Successie*, preliminary ruling of 3 July 1974, Case 7/74, ECR 1974 (Part II) at 764; United Nations Office of Legal Affairs, "Note to the Ministry of Foreign Affairs of [State], concerning privileges and immunities enjoyed by certain categories of United Nations personnel in [State]" *United Nations Juridical Yearbook* (New York: UN, 2013) 371 at 375.

143 United Nations Office of Legal Affairs, "Scope and effect of the privileges and immunities required under the 1946 Convention on the privileges and immunities of the United Nation for locally recruited staff", *United Nations Juridical Yearbook* (New York: UN, 1968) 212 at 214.

pay income taxes on their UN earnings in the United States and claim a reimbursement from the United Nations.[144]

The US approach gives rise to difficulties in determining the amount to be reimbursed to US nationals working in the United Nations. The income taxes one must pay in the United States depend not only on one's income from the UN but also on one's credits, tax deductions, and supplementary income sources. It is not always possible to determine which portion of the income taxes paid is attributable to emoluments received from the UN. Hence, disputes related to the amount of reimbursement of income taxes paid to the US government regularly arise between the UN and US nationals.[145]

Curiously, Canada and Turkey, also NATO member states, made no reservations to the provision granting fiscal privileges to NATO staff.[146] The United States proposed to insert a clause into Article 19 of the Ottawa Agreement, allowing it to tax its nationals, but other nations rejected the proposal.[147] Consequently, the United States conditioned its signature to the Ottawa Agreement upon the prior completion of the London Agreement[148] between the US government and the North Atlantic Council, which precluded the 'direct hire' of US citizens by NATO for positions in the secretariat. For many years, US citizens could only be seconded to NATO. In 1972, the United States government agreed to permit the direct hire of its nationals by NATO for middle and low-level positions in the secretariat and to exempt such officials from taxation.[149] The United States government subsequently rescinded this policy, but in the meantime, NATO had already hired US nationals. Questions arose as to whether US nationals recruited directly by NATO could continue enjoying fiscal exemptions even though the policy exempting them from taxation no longer existed. In the *Adair* case, the US Tax Court put the controversy to

144 The UN reimburses US nationals the amount of taxes paid to the US government from the Tax Equalization Fund which is replenished with deductions from salaries of UN staff members known as 'staff assessment'.

145 See for instance *Johnson v. Secretary-General of the United Nations*, 2012-UNAT-240 (United Nations Appeals Tribunal) and *McCloskey v. Secretary-General of the United Nations*, 2014-UNAT-424 (United Nations Appeals Tribunal).

146 Agreement on the status of the North Atlantic Treaty Organization, National Representatives and International Staff signed in Ottawa, 20 September 1951, 200 U.N.T.S. 3, Article 19: "Officials of the Organisation agreed under Article 17 shall be exempt from taxation on the salaries and emoluments paid to them by the Organisation in their capacity as such officials."

147 *Amaral v. Commissioner* (1988) 90 T.C. 802 (U.S. Tax Court).

148 Agreement between the United States and the North Atlantic Council, 5 U.S.T. 1098, T.I.A.S. 2992 (29 September 1951).

149 *Amaral v. Commissioner*, *supra* note 147.

rest by ruling that as soon as US nationals end their secondment and employment relationship with the United States government, they are exempt from income taxes because the United States made no reservations to the Ottawa Agreement.[150]

There is no logical explanation for denying fiscal privileges to UN staff members but granting them to NATO staff members. This inconsistency confirms that member states of international organisations are not obligated under their domestic legislation to levy income taxes on their nationals working for international organisations. Hence, making reservations to provisions that grant tax exemptions to officials of international organisations is unnecessary.

More worrisome practices, however, are disguised taxation attempts. States can be particularly creative in putting in place disguised taxation mechanisms. In one case, the authorities of a UN member state enacted legislation under which UN staff were required to turn over up to ten per cent of their monthly salary in order to apply for and obtain a passport renewal.[151] More recently, the authorities of another country required all international organisations to withhold and transfer to the government income taxes and contributions to the mandatory social welfare scheme from the salaries and emoluments paid to locally recruited international civil servants.[152]

During the Cold War, the Soviet Union and other Eastern European governments required all their nationals serving in international organisations to transfer a sizeable portion of their salaries to their governments.[153] Typically, for a salary of over 1,000 dollars, the staff member had an obligation to remit 500 dollars plus 90 per cent of the amount over 1,000 dollars. The Administrative Committee on Coordination[154] had noted in 1980 that "the exclusively international character of a staff member's obligations may also be adversely affected, should he be expected to turn over part of his emoluments

150 *Adair v. Commissioner* (1995) 70 T.C. 998 (U.S. Tax Court).

151 United Nations Office of Legal Affairs, "Letter to the Permanent Representative of Member State", *United Nations Juridical Yearbook* (New York: UN, 1972) at 188–189.

152 United Nations Office of Legal Affairs, "Note to [State] concerning the privileges and immunities enjoyed by United Nations officials from [State] taxation on the salaries and emoluments paid by the United Nations to its officials and from mandatory contributions to national social welfare schemes, which is also a form of taxation", *United Nations Juridical Yearbook* (New York: UN, 2015) at 299.

153 Theodor Meron, "Status and Independence of the International Civil Service" (1980) 167 *Recueil des Cours de l'Académie de Droit International* 289 at 326.

154 The Secretary-General established a Coordination Committee that was renamed the Administrative Committee on Coordination in 1949 (*Fourth Report of the Administrative Committee on Coordination to the Economic and Social Council*, UNESCOR, 1948, UN Doc E/1076, 1 at 3) and the Chief Executive Board for Coordination in 2001.

to his government".[155] These practices came to light when a Romanian national and a UNESCO staff member refused to turn over to his government a portion of his net income. The Romanian government initiated criminal proceedings against its citizen, triggering a razor-sharp exchange of letters between the Director General of UNESCO and the Romanian Ministry of Foreign Affairs.[156]

Of course, the opposite practice of subsidizing employment in the UN by wealthy countries was equally problematic. The Federal Republic of Germany, Japan and the United States were among the first nations to offer additional remuneration to their citizens working for international organisations.[157] Under the German legislation approved by the Bundestag in 1979, German citizens employed in international organisations could obtain additional remuneration of up to 80 per cent of the difference between the pay of the organisation's official and that of a German Federal or State civil servant posted abroad.[158] Japan, and the United States had slightly different rules; their nationals were guaranteed pay at least equivalent to their previous pay or to the pay that they would earn as a national public servant. After numerous complaints and *Notes Verbales* from the UN, supplementary payments offered by developed countries ceased.[159]

In NATO, however, United States citizens may still choose to retain their national emoluments during their secondment. In such cases, they continue to be remunerated by the United States government, which makes it impossible for NATO to ensure equality of treatment for all its staff. It also allows the US government to retain significant power and influence over American staff members.

---

155 Jacques Lemoine, *The International Civil Servant: An Endangered Species* (The Hague: Martinus Nijhoff Publishers, 1995) at 186.

156 Meron, *supra* note 52 at 336–337. See also Sorin Dumitrescu, "In the hands of the Securitate", *The UNESCO Courrier*, June 1990, at 45.

157 Genowefa Grabowska, "Independence of the International Civil Servants" (1988) 17 *Polish YB Int'l L* 61 at 70.

158 *Ibid.*

159 See para. 51 of the Secretary-General's Bulletin on the "Status, Basic Rights and Duties of UN Staff Members", UN Doc ST/SGB/2016/9, which reads as follows: "51. International civil servants should not accept supplementary payments or other subsidies from a government or any other source prior to, during or after their assignment with an organisation of the United Nations system if the payment is related to that assignment. Balancing this requirement, it is understood that Governments or other entities, recognising that they are at variance with the spirit of the Charter and the constitutions of the organisations of the United Nations system, should not make or offer such payments."

3 Actions by States That Undermine the Neutrality and Impartiality of International Civil Service

Few other practices can be as damaging to the independence of international civil servants as interference by member states in personnel administration matters, including appointments, promotions, and separations from service. International civil servants must be impartial and neutral and not rely on their countries of nationality. Otherwise, a staff member cannot uphold the oath of allegiance owed to the organisation.

3.1 *Interference in Personnel Management*

As early as 1952, the Commission of Jurists established by the Secretary-General expressed the view that the independence of the Secretary-General of the UN and his sole responsibility to the General Assembly for the selection and retention of staff should be recognised by all member states and if necessary asserted should it ever be challenged. The Commission cautioned that "[i]f the position of the Secretary-General in this respect were to be weakened, the whole conception of the responsibility of the staff of the United Nations would be impaired and the essential task of building up and maintaining an international civil service frustrated to the lasting detriment of the work of the United Nations."[160]

However, nations consider that the employment of their citizens in international organisations, especially at senior levels, is a matter of national importance. In fact, several governments have, as part of the Department of Foreign Affairs, a special service dedicated to the placement of nationals.[161] Consequently, they have always tried to influence decisions pertaining to the selection, appointment, promotion, and separation from service of international civil servants. There are two possible ways for member states to get involved in personnel matters: formal and informal. A formal involvement presupposes the existence of written rules and procedures requiring the IGO to seek and obtain the approval of its member nations before appointing,

160 On page 19 of the opinion of the Commission of Jurists of 29 November 1952 attached as Annex III to the Report of the Secretary-General of the United Nations to the United Nations General Assembly, UNGAOR, Sess. 7, Agenda Item 75, UN Doc. A/2364 (30 January 1953).

161 Valentina Mele, Simon Anderfuhren-Biget and Frédéric Varone, "Conflicts of Interest in International Organizations: Evidence from Two United Nations Humanitarian Agencies" (2016) 94:2 *Public Adm* 490; Meryll David, "Les stratégies d'influence des Etats membres sur le processus de recrutement des organisations internationales : le cas de la France" (2008) 2:126 *Rev Fr Adm Publique* 263.

promoting, or separating from service a staff member. An informal involvement refers to interference when no written rules or procedures allow a nation to participate or take part in the decision-making process, but it nevertheless attempts to do so by exerting political pressure on the chief administrative officer of the organisation. Both types of interference erode the independence of international secretariats and should not be tolerated.

3.1.1 Involvement Permitted under Written Rules or Procedures

In the United Nations System, the existing rules and regulations do not grant member states any decision-making power in appointing, promoting, and separating from service UN staff members. The General Assembly has entrusted the Secretary-General with the discretionary authority to appoint most staff at all levels.[162] The Secretary-General (or other UN officials acting on his behalf) has the ultimate authority to make the final selection based on objective factors, such as merit, geographical distribution, and gender balance. Nevertheless, a few senior appointments are governed by specific resolutions of the General Assembly. These include the appointment of the High Commissioner for Refugees, the Executive Director of the UN Environment Programme, the head of the Office of Internal Oversight Services, and a few other senior officials. The appointment of these officials may be subject to certain conditions, procedural requirements, or endorsements, including the General Assembly's approval.[163]

In the Eurocontrol Agency and NATO Support and Procurement Agency, the appointment of international civilian personnel to senior posts requires the endorsement of their governing bodies.[164] In another NATO agency, contract

---

162 *Human Resources Management*, GA Res 51/226, UNGAOR, 51st Sess, UN Doc A/RES/55/226 (1997) 1 at 8.

163 See *Assistance to Palestine refugees*, GA Res 302 (IV), UNGAOR, 4th Sess, UN Doc A/Res/302(IV) (1949) 23 for UNRWA; *Statute of the Office of the United Nations High Commissioner for Refugees*, GA Res 428 (V), UNGAOR, 5th Sess, UN Doc A/Res/428(V) (1950) 46 for UNHCR; *Establishment of the United Nations Conference on Trade and Development as an organ of the General Assembly*, GA Res 1995(XIX), UNGAOR,19th Sess, UN Doc A/Res/1995(XIX) (1964) 1 for UNCTAD; *Institutional and financial arrangements for international environmental cooperation*, GA Res 2997 (XXVII), UNGAOR, 27th Sess, UN Doc A/Res/2997(XXVII) (1972) 43 for UNEP; *High Commissioner for the promotion and protection of all human rights*, GA Res 48/141, UNGAOR, 48th Sess, UN Doc A/Res/48/141 (1993) 1 for OHCHR; *Review of the efficiency of the administrative and financial functioning of the United Nations*, GA Res 48/218B, UNGAOR, 48th Sess, UN Doc A/Res/48/218B (1994) 1 for OIOS; *Strengthening the mandate and status of the Commission on Human Settlements and the status, role and functions of the United Nations Centre for Human Settlements (Habitat)*, GA Res 56/206, UNGAOR, 56th Sess, UN Doc A/Res/56/206 (2002) 1 for UN Habitat.

164 See Article 30(d)(4) of the *Charter of the NATO Support and Procurement Organisation*, which provides that the Agency Supervisory Board (the organisation's governing body)

renewals of senior officials are subject to the governing body's approval.[165] Since consensus is required for any decision to be adopted in NATO entities, any member nation may singlehandedly block the proposal to appoint a selected candidate to a senior position or renew their contract. Although this happens rarely, selected candidates have been denied appointments because of such objections.

The Administrative Tribunal of the International Labour Organisation has already ruled that a policy which states that the appointment is subject to government endorsement or which requires a government's sponsorship is *ultra vires* because it is incompatible with the chief administrative officer's and staff members' obligation not to seek or receive instructions from any source external to the organisation. The held that the Director General of the International Atomic Energy Agency received instructions from an external source by allowing a member State to veto the appointment of a staff member. This also interferences with the paramount consideration of securing staff of the right calibre.[166]

3.1.2 Informal Interference

During the first decades of the UN's existence, some senior posts in its Secretariat were earmarked for certain nations, which is incompatible with Article 101.3 of the UN Charter. This provision provides that the paramount consideration in the employment of the staff is not their nationality but the necessity of securing the highest standards of efficiency, competence, and integrity.[167] Consequently, earmarking some positions for specific nations is at odds with this requirement. Hence, the General Assembly reiterated several times that "the principle that there should be no monopoly on senior posts by nationals of any State or group of States should be strictly observed and implemented."[168] Generally, no national of a member state should succeed

has the authority to approve the appointment of personnel of grade A5 and above. See also Statute of the EUROCONTROL Agency (Annex to the Eurocontrol International Convention relating to Cooperation for the Safety of Air Navigation, 523 U.N.T.S. 117), Article 13, paragraph 3, which provides "*appointments of Directors at Grade AD14 and AD 15 for a term of office of five years normally, renewable once, shall be subject to approval by the [Permanent] Commission*".

165 Human Resources Regulations of the NATO Communication and Information Organisation.

166 *Umar v. International Atomic Energy Agency*, Judgement 1733 (ILOAT).

167 Charter of the United Nations, art 101.3.

168 *Strengthening of the United Nations System*, GA Res 51/241, UNGAOR, 51st Sess, UN Doc A/Res/51/241 (1997) 1 at para 66 [*Strengthening of the United Nations System*]. See also

a national of that state on a senior post, and there should be no monopoly on senior posts by nationals of a state or group of states.[169] Nevertheless, historical analysis suggests that the nationals of some states are more likely to be appointed to certain senior posts. For instance, the Executive Director of UNICEF,[170] the Deputy High Commissioner for Refugees, and, since 1992, the Executive Director of the World Food Programme (WFP) have always been American nationals. The Under-Secretary-General in charge of the Office of Coordination for Humanitarian Affairs (OCHA) is frequently a British national, and the Under-Secretary-General for the Department of Peacekeeping Operations has been a French national since 1997.

In a report published in 2011, the Joint Inspection Unit of the United Nations noted that although the UN assured the Inspectors that no position was reserved for any member state, the information collected by the Inspectors showed that historically, certain positions are reserved for certain member states and that no Secretary-General has been immune to political pressure in this regard.[171]

By interfering in the selection process of a specific individual or on behalf of its nationals, states create, if not an expectation of reciprocation, then at least an appearance of such expectation. The impartiality and neutrality of officials parachuted by their nation into senior positions will likely be tainted throughout their tenure with the IGO. This affects the credibility of the secretariat and demoralises other staff members who make important career sacrifices by not seeking or receiving favours from their governments only to preserve their independence.

3.2 *Secondment*

The independence and neutrality of UN staff were often questioned in relation to the practice of some member states to second individuals from their national governments. During the Cold War, the only way for a national of the

---

Revitalization of the United Nations Secretariat, GA Res 46/232, UNGAOR, 46th Sess, UN Doc A/Res/46/232 (1992) 3 at para 3(e) [*Revitalizing of the UN Secretariat*].

169 Revitalization of the United Nations Secretariat, supra note 168 [Revitalizing of the UN Secretariat].

170 In his memoirs, Boutros Boutros-Ghali describes how the United States insisted that the Secretary-General of the UN appoint not just an American national but a specific individual to the post of UNICEF Executive Director. Boutros Boutros-Ghali, *Unvanquished* (London: I.B.Tauris, 1999) at 228.

171 M Deborah Wynes and Mohamed Mounir Zahran, "*Transparency in the selection and appointment of senior managers in the United Nations Secretariat*" Report by the Joint Inspections Unit, [2011] UN Doc. J/REP/2011/2, at para. 81.

USSR or an Eastern European country to work for the UN Secretariat was to be seconded to the UN by their government. The secondment arrangement between staff members from the Eastern Bloc and their governments compelled these members of personnel to return a large portion of their UN salary to their government. For obvious reasons, other member states of the UN frequently questioned the independence of these individuals until the matter was formally brought to the attention of the General Assembly. The Assembly decided that "[t]he practice of secondment of staff from government public service is consistent with Article 100 of the UN Charter."[172]

When seconded to the international organisation by their governments, staff members become the servants only of the IGO for the duration of their appointment, which means that seconded officials are supposed to owe no allegiance to their national governments. It is generally understood that staff members seconded by their government would embrace and act in accordance with the principles of neutrality expected of all staff members. Nevertheless, secondments are problematic because they allow member states to retain some control over the seconded staff. In particular, the member state has the discretion not to extend the secondment of its citizen and to recall the staff member. This occurred in the *Yakimetz* case. In 1977, Yakimetz, a national of the USSR, was offered a five-year fixed-term appointment, on secondment from the Soviet Government, as a Reviser in the Russian Languages Service. When Yakimetz found out that the Soviet government was contemplating replacing him with another individual, he claimed asylum in the United States, resigned from the Ministry of Foreign Affairs of the USSR and requested the Secretary-General to renew his appointment with the United Nations. Essentially, he attempted to change his employment status from "seconded staff member" to a regular staff member. The UN refused to renew Yakimetz's contract, and Yakimetz challenged the refusal before the UN Administrative Tribunal. The tribunal held that a staff member cannot unilaterally extract himself from a secondment, which is a tripartite agreement. Yakimetz presented an application for review of the Administrative Tribunal's judgment to the Committee on Applications for Review of Administrative Tribunal Judgments, in which he asked the Committee to request an advisory opinion of the International Court of Justice,[173] which it did. The International Court

172 *Human Resources Management*, GA Res 51/226, UNGAOR, 51st Sess, UN Doc A/RES/55/226 (1997) 1 at 8.

173 The Statute of the UN Administrative Tribunal contained a provision that allowed a UN member state, the Secretary-General, or the person in respect of whom the Administrative Tribunal has rendered a judgment to make a written application to a committee

of Justice upheld the administrative tribunal's judgment. It ruled that while the Secretary-General was not precluded from renewing the appointment of Yakimetz, despite the objection of the Soviet government, he did not have an obligation to do so. The Secretary-General was entitled to consider the wishes of a member state and the adverse consequences that the renewal of Yakimetz's contract could have on the UN.[174] The Administrative Tribunal of the ILO came to the same conclusion in the *Rosescu* case, where a Romanian national successfully challenged the IAEA's decision not to extend his contract based on instructions received from the Romanian government.[175] The ILOAT held that while the Director General of the IAEA could take into account the wishes of the Romanian government, he misused his authority by letting the interests of a member State prevail over those of the Agency without apparent reason.

These cases illustrate that member states can use secondment to retain control over and exert pressure on their nationals working in international organisations. As Dag Hammarskjöld had pointed out in a lecture delivered at Oxford University on 30 May 1960, "a national official, seconded by his government for a year or two with an international organisation, is evidently in a different position psychologically—and one might say, politically—from the permanent international civil servant who does not contemplate a subsequent career with his national government."[176] The fear of losing their employment exposes seconded staff members to improper interference by their country of nationality. For this reason, seconding staff from national governments has become rare in the United Nations. However, many other IGOs, including Interpol, NATO, and OSCE, continue employing seconded officials. In all three organisations mentioned above, a seconded staff member may be separated from service at the request of the seconding country, which is a significant impediment to their independence and neutrality.[177]

---

established for these purposes to request an advisory opinion of the International Court of Justice on the matter.

174 *Application for Review of Judgment No 333 of the United Nations Administrative Tribunal*, Advisory Opinion, [1987] ICJ Rep 18 [Review of Judgment No 333]. See also *Stepanenko v. Secretary-General of the United Nations*, Judgment 763 (United Nations Administrative Tribunal) (26 July 1996).

175 *Rosescu v. International Atomic Energy Agency*, Judgement No. 431 (ILOAT).

176 Dag Hammarskjöld, *The International Civil Servant in Law and in Fact: A Lecture Delivered to Congregation on 30 May 1961* (Uppsala: Dag Hammarskjöld Foundation, 2021) at 20.

177 NATO Civilian Staff Regulations, Art. 7.1 (vii); OSCE Staff Regulation 4.02(b); INTERPOL Staff Manual, Regulation 11.1(d).

Apart from secondments, retaining contractual links to national governments can also significantly hinder international civil servants' independence. As the former UN Under-Secretary-General for Political Affairs Jeffrey Feltman explains Under-Secretaries-General (USG) and Assistant-Secretaries-General (ASG) of the UN who rise from within the UN ranks (known as 'career appointees'), take the oath to UN impartiality quite seriously. "Others remain in varying levels of allegiance or sensitivity to their home governments, often because they expect to return to their government service after leaving the UN."[178] Feltman notes that a USG or ASG can serve the UN while on leave of absence from national service. Therefore, "the perception, if not always reality, is that one cannot be impartial on matters related to national polities if expected to return to national service after leaving the UN"; therefore, he recommends that those appointed at the USG or ASG level be required to resign from national government service. Feltman's rationale for limiting this requirement to USGs and ASGs as opposed to all international civil servants is unclear. After all, even most junior international civil servants must remain independent of their national government.

In summary, maintaining the independence of international secretariats requires states to respect the inviolability of the organisation's archives, premises, and assets. It requires them to shield IGOs against legal proceedings before their domestic courts even when alternative dispute resolutions have not been set up to deal with commercial or labour disputes. States should also fully exempt from taxes any transaction authorised by the organisation's constitutive document.

To preserve the independence of international civil servants, states have the incentive to respect the role of the chief administrative officer in deciding whether personal immunities (be it functional or diplomatic) apply and, if so, whether they should be waived. Unilateral determinations by states that privileges and immunities are inapplicable in certain situations defeat the purpose of having functional immunities. States should also stop requiring and granting *agréments* to international civil servants or declaring IGO officials *persona non grata* to prevent the selection and appointment of candidates they do not favour. States should also endeavour to exempt international civil servants from income taxes on emoluments received from international organisations.

178 Jeffrey Feltman, "Restoring (some) impartiality to UN senior appointments" (2020) *Cairo Rev Glob Aff.*

The impartiality and neutrality of international civil servants require them to sever all contractual links with their national apparatus and eliminate any substantial dependency on their government, including secondments from the national public service. Similarly, interference by member states in questions relating to personnel management, including selection, appointment, and separation from service, cannot be tolerated. Ideally, constitutive documents of international organisations or other treaty-level agreements should contain provisions prohibiting attempts to lobby in favour of or against specific candidates.

CHAPTER 4

Practices of International Organisations That Erode the Independence of International Secretariats and Their Staff

The previous chapter described practices of states and their governments that weaken the independence of international secretariats and international civil servants. This chapter focuses on practices of international organisations that erode the independence of their own secretariats and staff. The next chapter will cover acts and omissions of international civil servants that are detrimental to their own independence and that of international secretariats (Chapter V).

The first section of this chapter explores intergovernmental organisations' practices that erode their privileges and immunities. In contrast, the second section examines practices that weaken the privileges and immunities of international civil servants. The third and last section canvasses practices that undermine the neutrality and impartiality of international civil servants.

1 Acts and Omissions That Weaken Privileges and Immunities of IGOs

This section will examine privileges and immunities under two separate headings: (1) jurisdictional immunity and (2) fiscal privileges. Inviolability has been omitted because our extensive research revealed very few incidents where international organisations actively or significantly contributed to breaches of their inviolability. In most cases, international organisations were subjected to such violations and had to endure them simply because governmental actors of member states were in a position of power. For instance, in the early years of the Cold War, the US government was convinced that the UN Secretariat was sheltering American nationals who favoured communism.[1] Many Americans serving on the UN staff were called before Congressional committees to testify about their political views and allegations of espionage.[2] During this period, the UN Secretary-General Trygve Lie "permitted the FBI to enter the

1 Leon Gordenker, *The UN Secretary-General and Secretariat*, 2nd ed (New York: Routledge, 2010) at 30.

2 *Ibid.*

 | DOI:10.1163/9789004704596_006

UN premises, presumably shielded by a formal agreement with the United States from such intrusion, to question and sometimes interrogate members of the staff."[3] FBI agents were authorised to work in the United Nations building. They were obtaining information from the Department of Administrative and Financial Affairs, headed by an American national – Byron Price.[4] Brian Urquhart – an author and a long-serving senior official of the UN – criticised Trygve Lie for it, noting that his successor, Dag Hammarskjöld, promptly rectified this situation by cancelling that permission.[5] However, Trygve Lie may not have had a choice. He may have averted a more significant risk by consenting to the FBI's request to access UN premises and staff. The United States government likely made it impossible for Trygve Lie to deny FBI access to UN premises. The United States Congress was prepared to go to great lengths to ensure that US citizens belonging to communist or socialist parties did not secure employment in the UN. In fact, on 7 January 1953, Senator McCarran introduced into the United States Senate a bill which provided that any US citizen accepting an appointment with the United Nations, without first having his loyalty attested by the Attorney-General, was liable to imprisonment for five years or to a fine of $10,000.[6]

Many other types of breaches of the UN's inviolability can be found in the United Nations Juridical Yearbook; however, there is no evidence to suggest that international organisations have been wholly or even partially responsible for such transgressions.

1.1 *Acts and Omissions of IGOs That Undermine Their Jurisdictional Immunity*

As examined in Chapter 3, domestic courts of many states do not recognise the jurisdictional immunity of international organisations in three specific circumstances.

First, some treaties establishing international organisations or governing their legal status, privileges and immunities expressly limit their jurisdictional immunity.[7] Specifically, legal instruments may expressly deny jurisdictional

3 *Ibid.*

4 John Mathiason, *Invisible Governance: International Secretariats in Global Politics* (Bloomfield, CT: Kumarian Press, 2007) at 43.

5 Brian Urquhart, *Hammarskjöld* (New York: Harper and Row, 1972) at 58–62.

6 F Honig, "The International Civil Service: Basic Problems and Contemporary Difficulties" (1954) 30:2 *Int Aff* 175 at 176.

7 August Reinisch and Ulf Andreas Weber, "In the Shadow of Waite and Kennedy – The Jurisdictional Immunity of International Organizations, the Individual's Right of Access

immunity in relation to certain tort actions, such as car accidents, or specific acts, such as loans made by international development banks. International organisations have no control over this limitation of jurisdictional immunity because member states normally determine such restrictions before establishing the IGO. Therefore, this chapter will not address this scenario.

Second, domestic courts in many jurisdictions disregard the jurisdictional immunity of international organisations when such immunity is seen to breach an individual's right to access a court. In deciding when an IGO's jurisdictional immunity overrides an individual's right of access to a court, domestic courts consider, among other things, as a material factor whether there were reasonable alternative means to effectively protect the rights of the individual. The absence of internal dispute resolution mechanisms in an international organisation may lead national courts in some countries to disregard the IGO's jurisdictional immunity and entertain a dispute. Consequently, international organisations have an interest in ensuring that they have adequate internal dispute resolution mechanisms.

Third, some states refuse to recognise jurisdictional immunity to international organisations for *jure gestiones* acts.[8] In principle, international organisations do not have the authority to carry out activities not explicitly or implicitly permitted under their constitutive instruments. As implied by the ICJ, international organisations can perform only those activities that are required to fulfil their mandate.[9] There is an unwritten but refutable presumption that an activity performed by an international organisation is necessary to fulfil its mandate. This presumption is at risk when IGOs perform functions not part of their constitutional mandate. Activities not permitted by their constitutive documents are *ultra vires*[10] and expose them to the jurisdiction of national courts and tribunals. Therefore, it is paramount for international organisations not to engage in activities that are not necessary to fulfil their mandate.

Subsection 1.1.1 below will examine IGOs' failure to establish adequate dispute resolution mechanisms, whereas Subsection 1.1.2 will focus on activities

---

to the Courts and Administrative Tribunals as Alternative Means of Dispute Settlement" (2004) 1 *Int'l Org L Rev* 59 at 61.

8 Luca Pasquet, "Litigating the Immunities of International Organizations in Europe: The 'Alternative-Remedy' Approach and its 'Humanizing' Function" (2021) 36:2 *Utrecht J Int Eur Law* 192 at 193.

9 *Legality of the Threat or Use by a State of Nuclear Weapons*, Advisory Opinion, [1996] ICJ Rep 66 at para. 25.

10 August Reinisch, *The Privileges and Immunities of International Organizations in Domestic Courts* (Oxford: Oxford University Press, 2013) 9.

of IGOs not authorised by their constitutive instruments and not necessary for the fulfilment of their functions.

1.1.1 Failure to Establish Adequate Internal Dispute Resolution Mechanisms

An international organisation's ability to assert its privileges and immunities is closely intertwined with the existence of a suitable internal justice system capable of adequately addressing its needs and those of its staff.[11] The availability of alternative dispute settlement methods has been an essential consideration for national courts in deciding whether to grant jurisdictional immunity to international organisations.[12] Also, many instruments on privileges and immunities require international organisations to make adequate dispute resolution mechanisms available. For instance, Article VIII, Section 29(a) of the General Convention[13] and Article XXIV of the Ottawa Agreement[14] provide that the UN and NATO shall make provisions for appropriate modes of settlement of (a) disputes arising out of contracts or other disputes of a private law character to which the organisations are parties and (b) disputes involving officials of these organisations who by reason of their official position enjoy immunity, if immunity has not been waived.[15]

International organisations often fail in their duty to establish independent and functional mechanisms for adjudicating disputes. In most flagrant cases, they do not put in place any mechanism at all. In some instances, a mechanism may exist, but it is not independent.

It is not always apparent whether the failure to establish independent dispute resolution mechanisms is attributable to international organisations or their member states. In most cases, member states and international organisations are both responsible for such failures for different reasons. Although

11 Katherine Meighan and Gabriel Rodriguez-Rico, "To Join or Not to Join: A Comparative Analysis of Joining or Creating an International Administrative Tribunal" in Peter Quayle, ed., *The Role of International Administrative Law at International Organizations* (AIIB Yearbook of International Law, 2020) 119 at 120.

12 Reinisch, *supra* note 10 at 10.

13 Convention on Privileges and immunities of the United Nations, 13 February 1946, 1 U.N.T.S. 15.

14 Agreement on the status of the North Atlantic Treaty Organization, National Representatives and International Staff signed in Ottawa, 20 September 1951, 200 U.N.T.S. 3.

15 Convention on Privileges and immunities of the United Nations, 13 February 1946, 1 U.N.T.S. 15 and Agreement on the status of the North Atlantic Treaty Organization, National Representatives and International Staff signed in Ottawa, 20 September 1951, 200 U.N.T.S. 3.

member states approve and authorise the creation of dispute resolution mechanisms, they act on proposals made by IGOs. Normally, IGOs develop ideas and plans for setting up dispute resolution mechanisms. If IGOs do not set forth concrete and reasonable proposals, member states are not likely to take the initiative. Similarly, if IGOs propose costly internal justice systems, member states will be tempted to reject the idea. Consequently, IGOs need to develop and recommend dispute resolution mechanisms that are credible, independent, and cost-efficient.

1.1.1.1 *Failure to Establish Independent Dispute Resolution Mechanisms for Personnel*

An independent internal dispute resolution mechanism of an IGO first appeared in the League of Nations.[16] Initially, staff members of the League had a very precarious contractual status. They had fixed-term contracts and at the end of every seven-year-period there was "a sort of overhauling of the official's position, and if his work is not completely satisfactory, or it is decided to suppress the post, he may be dismissed or degraded without further ado."[17] The only legal redress that certain categories of staff had was an appeal directly to the League's Council.[18] In the International Labour Organisation, the situation was identical; the only recourse ILO staff had was to submit an appeal to ILO's governing body.

In 1925, the impracticality of this appellate procedure became abundantly clear when the Director of the Précis-Writing Department of the League – François Monod – claimed compensation from the League for dismissing him without cause by addressing an appeal to the League's Council.[19] As a political body, the League's Council was not equipped to adjudicate a legal dispute. Therefore, it decided to submit the case to a committee of three legal experts and declared in advance that it would adopt the conclusions of this body as its own decision.[20] The committee of three jurists released its decision the same year, awarding Monod 750 British pounds in

16 See Santiago Villalpando, "International Administrative Tribunals" in Jacob Katz Cogan, Ian Hurd and Ian Johnstone, eds, *The Oxford Handbook of International Organizations* (Oxford: Oxford University Press, 2016) at 1087.

17 Charles Howard-Ellis, *The Origin, Structure and Working of the League of Nations* (London: George Allen and Unwin, 1928) at 178.

18 Ivor LM Richardson, "The Legal Relation between an International Organization and Its Personnel" (1956) 2:2 *Wayne L Rev* 75 at 77.

19 "Second Meeting (Public and then Private)" (1925) 6:7 *League of Nations OJ* 853 at 858, item 1496.

20 *Ibid.*

damages.[21] This case highlighted the practical difficulties that may arise when a political organ composed of representatives from different countries, continents, and cultures is called upon to adjudicate a legal dispute between the organisation and its staff. Following the Monod case, another committee was formed to determine whether the League needed an internal judicial body competent to hear labour disputes. The committee issued a detailed report recommending the establishment of an internal administrative tribunal as an experiment. The tribunal would have jurisdiction over disputes between the League of Nations and its staff or the ILO and its staff.[22] The Assembly endorsed the recommendation and created the administrative tribunal of the League of Nations. During the 18 years of its operation, the League's administrative tribunal passed only 37 judgements.[23] Whilst the tribunal was not a very active judicial body, it paved the way for some 45 international administrative tribunals.[24] When the League was dissolved, the tribunal was transferred to the International Labour Organization and became the ILOAT.[25]

International organisations must offer their staff some form of legal recourse for challenging decisions that affect their terms of employment or conditions of service. The ILOAT ruled that international civil servants are "entitled to the safeguard of an impartial ruling by an international tribunal on any dispute with the employer".[26] The International Court of Justice noted in the *Effect of*

21 "Conclusions of the Committee for whose appointment provision was made in the Council resolution of June 8th, 1925, relating to a claim submitted by M Monod" (1925) 6:10 *League of Nations O J* 1409 at 1541, Annex 790. Monod was claiming 4,750 British pounds, which represented 475% of his annual salary of 1,000 British pounds.

22 "Report submitted to the Fourth Committee of the Assembly by the Sub-Committee on the Administrative Tribunal" (1927) *League of Nations O J, Special Supplement* 58 69, at 250.

23 Wolfgang Friedmann and Arghyrios A Fatouros, "The United Nations Administrative Tribunal" (1957) 11:1 *International Organization* 13 at 15. See also Bruno Michel de Vuyst, "The Use of Discretionary Authority by International Organizations in Their Relations with International Civil Servants" (1983) 12:Issues 2 & 3 *Denv J Int'l L & Pol'y* 237 at 256.

24 These include administrative tribunals, appeals boards, or arbitration tribunals of the following organizations: UN, ILO, NATO, WB, IMF, ADB, OAS, AfDB, EBRD, OPEC, CoE, BIS, EUMETSAT, IMO, OICA, ESM, Organisation Internationale de la Francophonie, OECD, OSCE, ESA, AU, Arab League, IDBG, Commonwealth Secretariat, PAHO, IADB, Caribbean Community, EU Satellite Centre, OCCAR, UNIDROIT, IDLO, Nordic Investment Bank, European Launcher Development Organization, European Space Research Organization, Mercosur, Black Sea Trade Development Bank, UNRWA, International Seabed Authority, ITLOS, IFAD, UPU, and GAVI.

25 Henry G Schermers and Niels Blokker, *International Institutional Law*, 6th ed (Leiden: Nijhoff, 2018) at 464.

26 *In re Rubio*, Judgment 1644 of 10 July 1997 (ILO Administrative Tribunal).

Awards advisory opinion that it would have been inconceivable for the UN to afford no judicial or arbitral remedy to its staff for the settlement of disputes which may arise between it and them. It added that establishing an internal tribunal to do justice between the organisation and the staff members was essential to ensure the efficient working of an organisation and to give effect to the paramount consideration of securing the highest standards of efficiency, competence and integrity.[27] The UN General Assembly also recognised that "a transparent, impartial, independent and effective system of administration of justice is a necessary condition for ensuring fair and just treatment of United Nations staff and"[28] and that such a system is "consistent with the relevant rules of international law and the principles of the rule of law and due process."[29] The Parliamentary Assembly of the Council of Europe also noted that "it would be unacceptable if the Council of Europe did not apply to its own staff the principles laid down in its Convention on Human Rights and the Social Charter" and therefore "it should be possible for individual staff members, the Staff Committee and the Trade Union(s) to make appeals".[30]

Well-advised international organisations usually have some form of independent dispute settlement mechanisms. The largest IGOs often have their own administrative tribunals. The UN Relief and Works for Palestine Refugees in the Near East, the International Labour Organisation, the Organization of American States, the League of Arab States, the African Union, the World Bank, the International Monetary Fund, the European Bank for Reconstruction and Development, the Asian Development Bank, the Inter-American Development Bank, the African Development Bank, the Council of Europe, the North Atlantic Treaty Organization, the Organisation for Security and Cooperation in Europe, the European Space Agency, the Caribbean Community, and the Commonwealth are among those organisations that have their own administrative tribunals.[31] A handful of IGOs have gone a step further and established two-tier dispute settlement systems that are equipped not only with

27 *Effect of awards of compensation made by the United Nations Administrative Tribunal*, Advisory Opinion, [1954] ICJ Rep 47 at 57 [Effect of Awards].

28 "Administration of justice at the United Nations", General Assembly resolution 61/261, UN Doc. A/Res/61/261 (4 April 2007).

29 "Administration of justice at the United Nations", General Assembly resolution 63/253, UN Doc. A/Res/63/253 (24 December 2008).

30 Recommendation 856 (1979) of the Parliamentary Assembly of the Council of Europe cited in Gerhard Ullrich, *The Law of the International Civil Service: Institutional Law and Practice in International Organisations* (Berlin: Duncker and Hublot, 2018) at 431.

31 These mechanisms are not always called administrative tribunals. Some have been designated as 'Arbitral Tribunal' (The Commonwealth) or 'Panel of Adjudicators' (OSCE).

tribunals of first instance but also appellate tribunals. For instance, the internal justice system of the United Nations consists of a UN Dispute Tribunal and a UN Appeals Tribunal.[32] The *Organisation Internationale de la Francophonie* is another organisation that has a two-tier system with an appellate tribunal. Nevertheless, such sophisticated systems are rather an exception.[33]

The majority of international organisations do not have their own administrative tribunals. While it may not be financially viable for tiny international organisations, such as the International Coffee Organisation with its 13 staff members,[34] the International Sugar Organization with its nine staff members,[35] or the International Tropical Timber Organization with its 30 staff members[36] to establish an administrative tribunal of their own, such organisations have at least two alternative solutions.

The first option is to recognise the jurisdiction of an existing international administrative tribunal that permits external organisations to recognise its jurisdiction and to submit disputes to it in exchange for a fee.[37] For instance, Article 2(10) of the Statute of the United Nations Appeals Tribunal allows specialised agencies of the United Nations to accept and submit to the terms of the jurisdiction of the Appeals Tribunal.[38] As the ordinary jurisdiction of the UN Appeals Tribunal is to hear and pass judgement on appeals against a judgement rendered by the UN Dispute Tribunal,[39] Article 2(10) of its Statute only requires specialised agencies to have impartial first instance processes so that the Appeals Tribunal does not become a trier of fact but instead remains an appellate court.

32 See the Statute of the United Nations Appeals Tribunal as adopted by the General Assembly in resolution 63/253 on 24 December 2008 and amended by resolutions 66/237, 69/203, 70/112, and 71/266.

33 https://www.francophonie.org/tribunal-dappel-88.

34 Annual Review 2019 of the International Coffee Organization at p. 27 available online: https://www.ico.org/documents/cy2019-20/annual-review-2018-19-e.pdf (accessed on 1 June 2022).

35 See International Sugar Organization's website: https://www.isosugar.org/aboutus/international-sugar-organization-team (accessed on 1 June 2022).

36 Organizational Chart of the ITTO Secretariat available online: https://www.itto.int/files/user/pdf/ITTO_Organizational_chart_web.pdf?1655976033 (accessed on 23 June 2022).

37 Meighan and Rodriguez-Rico, *supra* note 11 at 123 (The ILOAT, the United Nations Dispute Tribunal, the United Nations Appeals Tribunals, and the administrative tribunal of the Council of Europe adjudicate disputes that arise in many other IGOs).

38 General Assembly resolution 63/253, UN Doc. A/RES/ 63/253 (24 December 2008), amended by resolution 66/237 adopted on 24 December 2011, amended by resolution 69/203 adopted on 18 December 2014, amended by resolution 70/112 adopted on 14 December 2015 and amended by resolution 71/266 adopted on 23 December 2016.

39 Article 2 of the Statute of the United Nations Appeals Tribunal.

Similarly, Article II, paragraph 5 of the Statute of the ILOAT also allows an international organisation that meets certain criteria to recognise its jurisdiction and submit disputes to it.[40] As of July 2023, almost 60 organisations, some of which are as small as the International Organisation of Vine and Wine (OIV), the International Cocoa Organization (ICCO), and the International Bureau for Weights and Measures (BIPM) with 16, 20, and 72 staff members[41] respectively, have recognised the jurisdiction of the ILOAT.

The Administrative Tribunal of the Council of Europe has also been empowered to adjudicate "disputes between bodies attached to the Council of Europe and other international governmental organisations and their respective officials, should the appropriate authorities of such bodies or international governmental organisations so request".[42] The Central Commission for the Navigation of the Rhine, the Hague Conference on Private International Law and the Intergovernmental Organisation for International Carriage by Rail have signed an agreement with the Council of Europe recognising the jurisdiction of its Administrative Tribunal.[43]

Sometimes, international or regional courts may have jurisdiction to settle labour disputes between international organisations and their staff. For instance, the Court of Justice of the European Union adjudicates labour disputes between EU institutions and their staff.[44] The Court of Justice of the West African Economic and Monetary Union is competent to hear and adjudge disputes between the *Conseil de l'Entente* and its staff.[45] These courts are not administrative tribunals and do not specialise in labour law; they are courts of law with broad jurisdictions.

---

40 Statute of the Administrative Tribunal of the International Labour Organization, adopted by the International Labour Conference on 9 October 1946 and amended by the Conference on 29 June 1949, 17 June 1986, 19 June 1992, 16 June 1998, 11 June 2008, 7 June 2016, 17 June 2019, and 18 June 2021.

41 See IOVW's website www.oiv.int/js/lib/pdfjs/web/viewer.html?file=/ public/medias/7884/ organigramme-secr-tariat-oiv-2021-avril.pdf (accessed on 1 June 2022) and ICCO's and BIPM's LinkedIn accounts at: and https://www.linkedin.com/company/bipm/ and https://www.linkedin.com/company/international-cocoa-organization-icco/people/.

42 Article 15.1 of the Statute of the Administrative Tribunal of the Council of Europe (Appendix XI to the Staff Regulations). See also Resolution CM/Res(2014)4 adopted by the Committee of Ministers on 11 June 2014.

43 https://www.coe.int/en/web/tribunal.

44 Regulation No 31 (EEC), 11 (EAEC), laying down the Staff Regulations of Officials and the Conditions of Employment of Other Servants of the European Economic Community and the European Atomic Energy Community, O.J. 45, 14.6.1962, p. 1385, Article 91.

45 Article 113 of Conseil de l'Entente Staff Regulations of 2012.

In the past, the International Court of Justice also gave binding advisory opinions to UN agencies in employment disputes. The Statute of the ILOAT allowed some international organisations of the UN system to challenge a decision of the administrative tribunal before the International Court of Justice by requesting an advisory opinion.[46] This procedure was available to international organisations only; staff members of the same organisations did not have a similar or equivalent right. Essentially, this was a right of appeal granted only to the employer. In an advisory opinion issued in 2012, the ICJ criticised this mechanism as contrary to the principles of equality of access to justice and equality of arms.[47] Consequently, in June 2016, the ILOAT Statute was amended, and the possibility of seeking advisory opinions from the ICJ in labour disputes was removed.[48]

The Statute of the former UN Administrative Tribunal, which was abolished on 31 December 2009, also contained a provision that allowed a UN member state, the UN Secretary-General, or the person in respect of whom the UN Administrative Tribunal had rendered a judgment to make a written application to a committee[49] established to examine and decide on requests for authorisation to seek an advisory opinion of the International Court of Justice on a labour dispute. The ICJ had jurisdiction to review the judgment on the ground that the tribunal had exceeded or failed to exercise its jurisdiction, had erred on a question of law relating to the provisions of the *Charter of the United Nations*, or had committed a fundamental error in procedure, which has occasioned a failure of justice. In 1994, at the request of the General Assembly, the UN Secretary-General reviewed the procedure for recourse to

46 Statute of the International Labour Organization Administrative Tribunal, art XII, as amended by the International Labour Conference at its 105th Session in June 2016. Article XII of the Statute and article XII of its Annex – which enabled only the defendant organizations to challenge a decision of the ILO Administrative Tribunal before the International Court of Justice – was removed. The provisions had been criticised as being contrary to the principles of equality of access to justice and equality of arms (see *Judgment No. 2867 of the Administrative Tribunal of the International Labour Organization upon a Complaint Filed against the International Fund for Agricultural Development*, Advisory Opinion, [2012] ICJ Rep 10).

47 *Ibid.*

48 ILO resolution concerning the Statute of the Administrative Tribunal of the International Labour Organization (7 June 2016); see also *Initial review of the jurisdictional set-up of the United Nations common system*, Report of the Secretary-General, UN Doc. A/75/690 (15 January 2021) at para. 122.

49 The Committee on Applications for Review of Administrative Tribunal Judgements was composed of the representatives of UN Member States who had served on the General Committee of the most recent regular session of the General Assembly.

the International Court of Justice and concluded that it "has not proved to be a constructive and useful element of the appeal system available within the Secretariat".[50] Therefore, the General Assembly repealed the procedure from the statute in 1995.[51]

A second solution small international organisations can opt for is to set up their own *ad hoc* mechanisms with arbitrators on standby in case disputes arise. For instance, the European Stability Mechanism (ESM) and the Financial Stability Institute (BIS) set up an arbitral tribunal composed of five judges that is not in session unless convened.[52] The tribunal established by ESM has not yet convened because no ESM staff member has thus far submitted a grievance. Article 15 of Staff Regulations of the Energy Community[53] provides that disputes between the Secretariat of the Energy Community and its staff shall be settled by a tribunal composed of a single arbitrator appointed by the Secretary-General of the Permanent Court of Arbitration.[54] Staff Rules of the International Anti-Corruption Institute provides that its "Appeals Tribunal shall consist of one active or retired professional judge" unless the dispute is complex or relates to summary dismissal, in which case "two more experts with relevant professional knowledge, at least one of whom is of the legal profession, shall be members of the Appeals Tribunal".[55]

Establishing ad hoc arbitration tribunals allows small IGOs to argue credibly that they offer their staff members a reasonable alternative for resolving internal disputes, and, therefore, national courts must uphold their jurisdictional immunity.

---

50 See Review of the Procedure Provided for under Article 11 of the Statute of the Administrative Tribunal of the United Nations, Report of the Secretary-General, UN Doc. A/C.6/49/2 (17 October 1994) paras. 16–18, and 37.

51 Review of the procedure provided for under article 11 of the Statute of the Administrative Tribunal of the United Nations, General Assembly resolution 50/54, UN Doc. A/RES/50/54 (11 December 1995).

52 See the websites of these two IGOs at https://www.esm.europa.eu/how-we-work/composition-tribunal and https://www.bis.org/about/at_bis.htm?m=2517 (accessed on 2 June 2022).

53 The Energy Community is an intergovernmental organisation founded in 2005 in Athens that creates a pan-European energy market. The primary objective of this organisation is to extend the EU internal energy market rules and principles to countries in South-East Europe, the Black Sea region and beyond on the basis of a legally binding framework.

54 Energy Community Staff Regulations as adopted by the Ministerial Council on 18 December 2007.

55 Staff Rules of the International Anti-Corruption Institute (March 2018), Art. 20.2.

Many international organisations do not offer any dispute resolution mechanism to their staff. The Black Sea Economic Cooperation Organization,[56] the North-East Atlantic Fisheries Commission,[57] the Asian-African Legal Consultative Organization,[58] the Commission for the Conservation of Antarctic Marine Living Resources,[59] the Arctic Council[60] and many other small IGOs fall into this category. This approach poses a significant risk to the independence of their secretariats and staff. National courts may feel compelled to decide internal employment disputes simply because staff members have no alternative legal recourse.

Other IGOs rely solely on peer-review committees or hierarchical reviews where a panel composed of three or five different staff members convenes to examine the complaint or grievance and to provide a recommendation to the organisation's chief administrative officer. The United Nations Appeals Tribunal has already concluded that such mechanisms are not independent because the executive head of the organisation retains the authority to make the final decision:

> As we understand it, the Secretary-General of the IMO says (and the Staff Regulations and Rules specify) that the SAB is the neutral element in that first instance process. However, even if what was issued by the SAB was a "decision", it was nevertheless only advisory or recommendatory. It gave advice to the Secretary-General of the IMO, who cannot himself be regarded as a neutral part of the process. That is because he is both

56 The author obtained this information from an official of the Black Sea Economic Cooperation Organization (copy of the summary of the interview on file with the author).

57 The North-East Atlantic Fisheries Commission has a secretariat composed of six staff members. The only rule that governs employment dispute resolutions within the Commission provides that "Any questions arising from application of these Rules shall be resolved by the Secretary following consultation with the President of the Commission. Should there be any conflict between a staff member and the Secretary which cannot be resolved in this manner, it shall be resolved by the staff member and Secretary in question in direct consultation with the President of the Commission."

58 Administrative, Financial and Staff Regulations of the Asia-Africa Legal Consultative Organization available online at www.aalco.int/Administrative%20Financial%20and%20Staff%20Regulations.pdf (last accessed on 30 July 2022).

59 Staff Regulations of the Commission for the Conservation of Antarctic Marine Living Resources of 2019 available online at www.ccamlr.org/en/system/files/e-pt7_2.pdf (last accessed on 30 July 2022).

60 Terms of Reference and Staff Rules of the Secretariat of the Arctic Council available online at www.arctic-council.org/about/secretariat/.

the employer's representative and the original decision-maker appealed against by Ms. Spinardi.[61]

Therefore, while this type of legal recourse is better than no legal recourse at all, it is not sufficiently independent to shield IGOs from the intervention of national courts. As mentioned in Chapter 3, some national courts examine not only whether a dispute settlement mechanism exists but also whether the mechanism is reasonable and adequate.

A few international organisations prefer a solution which consists of referring grievances or appeals to the IGO's governing body or to a panel composed of representatives of member states. They reckon that if the final decision remains with the delegates of member states, the mechanism is sufficiently independent. For instance, Staff Rule 805 of the International Tropical Timber Organization provides that appeals against the Executive Director's decision may be referred to a five-member panel composed of the Chair and Vice-Chair of the Council and the Chairs of three of the Committees.[62] Similarly, Article 13 of the Staff Regulations of the South Pacific Fisheries Management Organization provides that certain categories of disputes must be referred to the chairperson of the organisation's governing body, who is empowered to adjudicate it in consultation with members of the governing body.[63] The League of Nations had retained a similar dispute resolution mechanism until 1925. However, the *Monod* case revealed that "the right of direct appeal by a career servant to the League Council [was] cumbersome and unsuccessful since that body was eminently political and not suited for judicial functions".[64] For this reason, the League's Council referred the Monod case to a committee of jurists and, at the same time, began exploring the feasibility of

61 *Spinardi v. Secretary-General of the International Maritime Organization*, 2019-UNAT-957 (United Nations Appeals Tribunal) at para. 26; *Dispert and Hoe v. Secretary-General of the International Maritime Organization*, 2019-UNAT-958 (United Nations Appeals Tribunal) at para. 19 and *Sheffer v. Secretary-General of the International Maritime Organization*, 2019-UNAT-949 (United Nations Appeals Tribunal) at para. 26. See also *Rolli v. World Meteorological Organization*, 2019-UNAT-952 (United Nations Appeals Tribunal) at para. 29; *Webster v. Secretary-General of the International Seabed Authority*, 2020-UNAT-983 (United Nations Appeals Tribunal) at para. 42.

62 Staff Regulations and Rules of the International Tropical Timber Organization, Third Edition, as revised in November 2018.

63 Staff Regulations of the Commission of the South Pacific Fisheries Management Organization, amended in February 2020, Regulation 13.2.

64 David J Padilla, "The Administrative Tribunal of the Organization of American States" (1981) 50:Issues 3–4 *Rev Jur UPR* 479.

establishing an administrative tribunal.[65] Moreover, dispute resolution mechanisms that consist of representatives of member states are not independent or impartial. It is worth recalling that independence refers to independence from member states and their governments. Referring internal labour disputes to national delegates defeats the purpose of having jurisdictional immunities from national courts.

Furthermore, even where staff members of certain international organisations have access to an independent dispute settlement system, some categories of personnel of the same organisations may not have access to it. For instance, consultants and individual contractors of the United Nations do not have standing before the UN Dispute Tribunal.[66] Therefore, their employment contract usually contains a clause for settling work-related disputes through international arbitration. The dispute resolution mechanism available to staff members of the Hague Conference on Private International Law is binding arbitration under the auspices of the Permanent Court of Arbitration.[67] Organisations that opt for this solution expose themselves to significant legal risk because arbitration proceedings are costly and onerous. To pursue any dispute or challenge routine administrative decisions, members of personnel are required to disburse extensive arbitration fees. Domestic courts may view the arbitration clause of these organisations as unconscionable, declare it invalid and entertain the dispute by lifting their jurisdictional immunity. The Supreme Court of Canada disregarded an arbitration clause in a contract between Uber and one of its drivers and ruled that Canadian courts had jurisdiction to hear the dispute. The Court concluded that arbitral proceedings are too costly, making the arbitration clause in the contract unconscionable.[68] In

65 Kenneth S Carlston, "International Administrative Law: A Venture in Legal Theory" (1959) 8:2 *J Pub L* 329 at 342.

66 *Megerditchian v. Secretary-General of the United Nations*, United Nations Dispute Tribunal, UNDT/2010/035, affirmed by the United. Nations Appeals Tribunal in 2010-UNAT-088; *Mialeshka v. Secretary-General of the United Nations*, UNDT/2011/055 (United Nations Dispute Tribunal); Sanchez *Calero v. Secretary-General of the United Nations*, UNDT/2015/074 (United Nations Dispute Tribunal). In a recommendation in paragraph 40 of the Report of the Advisory Committee on Administrative and Budgetary Questions (ACABQ) (UN Doc. A/76/499), endorsed by the General Assembly in paragraph 2 of its resolution (UN Doc. A/Res/76/242), the Secretary-General was requested to provide in his report further information, including on the financial implications, of expanding the mandate of the Office to include non-staff personnel.

67 Rishi Gulati and Thomas John, "Arbitrating Employment Disputes Involving International Organizations" in Peter Quayle, ed, *The Role of International Administrative Law at International Organizations* (Leiden: Brill, 2021). See also article 62.4 of Staff Rules of the Hague Conference on Private International Law (2021).

68 See, for instance, *Uber Technologies Inc v. Heller*, 2020 SCC 16 (Supreme Court of Canada).

Canadian contract law, unconscionability is a widely accepted equitable doctrine that allows courts to set aside unfair agreements resulting from unequal bargaining power. This doctrine protects vulnerable or unduly disadvantaged parties and provides relief from improvident contracts. Similar doctrines protecting weaker parties or mitigating the inequality of bargaining power exist in other jurisdictions under different names or designations. There is no reason to believe that the Supreme Court of Canada would have reached a different conclusion if the respondent had not been a multinational corporation (in this case, Uber) but instead an international organisation.

The privileges and immunities of international secretariats, and by extension their independence, are at risk when the IGO does not offer its staff a robust internal dispute resolution mechanism. In such cases, aggrieved staff members may submit internal labour disputes to national courts and argue that no alternative dispute resolution forum has been made available to them by the international organisation. National courts in many countries have espoused the Waite and Kennedy test of the European Court of Human Rights, regarding 'reasonable alternative means of redress' as a requirement for recognising jurisdictional immunity to international organisations.[69] If national courts of the relevant country subscribe to the view that one's right to a reasonable dispute resolution alternative trumps the jurisdictional immunity of international organisations, they will likely hear the case and interfere with the independent functioning of the IGO.

Moreover, the lack of an independent and credible dispute resolution mechanism also undermines the independence of international civil servants because there is always the possibility that the decisions of administrative officials regarding their subordinates can be arbitrary or based on extraneous reasons. "The mere existence of such a possibility tends to make the subordinate feel dependent on his superior's whims and thus divert[s] his attention from service to personal considerations."[70] Considering the number of alternative solutions IGOs can opt for, international organisations can have no excuse for not establishing adequate legal recourses.

---

69 August Reinisch, "Privileges and Immunities" in Jacob Katz Cogan, Ian Hurd and Ian Johnstone, eds, *Oxford Handbook of International Organisations* (Oxford: Oxford University Press, 2016) at 1064.

70 Friedmann and Fatouros, *supra* note 23 at 13.

1.1.1.2 *Failure to Establish Independent Dispute Resolution Mechanisms for Unsuccessful Bidders*

Public procurement is another area where international organisations often fail to set up adequate dispute resolution mechanisms. As public entities, intergovernmental organisations are normally required to purchase goods and services through competitive solicitation processes.[71] Typically, procurement processes begin with solicitations or requests for proposals. The public body seeking to procure goods or services publishes detailed specifications of goods or services sought and invites individuals, organisations, and other entities to compete for the contract by submitting their tenders within prescribed time limits. After the expiration of the deadline, all technically compliant proposals are compared and – based on pre-determined criteria – the contract is awarded to one of the bidders. When a contract is awarded to a specific bidder, the successful bidder's status changes from bidder to contractor. As a result, the bidder acquires not only the commercial benefits of the contract but also fundamental guarantees, including the right to institute arbitration proceedings in case the IGO breaches the terms of the contract. In contrast with contractors, unsuccessful bidders do not enjoy the same procedural rights because they do not become parties to a contract with the IGO. Legal recourses available to vendors during the competitive solicitation process vary from organisation to organisation, ranging from no provision of accountability mechanisms at all to review by national courts.[72] When present, mechanisms open to unsuccessful bidders can be classified into four models: informal appeals to the representatives of the member states within the organisations, hierarchical administrative appeals, administrative appeals to independent bodies, and judicial review by national courts.[73] In some organisations, a combination of remedies is available.

In the United Nations System, the UN, UNDP, UNOPS, UNHCR, UNICEF, UNIDO and UNRWA have established formal procurement challenge mechanisms consisting of a recourse to the administrative authority that took the decision or to a higher level one.[74] Of these organisations, the United Nations

71 See for instance Regulation 5.13 and Rule 105.14 of the United Nations Financial Regulations and Rules, UN Doc. ST/SGB/2013/4; Article 32.1(a) of the NATO Financial Regulations C-M(2015)0025; Article 10.1 of Procurement Contract Rules of the Organization of American States, Executive Order 00–01, Corr.1.

72 Elisabetta Morlino, *Procurement by International Organizations* (Cambridge University Press, 2019) at 332.

73 *Ibid.*

74 "Procurement reforms in the United Nations system", Joint Inspection Unit, UN Doc. JIU/NOTE/2011/1 at para. 195.

comes closest to establishing an independent mechanism. In 2009, it created an Award Review Board (ARB) – "an independent procurement challenge system established to review vendors' submissions to determine whether they were treated correctly and evaluated fairly".[75] The board is composed of external experts convened to examine complaints. They are remunerated only for work actually performed. Nevertheless, this Board makes recommendations to the Under-Secretary-General for Management, who then decides whether to accept the board's conclusions. The Under-Secretary-General for Management refused to follow the ARB's recommendation in the only case where it sided with the vendor.[76] This deprives the mechanism of its independence because the ultimate decision-maker is an official of the organisation. Many UN organisations lack any formal mechanism that could allow a vendor to challenge their procurement-related decisions.[77]

While the absence of an appeal mechanism appears to be the norm among international organisations, it is an anomaly in most domestic systems. In the European Union, *Council Directive 89/665/EEC, commonly known as the 'Remedies Directive',* requires all EU member states to ensure that decisions taken by contracting authorities may be challenged before and reviewed by independent bodies or courts of law.[78] The *Public Contracts Regulations* 2015 of the United Kingdom,[79] the *Canadian International Trade Tribunal Act*,[80] and the *Contract Disputes Act* of the United States,[81] also allow bidders to initiate proceedings before their national courts. Naturally, national courts expect bidders to be given access to some form of independent appeal mechanism for challenging procurement-related decisions. A bidder or vendor with no legal recourse may turn to national courts and request that the jurisdictional immunity of the organisation be lifted so that its grievance or complaint can be heard by an independent court. The mere possibility that national courts may be inclined to lift the jurisdictional immunity of an IGO to adjudicate a commercial dispute is a risk to its independence and is sufficient to justify the

75 "Procurement activities in the United Nations Secretariat", Report of the Advisory Committee on Administrative and Budgetary Questions, UN Doc. A/71/823 (2 March 2017) at para. 17.

76 *Ibid.*

77 "Procurement reforms in the United Nations system", *supra* note 74 at para. 195.

78 Council Directive 89/665/EEC of 21 December 1989 on the coordination of the laws, regulations and administrative provisions relating to the application of review procedures to the award of public supply and public works contracts.

79 Public Contracts Regulations, 2015 United Kingdom Statutory Instruments No. 102, Part 3.

80 Canadian International Trade Tribunal Act, RSC 1985, c 47 (4th Supp), Sect. 30.11 and 30.12.

81 Contract Disputes Act, 41 U.S. Code Chapter 71, paras. 7104 and 7107.

establishment of an independent arbitration board or tribunal. Hence, all well-advised intergovernmental organisations should establish independent dispute resolution mechanisms for unsuccessful bidders and potential suppliers.

NATO Support and Procurement Agency (NSPA) is establishing a dispute settlement system for bidders and suppliers, which could serve as a model for other international organisations. The dispute settlement mechanism provides a recourse to three categories of bidders and suppliers. The first category of bidders that have access to this mechanism are firms seeking to challenge the agency's decisions to award a contract to a competitor. The second category consists of bidders who allege that the advertised requirements are unduly restrictive and unfairly exclude them from the competitive solicitation process. The third category includes vendors that NSPA suspended or debarred from submitting proposals for fraudulent or corrupt activities. This new board is composed of external and independent experts. Unlike the Award Review Board of the United Nations, which makes recommendations only, NSPA's board makes legally binding decisions, acting like an arbitral tribunal. The executive head of the agency does not have the discretion to disregard or deviate from the board's decision.[82]

1.1.2 Activities Not Authorised by Constitutive Instrument

Unlike states, international organisations do not possess a general competence. They are governed by the 'principle of speciality', which means that "they are invested by the states which create them with powers, the limits of which are a function of the common interests whose promotion those states entrust to them."[83] The Permanent Court of International Justice explained this basic principle in the following terms:

> As the European Commission [of the Danube] is not a State, but an international institution with a special purpose, it only has the functions bestowed upon it by the Definitive Statute with a view to the fulfilment of that purpose, but it has power to exercise these functions to their full extent, in so far as the Statute does not impose restrictions upon it.[84]

Functions and powers vested in the organisation need not be explicitly listed or mentioned in its constitutive instruments. The PCIJ had already acknowledged

82 Terms of Reference of the Award Review and Debarment Board of NSPA.

83 *Legality of the Threat or Use by a State of Nuclear Weapons*, Advisory Opinion, *supra* note 9 at para 25.

84 *Jurisdiction of the European Commission of the Danube* (1927) PCIJ (Ser B) No 14 at 64.

in an earlier advisory opinion that an organisation had implicit powers to undertake acts necessary to fulfil its mandate.[85] In this specific case, the Court was asked to determine whether the International Labour Organization could prohibit night shifts in bakeries for employees and owners of bakeries. The PCIJ concluded that if the ILO could not prohibit night work by owners and employers, it would be prevented from accomplishing its mission to assure humane labour conditions and the protection of workers.

Chapter 2 established that an essential distinction between the jurisdictional immunity of states and that of international organisations relates to their scope. Most national courts interpret sovereign immunity (jurisdictional immunity of states) restrictively. While they recognise that foreign states enjoy immunity concerning juri imperii or sovereign acts, they refuse to grant jurisdictional immunity concerning commercial acts.[86] International organisations, conversely, tend to enjoy broader jurisdictional immunity in many but not all countries. Chapter 3 described the practice of national courts when interpreting and applying privileges and immunities of international organisations as erratic and inconsistent. In many countries, international organisations enjoy absolute jurisdictional immunity; in others, namely the United States, Canada, Brazil, Kenya, and Russia, they enjoy restrictive (or functional) immunity. In countries where national courts do not recognise to international organisations jurisdictional immunity in relation to acts that they regard as commercial, IGOs must be particularly careful not to engage in activities not authorised by their constitutive instruments. Acts that do not fall squarely within their mandate will likely be interpreted as commercial and subjected to judicial scrutiny by national courts. Therefore, international organisations must carry out activities that are expressly or impliedly part of their mandate.

Unfortunately, many international organisations engage in unrelated activities to their mandate and mission. For instance, the United Nations Office at Nairobi operates an enormous sports complex with tennis and squash courts, basketball and football pitches, and an open swimming pool accessible to UN staff and embassies. It also operates a fuel station for staff members of the UN System and personnel of embassies.[87] Both activities can generate third-party liability resulting from an injury or environmental damage. To evade

85 *Competence of the ILO to Regulate Incidentally the Personal Work of the Employer* (1926) PCIJ (Ser B) No 13 at 18.

86 Hazel Fox and Philippa Webb, *The Law of State Immunity*, 3d ed (Oxford: Oxford University Press, 2013) at 673–674.

87 https://www.unon.org/content/commercial-operations-unit See also https://dcs.unon.org/site-facilities-0.

such liability, the UN cannot rely on its jurisdictional immunity, particularly in Kenya, where the Court of Appeal at Nairobi has already ruled that the government of Kenya could not have possibly granted an international organisation absolute immunity from suits and legal process as this would have been contrary to international law.[88]

Similarly, at least one NATO agency used to operate a gas station between 1970 and 2022. If these activities had caused environmental harm or bodily injury, the agency could have been held liable by national courts because NATO does not provide alternative dispute resolution mechanisms to parties who sustain harm from such activities. Since there is no legal recourse for tort actions, national courts could disregard NATO's jurisdictional immunity and entertain the claims. This approach would be consistent with the *Waite and Kennedy* precedent of the European Court of Human Rights.[89] For this reason, in 2023, the NATO agency shut down and decommissioned its gas station.

1.2 *Acts and Omissions of IGOs That Undermine Their Fiscal Privileges*

As briefly covered in Chapter 2, the primary reason for exempting international organisations from taxes is not to minimise the cost of their operations but to ensure that individual member states do not interfere with the independent functioning of international organisations. If an intergovernmental organisation were subjected to the fiscal jurisdiction of its member states, the taxing authorities of those member states would have the means of exerting pressure and controlling, at least indirectly, the activities of the organisation. Consequently, any attempt by one of the member countries to tax an international organisation would allow such a country to exercise undue control over the organisation.[90] However, the corollary of this principle is that international organisations have a duty not to abuse their fiscal privileges. Whilst the host country cannot bolster its revenues by taxing the activities of international organisations, fiscal privileges enjoyed by international organisations should not become an unfair advantage used to compete with existing businesses. Therefore, international organisations must enjoy their fiscal privileges

88 *Tononoka Steels Limited v. Eastern and Southern Africa Trade and Development Bank*, [1999] KLR, Civil Appeal No. 255 of 1998 (8 May 1998).

89 *Waite v. Kennedy*, Application no 26083/94 (European Court of Human Rights, Grand Chamber).

90 Rutsel Silvestre Martha, "Exemptions from Taxes, Customs Duties, and Prohibitions on Imports and Exports" in August Reinisch, ed, *Convention on the Privileges and Immunities of the United Nations and Its Specialized Agencies* (Oxford: Oxford University Press, 2016) at 220.

sparingly and strictly adhere to their constitutive instruments and seat agreements. More specifically, they should not carry out economic activities not part of their mandate because such activities inevitably lead to an ambiguity that may negatively affect their privileges and immunities. If the economic activity undertaken by an international organisation is not 'official' or necessary to fulfil its mandate, it might be regarded as an economic or commercial activity and be taxed by the national authorities of the host nation. Taxing some activities will defeat the purpose of granting fiscal privileges to the international organisation even if most other activities remain tax-exempt. Indeed, once an IGO is subjected to the fiscal jurisdiction of the host nation, it is exposed to political interference, in which case exempting 'official' activities from taxes loses its primary objective. In such cases, the host nation might be tempted to tax all IGO activities not expressly authorised by its constitutive instrument.

The dispute that arose in 1982 between Germany and the European Molecular Biology Laboratory (EMBL) is a relevant illustration of such a scenario. EMBL is an intergovernmental organisation headquartered in Heidelberg, Germany. It was founded in 1974 to promote molecular biology research in Europe, train young scientists, and develop new technologies. On 10 March 1974, it concluded a Headquarters Agreement with Germany providing for privileges and immunities of the organisation.[91] Article 7 of the Headquarters Agreement provided for the exemption of EMBL from the payment of certain taxes with respect to its official activities. The relevant provisions of this agreement read as follows:

> 7.(1) Within the scope of its official activities, the Laboratory and its property and income shall be exempt from all direct taxes.
>
> 7.(2) When the Laboratory makes substantial purchases or uses substantial services, strictly necessary for the exercise of its official activities, in the price of which taxes or duties are included, appropriate measures shall be taken by the Federal Republic of Germany, whenever possible, to remit or reimburse the amount of such taxes or duties.

Article 9 of the same Agreement defined the phrase 'official activities' as activities that "include its administrative activities and those undertaken in pursuance of the purposes of the Laboratory as defined in the Laboratory Agreement."

91 Headquarters Agreement between the Federal Republic of Germany and the European Molecular Biology Laboratory of 10 March 1974.

EMBL operated a canteen and a guesthouse that generated revenues. German fiscal authorities required EMBL to pay taxes and duties on income generated from the operation of the canteen and guesthouse. EMBL argued that the canteen and the guesthouse were inseparably linked to its functions in that they catered for staff and visiting scientists. It also maintained that its interpretation of official activities was supported by state practice, asserting that there was a prohibition under international law upon host states gaining financial advantage by levying taxes from the presence of international organisations in their territories.

Germany, on the other hand, was of the view that 'official activities' were limited to functions of a scientific nature and did not extend to the supply of facilities such as a canteen and guesthouse because, notwithstanding the benefit to staff and guests of EMBL of such facilities, these did not come within the functions with which EMBL was charged under its constitutive agreements. According to the German position, the determining factor was whether the absence of a particular facility would prevent or impair the achievement of the goals of EMBL.

Following unsuccessful and protracted attempts to find an amicable solution to this issue through negotiations, the Director-General of EMBL informed the German government that, in accordance with Article 37(1) of the Headquarters Agreement, he intended to submit the questions relating to the interpretation of the Headquarters Agreement to an arbitration tribunal. The parties constituted the tribunal in January 1989 and agreed to submit their dispute to it.

The arbitration tribunal determined that the scope of official activities was to be determined by reference to the headquarters agreement between Germany and EMBL and the mandate of EMBL under its constitutive agreement.[92] It ruled that official activities were those undertaken to further the purposes of EMBL as defined in the agreement establishing the organisation. The tribunal held that activities of a specifically scientific nature, such as seminars, were official activities, as were the meals and accommodation placed at the disposal of the participants. However, where the supply of meals and accommodation was paid for, whether by staff or guests, this was not an official activity because the Establishing Agreement did not include the sale of goods and services as a function of EMBL, nor did EMBL have a function of making a profit. The tribunal held that although a canteen and guesthouse were useful, they were not strictly necessary. As a result of this finding, EMBL's

92 *European Molecular Biology Laboratory v. Federal Republic of Germany*, Award of 29 June 1990, 105 ILR 1.

activities became taxable under the German fiscal legislation, thereby eroding the organisation's fiscal privileges and independence from Germany.

This case exemplifies the importance of international organisations not undertaking activities unrelated to their mandate and mission and respecting the principle of specialty referred to in section 1.1.2 above.

2 Acts and Omissions of IGOs That Undermine Privileges and Immunities of International Civil Servants

Two types of omissions erode the privileges and immunities of international civil servants. The first category consists of a failure to assert the privileges and immunities of staff members when member states disregard or violate these privileges and immunities. The second category relates to omissions to take prompt and decisive action against staff members who commit misconduct or engage in behaviour that would normally trigger an individual's liability before a court of law.

2.1 *Failure to Assert Privileges and Immunities of Staff*

It is now well-recognised that international organisations owe a duty of care to their staff.[93] Many international organisations expressly recognise this duty in their staff regulations and rules, which require the chief administrative officer to ensure that the rights of staff members are protected.[94] Tribunals have also confirmed this duty. For instance, the International Court of Justice held in its advisory opinion on the *Reparation for Injuries* case that "in order that the agent may perform his duties satisfactorily, he must feel that this protection is assured to him by the Organization, and that he may count on it."[95] The organisation's protection ensures the independence of its agents.

---

93 Andrea de Guttry et al, eds, *The Duty of Care of International Organizations Towards Their Civilian Personnel: Legal Obligations and Implementation Challenges* (The Hague: T.M.C. Asser Press, 2018) at 36; Gerhard Ullrich, *The Law of the International Civil Service: Institutional Law and Practice in International Organisations* (Berlin: Duncker and Hublot, 2018) at 235–236.

94 See for instance Staff Regulations and Rules of the United Nations, UN Doc. ST/SGB/2018/1, Regulations 1.1(c) and 1.2(c); NATO Civilian Personnel Regulations, Articles 14.1 and 14.2; African Union Staff Regulations and Rules, AU Doc. Assembly/AU/4(XV), Regulation 3.2(a); OSCE Staff Regulations and Staff Rules (2018), OSCE Doc. SEC/3/03, Regulation 2.07.

95 *Reparation for injuries suffered in the services of the United Nations*, Advisory Opinion, [1949] ICJ Rep 174 at 183 [Reparation for Injuries].

In a 1964 judgment, the ILOAT reiterated that "it is the duty of the [International Labour Organization] to protect and assist its officials in the performance of their functions and in connection therewith".[96] The United Nations Dispute Tribunal pointed out in the *Bekele* case that procedures for asserting and protecting the privileges and immunities of staff members arrested and detained by local authorities are not in place merely to protect staff members and agents of the organisation. The organisation has an interest in ensuring that the authorities of a host country respect the rights, privileges, and immunities of its staff.[97]

Reference to the duty of care can also be found in the literature. Specifically, Crawford observed that functional protection "is closer to a duty on the part of the international organisation to protect its agents, which may even extend to a possible obligation of prevention if the agent finds himself in a difficult situation which has not yet resulted in actual injury."[98] Langrod believed that the protection assured by international organisations of international civil servants against pressures and manoeuvres of member states is a *sine qua non* condition of a truly impartial and independent secretariat.[99]

The cases below illustrate acts and omissions of intergovernmental organisations that erode and weaken the privileges and immunities of their staff. They relate to incidents where the organisation either surrendered its staff members to national law enforcement authorities or refused to intervene when national authorities were acting in clear breach of the privileges and immunities of international civil servants.

The *Mutiso*[100] case illustrates how international organisations can cause significant damage to the privileges and immunities of their staff. Mutiso worked as a driver for a UN political mission in Nairobi. He was suspected of participating in the mysterious disappearance of a UN vehicle from the United Nations compound. UN Security Services interrogated Mutiso but could not obtain any information corroborating their suspicion of his involvement. They then decided to hand him over to the Kenyan police for a more robust interrogation. The staff member was fingerprinted, held in custody, and subjected

96 *In re Jurado*, [1964] Judgment No. 70 (ILOAT) para. 11(3).

97 *Bekele v. Secretary-General of the United Nations*, UNDT/2010/175 (UN Dispute Tribunal) affirmed in 2012-UNAT-190 (UN Appeals Tribunal).

98 James Crawford, *State Responsibility: The General Part* (Cambridge: Cambridge University Press, 2013) at 594.

99 Georges Langrod, *La fonction publique internationale* (Leiden: Sythoff, 1963) at 191; see also Alain Plantey and François Loriot, *Fonction Publique Internationales*, 2d ed (Paris: CNRS Éditions, 2005) at 17.

100 *Mutiso v. Secretary-General of the United Nations*, UNDT/2015/059 (UN Dispute Tribunal).

to degrading interrogation techniques. Mutiso challenged the UN's internal investigation procedures and sought compensation from the UN Secretary-General for exposing him to undue hardship. The UN Dispute Tribunal chastised the organisation for putting the staff member in harm's way and failing to protect his fundamental rights. The tribunal referred the way the UN acted to the Secretary-General's attention and requested him to investigate the conduct of UN officials responsible for these actions.[101]

A staff member of UNESCO endured a similar treatment at the hands of French police in 1995. Mr. Awoyemi worked at UNESCO's headquarters in Paris. At 6:45 a.m., members of the drugs squad of the French police entered and searched Awoyemi's residence, questioned him and his wife, and then took the couple to the police headquarters, where they were detained and questioned for many hours. During the interrogation, Awoyemi learned that the French police had received a letter from the Director-General of UNESCO, in which it was alleged that someone sent to the staff member's supervisor anonymous threats.[102] For unknown reasons, suspicions fell on Awoyemi. When the staff member and his wife were finally released from custody, Awoyemi reported the incident to the organisation and sought its assistance in dealing with the French police. Having received no reply from UNESCO, the staff member pursued internal dispute resolution proceedings and eventually filed an appeal before the ILOAT. Based on the documentary evidence filed by both parties, the administrative tribunal concluded that it was impossible to determine whether the Director-General or another official of UNESCO may have expressed suspicions about who was to blame for the making of anonymous threats. Nevertheless, the tribunal held that the organisation was obligated to shield its staff from such violations.

IGOs may also breach their duty of care through negligence or recklessness. The International Criminal Court (ICC) was found to be reckless when it sent a group of ICC staff members on an official mission to Libya, where they were mistreated.[103] In June 2012, an Australian lawyer and a Lebanese interpreter took part in a mission to Libya which had been ordered by the ICC's Pre-Trial Chamber I in the context of proceedings concerning Muhammar Gaddafi's captured son Saif al-Islam against whom the ICC had issued an arrest warrant. The mission's primary objective was to ensure that the accused retained counsel of his choice to represent him in criminal proceedings. On 6 June 2012, shortly after meeting with the accused, the ICC officials were detained by local

101 *Ibid.*

102 *In re Awoyemi*, [1998] Judgement No. 1756 (ILOAT).

103 *A. v. ICC*, [2018] Judgment No. 4003 (ILOAT).

authorities and charged with various criminal offences relating to national security laws, including spying.[104] On 2 July 2012, following intense diplomatic efforts, the Libyan authorities released the staff members.[105] A post-incident review conducted by the Independent Oversight Mechanism revealed that the Registrar of the Court had failed in his duty to negotiate and reach an agreement with the Libyan authorities concerning the privileges and immunities of ICC personnel before authorising the mission. Based on these findings, one of the aggrieved staff members sought monetary compensation from the ICC. After several years of unsuccessful negotiations and attempts to settle the matter out of court, the ICC staff member filed an appeal before the ILOAT. The administrative tribunal found that the staff member's ordeal in Libya was a direct result of the ICC's failure to agree with the Libyan government on the privileges and immunities of its personnel.

In 2013, the United Nations Dispute Tribunal heard a dispute where a staff member of the United Nations was alleging that the UN jeopardised his safety and security while investigating allegations of misconduct implicating him.[106] The staff member was Palestinian with no citizenship or passport. The UN Office of Internal Oversight Services (OIOS) investigated the staff member's alleged involvement in an attempt to purchase a forged passport. As part of the investigation, OIOS wrote to dozens of countries asking them to ascertain that the staff member does not possess or travel with a forged passport. As a result of this communication, the staff member was periodically detained and interrogated by border officers of several countries when travelling on official business for the UN. Such negligent conduct by UN investigators is a wide-open invitation for member states to disregard the privileges and immunities of UN staff, including the inviolability of their official documents and devices. The UN Dispute Tribunal awarded monetary compensation to the staff member and requested the organisation to withdraw its prior communication to the border authorities of member states.

A more recent failure by an international organisation to ensure that the privileges and immunities of its staff are protected occurred during the financial crisis in Lebanon. In 2019, Lebanon's economy and financial institutions collapsed, causing a substantial liquidity shortage. Banks immediately froze

104 Mark Kersten, Tinker, "Tailor, Lawyer: ICC Staff Arrested in Libya", *Justice in Conflict* (12 June 2012) accessible online at: https://justiceinconflict.org/2012/06/10/tinker-tailor-lawyer-icc-staff-arrested-in-libya-for-spying/.

105 Hadeel Al Shalchi, "Libya frees detained ICC staff after apology", *Reuters* (2 July 2012) accessible online at: https://www.reuters.com/article/uk-libya-icc-idUKBRE8610K120120702.

106 *Lubbad v. Secretary-General of the United Nations*, UNDT/2013/132 (UN Dispute Tribunal).

accounts and imposed withdrawal limits. The Lebanese government recognised that UN staff members in the professional category were exempt from withdrawal restrictions; therefore, this category of staff was allowed to withdraw the entirety of their savings from Lebanese banks. However, UN staff members in the general service and related categories were treated as ordinary Lebanese citizens and were denied the right to transfer their savings to banks outside Lebanon.[107] Staff members in the general service category of the UN Economic and Social Commission for Western Asia (UN-ESCWA) headquartered in Beirut made several attempts to obtain assistance from the United Nations in representing their interests or in asserting their privileges and immunities under the host country agreement.[108] However, the Secretary-General informed his staff that the UN would not intervene on their behalf. Curiously, the legal basis for exempting staff members from the professional category applied equally to staff members in the general service category. Indeed, the host country agreement between the United Nations and Lebanon does not distinguish various categories of staff:

> *Article 12*: The officials of the Commission, regardless of their nationality, shall enjoy in Lebanon the following privileges, immunities and facilities: [...]
> (b) Immunity from personal detention and from seizure of their personal and official effects [...]
> (g) In regard to foreign exchange, including holding accounts in foreign currencies, enjoyment of the same facilities as are accorded to members of diplomatic missions accredited to the Government.[109]

In 2000, the government of Lebanon had already attempted to restrict the scope of this agreement to staff members in the professional and higher categories. It proposed amending the host country agreement with the United Nations to exclude nationals of Lebanon from the term 'official'. The United Nations rejected the proposal, recalling that the term 'official' includes "all

107 It is noteworthy that UN staff members do not need to have the citizenship of the host country to be employed in the general service category. In other word, a national of Syria could well be employed as a staff member in the general service category in Lebanon.

108 Interview with a serving staff member in the general service category of the UN-ESCWA held on 24 August 2022 (record of interview on file with the author).

109 Agreement concerning the Headquarters of the United Nations Economic and Social Commission for Western Asia, signed at Beirut on 27 August 1997, 1988 U.N.T.S. 339.

members of the staff of the United Nations, with the exception of those who are recruited locally and are assigned to hourly rates".[110] The UN Legal Counsel emphasised that "the definition allows for no distinction among staff members of the United Nations on the basis of nationality or residence, or according to whether they are internationally or locally recruited".[111] It is therefore incomprehensible that two decades later, the UN decided not to assert the privileges and immunities of its staff and to treat two different categories of personnel differently.

IGOs' failure to ensure that the privileges and immunities of their officials are respected undermines the independence of international civil servants. Knowing that they cannot rely on the protection of their employer, personnel of IGOs may feel compelled to please national authorities to avoid arrests, detentions, seizures of assets, and other forms of mistreatment. Furthermore, when despite IGOs' best efforts to prevent such violations, national authorities harass international civil servants, IGOs should treat such incidents as their highest priority. Concealing such problems from other states or the governing body is a strategic mistake. In addition to taking measures to address the problems bilaterally with the government of the recalcitrant state, IGOs should also report these incidents to their governing body thereby signalling that violations of this nature are international problems to be taken seriously by all member states. This approach may also result in other member states exerting pressure on the recalcitrant state to find a solution and avoid such actions in the future.

2.2 *Omissions to Take Prompt and Decisive Action against Staff Members Who Commit Misconduct*

An organisation's failure to take prompt and decisive action against international civil servants who commit misconduct may also adversely affect the independence of international secretariats and their staff in two different ways.

First, member states expect international civil servants to comply with local laws and international secretariats to be responsible stewards of funds entrusted to them to implement policy decisions. When international organisations fail to take appropriate actions to investigate and redress a situation which may involve misuse of funds, nations will naturally be tempted to scrutinise their decisions and internal functioning. Member states have already shown their readiness to intervene in the internal affairs of international

110 United Nations Office of Legal Affairs, "Meaning of 'officials' of Economic and Social Commission for Western Asia", *UN Juridical Yearbook* (New York: UN, 2000) 364, at 365.

111 *Ibid.*

organisations when serious incidents such as fraud, corruption, embezzlement, and other criminal conduct remain unaddressed. For instance, in 2018, a UNDP staff member alleged financial mismanagement, corruption, fraud and interference in internal audit processes in a UNDP-led project aimed at promoting energy efficiency in Russia.[112] He alleged that UNDP contracts were awarded to fake corporate entities belonging to family members and relatives of Russian officials. The whistle-blower became a victim of successive retaliatory actions affecting his contractual rights. He sought protection from the UNDP but obtained no assistance. Therefore, he felt compelled to turn to his country of nationality for assistance.[113] The donor countries became aware of the allegations and began insisting in writing that the UNPD Administrator investigate the allegations of embezzlement made by the staff member.[114] In November 2020, in response to UNDP's failure to investigate and correct the situation, the Netherlands decided to withhold some of its annual contributions to UNDP[115] while other countries continued to press for an objective investigation and concrete actions.

Second, international civil servants who become victims of abusive and inappropriate conduct expect protection from their employers. When they receive no protection or support from the organisation, they may feel compelled to seek the assistance of their national delegation or other governmental authorities, prompting interference from member states in the internal affairs of IGOs. The jurisprudence of international administrative tribunals is rife with cases where the IGOs neglected to take prompt action and allowed some senior officials to operate with immunity.[116] The ILOAT has already chastised several organisations for failing to investigate promptly after a formal

112 See *O'Brian v. Secretary-General of the United Nations*, UNDT/2021/166 (UN Dispute Tribunal).

113 Disclosure made by the Foreign Affairs and Trade of New Zealand under the Official Information Act of 1982 accessible online at: https://www.mfat.govt.nz/assets/OIA/OIA-2021-22/August/OIA-28160-UNDP-Governance-29-July-2022.pdf.

114 Letter dated 5 March 2020 from the governments of Australia, Austria, Belgium, Canada, Denmark, Finland, France, Japan, the Netherlands, New Zealand, Sweden and the United States of America addressed to Achim Steiner, Administrator of the United Nations Development Programme, See also Colum Lynch, "Aid Donors Blast UNDP for Resisting Appeals to Fight Corruption" *Foreign Policy* (7 December 2020).

115 Wendelmoet Boersema and Jeroen Tromellen, "Nederland bevriest VN-geld vanwege corruptie bij Russisch project" *Trouw* (28 January 2021).

116 See, for instance, *Dalgamouni v. Secretary-General of the United Nations*, UNDT/2016/094; *Wasserstrom v. Secretary-General of the United Nations*, UNDT/2012/092 and UNDT/2013/053.

complaint had been filed, holding that such failures constitute a breach of the IGO's duty of care toward the staff member:

> an accusation of harassment requires that an international organisation both investigate the matter thoroughly and accord full due process and protection to the person accused. Its duty to a person who makes a claim of harassment requires that the claim be investigated both promptly and thoroughly.[117]

The most disturbing example of this came to light in June 2022 when the BBC published an explosive article on sexual abuses in the United Nations.[118] One of the victims of sexual harassment interviewed by BBC worked during the relevant period as a senior advisor for UNAIDS. She recounts how she was sexually assaulted by the former deputy executive director of UNAIDS in the elevator of a hotel where the official event was taking place. The staff member launched a formal complaint of sexual harassment in 2015 and became a target of retaliation. The alleged harasser, on the other hand, retired comfortably from the UN in 2018 and was thanked for his 22 years of dedicated service. The victim received a final determination of her complaint only six years after launching it. The confusing letter issued by the human resources department stated that the UNAIDS accepted that she was sexually harassed over a protracted period but, regarding the allegation she was sexually assaulted in 2015, it concluded that "something traumatic happened to you consistent with your account of the situation", but the findings "did not meet the evidentiary standards".[119] The mere delay of six years to complete an investigation into one specific alleged incident is an egregious breach of the organisation's duty of care which may leave staff members with no other choice but to seek the assistance of their national authorities.

Another high-profile incident where an international organisation failed to take appropriate action and, in doing so, exposed itself to the scrutiny of member states was the *Kompass* case. Kompass – a Swedish national – worked during the relevant period as a Director of Field Operations in the Office of the High Commissioner for Human Rights. In 2014, he became aware that French

---

117 *C.E.S. v WHO*, [2007] Judgement No. 2642 (ILOAT) at para. 16, *H.F. v IAEA*, [2006] Judgement No. 2552 (ILOAT) at para. 8. See also *B. K.-M. v. WHO*, [2011] Judgement No. 2973 (ILOAT) and *K.E.G. v. WHO*, [2011] Judgement No. 2975 (ILOAT).

118 Sima Kotecha and Sarah Bell, "UN sexual abuse claims 'must be investigated'" *BBC News* (21 June 2022) accessible online: https://www.bbc.com/news/world-61826551.

119 *Ibid.*

peacekeeping troops were sexually exploiting children in the Central African Republic. He reported these allegations to the Deputy High Commissioner for Human Rights, but OHCHR took no action for several months. In the meantime, Kompass sought the intervention of France by disclosing the allegations to the Deputy Ambassador of France. Kompass was suspended by the UN for allegedly disclosing internal documents to a member state. The real reason for the suspension may have been that the then-High Commissioner for Human Rights was embarrassed that he had taken no action for months to prevent the abuse of children. Kompass challenged the suspension, and the UN Dispute Tribunal ordered his reinstatement.[120] He was subsequently cleared of any wrongdoing. As this was not the UN's first attempt to conceal incidents of sexual exploitation and abuse, its inadequate response led member states to question and scrutinise the organisation's internal processes for dealing with allegations of sexual exploitation and abuse. It is noteworthy that the first wave of allegations of sexual crimes, including rape, sexual assault, and sex trafficking, against UN personnel was widely reported in the media in the 1990s in Cambodia, former Yugoslavia, and Somalia.[121]

However, it is important to point out that incidents do not need to be high-profile or give rise to scandals to affect the independence of international civil servants adversely. Any problematic behaviour that is not handled promptly may grow into a conflict warranting the intervention of parties external to the organisation, namely member states. Bullying, abuse of authority, and retaliation are the most common types of issues that push staff members of IGOs to seek the assistance of their country of nationality. The *Dalgamouni* case[122] offers a familiar and recurrent pattern of conflict avoidance by international organisations. Ms. Dalgamouni – a UN staff member – began experiencing problems with her supervisor after she refused to comply with instructions that seemed unlawful. As a result of her disobedience, she was subjected to abusive conduct at the hands of her supervisor. Her manager deprived her of work, moved her desk and working station into an empty building far away from the staff member's team, revoked her login credentials and access to electronic platforms, etc. Dalgamouni filed a complaint for abuse of authority and sought assistance from various offices of the UN. The organisation ignored her

120 *Kompass v. Secretary-General of the United Nations*, Order No. 99 (GVA/2015) (UN Dispute Tribunal).

121 Ai Kihara-Hunt, "Addressing Sexual Exploitation and Abuse" (2017) 21:1–2 *J Int Peacekeeping* 62–82 at 63.

122 *Dalgamouni v. Secretary-General of the United Nations*, UNDT/2016/094 (UN Dispute Tribunal).

requests and allowed this situation to last for 17 months. The abuse stopped only after the Dispute Tribunal ordered the UN to pay the staff member a hefty compensation and called on the Secretary-General to investigate the organisation's failure to prevent the abusive conduct of the supervisor for such a long period.[123] In such circumstances, the staff member had every right to request support and protection from her country of nationality. The Secretary-General would have been hard-pressed to resist interference from national authorities when the escalation of the conflict and the psychological harm suffered by the staff member were attributable entirely to his failure to act.

In one case, the staff member sued the IGO and her supervisor before national courts when her employer failed to address her complaints of sexual harassment.[124] Ms. Rendall-Speranza worked as an investment officer in the IFC. From the inception of her employment with the IFC, Ms. Rendall-Speranza was sexually harassed by her supervisor, who worked as the Director of the Europe Department of the IFC. As soon as Ms. Rendall-Speranza complained about the behaviour of her supervisor, she was physically threatened and assaulted. The staff member filed suit against IFC and her supervisor in the Superior Court of the District of Columbia. IFC and the supervisor invoked their jurisdictional and functional immunities, but the Court rejected their argument because the plaintiff was alleging tortious acts that were not performed by her supervisor in his official capacity and, therefore, did not fall within his functions as an IFC staff member.

To prevent nations from getting involved in the organisation's internal management and personnel administration, chief administrative officers of IGOs should follow existing processes. First and foremost, allegations of wrongful behaviour must be investigated promptly and thoroughly. If the investigation reveals that a staff member committed misconduct, the organisation should institute disciplinary proceedings and impose proportionate disciplinary sanctions. If, on the other hand, the investigation reveals that the allegations of misconduct were unsubstantiated, the staff member accused of misconduct should be cleared, and the charges against them should be dropped. In both cases, the organisation will have complied with its duty to take prompt action by completing an investigation into allegations of misconduct. Only when the organisation fails to initiate an investigation or complete it within a reasonable delay does it breach its duty of care and expose itself to external interferences.

---

123 *Ibid.* at para. 104.

124 *Rendall-Speranza v. Nassim* (1996) 942 F. Supp. 621 and 932 F. Supp. 19 (D.D.C.).

3 Failure by IGOs to Ensure the Independence of Their Staff from Governments of Member States

The chief administrative officers of international organisations must ensure that the independence and neutrality of international civil servants are respected.[125] They must resist political pressure from member states when making decisions that affect the rights and obligations of their staff. International organisations may fail to protect their staff against improper interference from governments of member states in three different ways.

First, they may fail to resist interference from governments of member states in selecting, recruiting, and promoting personnel. In such cases, international civil servants may lose their independence by feeling indebted to the government of the state, which intervened on their behalf or in support of their candidacy. Robert Cialdini, an eminent behavioural psychologist and recognised authority on persuasion techniques, argues that no human society does not subscribe to the rule of reciprocation. All humans feel obligated to the future repayment of favours, gifts, invitations, and the like.[126] This is the main reason why staff rules and regulations of many international organisations prohibit staff members from accepting gifts, favours, and gratuities from governments of member states.[127]

Second, international organisations should not make decisions that affect their staff based on perceptions and performance appraisals of governments. Assessing the performance of staff members is a core managerial function reserved for the employer. Appraisals may have important and long-lasting consequences on staff members' career progression. Therefore, staff members should not feel that member states may influence the appraisal of their performance as this would expose them to political pressure from governments.

Third, intergovernmental institutions may also yield to pressure from member states by terminating the employment contracts of staff or by separating from service members of personnel who are, for one reason or another, objectionable to national governments. Occasionally, international organisations

125 See Regulation 1.1(c) of UN Staff Regulations; *Stepanenko v Secretary-General of the United Nations*, Judgment 763 of 26 July 1996 (United Nations Administrative Tribunal); *Gaskins v Secretary-General of the United Nations*, UNDT/2010/119 (United Nations Dispute Tribunal); *Diop v Secretary-General of the United Nations*, UNDT/2012/029 (United Nations Dispute Tribunal).

126 Robert B Cialdini, *Influence: The Psychology of Persuasion* (New York: Harper, 2007) at 17–18.

127 See for instance the Staff Regulations and Rules of the United Nations, UN Doc. ST/SGB/2018/1, Staff Regulation 1.2(j) which provides that "No staff member shall accept any honour, decoration, favour, gift or remuneration from any Government.".

refused to select candidates whose government opposed their appointment. If international civil servants do not feel shielded by their organisation against such interference, they will be tempted to act in the interests of their national administration even when their actions or omissions are at odds with the interests of the organisation or of other member states.

3.1 *Independence from Member States in Decisions Pertaining to Selection and Appointment of Personnel*

In 1920, the founding members of the League of Nations established a commission of experts to explore and propose methods of work, recruitment, promotion, efficiency, number, and salaries of the staff. The chair and rapporteur of this commission was France's permanent representative Georges Noblemaire. In December of the same year, the commission released its report with several recommendations. Today, the report is known primarily for establishing the Noblemaire principle – which requires UN entities to offer emoluments at least equivalent to the highest-paying public administration.[128] However, the Noblemaire report contains many other significant recommendations. One such recommendation relates to the selection of the League's officials.[129] The commission stated that the League should recruit and promote their personnel based on merit only, recognising that this would preserve the independence of international civil servants by eliminating political influence by member states as a consideration in selection decisions.

In many international organisations, especially in the United Nations, senior appointments are still subject to political interference. Initially, an agreement had been reached at the Preparatory Commission of the UN and approved by the first General Assembly that the Secretary-General would have as his most senior assistants – designated as Assistant Secretaries-General – eight officials representative of the different political and regional groupings who were regarded as political appointees rather than as career civil servants.[130] It was accepted that the major powers and regional groups would nominate these Assistant Secretaries-General and that they would be expected to present the

128 See *United Nations common system: report of the International Civil Service Commission*, General Assembly resolution 50/208, UN Doc. A/RES/50/208 (9 February 1996) at 2.

129 Report submitted by the Fourth Committee to the Assembly on the conclusions and proposals of the Commission of Experts appointed in accordance with the resolutions adopted by the Assembly of the League of Nations at its meeting of December 17th, 1920 (26 September 1921) at 7.

130 Arthur W Rovine, *The First Fifty Years: The Secretary-General in World Politics 1920–1970* (Leiden: Sijthoff, 1970) at 211–212.

views of their particular government or group in their consultation with the Secretary-General.[131] "That this arrangement involved a departure from the obligations of Article 100 prescribing the exclusively international character of their responsibilities was conveniently ignored"[132] until Hammarskjöld proposed a reorganisation of the upper echelon of the Secretariat in 1953 by replacing political appointees with administrative officials called Under-Secretaries-General who would undertake political responsibilities only at the direction of the Secretary-General.[133]

Nonetheless, despite Hammarskjöld's structural reforms of the UN Secretariat, some senior posts in the UN continued to be earmarked for certain nations even though, under the *UN Charter*, the paramount consideration in the employment of the staff is not their nationality but the necessity of securing the highest standards of efficiency, competence, and integrity.[134] To rectify this anomaly, the General Assembly passed in 1997 a resolution clarifying that "the principle that there should be no monopoly on senior posts by nationals of any state or group of states should be strictly observed and implemented."[135] This resolution probably did not achieve the desired outcome because several high-profile posts in the UN continued to be occupied by nationals of specific nations. In his memoirs, the former Secretary-General Boutros Boutros-Ghali describes how the American State Secretary tried to impose not just an American national but a specific individual for the Executive Director of UNICEF.[136] It is well known that the posts of Executive Directors of UNICEF and WFP are still reserved for nationals of the United States.

The UN is not the only IGO where nations want to retain some influence in selection and recruitment decisions. In many international organisations, the appointment of senior officials requires the endorsement of their governing bodies.[137] However, this approach has been criticised by international

131 Oscar Schachter, "The International Civil Servant: Neutrality and Responsibility" in Robert S Jordan, ed, *Dag Hammarsjold Revisited: UN Secretary-General as a Force in World Politics* (Durham: Carolina Academic Press, 1983) at 44.

132 *Ibid.*

133 Urquhart, *supra* note 5 at 72.

134 Charter of the United Nations, Art. 101.3.

135 "Strengthening of the United Nations System", GA Res 51/241, UNGAOR, 51st Sess, UN Doc A/RES/51/241 (1997) 1 at para 66 [Strengthening of the United Nations System]. See also "Revitalization of the United Nations Secretariat", GA Res 46/232, UNGAOR, 46th Sess, UN Doc A/RES/46/232 (1992) 3 at para 3(e) [Revitalizing of the UN Secretariat].

136 Boutros Boutros-Ghali, *Unvanquished* (London: I.B. Tauris, 1999) at 227–228.

137 See for instance Article 30(d)(4) of the *Charter of the NATO Support and Procurement Organisation*, which provides that the Agency Supervisory Board (the organisation's governing body) has the authority to approve the appointment of personnel of grade A5 and

administrative tribunals on more than one occasion. An old ILOAT case illustrates how nations may abuse their influence if they are allowed to participate in decisions relating to the selection and promotion of international civil servants. This dispute arose in 1968 between the ITU (which was then called the WTU) and one of its translators.[138] The organisation refused to appoint a member of its linguistic personnel to a permanent post because a committee composed of national representatives objected to his appointment as a permanent translator. One of the countries explained that the staff member had refused to present himself for military service in that country and had accordingly been deprived of his nationality. The organisation informed the staff member that in accordance with instructions from the multinational committee, ITU would not appoint him to the permanent post. The staff member filed a complaint before the ILOAT. The tribunal ruled that an administrative decision affecting the rights of an international civil servant based on an objection from one nation could not be reconciled with the fundamental principle of the independence of an international organisation of its member states.[139]

In a more recent case, the IAEA published a vacancy announcement making it mandatory for candidates to obtain the endorsement of their government.[140] An internal staff member and a national of Pakistan applied for the vacant position but could not secure his government's support. Hence, the agency rejected his candidacy, triggering an appeal. The staff member challenged the refusal to select him before the ILOAT and argued that his government's endorsement should not have been an eligibility requirement. The Administrative Tribunal of the International Labour Organisation agreed with this argument and ruled that a policy which requires appointment decisions to be subject to government endorsement or sponsorship is *ultra vires* because it is incompatible with the chief administrative officer's and staff members' obligation not to seek or receive instructions from any source external to the organisation:

> For the Director General to allow a member State a veto on the appointment of a staff member is to "receive instructions" from an external source and an interference with the paramount consideration of securing staff of the right calibre.[141]

---

above; Article 21 of the Regulations of the Secretariat of the Association of Caribbean States; Article 25 of Council of Europe Staff Regulations; Article 68.2 of the Treaty for the Establishment of the East African Community; Article 3.03 (a) of OSCE Staff Regulations.

138 *In re Chadsey*, [1968] Judgement No. 122 (ILOAT).

139 *Ibid.* at 3.

140 *In re Umar*, [1998] Judgement No. 1733 (ILOAT).

141 *Ibid.* at para. 16.

International organisations should ensure that their selection, recruitment, and promotion policies do not permit participation by or interference from member states. Recruitment and promotion decisions must be based on competitive selection processes, which entails the existence of carefully drafted policies that consider candidates' competencies, qualifications, and skills as opposed to the amount of political support they can muster. While the wishes and preferences of member states may, in some cases, be a relevant consideration, they cannot be decisive in the decision-making process. The independence of international civil servants can be guaranteed only if selection decisions are founded on factors that relate to objectively verifiable criteria.[142] Similarly, to prevent nations from exploiting statutory gaps, selection processes must have detailed procedural rules so that there can be no opportunity for a country to intervene at any stage of the process. Most importantly, however, international organisations should not promulgate internal rules governing the selection and recruitment of personnel, allowing nations to participate in decisions that affect the careers of international civil servants.

3.2 *Independence from Member States in Decisions Pertaining to Performance Appraisal*

Performance appraisals play an important role in decisions relating to personnel of international organisations.[143] Poor performance appraisals may justify IGOs not extending or terminating their staff's appointment. Unsatisfactory performance may also deprive staff members of some benefits and entitlements, including periodic salary increments or an award of a permanent contract.[144] Consequently, only supervisors or other authorised officials of international organisations should carry out performance appraisals of staff members.[145] If member states are allowed to take part in appraising the performance of staff, they will inevitably have the power to influence decisions that affect the contractual situation of staff members, thereby undermining their independence. Many disputes arose when governmental officials of member states indirectly appraised a staff member's performance.

For example, in 1981, the ILOAT set aside the decision to terminate the appointment of a Pan-American Health Organization (PAHO) staff member for her alleged political activities and poor judgment. The staff member's superiors had received oral protests from the governments of El Salvador, Guatemala,

---

142 Plantey and Loriot, *supra* note 99 at 107.

143 *Ibid.* at 306.

144 *Ibid.* at 310.

145 *In re Sternfield*, [1972] Judgement No. 197 (ILOAT).

and Nicaragua based on which PAHO terminated the appointment of the staff member. The ILOAT found that the organisation had to seek concrete information and tangible evidence on the nature of political activities in which the staff member was said to have engaged. The tribunal implicitly held that the independence of international organisations requires them to reach findings and conclusions on the conduct of their staff independently.[146]

One of the first cases heard by the UN Dispute Tribunal established in 2010 related to an administrative decision affecting a staff member's rights that was founded on comments received from officials of member states. The *Gaskins* case[147] concerned a staff member of the UNDP in charge of managing a training program for the Sudanese judiciary. In carrying out his activities, Gaskins made decisions that upset some Sudanese judges. The Sudanese judiciary sent a letter to UNDP complaining about Gaskins' performance and requesting his replacement by another official. Without seeking additional information, UNDP replaced Gaskins, triggering an appeal before the United Nations Dispute Tribunal. The tribunal held that it was inconsistent with the high standards set by the *Charter* of the United Nations and the UN Staff Regulations to remove a staff member from his position solely as a response to a complaint or ultimatum by national authorities.[148]

Similar facts gave rise to another dispute before the same tribunal.[149] Mr. Diop worked in the UN Office for Drugs and Crime (UNODC) in close collaboration with the Ministry of Justice of Mali. In 2012, UNODC received a written complaint in which the minister of justice of Mali expressed his dissatisfaction with Diop's performance without providing any specific facts. UNODC decided not to extend Diop's contract based on this complaint. The staff member contested the decision before the UN Dispute Tribunal and prevailed. The tribunal ruled that the Secretary-General should not yield to political pressures from member states when making personnel decisions. The performance of a UN staff member should be assessed by his superiors and not by the national authorities of member states. The tribunal held that UNODC's decision not to renew Diop's contract and to separate him from service contravened Article 100 of the *UN Charter*.

146 *In re Troncoso*, [1981] Judgement No. 448 (ILOAT) at para. 8(b).

147 *Gaskins v. Secretary-General of the United Nations*, UNDT/2010/119 (United Nations Dispute Tribunal).

148 *Ibid.*

149 *Diop v. Secretary-General of the United Nations*, UNDT/2012/029 (United Nations Dispute Tribunal).

Similarly, in 2014, the ILOAT criticised the IAEA's decision to transfer a staff member following complaints about his conduct from governmental officials of the Islamic Republic of Iran. The tribunal held that unless the organisation investigates the allegations and determines that they are substantiated, it cannot take adverse decisions affecting the terms and conditions of a staff member's employment. The tribunal explained that "transferring him from his work with the Islamic Republic of Iran could also be seen as responding to the pressure put on the IAEA by the Iranian authorities when the IAEA must be, and be seen as, independent."[150]

In 2016, the ILOAT annulled Food and Agriculture Organization's decision not to extend a staff member's contract for poor performance, ruling that it was not made by the FAO in accordance with its internal rules and was unduly influenced by an official in the Ministry of Agriculture of Saudi Arabia.[151]

Most international organisations have policies and procedures for appraising the performance of their staff. Issues arise mostly when international organisations implement these policies and carry out performance appraisals. To maintain the independence of their staff, international organisations should issue clear instructions to all supervisors that while governmental officials may share with them their perception of international civil servants with whom they interact, this perception cannot constitute the basis for administrative decisions affecting the rights and obligations of staff under their supervision.

3.3 *Independence from Member States in Decisions Pertaining to Separation from Service of Personnel*

This part will canvass cases where international organisations failed to resist interference from the government of member states based on political and ideological reasons.

The ability of international secretariats to resist political interference from member states when deciding to separate from service staff members was first put to the test in the 1950s. During this period, US Senator Eugene McCarthy led a series of investigations against suspected communists in the UN. Various UN entities were accused of giving jobs to disloyal US citizens. A federal grand jury was set up in New York to investigate the alleged subversive activities by US citizens working in the United Nations. Dozens of American citizens employed by the United Nations appeared before the grand jury. Some of these staff members chose to testify, while others invoked their privilege

150 *C.C. v. IAEA*, [2014] Judgement No. 3412 (ILOAT).
151 *A.E. v. FAO*, [2016] Judgement No. 3593 (ILOAT).

under the Fifth Amendment of the US Constitution.[152] The US government was displeased with American staff members who refused to testify before the grand jury and requested the then Secretary-General of the UN, Trygve Lie, and the executive heads of other UN entities to terminate their appointment. The Secretary-General of the UN yielded to the pressure and dismissed twenty staff members because they had refused to answer whether they were engaged in subversive activities against the United States government. The Secretary-General determined that such a refusal constituted a "fundamental breach of the obligations laid down in the Staff Regulations."[153] The Director-General of UNESCO also separated from service a few UNESCO staff members facing a similar dilemma.[154] An article published in the New York Times on 7 December 1952 noted that "to United Nations staff workers this means that for better or worse the concept of an international civil service totally free from the influence of any government has been dropped, if not formally, at least in practice."[155]

These staff members contested their separation from service before the former UN Administrative Tribunal and the ILO Administrative Tribunal.[156] Both Administrative Tribunals ruled in favour of staff members and awarded hefty

152 This part is largely based on page 211 of my book – Alexandre Tavadian, *United Nations Law, Politics, and Practice* (Toronto: Irwin Law, 2021).

153 *Gordon v. Secretary-General of the United Nations*, Judgment 29 of 21 August 1953 (United Nations Administrative Tribunal) at 121. See also Judgments Nos. 28 to 37, A/DEC/28 to A/DEC/37 of the United Nations Administrative Tribunal.

154 *In re Leff*, [1954] Judgements Nos. 15 and 18 (ILOAT); *In re Duberg*, [1955] Judgement No. 17 (ILOAT); *In re Wilcox*, [1954] Judgement No. 19 (ILOAT); *In re Bernstein*, [1955] Judgement No. 21 (ILOAT); *In re Froma*, [1955] Judgement No. 22 (ILOAT); *In re Pankey*, [1955] Judgement No. 23 (ILOAT); *In re Van Gelder*, [1955] Judgement No. 24 (ILOAT).

155 AM Rosenthal, "Morale of UN Staff Shaken by Attacks: Loyal 90% of Employees Suffer With 10% Dismissed" *New York Times* (7 December 1952) Section E, page 6.

156 *Wallach v. Secretary-General of the United Nations*, Judgment 28 of 21 August 1953 (United Nations Administrative Tribunal); *Gordon v. Secretary-General of the United Nations*, Judgment 29 of 21 August 1953 (United Nations Administrative Tribunal); *Svenchansky v. Secretary-General of the United Nations*, Judgment 30 of 21 August 1953 (United Nations Administrative Tribunal); *Harris v. Secretary-General of the United Nations*, Judgment 31 of 21 August 1953 (United Nations Administrative Tribunal); *Eldridge v. Secretary-General of the United Nations*, Judgment 32 of 21 August 1953 (United Nations Administrative Tribunal); *Glassman v. Secretary-General of the United Nations*, Judgment 33 of 21 August 1953 (United Nations Administrative Tribunal); *Older v. Secretary-General of the United Nations*, Judgment 34 of 21 August 1953 (United Nations Administrative Tribunal); *Bancroft v. Secretary-General of the United Nations*, Judgment 35 of 21 August 1953 (United Nations Administrative Tribunal); *Elveson v. Secretary-General of the United Nations*, Judgment 36 of 21 August 1953 (United Nations Administrative Tribunal); *Reed v. Secretary-General of the United Nations*, Judgment 37 of 21 August 1953 (United Nations Administrative

monetary compensation. The ILOAT ruled that an international organisation "must enjoy the full sovereignty of its authority and must not be to any extent subject to external influence emanating from any one of its state members".[157] The UN Administrative Tribunal reached a similar conclusion regarding staff members of the UN Secretariat.

Since the UN did not have sufficient funds to pay the damages awarded by the tribunal, the Secretary-General turned to member states for a supplementary appropriation to cover these unanticipated expenses. Some member states objected, arguing that they had no obligation to pay for unexpected expenses they neither authorised nor caused. The Secretary-General was in a difficult position. On the one hand, the UN Administrative Tribunal had ordered him to pay monetary compensation to staff members he had dismissed, and on the other hand, he had no available funds to comply with the judgment. This deadlock led the General Assembly to seek an advisory opinion from the International Court of Justice. The Court was asked whether the General Assembly could refuse to give effect to an award of compensation made by the UN Administrative Tribunal in favour of UN staff members whose contracts of service had been unlawfully terminated. The ICJ concluded that as the final judgment of the Administrative Tribunal had binding force on the United Nations, the General Assembly, as an organ of the United Nations, must likewise be bound by the judgment.[158] Consequently, member states were compelled to increase their contribution so that the Secretary-General could compensate the aggrieved individuals. This incident underscored the importance of not allowing nations to interfere with personnel administration.

Following this saga, "President Truman eventually created a structure for advising the Secretary-General before appointments were made of candidates holding views objectionable to the United States."[159]

Soon after the purge of suspected communists by the United States government, countries from the Eastern Bloc began cracking down on their nationals suspected of sympathising with Western values and ideology. The well-known *Ballo* affair may have been the first such case. Ballo was an eminent translator of French literature and worked as the First Secretary of Czechoslovakia's

Tribunal); *Glaser v. Secretary-General of the United Nations*, Judgment 38 of 21 August 1953 (United Nations Administrative Tribunal). See also ILOAT cases *supra* note 154.

157 *In re Leff*, [1954] Judgement No. 15 (ILOAT) at 5.

158 *Effect of awards of compensation made by the UN Administrative Tribunal*, Advisory Opinion, [1954] ICJ Rep 47.

159 Leon Gordenker, *The UN Secretary-General and Secretariat*, 2nd ed (New York: Routledge, 2010) at 30.

embassy in Paris.[160] He was also a strong supporter of the 'Prague Spring'. Ballo received a two-year appointment as a senior official of UNESCO in July 1968. In August 1968, the USSR, Poland, Hungary, and Bulgaria invaded Czechoslovakia to stop Alexander Dubček's liberalisation reforms. A new government came to power in April 1969 and began cracking down on dissidents, including Ballo. In 1970, despite a strong performance record, the Director-General of UNESCO reluctantly renewed the staff member's appointment for one year. In 1971, Ballo's performance was again appraised as excellent by several supervisors, but the Director-General refused to endorse what he called "the laudatory assessment" of Ballo's performance.[161] There was little doubt that the Director-General was acting under pressure from the government of Czechoslovakia.[162] Ballo challenged the refusal to renew his appointment before the ILOAT and prevailed.

The defunct UN Administrative Tribunal adjudicated a quasi-identical case relating to a national of former Czechoslovakia in the *Levcik* case.[163] Similar disputes regularly arose between UN entities and nationals of socialist states, including the USSR, Romania, the German Democratic Republic, and China.[164]

In 1978, a Romanian national sought a renewal of his employment contract with UNESCO. The Director of the Division of Personnel wrote to the Permanent Representative of Romania, informing him of the organisation's intention to extend the staff member's appointment for five years. The Romanian authorities expressed reservations and asked the organisation not to proceed with the renewal. The Director-General complied with this request, and the staff member was separated from service. The staff member appealed his non-renewal. The ILOAT ruled that the executive head of an organisation is always bound to safeguard its interests and, where necessary, give them priority over the interests of member states. One area in which the interests of the organisation and

160 David Ruzié, "Le non-renouvellement des contrats à durée déterminée et l'ingérence des États. A propos de l'Affaire Ballo" (1972) 18 *Annuaire français de droit international* 378 at 379.

161 *In re Ballo*, [1972] Judgement No. 191 (ILOAT).

162 Ruzié, *supra* note 160 at 279.

163 *Levcik v. Secretary-General of the United Nations*, Judgement No. 192 of the UNaT (11 October 1974).

164 *Application for Review of Judgment No 333 of the United Nations Administrative Tribunal*, Advisory Opinion, [1987] ICJ Rep 18 [Review of Judgment No 333]; *Stepanenko v. Secretary-General of the United Nations*, Judgement No 763 (1996). See also *In re Rosescu*, [1980] Judgement No. 431 (ILOAT); *In re Stulz*, [1993] Judgement No. 1232 (ILOAT); *Qiu v. Secretary-General of the United Nations*, Judgment 482 of 25 May 1990 (United Nations Administrative Tribunal).

those of a member state may conflict is staff recruitment. The tribunal held that the Director-General is entitled to consult member states where such conflicts arise. The government may object if the candidate is a governmental official of that member state. However, the Director-General should not bow unquestioningly to the wishes of the government he consults. The IGO will be right to accede where the government of a member state expresses sound reasons for its opposition. However, the IGO cannot forgo deciding for the sole purpose of satisfying a member state. The tribunal recognised that an international organisation has an interest in being on good terms with all member states, but that is no valid ground to comply with the wishes of every one of them. For this reason, the tribunal concluded that the organisation breached its duty to resist political interference by deferring to the will of the Romanian authorities, even though they gave no compelling reasons for their opposition.[165]

The former Administrative Tribunal of the United Nations also criticised the UN Secretariat for separating from service staff members to please the government of China. This case revolved around employing three Chinese nationals seconded to the UN. When the secondment of these staff members was about to expire, the UN offered them an extension of their appointment. Anticipating China's refusal, Mr. Qiu proposed resigning from the Chinese government to receive an appointment with the UN. Before accepting Qiu's proposal, the organisation sought the Chinese government's views. Displeased with Qiu's unauthorised initiative, Chinese authorities replied that no further extension should be offered to its nationals. The UN complied with China's wishes and refused to appoint the three staff members. In the meantime, Qiu had already resigned and no longer had any employment links with the government of China.

Consequently, when the UN decided not to extend his appointment, he found himself without a job. Qiu contested the Secretary-General's decision before the UN Administrative Tribunal. Although the tribunal acknowledged that the Secretary-General had the right to consult the governments of member states, such consultations cannot fetter his discretion. The tribunal pointed out that the Secretary-General's discussions with member states should not contravene the principles of independence and neutrality referred to in Article 100 of the *UN Charter*.[166] By complying with the wishes of the Chinese government, the Secretary-General failed to act independently. In other words, the purpose of the consultative process must be analogous to a reference check

165 *In re Rosescu*, [1980] Judgement No. 431 (ILOAT) at 4.

166 *Qiu v. Secretary-General of the United Nations*, Judgment 482 of 25 May 1990 (United Nations Administrative Tribunal).

rather than an endorsement by a member state of the Secretary-General's choice.

In 1993, the ILOAT awarded damages to a Soviet national in circumstances like those of the *Qiu* case. Mr. Reznikov worked as a translator for the World Health Organization. When his appointment was about to expire, the government of the USSR recommended replacing him with another translator, whose name it provided upon the expiry of Reznikov's appointment. WHO complied with the wishes of the Soviet government, which led to an appeal by Reznikov. The ILOAT held WHO liable because "the Director-General took himself to be bound by the attitude of the government of the Soviet Union. In doing so, he mistook the limits of his own discretion."[167] The tribunal reiterated that in exercising their discretion, chief administrative officers of international organisations must observe the general principles that govern the international civil service and safeguard the independence of the organisation and officials alike.

In one case, the UN Secretary-General resisted pressure from the government of Burundi to separate from service the Deputy Executive Secretary of the Economic Commission for Africa (ECA) – a national of Burundi.[168] On several occasions in 1981 and 1982, the government of Burundi asked the Secretary-General and the Executive Secretary of ECA not to extend Mr. Manirakiza's appointment on the ground that his government required his services. The Secretary-General replied that the staff member was serving under a fixed-term appointment which, in accordance with the UN Staff Rules, could be extended at the Secretary-General's discretion. He pointed out that since the Executive Secretary of ECA had requested an extension of the staff member's appointment, the contract had been extended. The Secretary-General observed in his reply to Burundi that the Applicant was free to resign and to accept new responsibilities with his government, but his appointment would not be terminated without his consent. At this point, the government of Burundi revealed the real reason behind its request. It stated that the staff member was the author of a document which was of a political nature and was directed against the government of Burundi. The Secretary-General examined this allegation and concluded that while the staff member lacked judgment, his paper was not published and did not constitute misconduct.

The obligation of chief administrative officers of IGOs to protect the independence of their staff from national governments is far-reaching. They must resist political pressure from member states and shield the organisation from

---

167 *In re Reznikov*, [1993] Judgement No. 1249 (ILOAT) at 5.

168 *Manirakiza v. Secretary-General of the United Nations*, Judgement No. 663 of 22 July 1994 (United Nations Administrative Tribunal).

attempts to interfere in the administration and management of personnel. Even when the government of a member state declares a UN staff member undesirable or *persona non grata* and requests their immediate removal from the territory of that state, the Secretary-General has an obligation to demand an explanation or reasons from the member state. If the evicting state refuses to provide an explanation or provides an inadequate explanation, the Secretary-General has a duty to ensure that the staff member's rights under his employment contract are not adversely affected. This may entail a duty to relocate the staff member to another duty station and assign to him duties until the end of his contract.[169]

In some extreme cases, international organisations may even have an obligation not to accept a staff member's resignation if they believe that the staff member was acting under duress. UNESCO faced this scenario in the 1980s with a staff member from the former German Democratic Republic. While visiting East Berlin on behalf of UNESCO, the staff member was put under arrest and forced to sign a statement that he had been taken to hospital because of a heart attack. The staff member subsequently managed to inform the Director-General of UNESCO that the contents of the statement were not true and that he was detained in his country of nationality against his will. He later twice informed the Director-General of his intention to resign, but the Director-General refused to accept the resignation because he already had serious reason to doubt its genuineness. In the meantime, a military tribunal tried the staff member in secret and sentenced him to three years' imprisonment. After serving his sentence and being released from prison, the staff member was not allowed to leave the country and could not report for duty. The Director-General of UNESCO then received another letter from the staff member applying for early retirement and instructing UNESCO to surrender his entire pension to the Ministry for Foreign Affairs of the Republic. After some reflection, the Director-General of UNESCO granted the application, realising that it was likely signed under duress. Soon after the staff member was released, he sued UNESCO for separating him from service and releasing his pension to a third party. The ILOAT held that as soon as the Director-General of UNESCO became aware that the staff member had acted under duress, he had the duty, according to the general principles that guarantee the independence of international civil servants, to grant relief by denying the request for early retirement.[170]

169 *Hassouna v. Secretary-General of the United Nations*, UNDT/2014/094 (United Nations Dispute Tribunal).

170 *In re Stulz*, [1993] Judgement No. 1232 (ILOAT) at para. 4.

International organisations occupy a prominent place in maintaining the independence of their secretariats and staff from member states. They have an interest in establishing independent dispute resolution mechanisms for their members of personnel and unsuccessful bidders in commercial matters. Both categories of stakeholders may seek the intervention of national courts if they do not have any legal recourse for exercising their rights.

International organisations should also avoid activities that do not fall within their mandate and mission. This is particularly important in countries where the restrictive theory of jurisdictional immunity prevails.

Intergovernmental institutions also play a crucial role in protecting the privileges and immunities of international civil servants. They have a duty to assert their staff's functional immunities and fiscal privileges as soon as they become aware of incidents where national authorities disregard or ignore them. Nevertheless, to oppose interference from member states, IGOs must demonstrate that they promptly and fairly addressed the unbecoming conduct of their staff. This may include reporting criminal conduct to national law enforcement authorities, conducting investigations into allegations of embezzlement, fraud and corruption and, where necessary, initiating and completing disciplinary proceedings. Tackling abusive and fraudulent conduct expeditiously and fairly ensures that victims of such conduct do not feel ignored by the IGO and do not seek protection or assistance from member states.

Finally, international organisations should promulgate personnel management policies that expressly prohibit member states' involvement in decisions relating to selection, promotion, performance appraisal, and separation from service of staff members. International civil servants who feel indebted to their national government for advancing their careers or those who fear their government might obstruct their career progression cannot be truly impartial and neutral.

CHAPTER 5

Practices of Staff Members That Erode Their Independence and the Independence of International Secretariats

Chapter 2 identified three actors who play an essential role in preserving the independence of international secretariats and international civil servants. These three actors are: member states, IGOs, and international civil servants. Chapter 3 explored practices of member states that erode the independence of international secretariats, while Chapter 4 examined practices of international organisations. This chapter will focus on the practices of international civil servants.

This chapter consists of two sections. The first section examines the question of "to whom do international civil servants owe the obligation to do something or to abstain from doing something?" The second section explores the contents of international civil servants' obligations.

1 To Whom Do International Civil Servants Owe Obligations?

What is the relevance of knowing to whom international civil servants owe an obligation to do something or to abstain from doing something? Chapters 3 and 4 answered the following questions: (a) Who has an obligation to do something or refrain from doing something? and (b) what this obligation consists of. However, neither chapter explained to whom states and international organisations owe the duty to do or to abstain from doing certain things.

The reason for covering this question in Chapter 5 is simple. The nexus between member states' obligations and the independence of international secretariats and civil servants can be easily understood. For instance, it is relatively easy to grasp how member states' obligation to recognise an IGO's jurisdictional immunity can preserve its international secretariat's independence. It is also easy to draw a link between the obligation of member states to respect the functional immunities of international civil servants and their independence.

The link between IGOs' obligations and the independence of their secretariats and staff members is also often clear. For example, it is obvious that an IGO's failure to establish internal dispute resolution mechanisms can jeopardise its

 | DOI:10.1163/9789004704596_007

jurisdictional immunity and independence from states by exposing it to the jurisdiction of national courts and tribunals. It is equally easy to understand that the obligation of IGOs to assert the privileges and immunities of international civil servants fosters their independence.

However, it is not always easy to discern a connection between the obligations of international civil servants and their independence or the independence of international secretariats. Therefore, to appreciate fully how the obligations of international civil servants may impact their independence and the independence of international secretariats, we first need to identify the party to whom the obligation is owed.

At first glance, the relationship between member states, IGOs, and international civil servants is triangular in that each actor owes some obligations towards the two others, as illustrated by the diagram below.

Indeed, a literal reading of Article 100 of the United Nations Charter seems to provide support for this interpretation:

> **Article 100**
>
> 1. In the performance of their duties the Secretary-General and the staff shall not seek or receive instructions from any government or from any other authority external to the Organization. They shall refrain from any action which might reflect on their position as international officials responsible only to the Organization.
> 2. Each Member of the United Nations undertakes to respect the exclusively international character of the responsibilities of the Secretary-General and the staff and not to seek to influence them in the discharge of their responsibilities.

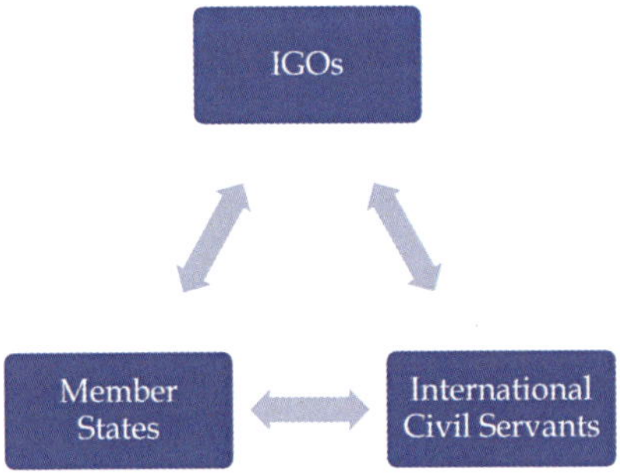

DIAGRAM 1 Triangular relationship between member states, IGOs, and international civil servants

Another element that may give the impression that international civil servants have certain obligations towards member states (and vice versa) is the nature of some obligations imposed on them. For instance, the obligation of international civil servants to comply with member states' local laws is, at first glance, owed to member states. One may view this as an obligation to be law-abiding citizens or residents and that it is owed to the country where the staff members perform their official functions. However, national legislations rarely – if ever – impose a general obligation on citizens and other residents to be law-abiding subjects. National laws usually prohibit certain acts and expect all residents present on the territory of that state, irrespective of their employment status, to comply. They do not distinguish between the conduct expected of the general population and that expected of international civil servants. From a state's viewpoint, there is no need to impose separate rules on international civil servants simply because prescriptive laws apply to all unless an explicit exception is carved out for certain categories of individuals.

The obligation to comply with local laws is often contained in staff rules and regulations promulgated by international organisations to regulate the conduct of their staff members. This obligation aims to avert undesired tensions between the IGO and its Host Nation, including the local community.[1] The IGOs have an interest in avoiding situations where they must choose between asserting or waiving the staff member's privileges and immunities, thereby putting the organisation in a delicate position vis-à-vis the host country. This obligation amplifies the rule, which provides that the privileges and immunities of the organisation afford no excuse to staff members for the non-performance of their private obligations.[2] It plays a crucial role in preserving the independence of international secretariats from the Host Nation. However, the link between this duty of international civil servants and the independence of international secretariats is not apparent.

The prohibition of engaging in political activities is another example of an obligation that international civil servants seemingly owe to member states. However, a closer look reveals that this obligation is not owed to states but to international organisations. Indeed, national laws do not normally prohibit international civil servants from engaging in political activities. This type of prohibition can often be found in international organisations' staff rules and regulations. The reason for this prohibition is twofold. First, the organisation has an interest in ensuring that its member states do not doubt the neutrality

1 Report on Standards of Conduct of the International Civil Service (1954) of the International Civil Service Advisory Board, UN Doc (Coord/Civil Service/5) paras. 53–54.

2 *Ibid.* at 55.

and impartiality of its staff. Second, the organisation is interested in ensuring that its staff's political activities do not irritate governments of member states and expose the organisation and its staff to political interference and harassment by national authorities.

Hence, a careful examination of the obligations of international civil servants leads to the conclusion that the relationship between the three actors (i.e., member states, IGOs, and international civil servants) is not triangular and is not necessarily direct. Undoubtedly, member states have direct obligations towards IGOs, and IGOs have direct obligations towards member states. It is equally indisputable that international civil servants have obligations towards their IGOs, and the IGOs have obligations towards their personnel. However, it is highly questionable that member states have direct obligations towards international civil servants, and international civil servants have direct obligations towards member states to preserve the independence of the international civil service. The relationship between these three actors appears linear as opposed to triangular; IGOs act as intermediaries between member states and international civil servants. This relationship is illustrated by the diagram below.

This second configuration, namely the absence of direct obligations between member states and international civil servants, is an essential component of independence. IGOs act as a buffer between member states and international civil servants. Any other arrangement could expose officials of IGOs to political pressures from governments of member states. Indeed, if, on the one hand, we assume that the relationship between a member state and international civil servants is governed by the administrative law of the concerned state, then any legal obligation would be enforceable before national courts. Under the administrative law of most democracies, legal obligations that individuals have towards a state and vice versa normally entail a corresponding right to demand compliance and the ability to enforce it. This would pose a significant risk to the independence of international officials since member states would have the power to exert pressure on international civil servants by threatening legal action for breaching their legal obligations. Correspondingly, international civil servants would be hard-pressed not to comply with the wishes of

DIAGRAM 2 Linear relationship between member states and IGOs, on the one hand, and between IGOs and International civil servants, on the other, with no direct relationship between member states and international civil servants

member states if they knew that governments of member states could enforce legal obligations directly against them through national courts.[3]

If, on the other hand, we assume that the relationship between a member state and international civil servants is governed by public international law, then there can be no direct rights and obligations between these two actors because, unlike states, individuals are neither primary nor secondary subjects of public international law. They constitute only the subject matter of intended legal regulation as such.[4] Individuals occasionally appear as legal persons on the international plane only in specific contexts.[5] Specifically, they are sometimes recognised as participants and subjects of international law in the fields of human rights law and investment protection.

Consequently, member states owe the duty to respect the functional immunities and fiscal privileges of international civil servants not to international civil servants (individuals) but to international organisations and other member states. This obligation is usually found in multilateral treaties between member states or the Seat Agreement (or Host Country Agreement) between the IGO and the host country. International civil servants are not party to such agreements and usually do not have standing before national courts to enforce a state's obligation to respect their privileges and immunities. The IGOs employing international civil servants are responsible for asserting their privileges and immunities and demanding compliance with the obligations of the concerned state.

It is also for this reason that conventions granting privileges and immunities to international civil servants often specify that the privileges and immunities enjoyed by international officials are conferred in the organisation's interests

---

3 *In re Leff,* [1955] Judgement No. 18 (ILOAT): "That it will suffice to realise that if any one of the seventy-two States and Governments involved in the defendant Organisation brought against an official, one of its citizens, an accusation of disloyalty and claimed to subject him to an enquiry in similar or analogous conditions, the attitude adopted by the Director-General would constitute a precedent obliging him to lend his assistance to such enquiry and, moreover, to invoke the same disciplinary or statutory consequences, the same withdrawal of confidence, on the basis of any opposal by the person concerned to the action of his national Government"; "That if this were to be the case there would result for all international officials, in matters touching on conscience, a state of uncertainty and insecurity prejudicial to the performance of their duties and liable to provoke disturbances in the international administration such as cannot be imagined to have been in the intention of those who drew up the Constitution of the defendant Organisation."

4 Malcolm N Shaw, *International Law,* 8th ed (Cambridge: Cambridge University Press, 2017) at 204.

5 Ian Brownlie, *Principles of Public International Law,* 7th ed (Oxford: Oxford University Press, 2008) at 65.

and not for the personal benefit of the individuals themselves'[6] International organisations not only have the authority to assert the privileges and immunities of their staff, but they can also waive them, particularly when the immunities can impede the course of justice.[7] Since officials of intergovernmental organisations rely on their employer to assert their privileges and immunities, they are obligated to report incidents involving the violation of these privileges and immunities to their employer.[8]

Now that we have identified to whom international civil servants owe the obligation to safeguard their independence, it is time to examine the nature of their obligations.

2 What Obligations Do International Civil Servants Have vis-à-vis Their IGOs?

In February 1946, the General Assembly called for the establishment by the Secretary-General of the UN of an International Civil Service Commission "to advise on the methods of recruitment for the Secretariat and on the means by which common standards of recruitment in the Secretariat and the specialised agencies may be ensured."[9] In 1948, the Administrative Committee on Coordination (present-day Chief Executives Board for Coordination or the 'CEB'), consisting of executive heads of UN System entities, established the International Civil Service Advisory Board (ICSAB) with terms of reference related mainly to questions of recruitment and personnel administration. The

6 See for instance Sec. 20 of the Convention on the Privileges and Immunities of the United Nations, 1 U.N.T.S. 15; Art. XXII of the Agreement on the status of the North Atlantic Treaty Organization, National Representatives and International Staff signed in Ottawa, 20 September 1951, 200 U.N.T.S. 3; Article 16 of the Supplementary Protocol No. 1 to the Convention for European Economic Co-operation on the Legal Capacity, Privileges and Immunities of the Organisation (OECD); Art. 17 of the Protocol (No. 7) on the Privileges and Immunities of the European Union O.J. C 326 (2012) 266–272.

7 See for instance Section 14 of the Convention on the Privileges and Immunities of the United Nations, 1 U.N.T.S. 15; Art. V of the Agreement on the status of the North Atlantic Treaty Organization, National Representatives and International Staff signed in Ottawa, 20 September 1951, 200 U.N.T.S. 3; Art. 17 of the Protocol (No. 7) on the Privileges and Immunities of the European Union O.J. C 326 (2012) 266–272.

8 See UN Administrative Instruction on "Reporting of Arrest or Detention of Staff Members, Other Agents of the United Nations and Members of their Families", UN Doc. ST/AI/299 (10 December 1982); Rule 2.03.2(b)(iii) of OSCE Staff Regulations and Rules, DOC.SEC/3/03 (2018); Article 23 para. 2 of Staff Regulations of Officials of the European Union.

9 *Organization of the Secretariat*, GA Res 13 (I), UN Doc A/RES/13(I) (1946) 14 at para. 6.

ICSAB was composed of nine experts[10] who "were 'who's who' of eminences from national public administrations."[11] In 1954, shortly after the commencement of the communist purge led by Senator McCarthy, the ICSAB issued Standards of Conduct expected of international civil servants.[12] This report was issued by an internal body but was not endorsed by an intergovernmental body. Therefore, it is not a legally binding document. Nevertheless, the report left its mark on international civil service law, becoming the first code of conduct for international public servants. It contained several broad principles that all staff members had to comply with.[13] These standards of conduct were ultimately transposed into prescriptive rules and incorporated into Staff Regulations and Rules of the UN as basic obligations applicable to all UN staff. They were also occasionally relied on by the UN and ILO administrative tribunals to adjudicate employment disputes. Although these standards of conduct were designed for the United Nations System, other international organisations drew inspiration from them and imposed similar duties and obligations on their members of personnel. The essence of these standards is that in addition to carrying out tasks assigned to them, international civil servants have "a duty to show such dignity of behaviour as not to harm the good name that the organisation must enjoy if it is to do its job properly."[14]

It would be impossible to list all the kinds of behaviour which are incompatible with the status of an international civil servant just like it would be futile to attempt to list the types of permissible conduct.[15] This is why it is important to identify and adopt standards of conduct. For this reason, the

10 For the exact composition of the ICSAB, see Fourth Report of the Administrative Committee on Co-ordination to the Economic and Social Council, UN Doc. E/1076, at 11, para. 32.

11 John Mathiason, *Invisible Governance: International Secretariats in Global Politics* (Bloomfield, CT: Kumarian Press, 2007) at 47.

12 See paragraph 52 of the Tenth Report of the Administrative Committee on Co-ordination to the Economic and Social Council, UN Doc. E/2161 and Corr.1: "Acting upon a proposal by the Director-General of ILO, [the Administrative Committee on Coordination] further agreed to request the ICSAB to study the question of standards of professional conduct in the international civil service. Without wishing to limit the scope of the Board's review, the Committee suggested that the review should include matters of conduct which had a bearing on the personal integrity, loyalty and professional reputation of officials, and the maintenance by them of high standards of courtesy, objectivity and disinterestedness."

13 Alexandre Tavadian, *United Nations Law, Politics, and Practice* (Toronto: Irwin Law, 2021) at 471–472 (footnote 152).

14 *In re Souilah*, [1997] Judgement No. 1584 (ILOAT) at para. 9.

15 Aghnides H E Thanassis, "Standards of Conduct of the International Civil Servant" (1953) 19:1 *Int Rev Adm Sci* 179 at 180.

ICSAB observed in its 1954 Report that the wide range of obligations owed by international civil servants to their employer fall into four broad categories. These are (a) obligations relating to integrity, (b) obligations relating to loyalty, (c) obligations relating to independence, and (d) obligations relating to impartiality and neutrality.[16] The ILOAT confirmed this view in Judgement 1061.[17] In deciding whether these four principles are still relevant, and if so, whether they have become universal, this work assessed their prevalence in legal texts of 35 randomly selected international organisations. Essentially, to test the hypothesis that integrity, loyalty, independence, and impartiality are universally recognised principles applicable to all international civil servants, I reviewed constitutive documents, staff regulations, codes of conduct, and other statutory documents of these 35 international organisations. This review revealed that all four principles are expressly recognised as such in all 35 institutions, thereby supporting the hypothesis that these four principles can be regarded as universal.

Although integrity, loyalty, independence, and impartiality appear universally recognised, they are nevertheless principles. Principles are standards that must be observed primarily because it is a requirement of justice or fairness or some other dimension of morality.[18] Principles are not rules; they underlie, explain, or provide reasons for rules. Where rules answer the question *what*, principles answer the question *why*.[19] Principles act as a guide in the process of interpreting rules. International organisations operationalise these principles by promulgating staff rules and regulations that contain detailed legal norms that either impose desirable conduct or prohibit undesirable conduct. International organisations have different approaches to implementing the principles. Some IGOs promulgate a few catch-all rules, such as "staff members shall conduct themselves in a manner befitting their status". This wording is so broad that it can encompass almost any type of wrongful conduct. Other international organisations issue more targeted and specific rules. The Staff Regulations and Rules of the United Nations provide a good illustration

16 Report on Standards of Conduct of the International Civil Service, *supra* note 1 at paras. 4–8.

17 *In re Dodi*, [1991] Judgement No. 1061 (ILOAT) at para. 5: "Integrity, loyalty to the international civil service, independence and impartiality are the standards required of an international civil servant".

18 Ronald Dworkin, *Taking Rights Seriously* (Cambridge: Harvard University Press, 1977) 25.

19 Gerald Fitzmaurice, "The General Principles of International Law considered from the Standpoint of the Rule of Law" (1957) 92 *Recueil des Cours de l'Académie de Droit International* 7.

TABLE 2 List of intergovernmental organisations where the principles of integrity, loyalty, impartiality, and independence are recognized

	Organisation
1.	United Nations (UN)[a]
2.	North Atlantic Treaty Organization (NATO)[b]
3.	European Union (EU)[c]
4.	Organisation for Economic Co-operation and Development (OECD)[d]
5.	Organization for Security and Cooperation in Europe (OSCE)[e]
6.	African Union (AU)[f]
7.	Arctic Council[g]
8.	Association of Caribbean States[h]
9.	Organization of the Black Sea Economic Cooperation[i]
10.	Central Commission for the Navigation of the Rhine[j]
11.	Commission for the Conservation of Antarctic Marine Living Resources[k]
12.	Commission for the Conservation of Southern Bluefin Tuna[l]
13	Conseil de l'Entente[m]
14.	Council of Europe[n]
15.	European Bank for Reconstruction and Development (EBRD)[o]
16.	INTERPOL[p]
17.	Organization of American States (OAS)[q]
18.	European Patent Office (EPO)[r]
19.	International Tropical Timber Organization[s]
20.	World Trade Organization (WTO)[t]
21.	International Criminal Court (ICC)[u]
22.	International Renewable Energy Agency (IRENA)[v]
23.	World Agroforestry[w]
24.	Islamic Organization for Food Security[x]
25.	Pacific Community[y]
26.	Hague Conference on Private International Law (HCCH)[z]
27.	Organization for the Prohibition of Chemical Weapons (OPCW)[aa]
28.	International Organization International Thermonuclear Experimental Reactor (ITER)[bb]
29.	Pan-American Health Organization (PAHO)[cc]
30.	International Agency for Research on Cancer (IARC)[dd]
31.	Nordic Development Fund (NDF)[ee]
32.	South Pacific Regional Fisheries Management Organization (SPRFMO)[ff]
33.	Inter-American Institute for Cooperation on Agriculture (IICA)[gg]
34.	Eurocontrol[hh]

TABLE 2 List of intergovernmental organisations where the principles of integrity, loyalty, impartiality, and independence are recognized (*cont.*)

Organisation
35. European Stability Mechanism (ESM)[ii]

a Charter of the United Nations and Staff Regulations and Rules of the United Nations, UN Doc. ST/SGB/2018/1/Rev.2.
b NATO Civilian Personnel Regulations and NATO Code of Conduct.
c Regulation No 31 (EEC), 11 (EAEC), laying down the Staff Regulations of Officials and the Conditions of Employment of Other Servants of the European Economic Community and the European Atomic Energy Community, Articles 11, 12, 17(a).
d OECD Staff Regulations, Rules, and Instructions of January 2023, Regulations 2 and 3.
e OSCE Staff Regulations and Staff Rules, DOC.SEC/3/03 (updated on 6 July 2018), Regulation 2.01(a) and Rule 3.07.1(b).
f African Union Staff Regulations and Rules, Assembly/AU/4(XV), (2010), Regulations 2.1(b), 3.3(b) and (h), Rule 4.1(b).
g Staff Rules of the Arctic Council Secretariat, Articles 2.2 and 2.4.
h Revised Staff Manual of the Secretariat of Caribbean States, Eighteenth Ordinary Meeting of the Council of Ministers, Agreement No. 6/13 (2013), Articles 1.1, 1.3, 1.5.
i Regulations for the Staff of the Permanent International Secretariat of the Organization of the Black Sea Economic Cooperation, Approved by the First Council of Ministers (Thessaloniki, 27 October 1999), Rule III, paragraphs 1, 3, and 6.
j Règlement du personnel du Secrétariat de la Commission Centrale (arrêté par la résolution CCR 1979-II-45 bis, modifié par les résolutions CCR 2012-I-23, CCR 2012-I-24, CCR 2014-II-26, CCR 2016-II-24, CCR 2018-I-21 et CCR 2021-II-27), Art. 3, 4, and 11.
k Staff Regulations, as adopted at CCAMLR-XXXI (2012), amended at CCAMLR-XXXVII (2018) and amended at CCAMLR-38 (2019), Regulations 1.2.3(a) and (d), 1.9.2.
l Staff Regulations adopted at the Reconvened First Annual Meeting on 11 September 1995 and amended at the Third Annual Meeting on 24 – 28 September 1996, Regulations 2.3, 2.5, and 6.2.
m Règlement portant statut du personnel du Secrétariat Exécutif du Conseil de l'Entente (5 September 2012), Art. 7 and 10.
n Staff Regulations and Staff Rules of 1 January 2023 of the Council of Europe, consolidated version of the Staff Regulations as they appear in Resolution CM/Res(2021)6-consolidated adopted by the Committee of Ministers on 22 September 2021 at the 1412th meeting of the Ministers' Deputies, and amended by Decision CM/Del/Dec(2022)1434/11.2, on 11 May 2022, at the 1434th meeting of the Ministers' Deputies and by Resolution CM/Res(2022)66, on 14 December 2022 at the 1452nd meeting of the Ministers' Deputies, and the Staff Rules, as adopted by the Secretary-General on 30 December 2022. This version is in force as from 1 January 2023. See also Code of Conduct of 1 January 2023.
o EBRD Staff Regulations, Sections 3(a), 4(a) and Code of Conduct for EBRD personnel.
p INTERPOL Staff Manual, II.C/SREG/GA/1987(2006)] [II.C/SRUL/EC/1988(2021), Regulation 1.3(3) and Rule 1.2.2.
q Staff Rules of the General Secretariat of the Organization of American States, Rules 101.6, 101.7, and 104.6.
r EPO Service Regulations for permanent and other employees (January 2023), Art. 14(a).

TABLE 2 List of intergovernmental organisations where the principles of integrity, loyalty, impartiality, and independence are recognized (*cont.*)

s ITTO Staff Regulations and Rules (third edition revised in November 2018) adopted by the International Tropical Timber Council through Decision 3(LII), Regulation 1.5 and Code of Ethics for ITTO Personnel, CFA(XXXVII)/8.
t WTO Staff Regulations and Rules WT/L/282 (21 October 1998), Regulations 1.1, 1.4, 1.5, and 1.12.
u ICC Staff Regulations, ICC-ASP/2/10 (September 2003), Regulation 1.2(e) and (f).
v Staff Rules for the International Renewable Energy Agency, A/2/11 (January 2012), Rules 102.1(a), 102(3)(c) and IRENA Code of Conduct, para. 7.
w Human Resources Policy Manual (revised in April 2018), Art. 1.13.2, and 1.9.
x Personnel Regulations of the Islamic Organization for Food Security, OIC/GA-IOFS/2016/PER.REG, Art. 3, 7, and 20.
y Staff Regulations of the Secretariat of the Pacific Community (2001), Regulations 3(a), 15(b).
z HCCH Staff Rules applicable to officials and personnel of the organisation (1 July 2021), Art. 3 and 4.
aa Staff Regulations and Interim Staff Rules, OPCW Director-General's Bulletin OPCW-S/DGB/26, dated 12 December 2017 and as amended by OPCW-S/DGB/28, dated 21 December 2018. Regulation 1.5, Rules 1.1.01 and 1.2.01.
bb ITER Organization Code of Conduct, version 2.2 (December 2018).
cc PAHO Staff Rules and Staff Regulations (July 2015), Art. 1.3, 1.5, 1.10, and 4.2.
dd Ethical Principles and Conduct of IARC staff (May 2017).
ee Code of Conduct for the Staff of the Nordic Development Fund, approved by the Board of Directors on 21 November 2017.
ff Staff Regulations of the Commission, amended in February 2020, Regulations 2.2, 3.8–3.10, 3.18, and 3.20.
gg Code of Ethics of IICA (2016), paras. A.1, B.2, C and C.1.
hh Staff Regulations governing officials of the EUROCONTROL Agency, edition of March 2021, Articles 16, 17, and 17(a).
ii Code of Conduct of the European Stability Mechanism (4 February 2021), Articles 4.1, 4.2, 4.3, and 4.4.

of relatively complete rules relating to desirable and prohibited conduct. Many of these rules can also be found in staff rules and regulations of other IGOs.

For instance, staff members have a duty to uphold and respect such principles as faith in fundamental human rights, dignity and worth of the human person and the equal rights of men and women. They must exhibit respect for all cultures and not harass, threaten, intimidate, or discriminate against any individual or group of individuals or otherwise abuse the power and authority vested in them.[20] Sexual exploitation and abuse are particularly serious forms of misconduct.[21]

20 Regulation 1.2(a) and Rules 1.2(f) & (g) of Staff Regulations and Rules of the United Nations, UN Doc. ST/SGB/2018/1/Rev.2; Article 12.1.4 of NATO Civilian Personnel Regulations; Rule 101.8 of Staff Rules of OAS General Secretariat.

21 Regulation 10.1(b) and Rule 1.2(e) of Staff Regulations and Rules of the United Nations, UN Doc. ST/SGB/2018/1/Rev.2.

Most international organisations require their staff to exhibit the highest standards of efficiency, competence, diligence, and integrity.[22] They must always conduct themselves in a manner befitting their status as international civil servants. They cannot engage in any activity that is incompatible with the proper discharge of their duties. In particular, they must avoid any action and any public pronouncement that may adversely reflect on their status or on the integrity, independence and impartiality that are required by that status.[23] Complying with local laws and honouring private obligations are a fundamental duty of all international civil servants.[24] It is prohibited for staff of IGOs to use their office or knowledge gained from their official functions for private gain or for the private gain of any third party, including family, friends and those they favour.[25] Intentionally misrepresenting their functions, official title or the nature of their duties is also a serious breach of their obligations.[26] Similarly, altering, destroying, falsifying, or rendering useless official documents is sanctionable conduct as well.[27]

International civil servants are not permitted to seek or accept instructions from any government or any other source external to the organisation in performing their duties.[28] The opposite is also true – they should not seek to influence member states or organs of international organisations, particularly

22 Regulation 1.2(b) of Staff Regulations and Rules of the United Nations, UN Doc. ST/SGB/2018/1/Rev.2; Article 27 of Staff Regulations of Officials of the European Union; Rule 104.6 of Staff Rules of the OAS General Secretariat; Regulation 2.1(3) of Interpol Staff Manual, II.C/SRUL/EC/1988(2021).

23 Regulation 1.2(f) of Staff Regulations and Rules of the United Nations, UN Doc. ST/SGB/2018/1/Rev.2; Regulation 2.01(a) of OSCE Staff Regulations and Staff Rules, DOC.SEC/3/03 (2018); Article 12 of Staff Regulations of Officials of the European Union; Article 13.2 of NATO Civilian Personnel Regulations; Regulations 1.3(1) and (3) of Interpol Staff Manual, II.C/SRUL/EC/1988(2021).

24 Rule 1.2(b) of Staff Regulations and Rules of the United Nations, UN Doc. ST/SGB/2018/1/Rev.2; Regulation 2.03(c) of OSCE Staff Regulations and Staff Rules, DOC.SEC/3/03 (2018); Rule 101.9(b) of Staff Rules of OAS General Secretariat.

25 Regulation 1.2(g) of Staff Regulations and Rules of the United Nations, UN Doc. ST/SGB/2018/1/Rev.2; Regulation 2.01(c) of OSCE Staff Regulations and Staff Rules, DOC.SEC/3/03 (2018); Regulation 1.3(6) of Interpol Staff Manual, II.C/SRUL/EC/1988(2021).

26 Rule 1.2(h) of Staff Regulations and Rules of the United Nations, UN Doc. ST/SGB/2018/1/Rev.2.

27 Rule 1.2(i) of Staff Regulations and Rules of the United Nations, UN Doc. ST/SGB/2018/1/Rev.2.

28 Regulation 1.2(d) of Staff Regulations and Rules of the United Nations, UN Doc. ST/SGB/2018/1/Rev.2; Regulation 2.01(b) of OSCE Staff Regulations and Staff Rules, DOC.SEC/3/03

to secure support for improving their personal situation or for blocking or reversing unfavourable decisions regarding their employment status.[29] Whilst staff members may exercise the right to vote, their participation in any political activity must be consistent with, and should not reflect adversely on, the independence and impartiality required by their status as international civil servants.[30] The staff of international secretariats are also expected to exercise the utmost discretion with regard to all matters of official business. They are not supposed to communicate to any external party any information known to them by reason of their official position that they know has not been made public.[31]

Staff members are not supposed to accept honours, decorations, favours, gifts or remuneration from a non-governmental source without first obtaining the approval of the organisation.[32] They are not authorised to offer or promise such gifts, favours, and remuneration to others with a view to causing them to perform, fail to perform, or delay the performance of official duties.[33] They must disclose conflicts of interest as soon as they become aware that their personal interests interfere with their official duties and responsibilities or may reflect poorly on their loyalty, integrity, independence and impartiality.[34] Outside occupations or employment are also frowned upon, particularly if

(2018); Article 11 para. 1 of Staff Regulations of Officials of the European Union; Regulation 1.2(2) of Interpol Staff Manual, II.C/SRUL/EC/1988(2021).

29 Rule 1.2(j) of Staff Regulations and Rules of the United Nations, UN Doc. ST/SGB/2018/1/Rev.2.

30 Regulation 1.2(h) of Staff Regulations and Rules of the United Nations, UN Doc. ST/SGB/2018/1/Rev.2; Rule 101.6 of Staff Rules of the OAS General Secretariat; Regulation 1.3(2) of Interpol Staff Manual, II.C/SRUL/EC/1988(2021).

31 Regulation 1.2(i) of Staff Regulations and Rules of the United Nations, UN Doc. ST/SGB/2018/1/Rev.2; Regulation 2.02 of OSCE Staff Regulations and Staff Rules, DOC.SEC/3/03 (2018); Article 17.1 of Staff Regulations of Officials of the European Union; Articles 12.1.5(a) and (b) of NATO Civilian Personnel Regulations; Regulation 1.4(1) of Interpol Staff Manual, II.C/SRUL/EC/1988(2021).

32 Regulation 1.2(j) and Rule 1.2(m) of Staff Regulations and Rules of the United Nations, UN Doc. ST/SGB/2018/1/Rev.2; Rule 2.01.1 of OSCE Staff Regulations and Staff Rules, DOC.SEC/3/03 (2018); Article 11 para. 2 of Staff Regulations of Officials of the European Union; Articles 12.2.3 and 12.2.4 of NATO Civilian Personnel Regulations; Regulation 1.3(5) of Interpol Staff Manual, II.C/SRUL/EC/1988(2021).

33 Rule 1.2(k) of Staff Regulations and Rules of the United Nations, UN Doc. ST/SGB/2018/1/Rev.2.

34 Regulation 1.2(m) and Rule 1.2(q) of Staff Regulations and Rules of the United Nations, UN Doc. ST/SGB/2018/1/Rev.2; Article 11(a) of Staff Regulations of Officials of the European Union; Regulation 1.3(3) of Interpol Staff Manual, II.C/SRUL/EC/1988(2021).

they conflict with the staff member's official functions or status of an international civil servant.[35]

The remainder of this chapter will attempt to define the principles of integrity, loyalty, independence, impartiality, and neutrality in separate sections. Under each principle, it will identify types of conduct that interfere with international civil servants' independence.

Staff rules and regulations governing the conduct of international civil servants do not usually specify which one of the four principles listed above certain obligations and prohibitions aim to uphold. The same wrongful conduct can transgress several principles at once. For instance, a staff member who steals the organisation's property breaches his obligation of loyalty and fails to meet the required standards of integrity. Similarly, a staff member who, without authorisation, discloses sensitive information to the government of his country not only exhibits disloyalty and dishonesty but also fails to act independently and impartially.

2.1 *Obligations Relating to Integrity*

The UN Charter makes integrity a fundamental, if not paramount, standard of conduct expected of UN staff.[36] This requirement is universal in that most international organisations impose this obligation on all members of their personnel.[37] Neither the UN Charter nor other legal instruments referring to this obligation provide an exhaustive definition of the word 'integrity'. Black's Law Dictionary defines the term 'integrity' as used in legal texts prescribing the qualifications of public officers as: "soundness or moral principle and character, as shown by one person dealing with others".[38] According to the UN Staff Regulations, "the concept of integrity includes [...] probity, impartiality, fairness, honesty and truthfulness in all matters affecting their work and status".[39] The International Civil Service Advisory Board noted in 1954 that while

---

35 Regulations 1.2(o) and (p) and Rules 1.2(s) and (t) of Staff Regulations and Rules of the United Nations, UN Doc. ST/SGB/2018/1/Rev.2; Article 12(b) of Staff Regulations of Officials of the European Union; Article 12.2.1(b) of NATO Civilian Personnel Regulations; Rule 101.4 of the Staff Rules of OAS General Secretariat; Regulation 1.3(4) of Interpol Staff Manual, II.C/SRUL/EC/1988(2021).

36 Article 101.3 of the United Nations Charter.

37 Alain Plantey and François Loriot, *Fonction Publique Internationales*, 2d ed (Paris: CNRS Éditions, 2005) at 88, at para 275.

38 Bryan A Garner, ed, *Black's Law Dictionary*, deluxe ninth ed (St Paul, MN: West, 2009).

39 Regulation 1.2(b) of Staff Regulations and Rules of the United Nations (2018), UN Doc. ST/SGB/2018/1/Rev.2.

perhaps not subject to exhaustive and precise definition, integrity must be judged on the basis of the total behaviour of the person concerned:

> Such elementary personal or private qualities as honesty, truthfulness, fidelity, probity and freedom from corrupting influences are clearly included. For the international official, however, the Charter also requires integrity as a public official, and especially as an international public official. Perhaps the clearest expression of this is the fact that he has dedicated himself to regulate his conduct with the interests of the international organization only in view. It follows that he must subordinate his private interests and avoid placing himself in a position where those interests would conflict with the interests of the organization he serves.[40]

Integrity is a broad concept applicable to various situations and scenarios.[41] It comprises a degree of selflessness or, to use the French term, '*désinéressement*'.[42] The most frequent instances where international civil servants fail to uphold the highest standards of integrity include:

- Failure to respect the dignity of others (including abuse of authority, harassment, sexual harassment, discrimination, as well as sexual exploitation and abuse);[43]
- Offences motivated by financial gains (including theft, fraud, corruption, embezzlement, misappropriation, falsification of claims, and acceptance of gifts and favours);[44]

---

40 Report on Standards of Conduct of the International Civil Service, *supra* note 1 at para. 4.

41 Gerhard Ullrich, *The Law of the International Civil Service: Institutional Law and Practice in International Organisations* (Berlin: Duncker and Hublot, 2018) at 411.

42 Plantey and Loriot, *supra* note 37 at 231.

43 See for instance *Clark & Gelbert v. Secretary-General of the United Nations*, UNDT/2013/091 (UN Dispute Tribunal); *Delaunay v. Registrar of the International Court of Justice*, 2019-UNAT-939 (UN Appeals Tribunal); *Adriantseheno v. Secretary-General of the United Nations*, 2021-UNAT-1146/Corr.1 (UN Appeals Tribunal); *Khan v. Secretary-General of the United Nations*, 2014-UNAT-486 (UN Appeals Tribunal); *Conteh v. Secretary-General of the United Nations*, 2021-UNAT 1171 (UN Appeals Tribunal); *J.M. v. NATO Communications and Information Agency*, NATO AT Judgment No. 2019–06 (8 April 2019); *H. v. ITU*, [2022] Judgement No. 4578 (ILOAT); *M. v. Global Fund*, [2022] Judgment No. 4579 (ILOAT).

44 See Information Circulars of the United Nations Secretariat, "Practice of the Secretary-General in disciplinary matters and cases of criminal behaviour" UN Docs. ST/IC/2017/33, ST/IC/2016/26, ST/IC/2015/22, ST/IC/2014/26, ST/IC/2013/29, ST/IC/2012/19. See also *In re Umar*, [2001] Judgement No. 2038 (ILOAT); *Fichtner v. Commission of the European Communities*, European Court Reports 2003 I-A-00007, Case T-75/00, ECLI:EU:T:2003:9; *Mariki v. Secretary-General of the United Nations*, UNDT/2014/138 (UN Dispute Tribunal); *Fernandez v. Inter-American Development Bank*, IDBAT Judgement No. 74 (29 July 2011);

- Conflicts of interest (including unauthorised outside activities or publications, personal relationships, personal financial and business interests);[45]
- Failure to honour private obligations (including the commission of criminal offences and failure to pay alimonies, child support, private loans, and rent).[46]

International organisations have collectively imposed thousands of disciplinary measures on their members of personnel. Hundreds of judgements issued by various international administrative tribunals deal with reviews of disciplinary proceedings and sanctions.[47] Although international civil servants are expected to meet standards of conduct much more exacting than ordinary legal standards,[48] it does not shock the public's conscience to see that, as all humans, international officials often make mistakes, some of which are sufficiently serious to lead to disciplinary measures. Consequently, most cases where international civil servants are disciplined do not attract much attention or go entirely unnoticed. It would, therefore, seem accurate to postulate that not all breaches of integrity necessarily affect the independence of international secretariats and that of international civil servants.

Nevertheless, instances where violations of standards by international officials make the headlines almost invariably have a destructive effect on the reputation and trustworthiness of international secretariats and international

J. v. Asian Development Bank, ADBAT Judgement No. 116 (2 October 2018); *M. v. Asian Development Bank*, ADBAT Judgement No. 119 (2 October 2018).

45 See *Vedel v. Secretary-General of the United Nations*, UNDT/2019/110 (UN Dispute Tribunal); *Kamara-Joyner v. Secretary-General of the United Nations*, UNDT/2022/089 (UN Dispute Tribunal) currently under appeal; *Akello v. Secretary-General of the United Nations*, 2013-UNAT-336 (UN Appeals Tribunal).

46 See Information Circulars of the United Nations Secretariat, "Practice of the Secretary-General in disciplinary matters and cases of criminal behaviour" UN Docs. ST/IC/2017/33, ST/IC/2016/26, ST/IC/2015/22, ST/IC/2014/26, ST/IC/2013/29, ST/IC/2012/19. See also *Benamar v. Secretary-General of the United Nations*, 2017-UNAT-797 (UN Appeals Tribunal); *Kubwimana v. Secretary-General of the United Nations*, Order No. 088 (NBI/2015) (UN Dispute Tribunal); *Kozul-Wright v. Secretary-General of the United Nations*, 2018-UNAT-843 (UN Appeals Tribunal).

47 For instance, according to the Report of the Secretary-General on the Administration of Justice of the United Nations (UN Doc. A/76/99 at 9 and A/77/156 at 10), in 2020 and 2021, the UN Dispute Tribunal alone adjudicated disciplinary matters in 9% and 17% of cases (or 19 cases in 2021 and 36 cases in 2020).

48 UNGAOR, 8th sess., agenda item 51, Report of the Secretary-General of the UN on Personnel Policy, UN Doc. A/2533 (2 November 1953) at para. 72.

civil servants.[49] A review of academic journals and news articles published by notable media outlets reveals that three types of conduct attract the most attention and erode the reputation and credibility of international secretariats and international civil servants in the eyes of states and the public. These three categories of conduct are (a) reprehensible or unethical acts by very senior or executive officials of IGOs, (b) major fraud and corruption by international civil servants, and (c) sexual exploitation and abuse by international civil servants.

2.1.1 Unethical Conduct by Executive Officials of IGOs

The first notorious case of unethical conduct by the executive head of an international organisation was Joseph Avenol's attempt to evade his private obligations towards his former spouse when he unsuccessfully invoked the privileges and immunities enjoyed by the Secretary-General of the League of Nations in legal proceedings instituted by his ex-wife for family support.[50] Avenol was the second Secretary-General of the League of Nations. Due to his divorce proceedings, a French court ordered him to pay his ex-wife 12,500 francs per month as spousal support.[51] He appealed against this order, asserting that as Secretary-General of the League, he enjoyed diplomatic privileges and immunities under Article 7 of the Covenant of the League and had jurisdictional immunity before the courts of all member states of the League, including those of France. The French court rejected this argument for being a "flagrant contradiction to the sacred and profound sentiment of justice".[52]

Another Secretary-General whose conduct "has done immense damage [...] to the United Nations"[53] was Kurt Waldheim. In March 1986, after Waldheim had completed his second five-year term as Secretary-General of the UN and while he was campaigning for the presidency of Austria, reports emerged that while serving as an officer in the German armed forces in World War II in the Balkans, he had participated in ethnic cleansing.[54] It became clear that

49 On how reputational pressures affect IGOs, see Kristina Daugirdas, "Reputation as a Disciplinarian of International Organizations" (2019) 113:2 *Am J Int Law* 221; Ian Johnstone, "Do International Organizations Have Reputations Editorial" (2010) 7:2 *Int'l Org L Rev* 235–240.

50 Niels Blokker, "International Organizations: The Untouchables" (2014) 10:2 *Int'l Org L Rev* 259 at 263.

51 *Ibid.*

52 *Ibid.*

53 Brian Urquhart, *A Life in Peace and War* (New York: Harper and Row Publishers, 1987) at 227.

54 Boutros Boutros-Ghali, *Unvanquished* (London: I.B.Tauris, 1999) at 222.

Waldheim had "lied for nearly forty years about his war record".[55] In April 2001, the CIA released declassified material on Kurt Waldheim, confirming that the British and American intelligence services knew as early as 1945 that Waldheim was a junior officer in a Nazi intelligence unit in the Balkans, which was renowned for its brutalities. However, the document had been forgotten or misplaced when Waldheim was recommended for the position of the UN Secretary-General. Waldheim's attempt to conceal his past dented the prestige and credibility of the Secretary-General's office.

Several heads of major international organisations have resigned in recent years because of questions about their ethical conduct. For instance, in November 2018, the Secretary-General of the United Nations asked the UNEP Executive Director, Erik Solheim from Norway, to resign after an audit revealed that he had spent almost 500,000 US dollars on air travel and hotels within 22 months. Many of the trips were personal as opposed to justified by his functions. His unethical conduct attracted severe criticism and led some nations to withhold their funding of very important projects.[56]

In November 2019, the Commissioner-General of UNRWA, Pierre Krähenbühl from Switzerland, was urged to resign from his post following the findings of an internal investigation that he and his 'inner circle' abused their authority for personal gain and retaliated against anyone who dared to raise objections.[57]

In May 2022, the Executive Director – Grete Faremo from Norway – and the Assistant Executive Director of UNOPS resigned after a New York Times report revealed questionable investments of funds which exposed the organisation to a loss of 20 million dollars.[58] Faremo and her leadership team awarded contracts to an acquaintance without a competitive solicitation process, including a three-million contract for a pop song and a videogame allegedly designed to help protect oceans. A subsequent article in the New York Times remarked that the incident had damaged the credibility of the United Nations and weakened the trust of donor countries at a time when the organisation is seeking major funding infusions for an array of global crises.[59] The United States, which sits

55 Urquhart, *supra* note 53 at 227.

56 Damian Carrington, "UN environment chief resigns after frequent flying revelations" *The Guardian* (20 November 2018).

57 UNRWA boss resigns amid probe into misconduct claims, *Aljazeera* (6 November 2019) available online at: www.aljazeera.com/news/2019/11/6/unrwa-boss-resigns-amid-probe-into-misconduct-claims.

58 David A Fahrenthold and Farnaz Fassihi, "A Pot of U.N. Money. Risk-Taking Officials. A Sea of Questions." *New York Times* (7 May 2022).

59 Farnaz Fassihi, "Reforms Are Imposed on U.N. Agency That Made Questionable Investments" *New York Times* (10 June 2022).

on the agency's executive board, has suspended its funding to UNOPS, until such time as appropriate law enforcement action is taken against all wrongdoers. Finland followed suit by suspending all its funding to UNOPS and by reviewing its donations to other UN agencies.[60] The Governing Body of UNOPS commissioned KPMG to conduct an audit of UNOPS's oversight mechanisms.

The UN is not the only organisation whose senior officials breach basic ethical standards. The European Commission has also had its share of unscrupulous conduct by senior officials. One notorious case is that of Edith Cresson, whose dishonourable behaviour was found not to be criminal but undermined the European Commission reputation. Cresson, a former prime minister of France, was appointed as the European Commissioner for Research, Science and Technology – a position she held between 1995 and 1999. During her term of office at the Commission, she wished to appoint one of her close acquaintances as a 'personal adviser'. Cresson was informed that because her acquaintance was 66 years old, he could not be appointed as a member of a Commissioner's Cabinet. To circumvent this rule, Cresson engaged him as a visiting scientist, even though he was a dental surgeon and had no scientific expertise to offer. She also improperly awarded contracts to another close acquaintance during the same period. Following a complaint by a Member of Parliament, Belgian authorities launched criminal proceedings against Cresson. In 2004, the Court in Brussels decided that no further action should be taken in the case, taking the view that this was not a criminal offence. On the other hand, the Commission, pressured by EU member states, pursued disciplinary proceedings against Cresson and sought to withhold her pension benefits, leading to a dispute before the European Court of Justice.[61] This incident exposed the Commission to various forms of scrutiny by EU member states, including investigations and audits.

Most recently, the former President of the European Court of Auditors, Klaus-Heiner Lehne from Germany, was accused of receiving benefits to which he was not entitled. In November 2021, a French news outlet released the conclusions of its investigation into allegations of financial misappropriations by Lehne.[62] It was alleged that Lehne had received more than 325,000 euros

---

60 Press Release by Finland's Ministry of Foreign Affairs, "Investigation of possible misconduct at the United Nations Office for Project Services (UNOPS)" (14 April 2022).

61 *Commission of the European Communities v. Édith Cresson*, Case No. C-432/04, ECLI:EU:C:2006:455 (judgement of the Court of Justice of the European Union of 11 July 2006) at paras. 28–29.

62 Jean Quatremer, "Fraudes à la tête de la Cour des comptes européenne", *Libération* (26 November 2021) available online at www.liberation.fr/international/fraude-au-sommet-de-la-cour-des-comptes-europeenne-20211126_UGCXGTDBNNHUDNOEVCEWG2AONQ/.

in accommodation allowances in Luxembourg, whereas he spent most of his time in Germany and had a 'shell address' in Luxembourg for the sole purpose of receiving the allowances.[63] The breach of trust by the President of an institution symbolising responsible spending of EU money led to a series of probes by the EU parliament and member states.[64]

Unethical conduct by senior officials of IGOs invariably leaves the impression that their senior management is unable to lead the organisation. Hence, delegates of member states often stop short of assuming a management role but go so far as to demand justifications for day-to-day management decisions such as relatively small expenditures and investments. In addition, unethical conduct by senior leadership almost inevitably leads to invasive probes, audits, and investigations by governments of member states or third parties, including consultancy and audit firms. IGOs whose leadership made questionable decisions or acted unethically are not able to object or push back on undesired interferences from member states. They are compelled to endure and passively observe the 'raid' by member states. This leads to the weakening of IGOs and the erosion of their immunities. This, in turn, results in a gradual loss of IGOs' independence and autonomy.

2.1.2 Large-Scale Fraud and Corruption

A second type of erosive conduct that often makes headlines is fraudulent and corrupt practices on a large scale by international civil servants. The Oil-for-Food fiasco is arguably the worst financial scandal in the UN's history.

The Security Council established the Oil-for-Food program in response to complaints that the population of Iraq was disproportionately affected by the international economic sanctions aimed at the demilitarisation of Saddam Hussein's regime. The program allowed the sale of Iraqi oil in exchange for necessities such as food and medicine. It was designed to offer humanitarian assistance to the Iraqi population without allowing Saddam Hussein's regime to boost its military power. In 2004, official documents of the Iraqi Oil Ministry were leaked to the media, exposing bribery and kickbacks by hundreds of

63 John Monaghan, "MEPs to probe EU auditors' expenses after media allegations", *Luxembourg Times* (1 December 2021) available online: www.luxtimes.lu/en/european-union/meps-to-probe-eu-auditors-expenses-after-media-allegations-61a765d5de135b92363b5bfe.

64 Jeremy Zabatta, "Luxembourg EU Court of Auditors member under scrutiny", *Delano* (9 February 2022) available online: https://delano.lu/article/lux-embourg-eu-court-of-audito.

high-ranking officials, including UN personnel and former Secretary-General Kofi Annan's son – Kojo Annan – from the Iraqi government.[65] Essentially, individuals and organisations were awarded contracts to sell Iraqi oil on the international market. The seller kept a small transaction fee of $0.50 per barrel of oil sold. To secure a contract, some sellers agreed in advance to refund a part of the commission to the Hussein administration as a kickback.

Similarly, contracts for buying humanitarian goods through the program were offered to those companies that agreed in advance to return a percentage of their profits to the Hussein regime as a bribe. When the scandal erupted, UN Secretary-General Kofi Annan set up a seventy-five-member independent inquiry committee, presided over by Paul Volker, the former chief of the US Federal Reserve.[66] Following the release of the committee's final report, two UN staff members were prosecuted, fined, and convicted for corruption. An investigative body of the United States Senate concluded that the Oil-for-Food program had allowed the Hussein administration to sell oil worth over US$13 billion in violation of the embargo. The Iraqi regime collected billions more through illegal commissions, bribes, and kickbacks through the program. The Oil-for-Food program had seriously damaged the image of the United Nations for decades.[67]

In 2007, the UN came into the limelight again when the Washington Post reported that a UN taskforce had uncovered a "pervasive pattern of corruption and mismanagement involving contracts for fuel, food, construction and other services for peacekeeping operations."[68] Ten UN procurement officials had been charged with misconduct for allegedly soliciting bribes and rigging bids for peacekeeping forces in Congo and Haiti. The amount embezzled exceeded 610 million US dollars, prompting the US government to press for a probe into UN activities in peace operations.[69]

In 2017, credible reports of systemic corruption by UNHCR staff members were made in Kenya and Uganda. Asylum seekers, refugees, and internally

---

65 Ewen MacAskill, "Oil-for-Food Report Condemns Corrupt UN", *The Guardian* (7 September 2005): https://www.theguardian.com/world/2005/sep/07/iraq.ewenmacaskill.

66 Gonzalo Villalta Puig, "Unethical Conduct in the Performance of International Government Contracts: AWB Ltd. and the United Nations Oil-for-Food Programme" (2007) 37:1 *Public Contract Law J* 59–66 at 60.

67 This paragraph is largely based on pages 67–68 of my book, *supra* note 13 at 67–68.

68 Colum Lynch, "UN Finds Fraud, Mismanagement in Peacekeeping", *The Washington Post* (18 December 2007).

69 Claudia Parsons, "US Urges Probe into UN Peacekeeping Fraud Report", *Reuters* (18 December 2007): https://www.reuters.com/article/us-un-corruption-idUSN1849413720071218.

displaced persons were allegedly paying 2500 US dollars per person to get resettled to Western countries. The corruption scheme consisted of UNHCR staff members taking bribes from individuals not facing an imminent risk of persecution, issuing them fake ID documents by giving them the identity of real refugees or persons in need of protection and resettling them in other countries. As a result, persons ineligible for resettlement were buying a new identity and life in developed countries, while refugees and displaced persons facing imminent danger who were on the verge of being resettled to Western countries were unknowingly losing their right to be ever resettled.[70]

Large-scale corruption scandals undermine the credibility of international organisations and attract unwanted attention from all quarters, particularly from governments of member states. International civil servants who engage in such behaviour do tremendous damage not only to their organisations but also to the international civil service.

2.1.3 Sexual Exploitation and Abuse

Sexual exploitation and abuse by intergovernmental organisations is not a new phenomenon in conflict areas. The UN, the media, and nongovernmental organisations have reported instances of UN personnel participating in sexual exploitation and abuse, which included human trafficking in Cambodia, Bosnia and Herzegovina in the early and late 1990s, and Kosovo, Timor-Leste, and West Africa in the early 2000s.[71] Nevertheless, the issue became the focus of public attention in 2002 because of widely reported instances of such behaviour by humanitarian workers in West Africa.[72] On 26 February 2002, a headline that read 'Child Refugee Sex Scandal' appeared on BBC News, revealing the sexual exploitation of children in refugee camps by staff members of various aid organisations and UN agencies, including the UNHCR.[73] The allegations of sexual exploitation and abuse of refugees referred to in the article had occurred in Guinea and Sierra Leone. In response to these allegations, in April 2003,

70 Charlotte Hauswedell, "UNHCR Probing Corruption in Resettlement Cases in Uganda, Kenya". *InfoMigrants* (10 January 2020): https://www.infomigrants.net/en/post/22018/unhcr-probing-corruption-in-resettlement-cases-in-uganda-kenya.

71 Anna Shotton, "A Strategy to Address Sexual Exploitation and Abuse by United Nations Peacekeeping Personnel Perspective" (2006) 39:1 *Cornell Int Law J* 97–108 at 98.

72 Anthony J Miller, "Legal Aspects of Stopping Sexual Exploitation and Abuse in U.N. Peacekeeping Operations Perspective" (2006) 39:1 *Cornell Int Law J* 71–96 at 72.

73 "Child Refugee Sex Scandal", *BBC News* (29 February 2002): http://news.bbc.co.uk/2/hi/africa/1842512.stm See also Kate Grady, "Sex, Statistics, Peacekeepers and Power: UN Data on Sexual Exploitation and Abuse and the Quest for Legal Reform" (2016) 79:6 *Mod Law Rev* 931–960.

the UN General Assembly requested the Secretary-General "to maintain data on investigations into sexual exploitation and related offences, irrespective of age and gender, by humanitarian and peacekeeping personnel, and all relevant actions taken thereon".[74] Data collection was clearly insufficient as occurrences of sexual exploitation and abuse only intensified. In June 2004, BBC News published another article containing testimonies of victims of extreme sexual violence by UN peacekeepers in DRC.[75] This led to an investigation by the UN Office of Internal Oversight Services, which released a report concluding that UN military contingent personnel were involved in sexual exploitation of women and children in the Democratic Republic of the Congo.[76]

New allegations of sexual exploitation and abuse emerged a few months later, this time in the peacekeeping operation in Burundi.[77] In May 2006, the New York Times published the findings of a report by Save the Children UK, where it described how UN personnel and aid workers were sexually exploiting Liberian girls as young as eight in return for food and small favours.[78] The New York Times correctly remarked that "nothing discredits the United Nations more than the continuing sexual abuse of women and girls" – the people it is supposed to protect.[79]

In 2016, the UN Secretary-General Ban Ki-moon had to admit that despite the UN's efforts, sexual abuse by UN peacekeepers had become "a cancer in our system."[80] Six years later, his successor – Antonio Guterres – conceded that "despite clear gains, allegations [of sexual exploitation and abuse] implicating United Nations personnel regrettably continue to emerge."[81]

---

74 UNGA resolution 57/306 "Investigation into sexual exploitation of refugees by aid workers in West Africa", UN Doc. A/RES/57/306 at para. 10.

75 Kate Holt, "DR Congo's Shameful Sex Secret", *BBC News* (3 June 2004): http://news.bbc.co.uk/1/hi/world/africa/3769469.stm.

76 Report of the Secretary-General on the activities of the Office of Internal Oversight Services, "Investigation by the Office of Internal Oversight Services into allegations of sexual exploitation and abuse in the United Nations Organization Mission in the Democratic Republic of the Congo" UN Doc. A/59/661 (5 January 2005).

77 Susannah Price, "New Sex Misconduct Claims Hit UN", *BBC News* (17 December 2004): http://news.bbc.co.uk/2/hi/africa/4106515.stm.

78 Sarah Lyall, "Aid Workers Are Said to Abuse Girls", *The New York Times* (9 May 2006): https://www.nytimes.com/2006/05/09/world/africa/aid-workers-are-said-to-abuse-girls.html.

79 Elizabeth F Defeis, "U.N. Peacekeepers and Sexual Abuse and Exploitation: An End to Impunity" (2008) 7:2 *Wash Univ Glob Stud Law Rev* 185–214 at 189.

80 Kevin Sieff, "Members of a U.N. peacekeeping force in the Central African Republic allegedly turned to sexual predation, betraying their duty to protect", *The Washington Post* (27 February 2016): https://www.washingtonpost.com/sf/world/2016/02/27/peacekeepers/.

81 Report of the Secretary-General, "Special measures for protection from sexual exploitation and abuse" UN Doc. A/76/702 (15 February 2022) at para. 2.

The review of the cases above may give the impression that sexual exploitation and abuse are committed exclusively by UN military personnel as opposed to international civil servants. Whilst the incidences of sexual exploitation and abuse by military personnel are much more prevalent, there have been many cases where staff members of various UN entities have been accused of the same conduct in contexts other than peacekeeping. For instance, as a result of press reports of alleged sexual exploitation and abuse by WHO staff during an Ebola outbreak in DRC,[82] the WHO Director-General established an Independent Commission of Inquiry to investigate the allegations. The inquiry by the Commission led to findings of some form of sexual abuse by at least 21 staff members of WHO.[83]

Many other cases of sexual exploitation and abuse by UN staff members can be found in the jurisprudence of the UN Dispute Tribunal[84] as well as in the Information Circulars of the Secretary-General that the UN publishes to inform staff members of the practice of the Secretary-General in exercising his authority in disciplinary matters.[85] The author himself prosecuted several cases of SEA in refugee camps involving UN staff.

Instances of sexual exploitation and abuse by UN personnel are so damaging for the entire system and other staff members that even the General Assembly found it necessary to highlight in a preamble of its resolution dealing with sexual exploitation and abuse that "the actions of a few will not be allowed to tarnish the achievement of all".[86]

---

82 See Robert Flummerfelt and Ange Kasongo, "New Sex Abuse Claims Ebola Aid Workers Exposed in Congo", *Thomson Reuters Foundation*, 12 May 2021.

83 World Health Organization (WHO), "Final report of the independent commission on the review of sexual abuse and exploitation during the response to the 10th Ebola virus disease epidemic in the Democratic Republic of the Congo" (28 September 2021): https://www.who.int/publications/m/item/final-report-of-the-independent-commission-on-the-review-of-sexual-abuse-and-exploitation-ebola-drc.

84 *Erefa v. Secretary-General of the United Nations*, UNDT/2021/109 (UN Dispute Tribunal); *Muteeganda v. Secretary-General of the United Nations*, UNDT/2020/050 (UN Dispute Tribunal); *Gisage v. Secretary-General of the United Nations*, UNDT/2020/121 (UN Dispute Tribunal); *Kazagic v. Secretary-General of the United Nations*, UNDT/2016/086 (UN Dispute Tribunal).

85 See, for instance, Information Circulars, "Practice of the Secretary-General in disciplinary matters and cases of criminal behaviour, 1 July 2016 to 30 June 2017" UN Doc. ST/IC/2017/33 (13 October 2017) at paras. 58–59; "Practice of the Secretary-General in disciplinary matters and cases of criminal behaviour, 1 July 2015 to 30 June 2016" UN Doc. ST/IC/2016/26 (19 September 2016) at paras. 67–69.

86 UNGA resolution 76/303 "United Nations action on sexual exploitation and abuse" UN Doc. A/Res/76/303 (2 September 2022) preambular paragraph 4.

2.2 *Obligations Relating to Loyalty*

The International Civil Service Advisory Board noted in its 1954 Report that a second basic requirement is the necessity of developing and maintaining an international outlook based on loyalty to the international organisation. This 'international outlook' flows from an understanding of and loyalty to the objectives and purposes of the international organisation as outlined in its constitution, the acceptance of the oath of office and the basic obligation to serve wholeheartedly and completely the organisation's interests.[87] It is not a coincidence that before the publication of this report, in November 1952, the first chair of the ICSAB (who served as Under-Secretary-General in the League of Nations) – Aghnides Thanassis – had remarked during a conference held at the UN headquarters that "if there is one brief way of characterising the primary demand placed by the Charter and the staff regulations upon the international civil servant it is the demand of loyalty to the organisation and to its objectives."[88]

Loyalty is closely related to integrity. First, it "is the focal point of all duties of conduct".[89] Like integrity, there cannot be too much of it. Some have argued that because the opposite of loyalty evokes disloyalty, treachery, betrayal, and treason, nobody is opposed to it.[90] Another similarity between integrity and loyalty is that neither concept is often empirically studied, perhaps because making the concepts operational is difficult.[91] However, what exactly does loyalty mean? An etymological sidestep suggests that loyalty was always meant to be a positive attribute. 'Loyal' is traced back through old French *loial* and *leial* to Latin *legalis* and *legalem*. The root *leg* and *lex* in Latin designate law or legal. Hence, at some point in history, loyal meant compliant with the law or meeting the conditions required by it. It referred to being 'true to obligations' and 'faithful to the government'. Today, loyalty is a broader and more elusive notion with normative, symbolic, and emotional connotations. There is no common definition of the term in the literature. It has been defined as "a willingness to stick with the group",[92] "an allegiance to a concept outside the self, such as an

87 Report on Standards of Conduct of the International Civil Service, *supra* note 1 at para. 5.

88 Aghnides H E Thanassis, "Standards of Conduct of the International Civil Servant" (1953) 19:1 *Int Rev Adm Sci* 179 at 181.

89 Ullrich, *supra* note 41 at 409.

90 Jill W Graham and Michael Keeley, "Hirschman's Loyalty Construct Research on Hirschman's Exit, Voice, and Loyalty Model" (1992) 5:3 *Empl Responsib Rights J* 191–200.

91 Gjalt de Graaf, "The Loyalties of Top Public Administrators" (2011) 21:2 *J Public Adm Res Theory* 285 at 288.

92 R E Ewin, "Loyalty and Virtues" (1992) 42:169 *Philos Q* 403 at 418.

organisation",[93] a disposition not to criticise,[94] "willingness to sacrifice",[95] or devotion to some cause expressed in a "sustained and practical way, by acting steadily in the service of [t]his cause".[96] In the context of international civil servants, however, loyalty has a slightly narrower meaning. It is not allegiance; allegiance is more suitable to describe a relationship between a national government and its staff.[97]

The concept of loyalty to the international organisation, first introduced by Eric Drummond in the League of Nations, was described by a group of former senior officials of the League as follows:

> What is 'international loyalty'? It is not the denationalised loyalty of a man without a country. On the contrary, it is the conviction that the highest interests of one's own country are served best by the promotion of security and welfare everywhere, and the steadfast manifestation of that conviction without regard to changing circumstances.[98]

It was first codified in 1932 when the League added to its Staff Regulations a provision which stated that "the officials of the Secretariat of the League of Nations are exclusively international officials and their duties are not national, but international." A separate provision requiring them to make a declaration of loyalty was introduced during the same year.[99] These provisions have become very common. Similar rules can be found in staff rules and regulations of many IGOs, including entities of the United Nations System.

The duty of loyalty constitutes a fundamental obligation owed by every official to the institution to which the official belongs.[100] As a minimum, it requires the official to actively seek to preserve the relationship of trust between him and his institution by "refrain[ing] from conduct which reflects on his position

93 Elizabeth A Hoffmann, "Exit and Voice: Organizational Loyalty and Dispute Resolution Strategies" (2005) 84:4 *Soc Forces* 2313–2330 at 2314.

94 AH Birch, "Economic Models in Political Science: The Case of 'Exit, Voice, and Loyalty'" (1975) 5:1 *Br J Polit Sci* 69 at 75.

95 PH Werhane and RE Freeman (eds.), *Encyclopedic Dictionary of Business Ethics* 2nd ed. (Oxford: Wiley-Blackwell, 2006).

96 Josiah Royce, *The philosophy of loyalty* (New York: Macmillan, 1908) at 17.

97 Plantey and Loriot, *supra* note 37 at 88.

98 Mathiason, *supra* note 11 at 29.

99 "Amendment in the Staff Regulations", Office Circular Nos. 75 and 76 (12 November 1932).

100 *Connolly v Commission*, [1999] ECR-SC I-A-87 and II-463, Court of First Instance of the European Communities (First Chamber) of 19 May 1999 in Joined Cases T-34/96 and T-163/96, affirmed in *European Court Reports 2001 I-01611*, ECLI:EU:C:2001:127.

and is detrimental to the respect due to the institution and its authorities [and to] conduct himself, particularly if he is of senior grade, in a manner that is beyond suspicion."[101] The Administrative Tribunal of the World Bank specified that the duty of loyalty includes the obligation to avoid situations and activities that might (i) reflect adversely on the organisation, (ii) compromise operations of the organisation, and (iii) lead to real or apparent conflicts of interest.[102] As pointed out above, loyalty and integrity are interconnected; therefore, one's failure to uphold high standards of integrity often entails a breach of one's duty of loyalty and vice versa. This explains why international tribunals refer to the obligations of integrity and loyalty interchangeably. As the examples below reveal, in many instances, conduct characterised by international administrative tribunals as a breach of an official's duty of loyalty may also be regarded as a lapse of integrity. Behaviour found to be a breach of loyalty included:

- engaging in treasonous espionage;[103]
- promoting policies or theories which the organisation believes to be wrong or mistaken;[104]
- misusing the organisation's duty-free import privileges for the personal benefit of a family member;[105]
- writing and publishing a book that exposed the official's fundamental opposition to his employer's strategy, goals, and activities; [106]
- making public statements deprecating the official's institution, organisational unit, or colleagues;[107]
- submitting frivolous and vexatious complaints or making gratuitously accusatory statements made against the official's colleagues, organisation, or the host State;[108]

---

101 *Ibid.* at para. 128.

102 *A.J. v. IBRD*, WBAT Judgement No. 389 (25 March 2009) at para. 46; *G.N. v. IBRD*, WBAT Judgement No. 667 (3 June 2022) at para. 167; *F.Q. v. IFC*, WBAT Judgement 638 (16 November 2020) at para. 98.

103 *M.K. v. NATO Allied Air Command*, NATO AT Judgement No. 2017–023 (21 November 2017): A former NATO staff member served seven years in a German prison for spying for Russia.

104 *In re Stjernswärd*, [1998] Judgement No. 1732 (ILOAT).

105 *R.D.A.G. v. PAHO*, Judgement No. 3295 (ILOAT).

106 *Connolly v. Commission*, European Court Reports 2001 I-01611, ECLI:EU:C:2001:127 at para. 128.

107 *Williams v. Court of Auditors of the European Communities*, European Court Reports 1991 II-01293, ECLI:EU:T:1991:61 at para. 72.

108 *In Re Jurado*, [1966] Judgement No. 96 (ILOAT) at para. 5 and *J.-D. v. ILO*, [2018] Judgement No. 3982 (ILOAT) at para. 1; *In re Loomba*, [1970] Judgement No. 169 (ILOAT) at para. 4.

- engaging in outside activities without seeking prior authorisation;[109]
- writing a character letter (testimonial) for another staff member who has been tried for and convicted of paedophilia;[110]
- failing to disclose a conflict of interests;[111]
- taking sides with or showing political support for one party to a conflict;[112]
- falsely declaring being a national of an organisation's member state;[113] and
- lobbying government officials to improve the staff member's employment situation.[114]

Officials of international organisations may breach their duty of loyalty even when they are convinced that they are acting in the interests of the international community and of the organisation. The *Galbraith* case, described below, provides an example of such conduct.

In March 2009, the UN Secretary-General announced the appointment of Mr. Galbraith, a United States national, as Deputy Special Representative of the Secretary-General ("DSRSG") for the United Nations Assistance Mission in Afghanistan ("UNAMA"). This was the rank of Assistant Secretary-General ("ASG"). Galbraith's role was to assist his supervisor – the Special Representative of the Secretary-General ("SRSG") – in the performance of his diplomatic, political, and managerial responsibilities in connection with UNAMA. Soon after his appointment, Galbraith began having disagreements with the SRSG regarding the elections in Afghanistan in 2009 and UNAMA's role therein. He

---

109 *Nsabimana v. IFAD*, 2022-UNAT-1254 (UN Appeals Tribunal); *In re Moore*, [1995] Judgement No. 1405 (ILOAT); *Fichtner v. Commission of the European Communities*, European Court Reports 2003 I-A-00007, Case T-75/00, ECLI:EU:T:2003:9.

110 *Bissell v. Secretary-General of the UN*, UNDT/2020/084 (UN Dispute Tribunal). The staff member's actions were particularly negligent given her position of Director of the Global Partnership to End Violence Against Children in UNICEF.

111 *Vedel v. Secretary-General of the United Nations*, UNDT/2019/110 (UN Dispute Tribunal). In this case, a UNICEF staff member working in the procurement and supply failed to disclose that her husband held executive roles with UNICEF suppliers.

112 *Kuruc v. Secretary-General of the United Nations*, UNDT/2015/008 (UN Dispute Tribunal). A UNHCR staff member of Turkish nationality handed a white flag with the inscription "do not yield" to the Syrian President.

113 *L.G. v CERN*, [2007] Judgement No. 2569 (ILOAT).

114 *Banaj v. Secretary-General of the United Nations*, UNDT/2022/060 (UN Dispute Tribunal). To secure support for preserving her personal situation as the sole UNODC representative in Albania, the staff member lobbied government officials against the recruitment of a candidate who would hold a higher-ranking post. See also *Bel Ghazi v. WHO*, [1996] Judgement 1475 (ILOAT).

was of the view that the UN, namely UNAMA, had the responsibility of ensuring that the Afghan Independent Electoral Commission ("IEC") operated impartially and honestly. His supervisor, however, believed that the UN did not need to interfere in the activities of the IEC. Reports emerged in the media that electoral fraud may have occurred in Afghanistan.[115] In September 2009, Galbraith returned to the United States and gave an interview for a news article in Burlington Free Press in which he disclosed his disagreement with the SRSG over how to address allegations of widespread electoral fraud. He stated during his interview that he wanted to take a harsher line on the vote fraud issue than his supervisor. Following this interview, the UN Secretary-General thanked Galbraith for his services and terminated his contract. Galbraith challenged this decision before the UN Dispute Tribunal, arguing that the Secretary-General ended his employment without cause. The Dispute Tribunal rejected this argument, holding that,

> It is only possible for a mission to have and maintain a single policy line if there is a relation of full trust and cooperation between all the staff members, especially between the SRSG and the DSRSGs. [...] The Secretary-General acted in respect of this principle and his intervention was necessary in order to avoid any negative impact of the disagreement between the SRSG and the Applicant upon UNAMA's mandate at a very important time and consequently upon the relations between the mission, the Afghani government and the international community, so he did not abuse his discretionary power.[116]

Not all failures to exhibit loyalty pose a risk to the independence of international civil servants and of international secretariats. Most cases of disloyal conduct are dealt with confidentially through disciplinary proceedings without much ado. Nonetheless, some actions by a few may discredit entire teams and seriously undermine the organisation's reputation. Spying or acts of espionage by international civil servants for a government undoubtedly fall into this category of actions.

In February 2022, soon after Russia invaded Ukraine, the US government announced the expulsion of 12 Russian diplomats and one UN staff member for acts of espionage without, however, disclosing any details about the alleged

115 Jon Boone, "One in five Afghan ballots may be illegal, UN warns" *The Guardian* (24 August 2009): https://www.theguardian.com/world/2009/aug/24/afghan-elections-fraud-karzai.

116 *Galbraith v. Secretary-General of the United Nations*, UNDT/2013/102 (UN Dispute Tribunal) at paras. 69–70.

activities. The expelled UN staff member was allegedly a Russian intelligence operative working under the cover of a UN official.[117] This did not surprise people familiar with the UN and the Kremlin's long history of using the organisation for espionage. From the UN's earliest days, the Soviet government regarded the world body as an ideal cover. Over several decades, its intelligence had penetrated and subverted key parts of the UN, including the human resources and communications functions.

Details about Soviet intelligence tactics are still coming to light. In September 2021, the British Foreign & Commonwealth Office declassified a file entitled "Russian intelligence service operating under UN cover", revealing the USSR's sophisticated covert activities during the Cold War.[118] In the 1970s, the Soviet intelligence services had hundreds of operatives working in the UN in New York and Geneva. They controlled key parts of the UN's bureaucracy, including the Division for Policy Coordination in the Office of Personnel Services in New York and Personnel Services in Geneva.

In May 1978, the FBI arrested and prosecuted two Soviet staff members of the UN on espionage charges. They were attempting to procure US Navy antisubmarine warfare documents from an FBI undercover agent who posed as a US Navy officer. One of these individuals was an assistant to the Under-Secretary-General, and the second was a Human Resources Officer.[119] The two UN officials were arrested while trying to retrieve a microfilm that the FBI undercover agent had dropped in an orange juice carton. A third Russian citizen, attached to the Soviet mission at the UN, was also arrested but was subsequently released because he had diplomatic immunity.[120]

In July 1978, another staff member of the UN in Geneva – Viktor Suvorov – defected to British intelligence and revealed that his mission was to steal scientific and technical secrets from Western countries through the UN Conference on Trade and Development (UNCTAD).[121]

---

117 Michelle Nichols, "U.S. expels Russian Spy Working for United Nations – Spokesperson" *Reuters* (1 March 2022): https://www.reuters.com/world/us/us-says-expels-russian-spy-working-united-nations-2022-03-01/.

118 Calder Walton, "Soviet Espionage Under the Cover of Diplomacy" *The Cipher Brief* (16 March 2022): Soviet Espionage Under the Cover of Diplomacy.

119 Charles R Babcock, "Two Russians Are Indicted in Espionage" *The Washington Post* (31 May 1978).

120 Charles R Babcock, "FBI Arrests Two Soviets in Spying Case" *The Washington Post* (21 May 1978).

121 Luke Harding, "'Will they forgive me? No': ex-Soviet spy Viktor Suvorov speaks out" *The Guardian* (29 December 2018).

He later published a book describing the intricacies of the Soviet intelligence gathering through the UN.[122]

A few months earlier, the revelations made by Arkady Shevchenko, who worked as Under-Secretary-General in the UN Secretariat, had already shaken the UN Secretariat's reputation. Shevchenko sought political asylum and admitted that he was a KGB officer. Shevchenko's revelations were sensational; half of all Soviet nationals working for the UN in New York Geneva were intelligence officers or assigned to intelligence activities. Brian Urquhart – who also served as the Under-Secretary-General for political affairs under several Secretaries-General – corroborated this account, pointing out that Soviet nationals holding senior posts in the UN "seemed to be in a twenty-four-a-day competition to be first to relay the output of [his] office to the Soviet delegation".[123] In 1985, Shevchenko published a book, *Breaking with Moscow*, which shed light on the extent of damage inflicted on the UN Secretariat's good repute.[124] What exacerbated Shevchenko's conduct is that while spying for the Soviets, he was, at the same time, spying for the CIA as a double agent.[125]

Another seasoned spy from the USSR who worked as an Information Officer for the World Health Organization in Geneva was Ilya Dzhirkelov. He defected in 1980 and published a book in 1987 in which he explained the organisational structures and operational techniques of Soviet intelligence agencies.[126]

These high-profile defections and betrayals did not discourage the USSR. On the contrary, the number of its spies in the UN continued to increase. For instance, in 1980, the Swiss government estimated that of the 650 or so Soviet officials residing in Switzerland, at least 200 were engaged in espionage. In 1984, the Soviets had as many as 126 diplomats accredited to the UN in New York compared to 59 diplomats in the US mission and just 20 in the UK mission. The recently unveiled file of the British Foreign & Commonwealth Office indicates that most of these Soviet officials were conducting intelligence work.[127]

---

122 Viktor Suvorov, *Inside the Aquarium: The Making of a Top Soviet Spy* (New York: Macmillan, 1986).

123 Urquhart, *supra* note 53 at 290.

124 Arkady N Shevchenko, *Breaking with Moscow* (New York: Ballantine Books, 1985).

125 Robert D McFadden, "A Soviet Defector Says He Was a Spy for U.S. for Years" *The New York Times*, Section A, page 1 (4 February 1945).

126 Ilya Dzhirkelov, *Secret Servant: My Life with the KGB and the Soviet Elite* (New York: Harper Collins, 1987).

127 Calder Walton, "Soviet Espionage Under the Cover of Diplomacy" *The Cipher Brief* (16 March 2022): Soviet Espionage Under the Cover of Diplomacy.

NATO has had its share of spies. The most famous case of espionage in its history was the Pâques Affair.[128] In 1962, when the Cold War was in full swing, Georges Pâques – a prominent French civil servant – started work as Deputy Director of the NATO Press Service. This important position gave Pâques access to information discussed during high-level meetings and recorded in confidential documents. He also had impressive connections at NATO and in the French government, which exposed him to important dignitaries and officials from whom he could obtain valuable intelligence. For an extended period, Pâques disclosed NATO secrets to the Soviet Union.[129] Amongst the documents he transmitted to the USSR were plans related to psychological warfare, force posture, military exercises, and defence plans for Berlin. He also prepared extensive biographies of senior officials at NATO and within Allied governments. The French authorities apprehended Pâques in 1963 after receiving tips that the CIA collected from a former KBG spy. Pâques' trial became a highly publicised affair, attracting press worldwide. During the trial, Pâques explained the reason for his betrayal by advancing an unconvincing excuse:

> I'm a man of peace. I don't like the Soviets, but I'm also convinced that the Americans, with their very primitive ideas, are dangerous warmongers. So, I thought that to avoid an international conflict, leading inevitably to a global catastrophe, it was essential to restore the balance of power. This has always been my driving force.[130]

Although he was sentenced to life imprisonment, Pâques served less than seven years. The then President of France, Georges Pompidou, Pâques' classmate in *École Normale Supérieure*, pardoned him in 1970.[131]

In the recent past, another espionage case caused embarrassment to NATO. In 2013, Manfred Koenig, a NATO staff member of German nationality, was sentenced to seven years of imprisonment for selling secret data to Russian intelligence services.[132] Koenig worked as an IT expert at the Ramstein Air Force Base in western Germany. He was caught with USB sticks and top-secret plans

128 "The Pâques Affair", Declassified Memo of the Secretary-General of NATO, NATO Ref. PO/64/118 (25 March 1964) available online: https://archives.nato.int/uploads/r/null/2/1/217022/PO_64_118_ENG_NHQL672901.pdf.

129 "Georges Pâques, 79, French NATO Aide Jailed for Espionage", *The New York Times* (3 January 1994).

130 Thierry Wolton, *Le KGB en France* (Paris: Grasset, 1986) at 175.

131 Paul Veyne, "Naïvetés et noblesse de la trahison" (1985) 81 *L'Histoire* at 22.

132 *M.K. v. NATO Allied Air Command*, NATO AT Judgement No. 2017–023 (21 November 2017).

of American land and air operations on his computer. Criminal proceedings revealed that Koenig was attempting to sell passwords to top-secret computer programs for military operations. The Russian secret services FSB had already paid him 5 million dollars.[133] This treason made some NATO member nations reluctant to share sensitive information with NATO and its various subsidiary entities.

Do acts of spying or espionage represent disloyalty or lack of independence? It is probably both. However, it fits better under disloyal conduct because spies steal secrets or gather information that is usually unrelated to their official functions. They often perform well their ostensible work for international organisations because it provides them a suitable cover. For example, a Human Resources Officer trying to obtain and transmit military secrets does not perform functions related to personnel administration. He does not take instructions from external sources when carrying out his roles and responsibilities as a human resources officer. Problematic conduct points to a lack of independence when international civil servants seek or accept instructions from external sources on how they perform their official functions.

2.3 *Obligations Relating to Independence*

The Advisory Board observed that a third requirement closely related to international loyalty is independence. The word *independence, as defined in Chapter 2 of this book*, is broad and includes notions of loyalty, impartiality, and integrity. This section explores the meaning of the word *independence* as the International Civil Service Advisory Board used it in its 1954 report. The Advisory Board used the term *independence* in the narrow sense of the word, noting that the international civil servant must, in the exercise of his functions, remain independent of any authority outside the organisation he serves and that his conduct should at all times reflect such independence:

> In taking his oath of office he has undertaken an obligation not to seek or accept instructions in regard to the performance of his duties from any government or other authority external to his organization. It is not only the strict letter of this oath but the spirit which must be understood and adhered to.[134]

---

133 Allan Hall, "German spy caught selling top secret U.S. battle plans while working for NATO is jailed for seven years" *Daily Mail* (20 November 2013): https://www.dailymail.co.uk/news/article-2510548/German-spy-caught-selling-secret-U-S-battle-plans-working-NATO-jailed-seven-years.html.

134 Report on Standards of Conduct of the International Civil Service, *supra* note 1 at para. 7.

Viewed from this angle, independence refers to the ability of international civil servants to make decisions and perform official acts free of external influence. Lack of independence is, to a certain extent, a form of disloyalty, but it is less egregious and not always premeditated. Sometimes, staff members' lack of independence may be due to circumstances and conditions beyond their control. For instance, a staff member may work on a project funded entirely by one country. If the country ceases to fund the project, the organisation may have two options. It may either (a) transfer the staff member to another vacant post and continue employing him on other projects or (b) abolish the staff member's post and separate him from service. Unless the staff member is confident that the organisation will opt for the first alternative, he may be inclined to do everything he can to gain and maintain the donor state's trust and confidence. In such a case, it is only normal that the staff member may not be entirely independent of a member state for reasons beyond his control. Similarly, if the international organisation assigns a staff member to work on an exclusively national project under the control and command of a member state's government, the staff member's independence is jeopardised by the organisation itself. However, when a staff member has not been given any reason to fear adverse consequences, he has no excuse for taking instructions from a member state's government to carry out his activities.

A case in point is the recent saga at the World Bank. In September 2021, the World Bank released an independent investigation report prepared by external investigators into the involvement of senior World Bank management in data manipulation.[135] The investigation found that Bank officials altered data to benefit China and Saudi Arabia in its flagship 'Doing Business' report, which ranks countries according to their business regulations. The 'Doing Business Index', first published by the World Bank in 2002, ranked countries on several aspects of business regulation, from the time it took to get a construction permit or clear customs to more controversial measures like the scope of labour rights or corporate tax rates.[136] While these reports did not attract much interest in many Western countries, Doing Business indexes often made headlines

135 Ronald C Machen Matthew et al., Investigation Findings and Report to the Board of Executive Directors "Investigation of Data Irregularities in *Doing Business 2018 and Doing Business 2020*" (15 September 2021): https://thedocs.worldbank.org/en/doc/84a922cc9273b7b120d49ad3b9e9d3f9-0090012021/original/DB-Investigation-Findings-and-Report-to-the-Board-of-Executive-Directors-September-15-2021.pdf.

136 See for instance "Doing Business 2020 Report: Comparing Business Regulation in 190 Economies" (Washington DC: World Bank, 2020): https://documents1.worldbank.org/curated/en/688761571934946384/pdf/Doing-Business-2020-Comparing-Business-Regulation-in-190-Economies.pdf.

in major international newspapers. Some governments were so interested in these reports and how they scored on the index that they set up entire governmental units to maximise their score.

The investigation revealed that in the month leading up to the publication of the Doing Business report, outreach from senior Chinese officials to Bank leaders over the country's ranking in Doing Business intensified. In some private meetings with World Bank senior officials, Chinese delegates exerted pressure, expressly mentioning that "if China's ranking improved, everyone would be relieved."[137] A senior Chinese delegate had dinner with Kristalina Georgieva (the current IMF executive head), during which he emphasised her role as the responsible person at the Bank to ensure that China's reforms were acknowledged in the report.[138] Georgieva then asked her team to explore ways to alter the methodology so that China's score did not drop. Georgieva and her colleagues had no reason to fear retaliation from the Chinese government against them. Hence, there was no reason to alter the methodology to please the Chinese government.

When this report was released, Georgieva was already the Managing Director of IMF. The allegations were perceived to be so damaging that the Economist magazine called for Georgieva to step down.[139] She was spared when the IMF executive board announced it had complete confidence in her "leadership and ability to continue to effectively carry out her duties."[140] Nevertheless, former staff, government officials, and outside experts pointed out that "regardless of whether IMF chief Kristalina Georgieva was to blame for changes to World Bank data in 2017 that benefited China, the scandal has dented the research reputations of both institutions [i.e. the World Bank and IMF]."[141]

A recent empirical study revealed that another factor affecting international civil servants' independence is not their seniority or rank but "proximity to the local environment", which makes them vulnerable "to local patronage, political

137 *Ibid.*, at para. 5.

138 *Ibid.*

139 "Why the Head of IMF Should Resign", *The Economist* (25 September 2021): https://www.economist.com/leaders/2021/09/25/why-the-head-of-the-imf-should-resign.

140 Bjarke Smith-Meyer, "IMF chief Kristalina Georgieva survives China scandal: What you need to know", *Politico* (12 October 2021): https://www.politico.eu/article/georgievas-scandal-geopolitics-china-and-data-tampering/.

141 Andrea Shalal and David Lawder, "Analysis: World Bank, IMF face long-term damage after data rigging scandal", *Reuters* (4 October 2021): https://www.reuters.com/business/world-bank-imf-face-long-term-damage-after-data-rigging-scandal-2021-10-04/.

pressures and expectations from the local community."[142] The same study established that when staff members are recruited from outside their country of nationality, they undergo what the authors call a "national identity dilution". It blurs national identities and perspectives. They are then more likely to lose their national perspective through a mechanism of alienation and to acquire a new international identity through assimilation. They acquire an international *esprit de corps* and are less vulnerable to external influences. The study found that even locally recruited staff members who perform administrative and clerical functions are less independent of the government of a member state than internationally recruited staff with political roles and managerial responsibilities. According to the authors, although locally recruited staff members do not make strategic decisions, they have access to information that member states consider valuable.[143]

Hence, to minimise the influence of member states on international organisations, international civil servants should, whenever possible, regularly change duty stations. Mobility fosters a 'supranational' identity. Where rotation is not feasible either because they are recruited locally or cannot secure suitable positions in other duty stations, international civil servants should avoid fraternising with governmental officials or getting involved in national and local politics. Similarly, international civil servants should sever all links with their national public service to avoid financial dependence before assuming international functions. Secondments or leave without pay from national public service allow sending governments to retain some influence over their nationals.

2.4 *Obligations Relating to Impartiality and Neutrality*

The 1954 report of the International Civil Service Advisory Board mentioned impartiality as the fourth and last category of obligations owed by international civil servants. The Advisory Board observed that impartiality implies objectivity, lack of bias, tolerance, and restraint – particularly when political or religious disputes or differences arise. It acknowledged that even though personal views and convictions of staff members remain inviolate, they do not have the freedom of "a private person to take sides, to enter a dispute as a partisan, or publicly to express his convictions on matters of a controversial nature, either singly or as a member of a group", adding that "just as the practice of

---

142 Valentina Mele, Simon Anderfuhren-Biget and Frédéric Varone, "Conflicts of Interest in International Organizations: Evidence from Two United Nations Humanitarian Agencies" (2016) 94:2 *Public Adm* 490 at 504.

143 *Ibid.*

impartiality will strengthen the secretariat, repeated instances of partiality, or bias, will do serious harm to the organisation."[144] The description above conflates aspects of impartiality with neutrality. As pointed out in Chapter 2, although the two terms designate related but different concepts, the notions of impartiality and neutrality are often used interchangeably in the context of public service. Consequently, in the interests of simplicity, this book refers to both principles even when using only one of these terms.

Impartiality involves respect and tolerance for and willingness to understand different points of view, cultures, ethnicities, religions, and political beliefs. It requires international civil servants to work with people of all nationalities, religions, and cultures without prejudice or bias. An impartial civil servant is conscious of how proposals, events and statements of opinion may appear to various nationalities and cultures. Impartiality involves the exercise of judgment and restraint in all expressions of view, whether public or private. Expressions that could be construed as biased or intolerant, particularly concerning national interests or political issues with which the organisation is confronted, are a breach of impartiality and neutrality. While staff members of IGOs are not expected to relinquish their personal or political views or their cultural and national characteristics, they cannot allow these views and characteristics to cloud their judgment. Impartial international civil servants can easily reconcile their personal views with their international obligations. "What is essential is not the absence of personal, political, or national views, but rather restrained at all times, not merely during working hours, and the expression of such views."[145] This is particularly important when international civil servants deal with conflicts or disputes opposing two or more member states. If, in the treatment of such conflicts, international officials conduct themselves as delegates by sponsoring or promoting the views of one of the parties to the dispute, they will inevitably defeat the aim of international cooperation through multilateral institutions and incidentally put an end to their usefulness to the organisation since, by definition, they cease to be international officials and revert to the status of national agents.[146]

The four examples below illustrate problematic conduct contrary to an international civil servant's duty of impartiality and neutrality.

Each year since 2002, the United Nations has held a forum on indigenous issues. The Forum was established by the Economic and Social Council (ECOSOC) in 2000 as a high-level advisory body on indigenous issues related

144 Report on Standards of Conduct of the International Civil Service, *supra* note 1 at para. 8.
145 *Ibid.* at para. 5.
146 Thanassis, *supra* note 88 at 186–187.

to economic and social development, culture, the environment, education, health, and human rights.[147] In April 2017, Dolkun Isa, a Uighur activist and President of an NGO called 'World Uighur Congress' based in Germany, had duly registered for the conference and intended to participate in the forum. During this period, a former Chinese diplomat appointed to the post of the Under-Secretary-General for the UN Department of Economic and Social Affairs ordered Isa's expulsion from the forum. Following protests from American and German diplomats, Isa was eventually allowed to return.[148] Wu later boasted about his actions on Chinese state television CCTV, stating that "when it comes to Chinese national sovereignty and security, we will undoubtedly defend our country's interests."[149] In 2018, under pressure from the Chinese government, the UN again denied Isa access to the UN Indigenous Forum, citing security concerns. This is an evident example of partial and biased conduct by international civil servants and the UN Secretariat.

Another incident where UN officials exhibited partial and biased conduct occurred in Ethiopia. In October 2021, two senior United Nations officials were recalled from Ethiopia after audio recordings containing criticism of senior UN officials were released online.[150] In the tapes, the Directors of UNFPA and IOM tell a freelance journalist during an unauthorised interview that top UN officials are wrong to sympathise with forces from the northern Tigray region who are fighting Ethiopia's government. During the interview, one of the UN officials called the Tigrayan minority "dirty" and "vicious".[151] These remarks were severe because there was already considerable tension between the UN and the Ethiopian government. The UN made repetitive calls requesting the Ethiopian government to allow humanitarian aid to reach certain pockets of the Tigrayan population. Perceiving these demands as criticism, Ethiopia expelled several UN staff members for taking sides.

---

147 "Establishment of a Permanent Forum on Indigenous Issues", ECOSOC Resolution 2000/22, UN Doc.: E/2000/22 (28 July 2000).

148 "In the UN, China uses threats and cajolery to promote its worldview", *The Economist*, 7 December 2019 edition; Colum Lynch, "U.S. Once Jailed Uighurs, Now Defends Them at U.N.: China tries to silence the group and lashes out at a U.S. diplomat" *Foreign Policy* (25 May 2018).

149 Anne Applebaum, "How China Outsmarted the Trump Administration", *The Atlantic* (11 October 2020): https://www.theatlantic.com/magazine/archive/2020/11/trump-who-withdrawal-china/616475/.

150 Maggie Fick, "U.N. officials recalled from Ethiopia over audio recordings" *The Reuters* (13 October 2021).

151 "UN recalls Ethiopia migration head over Tigray war remarks", *France24* (11 October 2021): www.france24.com/en/live-news/20211011-un-recalls-ethiopia-migration-head-over-tigray-war-remarks.

When the audio recordings of this unauthorised interview were leaked, the IOM immediately suspended and subsequently dismissed its Director in Ethiopia. However, a few months later, in November 2022, the Ethiopian government rewarded the dismissed staff member by appointing her as the Representative of the Intergovernmental Authority on Development (IGAD) to the African Union.[152]

A less blatant violation of the principle of impartiality occurred in 2022 in Palestine, where it was alleged that a UN staff member had breached her duty of impartiality and neutrality. The head of the UN Office for the Coordination of Humanitarian Affairs (OCHA) in the Occupied Palestinian Territory twitted "Relieved to see a ceasefire agreed ending hostilities impacting both Palestinians and Israeli civilians. Such indiscriminate rocket fire of Islamic Jihad provoking Israeli retaliation is condemned".[153] The staff member came under massive criticism, particularly from pro-Palestinian activists, for taking sides and apportioning blame in a conflict. Although she subsequently apologised for her Tweet, the UN removed her from the post. Israel criticised the UN for preventing its staff members from telling what it perceived to be the truth. This incident illustrates how a single imprudent comment may be viewed by some as partial and biased conduct.

The officials' conduct and attitude may make the difference between success and failure of the organisation. After all, international organisations consist of people and cannot be better than the people serving them.[154] Scenarios of wrongful and unethical conduct are limitless; therefore, listing all forms of desirable and prohibited behaviour is not always possible. For this reason, desirable conduct is expressed in terms of principles, namely independence, impartiality, integrity, and loyalty. The most egregious transgressions of these four standards undermine the credibility of international secretariats, significantly reduce the value-added of international organisations in the eyes of member states, lead to excessive scrutiny by national administrations, and eventually erode the independence of international secretariats.

152 Gebrekirstos Gebremeskel, "Ethiopian Regime Rewards Maureen Aching an IGAD Job for her anti-Tigrayan work at UN Ethiopia" Tghat (28 November 2022): www.tghat.com/2022/11/28/ethiopian-regime-rewards-maureen-aching-an-igad-job-for-her-anti-tigrayan-work-at-un-ethiopia/.

153 Jacob Magid, "Senior UN official loses her post after tweet condemning PIL rocket fire at Israel", *The Times of Israel* (13 August 2022).

154 Thanassis, *supra* note 88 at 186.

Conclusion and Recommendations

International secretariats are microcosms of multilateralism. A well-functioning and credible secretariat is indicative of healthy cooperation in a particular field. Conversely, an ineffective secretariat is usually a sign of a dysfunctional cooperation system. If nations and individuals cannot build international secretariats animated by the desire to foster international cooperation, they will stand no chance of creating a united world.[1]

As discussed in Chapter 1, initially, the main reason for creating permanent and integrated machinery for collective action (i.e., embryonic forms of international institutions) was the will to centralise the activities of states. The desire to achieve *une centralité quelconque* through a multinational arrangement was mentioned by Prussia as early as 1815.[2] International secretariats also helped states to avoid gaps between two conferences, ensure continuity in agreements reached during previous conferences, and prevent prolonged interruptions between meetings from thwarting the benefits of cohesion achieved by contracting nations.[3] Initially, primitive forms of international secretariats employed national public servants. There is evidence only towards the end of the 19th century that nations preferred cooperation but were reluctant to collaborate because they did not trust one another.[4] Yet, they also knew that the success of international cooperation largely depended on the amount of trust among them. Hence, they needed international institutions to remedy this mistrust.[5] Nevertheless, it was also evident to states that institutions could be effective and credible go-betweens only if they were neutral and impartial. The opposite is equally true: international institutions could exacerbate the existing mistrust if they favoured some member nations to the detriment of others.

1 Aghnides HE Thanassis, "Standards of Conduct of the International Civil Servant" (1953) 19:1 *Int Rev Adm Sci* 179 at 187.

2 Congrès de Vienne: Recueil de pièces relatives à cette assemblée, des déclarations qu'elle a publiées, des protocoles de ses délibérations et des principaux mémoires qui lui ont été présentés, Tome III (Paris: Librairie Grecque Latine Allemande, 1816), p. 280.

3 Georges Langrod, *La fonction publique internationale* (Leiden: Sythoff, 1963) at 191; See also Alain Plantey and François Loriot, *Fonction Publique Internationales*, 2d ed (Paris: CNRS Éditions, 2005) at 31.

4 Brian C Rathbun, "Before Hegemony: Generalized Trust and the Creation and Design of International Security Organizations" (2011) 65:2 *Int Organ* 243 at 246.

5 Xu Yi-Chong and Patrick Weller, "To Be, But not To Be Seen: Exploring the Impact of International Civil Servants" (2008) 86:1 *Public Adm* 35 at 42.

 | DOI:10.1163/9789004704596_008

Consequently, from the 1870s until the creation of the League of Nations, states experimented with international secretariats, steadily adding structural and institutional safeguards to increase their independence from the governments of member states. Some initial measures consisted of recruiting officials from nations other than the host state and placing international secretariats under the authority and control of a multinational governing body instead of the host nation's government. In a few cases, international officials were even granted limited privileges and immunities.

Looking back in history, the League of Nations may seem to have appeared out of nowhere. However, as mentioned above, the Concert of Europe, The Hague Conferences, and public international unions appeared as the forerunners of the League.[6] "The foundation of the League was little more than an attempt to recognise that international conferences were becoming a regular and frequently recurring part of international practice."[7] The League's Covenant was innovative, but its institutional features were not entirely novel. International secretariats and civil servants existed before the League's creation. Similarly, multinational governing bodies and simple forms of immunities had already been introduced before the League's establishment.

Nevertheless, the League, and to some extent the ILO, were the turning point in the evolution of international secretariats mainly because they became the first intergovernmental institution that expressly expected their staff to be truly 'international.' Staff were required to pledge loyalty to the organisation and to act in the interests of the organisation only. It is noteworthy that apart from staff regulations, no legal instrument of the League imposed any obligations on member states or its staff to safeguard the independence of the League's secretariat and civil service. As seen in Chapter 1, the Secretary-General of the League, Sir Eric Drummond, was instrumental in shaping and safeguarding the principle of independence, even though he had no analogy or precedent to guide him in setting up an independent civil service. Despite Eric Drummond's remarkable efforts, the independence of international secretariats and civil servants remained a nascent concept under the League. Independence was an ambiguous and abstract notion; it was poorly understood and did not attract much attention. This concept began taking shape with the establishment of the United Nations and continues to evolve.

---

6 Inis L Jr Claude, *Swords into Plow Shares: The Problems and Progress of International Organization*, 4th ed (New York: Random House, 1984) at 42–44.

7 Charles Howard-Ellis, *The Origin, Structure and Working of the League of Nations* (London: George Allen and Unwin, 1928) at 67.

Chapter 2 argued that independence must be from member states.[8] It is recognised that the independence of the international functionaries is designed to liberate them from individual state influence.[9] It shields international secretariats and their staff from improper interferences or political pressures so that they are not inclined to act in the interests of certain member states to the detriment of others. Its purpose is to ensure that officials of IGOs have nothing to lose by doing what is right and nothing to gain by doing what is wrong so that they can devote their best efforts to the conscientious performance of their duties. Independence is intrinsically linked to the credibility of the international organisation and the trust nations place in bureaucratic machinery designed to promote international cooperation. Consequently, all actors interested in or responsible for enhancing international cooperation must safeguard the independence of international secretariats and officials.

The main stakeholders of international cooperation are states. As such, they are interested in preserving the independence of institutions through which they cooperate. Each member state owes an obligation towards all other states not to undermine the independence of institutions they collectively set up to facilitate their cooperation. If member states do not protect the independence of international civil service, international organisations cannot be trustworthy agents and will be unable to facilitate inter-state cooperation. Without such independence, IGOs cannot ensure that their secretariats and staff carry out their official functions impartially and neutrally. Impartiality and neutrality of international civil service is a *sine qua non* condition of member states' trust. And if member states do not trust international civil servants, they will have no incentive to create intergovernmental organisations. A lack of confidence in international institutions can erode the fabric of international cooperation. Let us recall that two out of four purposes for establishing the United Nations were "to achieve international cooperation in solving international problems of an economic, social, cultural, or humanitarian character, and in promoting and encouraging respect for human rights and fundamental freedoms for all without distinction as to race, sex, language, or religion" and "to be a centre for harmonising the actions of nations in the attainment of these common ends."[10] The UN cannot achieve either goal unless its secretariat and civil servants are impartial and neutral. The same logic applies to any intergovernmental

8 Michael Barnett and Martha Finnemore, *Rules for the World: International Organizations in Global Politics* (Ithaca: Cornell University Press, 2012).

9 David B Michaels, *International Privileges and Immunities A Case for a Universal Statute* (The Hague: Martinus Nijhoff, 1971) at 21.

10 Charter of the United Nations, Articles 1(3) and 1(4).

organisation set up to help nations cooperate in a specific field. Hence, it is in the best interests of all member states to protect the independence of international secretariats and their personnel.

Although member states are the main stakeholders, they are not the only actors interested in protecting the independence of intergovernmental institutions, international secretariats, and civil servants. International organisations also have a vested interest in preserving the independence of their secretariats and personnel. Like any bureaucracy, intergovernmental organisations "are interested in power, prestige and amenities."[11] They try to maximise their budget, staff, and independence to achieve these objectives.[12] Since their survival depends on their ability to remain independent, they have a strong incentive to foster the independence of their secretariat and staff. For this very same reason, international officials also have an interest in preserving their independence and the independence of their secretariats, without which they can have no employment as international civil servants. One scholar points out that international civil servants are recruited from highly diverse backgrounds; therefore, "there is little else they can agree on but to pursue their common bureaucratic interest."[13] They know that unless their bureaucratic apparatus is independent, it cannot be successful in facilitating international cooperation and states will have no incentive to continue funding ineffective institutions.[14] Hence, all three actors – states, international organisations, and international civil servants – are motivated to maintain the independence of international secretariats and staff. And yet, all three categories of actors frequently and often knowingly fail to act in their interests through actions and omissions that erode this independence.

Chapters 3, 4, and 5 of this work describe practices that erode the independence of international secretariats and their personnel.

As explored in Chapter 3, the independence of international secretariats and international civil servants requires states to take several measures. First, they must enable international secretariats to act on behalf of the international organisation on the territory of any member state. Without such autonomy, the IGO will rely on the host nation or all member nations to fulfil routine and simple tasks. Such reliance could expose the secretariat to undue pressure

---

11 Roland Vaubel, "Bureaucracy at the IMF and the World Bank: A Comparison of the Evidence" (1996) 19:2 *The World Economy* 195 at 195.

12 *Ibid.*

13 *Ibid.*

14 See for instance Sandhya Chandrasekhar, "Cartel in a Can: The Financial Collapse of the International Tin Council" (1989) 10:2 *Northwest J Int Law Bus* 309.

from national governments. For this reason, international secretariats are given not only an international juridical personality but also a domestic one.

Chapter 3 also linked the independence of international secretariats with the privileges and immunities of international organisations. To avoid harassment by national law enforcement authorities, independence requires member states to respect the inviolability of the international organisation's premises, assets, documents, and archives. Similarly, to prevent governments from interfering with the activities of the IGOs through national judicial authorities, independence requires member states to recognise jurisdictional immunity to international organisations. For the same reason, international organisations are generally shielded against harassment by taxation authorities, which usually entails an obligation of member states to grant international organisations fiscal privileges.

The obligations of member states described in Chapter 3 also extend to preserving the independence of international civil servants, which is like that of international secretariats in many regards with a few variations. For instance, whilst international organisations, and by extension their secretariats, should normally enjoy broad jurisdictional immunity, most international civil servants are entitled to functional immunities only.[15] These immunities protect international civil servants against abusive or frivolous legal proceedings by national authorities for acts carried out or words spoken in the performance of their official duties. To ensure that this protection is meaningful and effective, nations must expressly recognise that the authority to decide whether the international civil servant committed the alleged wrongful act while performing their official functions belongs to the executive head of the IGO. States should resist the temptation to make such determinations unilaterally.

Like international organisations, international officials should also enjoy fiscal privileges. However, unlike IGOs, international civil servants are generally exempt from income taxes only in relation to emoluments received from the IGO and not on revenues from sources unrelated to their international functions.

Chapter 4 examined acts and omissions of international organisations that erode the independence of their secretariats and personnel. When international organisations exceed their constitutional mandate and engage

15 Although a few high-ranking officials of international organisations enjoy immunities ordinarily accorded to diplomatic agents or envoys, such immunities are not well suited in the context of international organisations as there is no "sending state" (within the meaning of the Vienna Convention on Diplomatic Relations) which can ultimately exercise jurisdiction over an international official.

in activities not explicitly or implicitly authorised by their constitutive instruments, they undermine their jurisdictional immunities and expose themselves to legal proceedings before national courts. Likewise, when international organisations do not offer adequate legal recourses that an individual is reasonably expected to have in an internal legal order, they inevitably invite domestic courts to disregard their jurisdictional immunities and entertain disputes to which they are a party. Hence, to discourage national courts from getting involved in internal disputes, international organisations should propose to their member states to establish adequate dispute resolution mechanisms for settling contractual, pre-contractual, employment, and pre-employment disputes with bidders, contractors, members of personnel, and candidates for vacant posts.

International organisations also have a responsibility to protect the independence of their staff. There are several measures that international organisations may take to ensure that their members of personnel remain impartial and neutral. First, they must assert the privileges and immunities of international officials each time they become aware of their breaches by national authorities. Second, to prevent external pressures in matters of personnel administration, IGOs should adopt policies governing recruitment, promotions, and separations from service based on meritocracy. Such policies should be very detailed and contain sequential and transparent steps for completing competitive processes for recruiting and promoting members of personnel. Policies should also prohibit separations from service based on demands from member states. Personnel administration policies must eliminate any opportunity for member states to intervene in decision-making. This will disincentivise serving staff members or candidates for vacant posts from seeking support from the governments of their country of nationality. Furthermore, to reinforce an international *esprit de corps*, international secretariats should endeavour to recruit geographically and culturally diverse teams to dilute the national identities and encourage the formation of an international outlook. To achieve further internationalisation of their staff, international organisations should promote or, where appropriate, impose geographical mobility, requiring staff to move periodically between duty stations.

Chapter 5 covered acts and omissions of international civil servants that erode their independence and the independence of their secretariats. International civil servants are expected to meet standards of conduct much more exacting than ordinary legal standards[16] not only while performing their

16 UNGAOR, 8th sess., agenda item 51, Report of the Secretary-General of the UN on Personnel Policy, UN Doc. A/2533 (2 November 1953) at para. 72.

official functions but also in their personal lives. They owe the obligation to conduct themselves at all times in a manner befitting the status of an international civil servant to the IGO employing them. Staff rules or regulations of most international organisations describe the types of conduct that are prohibited. The most detailed rules this research revealed are those contained in the Staff Regulations and Rules of the United Nations.[17] Nevertheless, irrespective of how intricate the staff rules and regulations of a specific international organisation are, international officials must, in addition to carrying out tasks assigned to them, strive "to show such dignity of behaviour as not to harm the good name that the organisation must enjoy if it is to do its job properly."[18] This means they must exhibit integrity, loyalty, impartiality, neutrality, and independence. Only if staff members honour these essential obligations can the IGO effectively protect them against political interference. As discussed in Chapter 5, most transgressions of the highest standards of conduct lead to disciplinary proceedings and culminate in sanctions without affecting the independence of international officials or their secretariats. However, the most egregious types of wrongful conduct can disproportionately affect the independence of international secretariats and their staff.

1 Concluding Remarks on the Nature of Independence as a Concept and Its Practical Application

The main purpose of this work was to explore the genesis and meaning of the concept of independence of the international civil service. The impetus of this research was also its main challenge – interpretations of the term 'independence' used in the context of international secretariats and civil servants are as many as the number of international organisations. There are no member states, international organisations, or civil servants who, on a conceptual level, flatly reject the need for international secretariats and civil servants to be independent. All states and international organisations firmly believe that international secretariats and civil servants must have a reasonable degree of independence to fulfil their mission. The review of staff regulations, staff rules, and codes of conduct of 35 IGOs carried out in Chapter 5 demonstrates that the independence of the international civil service is a universally accepted principle, even if it is not interpreted and applied consistently. Nevertheless,

17 The standards of conduct listed in the Staff Regulations and Rules of the United Nations are based on the 1954 report of the International Civil Service Advisory Board.

18 *In re Souilah*, [1997] Judgement No. 1584 (ILOAT) at para. 9.

it is not yet clear whether the independence of the international civil service exists only when it is expressly recognised in the constitutive documents of international organisations or whether it applies even when treaties establishing international organisations are silent on this point. In other words, is the independence of the international civil service a notion that can derive exclusively from a treaty or has it become a general principle? This concept is so firmly grounded that it can reasonably be regarded as a general principle of law within the meaning of Article 38.1(c) of the Statute of the International Court of Justice. This question is important because not all constitutive instruments for international organisations contain identical or similar guarantees of independence. If the independence of the international civil service requires an express written recognition in a treaty or an international agreement, then certain international organisations necessarily enjoy a greater degree of independence. If, on the other hand, the independence of the international civil service has become a general principle of law, then the absence of an express recognition in a treaty or international agreement is not a decisive element in determining the degree and scope of that independence.

1.1 *Independence of International Civil Service as a General Principle of Law*

Article 38.1(c) of the Statute of the International Court of Justice provides that the "Court, whose function is to decide in accordance with international law such disputes as are submitted to it, shall apply [...] the general principles of law recognised by civilised nations." The phrase 'law recognised by civilised nations' is not only 'anachronistic' and 'unjustified',[19] but also vague. It is unclear which legal systems should be considered and how many must recognise the principle.[20] This relic of European supremacism is today regarded as a term of art referring merely to states with well-developed legal systems and implying no racial or cultural prejudice.[21]

A term that is even more difficult to evaluate is the adjective 'general'. What characteristics does a principle need to have to become a *general* principle of law within the meaning of Article 38.1(c) of the ICJ Statute?

19 *North Sea Continental Shelf*, Separate Opinion of Judge Fouad Ammoun, [1969] ICJ Rep 3 at 134.

20 Imogen Saunders, *General Principles as a Source of International Law: Art. 38(1)(c) of the Statute of the International Court of Justice* (Oxford: Hart Publishing, 2020) at 15.

21 Christopher A Ford, "Judicial Discretion in International Jurisprudence: Article 38(1)(c) and 'General Principles of Law'" (1994) 5 *Duke Journal of Comparative & International Law* 35 at 65.

Two main approaches exist for finding general principles of law. According to the first approach – the comparative approach – a principle can be regarded as 'general' when it is recognised within the municipal systems of the majority of states or when it can be drawn from principles of international law.[22]

The second approach – called 'categoricism'[23] – identifies general principles as those "that have a universal validity as found in the law of nature or [...] a reflection of the legal conscience of civilised peoples and are foundational so that the superstructure of all law is built upon them."[24] Where the comparative approach requires a horizontal generality, assessed laterally across legal systems, *categoricism* requires a more vertical generality, looking to abstractions of principles rather than lateral commonality.[25]

The independence of international secretariats and civil servants can be characterised as a general principle of law under both approaches. For instance, if one applies the first approach, one can distil this principle from the judgements of international and national courts and tribunals, international legal instruments, and national laws. The ICJ, national courts, and international administrative tribunals have often associated the independence of the international civil service with the proper functioning of international organisations.[26] Moreover, the establishment of intergovernmental organisations

22 Report of the International Law Commission, UN Doc. A/78/10 (24 April – 2 June and 3 July – 4 August 2023) at 9; See also International Law Commission, *First Report on General Principles of Law*, UN Doc. A/CN.4/732 (29 April–7 June and 8 July–9 August 2019) at paras. 174 and 253: "For purposes of the present section, it suffices to note that, despite the different approaches in the literature, there seems to be agreement on the point that recognition in the sense of Article 38, paragraph 1 (c), can take place at the international level, without the need to look at the national legal systems of States. As shown in the next section, this position appears to be somewhat supported by the practice of States and the decisions of international courts and tribunals. [...] General principles of law comprise those: (a) derived from national legal systems; (b) formed within the international legal system."

23 Ford, *supra* note 21 at 72.

24 Frances T Freeman Jalet, "The Quest for the General Principles of Law Recognized by Civilized Nations – A Study" (1963) 10:5 *UCLA Law Rev* 1041 at 1085. See also Oscar Schachter, "International law in theory and practice: General course in Public International Law" (1982) 178 *Collected Courses of the Hague Academy of International Law* 9 at 74–75.

25 Saunders, *supra* note 20 at 16.

26 *Reparation for injuries suffered in the services of the United Nations, Advisory Opinion*, [1949] ICJ Rep 174; *Difference Relating to Immunity from Legal Process of a Special Rapporteur of the Commission on Human Rights*, Advisory Opinion, [1999] ICJ Rep 62; *JMB v Organisation for the Prohibition of Chemical Weapons*, [2003] Judgement No 2232 at para. 16 (ILOAT); *Bertucci v Secretary-General of the United Nations*, 2010-UNAT-062 (UN Appeals Tribunal). Contra *Ligue des États arabes c. T.M.*, No. S990103FV 12 March 2001 (Cour de cassation of Belgium) p. 390–395; *Groupement d'entreprises Fougerolle c. CERN*,

is usually accompanied by legal instruments that guarantee at least to some degree their independence. These guarantees can be contained in separate treaties on the status, privileges, and immunities of the organisation[27] or in host-country agreements.[28] Such guarantees can also be found in many constitutive instruments of international organisations.[29] There are no significant IGOs whose independence has been left entirely unaddressed. Similarly, many states have laws dedicated to international organisations, containing specific measures for protecting their independence.[30] Therefore, the concept of

---

21 December 1992 (Tribunal Fédéral suisse): « Les raisons de cette différence doivent, notamment, être recherchées dans le fondement juridique même de l'immunité octroyée aux organisations internationales, à savoir une convention internationale et non pas une règle de droit international général ».

27 See *Convention on Privileges and Immunities of the United Nations*, 13 February 1946, 1 U.N.T.S. 15; *Agreement on the status of the North Atlantic Treaty Organisation, National Representatives and International Staff* signed in Ottawa, 20 September 1951, 200 U.N.T.S. 3; *Supplementary Protocol No. 2 to the Convention on the OECD*, 14 December 1960, 888 U.N.T.S. 179; *General Convention on the Privileges and Immunities of the Organisation of African Unity*, 25 October 1965, 1000 U.N.T.S. 394.

28 See, for instance, the Headquarters Agreement between the Organisation of American States and the Government of the United States of America, 11 U.N.T.S. 11; Agreement between the Government of the Republic of Indonesia and the Association of Southeast Nations (ASEAN) on Hosting and Granting Privileges and Immunities to the ASEAN Secretariat; Agreement between the International Atomic Energy Agency ('IAEA') and the Republic of Austria regarding the Headquarters of the IAEA, 11 December 1957, 229 U.N.T.S. 110; Agreement between the United Nations and the United States of America regarding the Headquarters of the United Nations, UN Doc. A/RES/169(II); Agreement regarding Headquarters of the Organisation of the Petroleum Exporting Countries ('OPEC'), 18 February 1974, 2098 U.N.T.S. 416; Headquarters Agreement between the Federal Republic of Germany and the European Molecular Biology Laboratory of 10 March 1974; Agreement concerning the Headquarters of the United Nations Economic and Social Commission for Western Asia, signed at Beirut on 27 August 1997, 1988 U.N.T.S. 339.

Agreement between the International Atomic Energy Agency ('IAEA') and the Republic of Austria regarding the Headquarters of the IAEA, 11 December 1957, 229 U.N.T.S. p. 110.

29 See, for instance, Articles 100 and 105 of the *UN Charter*; Articles 133 and 134 of the *OAS Charter*; Article VIII of the *Agreement for the establishment of the IDLO*; Article 19 of the *Convention on the OECD*; Article 30 of the Constitution of the INTERPOL; Articles 8(b) and 9 of the Charter of ASEAN.

30 See for instance International Organisations Immunities Act of the United States, Foreign Missions and International Organisations Act of Canada, The International Organisations Act of the United Kingdom, Diplomatic Relations and Immunities Act of Ireland, International Organisations (Privileges and Immunities) Act of Australia, Diplomatic Privileges and Immunities Act of New Zealand, Privileges and Immunities Act of Kenya, Diplomatic Immunities and Privileges Act of Nigeria, and Ordonnance n° 2022–533 du 13 avril 2022 définissant la nature, les conditions et les modalités d'octroi par le Gouvernement de privilèges, immunités et facilités à des organisations internationales,

independence of the international civil service appears to be well-recognised internationally and by most legal systems. Under the comparative approach, this is a decisive criterion for establishing that the independence of the international civil service is a general principle of law.

If one applies the second approach – that of *categoricism* – the history of intergovernmental institutions covered in Chapter 1 reveals that the international community of states moved from primitive structures of multinational bureaucracies to modern forms of international organisations primarily to ensure their independence from some member states. Chapter 2 drew a link between the credibility of international organisations and their independence on the one hand and international cooperation and trustworthiness of intergovernmental bodies on the other. Two centuries of evolution of intergovernmental bureaucracies seem to support the view that the independence of the international civil service is a general principle of law. International river commissions, bureaux, and unions began functioning with national civil servants and were part of a bureaucracy placed under the command and control of a national administration. Over a century, states took small but essential steps to enhance the independence of international bureaucracies from their member states. Multinational governing bodies gradually gained control over international institutions and took upon themselves the responsibility to appoint the chief administrative officer. States then reinforced the independence of functionaries by placing them under the authority of this chief administrative officer, thereby increasing the degree of separation between governments and international institutions. The question of the independence of international civil servants and their ties to the governments of member states was addressed head-on at the time of establishing the League of Nations. The views expressed in the Balfour and Noblemaire reports unequivocally tied the independence of international civil servants to their ability to remain loyal, impartial, and neutral.[31] The Preparatory Commission of the United Nations further reinforced this link.[32] Most international organisations with permanent secretariats have some constitutional safeguards (codified in legal agreements) protecting the

---

des agences décentralisées de l'Union européenne et à certaines associations ou fondations of France.

31 AJ Balfour, "Procès-verbal of the Fifth Session of the Council of the League of Nations, Report relating to Staff of the Secretariat" (1920) 1:4 *League of Nations OJ* 115 at 137; *Report submitted by the Fourth Committee to the Assembly on the conclusions and proposals of the Commission of Experts appointed in accordance with the resolutions adopted by the Assembly of the League of Nations at its meeting of December 17th, 1920* (26 September 1921) at 8.

32 Report of the Preparatory Commission of the United Nations, UNCIO, 1945.

independence of their civil service. This is an acknowledgement that without independence, international organisations cannot effectively facilitate international cooperation because states rely heavily on neutral intermediaries to increase their mutual trust. Consequently, the independence of the international civil service is so deeply ingrained in our conception of intergovernmental organisations that we cannot imagine IGOs whose functionaries would take instructions from or be otherwise dependent on member states. This situation also supports the view that the independence of international civil service may have crystalised as a general principle of law under the second approach of *categoricism* as well.

1.2 *Inconsistencies in the Application of the Principle of Independence*

States and international organisations operationalise the principle of independence differently. There is no common understanding or interpretation of this concept, with a few exceptions. States and international organisations share views only on a few fundamental characteristics of independence of international secretariats and civil servants. For instance, they agree that international secretariats must enjoy a certain degree of autonomy and have a distinct will or *volonté distincte*. As Majone puts it, independence in the context of intergovernmental institutions means that states' preferences may differ from those of the institution of which they are members.[33] Abbott and Snidal call this form of independence "the authority to act with a degree of autonomy, and often with neutrality, in defined spheres."[34] Neutrality implies that the IGO "has the ability to operate in a manner that is insulated from the influence of other political actors – especially states."[35] As a corollary of this conceptualisation, it is understood by all that international secretariats and civil servants cannot favour one member state over another. Therefore, the prohibition for international officials to seek instructions from member states and for member states to influence international officials is common in many IGOs.

Other similarities can be observed in relation to measures adopted by states and IGOs to strengthen the independence of international secretariats and civil service. Specifically, most intergovernmental organisations enjoy some privileges and immunities on the territory of their member states, especially

33 Giandomenico Majone, "Two Logics of Delegation: Agency and Fiduciary Relations in EU Governance" (2001) 2:1 *European Union Politics* 103 at 110.

34 Kenneth W Abbott and Duncan Snidal, "Why States Act through Formal International Organizations" (1998) 42:1 *Conflict Resol* 3 at 9.

35 Yoram Z Haftel and Alexander Thompson, "The Independence of International Organizations: Concept and Applications" (2006) 50:2 *J Confl Resolut* 253–275 at 256.

the host state. International civil servants typically enjoy some privileges and immunities as well. This is not surprising because even the abundant academic literature on this topic tends to study the independence of international organisations primarily through the prism of privileges and immunities.[36]

However, apart from these broad commonalities, member states and intergovernmental organisations do not consistently interpret and apply independence as it relates to IGOs. They implement the principle differently. In relation to state practices, one can observe significant differences in the way states recognise IGOs' legal personality, domestic courts apply jurisdictional immunity enjoyed by IGOs, tax authorities grant fiscal privileges, or delegates interfere with decisions pertaining to personnel administration.

Notable differences also exist in the practices of international organisations, namely in their choice of internal dispute resolution mechanisms, personnel administration policies, codes of conduct, the extent to which they protect their members of personnel from interferences by governments, and other internal arrangements. Considerable differences can be observed in the attitudes and conduct of international civil servants as well. Behaviour that is unethical in some organisations may be widespread in others. For instance, outside activities that are prohibited in some organisations may be permitted in others, and frequent interactions with delegates of member states may be frowned upon in some IGOs but tolerated in others. Functionaries of some organisations do not believe they are accountable for their actions outside of working hours and premises of their employer, while officials of other IGOs

---

36 Kuljit Ahluwalia, *The Legal Status, Privileges and Immunities of the Specialized Agencies of the United Nations and Certain Other International Organisations* (The Hague: Martinus Nijhoff, 1964); CF Amerasinghe, *Principles of the Institutional Law of International Organisation*, 2nd ed (New York: Cambridge University Press, 2005); Niels Blokker, "International Organisations: The Untouchables" (2014) 10:2 *Intl Org L Rev* 259; Edward Chukwuemeke Okeke, *Jurisdictional Immunities of States and International Organisations* (Oxford: Oxford University Press, 2018); Maxwell Cohen, "The United Nations Secretariat – Some Constitutional and Administrative Developments" (1955) 49:3 *Am J Int Law* 295–319; Éric David, *Droit des Organisations Internationales* (Bruxelles: Bruylant, 2016); Norman A Graham and Robert S Jordan, *The International Civil Service: Changing Role and Concepts* (New York: Pergamon Press, 1980); Josef L Kunz, "Privileges and Immunities of International Organisations" (1947) 41:4 *Am J Int Law* 828–862; Jacques Lemoine, *The International Civil Servant: An Endangered Species* (The Hague: Martinus Nijhoff Publishers, 1995); Theodor Meron, "Status and Independence of the International Civil Service" (1980) 167 *Recueil des Cours de l'Académie de Droit International* 289; Anthony J Miller, "Privileges and Immunities of United Nations Officials" (2007) 4:2 *Int Org Law Rev* 169–258; Plantey and Loriot, *supra* note 3; S M Schwebel, "The International Character of the Secretariat of the United Nations" (1953) 30 *Brit YB Int'l L* 71–115; Michaels, *supra* note 9.

firmly believe that their conduct should always be irreproachable because it reflects on the reputation of the IGO.

Chapters 3, 4, and 5 illustrated differences in understanding and applying the concept of independence through concrete examples. What makes a specific practice acceptable or tolerable in one organisation but not in others? Why are the best practices and measures advocated by some IGOs for preserving the independence of international secretariats and officials unacceptable to other IGOs? Some may call this phenomenon 'unity within diversity'[37] others call it 'diversity within unity'.[38]

Several reasons may explain why intergovernmental organisations interpret and apply independence differently. One of the main reasons may be related to the organisation's history. An organisation operating in a certain way for several years cannot envisage fundamentally different ways of functioning. Values, beliefs, and practices that exist for extended periods become part of an organisation's institutional culture. As Plischke puts it, "existing practice tends to become the accepted way of life – the *de facto* situation crystallising as *de jure* behaviour."[39] The way an organisation begins to interact with its member states and officials – particularly its ability to secure greater autonomy from nations and instil an international *esprit de corps* in its staff – depends primarily on the personality of its first chief administrative officer. The values and beliefs of the first chief administrative officer can be decisive in shaping the organisation's institutional culture. The leadership style of the first executive head of an organisation matters a great deal in secretariat development from the outset when the first executive head introduces national bureaucratic traditions.[40] Chapter 1 showed how Eric Drummond introduced the Westminster tradition of independent, neutral, and anonymous civil service in the Secretariat of the League and how this had a positive influence during the first ten years of the League's existence. In Chapter 4, we saw the fundamental mistake made by the first Secretary-General of the UN – Trygve Lie – when he dismissed American citizens suspected of sympathising with communist regimes. This mistake opened the door for similar interference by other member states throughout the UN's existence. Hence, an organisation's civil service

37 Henry G Schermers and Niels Blokker, *International Institutional Law*, 6th ed (Leiden: Nijhoff, 2018) at para 22.

38 Franck Elong Mboulé, *Le régime juridique des biens des organisations internationales* (Geneva: Schulthess Médias Juridiques, 2022) at 693.

39 Foreword by Professor Plischke in Michaels, *supra* note 9 at xi.

40 Bob Reinalda, *International Secretariats: Two Centuries of International Civil Servants and Secretariats* (Routledge, 2020) at 4.

is more likely to be independent if its first chief administrative officer instils the importance of independence during the first years of the organisation's existence.

Another important variable that may determine the degree of independence of an international secretariat and its personnel is the funding mechanism. Some of the most contentious political struggles that have imperilled international organisations have swirled around their financing.[41] International organisations that depend on voluntary funding are more vulnerable to political interferences and are structurally less independent than those funded through assessed appropriations.[42] Precarious funding compels international organisations to tolerate interference. For instance, an organisation funded through voluntary contributions may be willing to accept seconded staff or officials loaned by national administrations to satisfy its personnel needs. Similarly, to obtain funding for some projects, the organisation may feel compelled to comply with the instructions of the donor nation.

Another factor that may impact the independence of an international secretariat and its staff is the mandate of the intergovernmental organisation. The International Bureau of Weights and Measures, the International Hydrographic Organisation, and the Universal Postal Union have a technical mandate that can be interpreted and understood more easily than that of the United Nations, the European Union, or the African Union. Since the activities of technical IGOs are seldom controversial, they are less likely to conflict or interfere with the sovereign powers of their member states. Hence, there may be little incentive for member states to influence the actions of such organisations. For this same reason, technical organisations may not find it necessary

41 Jeffrey Laurenti, "Financing" in Thomas G Weiss and Sam Daws, eds, *Oxford Handbook of the United Nations*, 2nd ed (New York: Oxford University Press, 2018) at 250. Although the United States is often associated with the use of non-payment of its assessed contributions to bend the United Nations to its will, the first financial crisis experienced by UN was triggered by France and USSR when they refused to pay their respective shares of the expenses for the peacekeeping missions in Suez (UNEF I) and Congo (ONUC). The General Assembly sought from the International Court of Justice an Advisory Opinion on the obligation of all member states to pay for peace and security operations carried out by a limited number of nations. In the *Certain expenses of the United Nations (Article 17, paragraph 2, of the Charter)*, Advisory Opinion, [1962] ICJ Rep 151, the ICJ determined that the phrase "expenses of the Organisation" found in Article 17 of the UN Charter must be understood as "the amounts paid out to defray the costs of carrying out its purposes [including] the political, economic, social, humanitarian, and other purposes of the United Nations."

42 Alexandre Tavadian, *United Nations Law, Politics, and Practice* (Toronto: Irwin Law, 2021) at 207.

to put in place extensive safeguards to protect the independence of their secretariats and functionaries. Organisations with political or broad mandates are more likely to encroach on the sovereign prerogatives of their member states. Thus, member states will try to retain some control over the decisions and actions of the organisation.

The location of the organisation's headquarters or offices may also affect the independence of its secretariat and staff. Chapter 3 contrasted the approach of the Supreme Court of the United States in the *Jam* case,[43] which eroded the jurisdictional immunity of the International Finance Corporation, with that of the Dutch Supreme Court, which recognised the jurisdictional immunity of the Supreme Headquarters Allied Powers Europe of NATO based on international customary law.[44] In the first case, the Supreme Court of the United States disregarded a treaty provision expressly requiring signatory states to respect the jurisdictional immunity of the IFC. In contrast, in the second case, the Dutch Supreme Court recognised the jurisdictional immunity of SHAPE even though it was not expressly identified in a written instrument. Therefore, an organisation's independence may depend on the policies and approaches adopted by the legislative, executive, and judicial branches of the host nation's government.

While these reasons may explain differences in the interpretation and application of independence among international organisations, they do not justify these differences. The independence of international secretariats and civil service is a fundamental principle that nurtures member states' trust in international bureaucracies and cooperation. The values and personalities of the first chief administrative officer should not determine the extent to which the institution's civil service is independent of its member states. Similarly, the funding mechanism cannot prescribe the degree of independence enjoyed by an international secretariat and its staff. Even the technical nature of an organisation's mandate is irrelevant in assessing how much independence its secretariat and officials need.

The essential characteristics of independence remain the same from one organisation to another. The only variable that can change is the degree of independence the secretariats and civil servants of different organisations enjoy. In other words, if we place international organisations on a spectrum

---

43 *Jam v. International Finance Corporation*, 139 S Ct 759 (2019), S I.B.

44 *Supreme Site Services v. Supreme Headquarters Allied Powers Europe* (*SHAPE*), Judgement of 24 December 2021. See also *Spaans v. Iran-United States Claims Tribunal*, Judgement of 20 December 1985, ECLI:NL:HR:1985:AC9158; *Eckhardt v. Eurocontrol* (*No. 2*) (1985) 16 NYIL 464 judgement of 12 January 1984 (Maastricht District Court).

(or continuum) of independence, some organisations' secretariats and civil servants will inevitably be less independent than those of other international organisations.[45] Hence, an organisation whose secretariat and staff enjoy little independence necessarily accepts a greater risk of political interference by its member states. Whether or not such interference occurs is irrelevant to determining the degree of an organisation's independence from its member states. States may be tempted to exert pressure on intergovernmental organisations only in certain circumstances, namely in times of crisis. As Michaels correctly points out, "in time of strife, and faced with the fluid and violent atmosphere of periods of national and international stress, [measures for preserving their independence] become safeguards and necessities for the accomplishment of the duties incumbent upon international officials."[46]

To measure the degree of independence enjoyed by secretariats and staff members of various organisations and to assess their tolerance to risk, one needs a standardised definition of independence and objective yardsticks for measuring degrees of independence. The dimension of independence has attracted less attention from scholars than other dimensions of institutional variation and design, including the degree of formality, hierarchy, legalisation, and institutionalisation.[47]

This work deconstructs independence by breaking it down into actors and their corresponding obligations. It demonstrates that member states, IGOs, and international civil servants are responsible for preserving this independence. The principle can be upheld only if all three actors comply with their obligations in good faith. If either one category of these three actors fails to comply with its obligations, the independence will be imperfect or partial.

45 Haftel and Thompson, *supra* note 35 at 260.

46 Michaels, *supra* note 9 at 27.

47 Judith Goldstein et al., eds. *Legalization and World Politics* (Cambridge, MA: MIT Press, 2001); Charles Lipson, "Why are some international agreements informal?" (1991) 45 *International Organisation* 495; David Lake, *Entangling Relations: American Foreign Policy in Its Century* (Princeton, NJ: Princeton University Press, 1999); Yoram Z Haftel, "From the outside looking in: The effect of trading blocs on trade disputes in the GATT/WTO" (2004) 48 *International Studies Quarterly* 121; Stone Sweet, Alec, Wayne Sandholtz, and Neil Fligstein, eds. *The institutionalization of Europe* (New York: Oxford University Press, 2001); Katja Weber, "Hierarchy amidst anarchy: A transaction costs approach to international security cooperation" (1997) 41 *International Studies Quarterly* 321.

2 Recommendations for Operationalizing the Principle of Independence

The previous section posited that the independence of international civil service is so ubiquitous in international law and national laws and indispensable to international cooperation that it can be regarded as a general principle of law. Nevertheless, designating a particular standard or legal norm as a general principle of law does not necessarily assist in understanding how it should be applied. As explained in Chapter 5, principles are not legal rules. Principles must be observed because they require justice, fairness, or some other dimension of morality.[48] They underlie, explain, or provide reasons for rules. Whereas rules answer the question *what*, principles answer the question *why*.[49] They act as a guide in the process of interpreting rules. Principles cannot be applied as easily as rules, which is why states and international organisations operationalise the principle of independence so differently. To harmonise the interpretation and application of this principle, we need rules governing the independence of international secretariats and officials. Rules can successfully harmonise the application of principles only if they are embraced universally.

The easiest way to achieve a universal codification of rules on the international plane is through the UN General Assembly. General Assembly declarations, resolutions, and decisions[50] usually are not binding on member states and do not normally set legal norms. They are not regarded as a formal source of international law.[51] Although, in most cases, General Assembly resolutions are only recommendatory, they often lead to the formation of international rules in two different ways.

First, a General Assembly resolution can lead to the adoption of international conventions. For example, the Universal Declaration of Human Rights

48 Ronald Dworkin, *Taking Rights Seriously* (Cambridge: Harvard University Press, 1977) 25.

49 Gerald Fitzmaurice, "The General Principles of International Law considered from the Standpoint of the Rule of Law" (1957) 92 *Recueil des Cours de l'Académie de Droit International* 7.

50 From a legal point of view, there is no difference between these three types of actions; they all have the same legal status. From a political or symbolic viewpoint, General Assembly declarations connote high political importance and almost invariably embrace particularly significant legal principles.

51 Pursuant to Article 38(1)(a) of the Statute of the International Court of Justice, the only formal sources of international law are: international conventions, international custom, general principles of law, and judicial decisions and the teachings of the most highly qualified publicists of the various nations, as subsidiary means for the determination of rules of law.

of 1948 is an important General Assembly declaration. In its initial form, it was not a legally binding instrument, but it led to a series of legally binding conventions, such as the International Covenant on Civil and Political Rights and the International Covenant on Economic, Social, and Cultural Rights. Similarly, several resolutions on the question of peaceful use of outer space[52] resulted in an international treaty.[53]

Second, declarations and resolutions can trigger the formation of new customary international norms or help crystallise an emerging customary international law.[54] They can become customary rules if member states adopt a uniform and consistent practice of complying with them and feel compelled to respect them. A General Assembly resolution may even allow the International Court of Justice to rely on it in support of its reasoning aimed at clarifying the obligations of member states and international organisations in protecting the independence of the international civil service.[55]

The General Assembly may also direct the International Law Commission to propose rules for protecting the independence of international secretariats and functionaries. Specifically, paragraph 13(a) of the UN Charter mandates the General Assembly to initiate studies and make recommendations for the purpose of "encouraging the progressive development of international law and its codification." In 1947, the General Assembly established the International Law Commission (ILC) to discharge this responsibility.[56] The ILC consists of

52 *Question of the Peaceful Use of Outer* Space, General Assembly Resolution 1348 (XIII), UN Doc A/RES/1348(XIII) (13 December 1958); *International Cooperation in the Peaceful Use of Outer Space*, General Assembly Resolution 1472 (XIV), UN Doc A/RES/1472(XIV) (12 December 1959); *International Cooperation in the Peaceful Use of Outer Space*, General Assembly Resolution 1721 (XVI), UN Doc A/RES/1721(XVI) (20 December 1961); *International Cooperation in the Peaceful Use of Outer Space*, General Assembly Resolution 1802 (XVII), UN Doc A/RES/1802(XVII) (14 December 1962); *Declaration of Legal Principles Governing the Activities of States in the Exploration and Use of Outer Space* General Assembly Resolution 1962(XVIII), UN Doc A/RES/1962(XVIII) (13 December 1963).

53 Treaty on Principles Governing the Activities of States in the Exploration and Use of Outer Space, Including the Moon and Other Celestial Bodies, annexed to the General Assembly Resolution 2222(XXI), UN Doc A/RES/2222(XXI) (19 December 1966).

54 See Ian Brownlie, *Principles of Public International Law*, 7th ed (New York: Oxford University Press, 2008) at 15.

55 See *Review of the Role of the International Court of* Justice, General Assembly Resolution 3232 (XXIX), UN Doc A/RES/3232(XXIX) (12 November 1974) Preamble.

56 *Establishment of an International Law Commission*, General Assembly Resolution 174(II), UN Doc A/RES/174(II) (21 November 1947). As a document simply annexed to a resolution of the General Assembly, the Statute of ILC does not have the status of a treaty. Hence, it may be amended by a subsequent resolution of the General Assembly.

thirty-four members elected by the General Assembly from a list of candidates nominated by the governments of member states. ILC members must be "persons of recognised competence in international law." They are recognised experts or practitioners in both doctrinal and practical aspects of international law. They are selected from various segments of the international legal community, such as academia, the diplomatic corps, national governments, and international organisations. The members of the commission sit in their individual capacity and not as representatives of their governments. The International Law Commission's role includes preparing draft conventions and non-binding legal instruments (*soft law*) on subjects not yet regulated by international law or where the law has not yet been sufficiently developed by state practice. The ILC also has the responsibility to formulate and systematise rules of international law in fields where there has already been long state practice. The work of the ILC has led to the creation of several important treaties and other instruments of international law, including the Vienna Convention on the Law of Treaties, the Vienna Convention on Succession of States in Respect of Treaties, the Vienna Convention on Diplomatic Relations, and the Draft Articles on the Responsibility of States for Internationally Wrongful Acts.

The UN General Assembly can mandate the ILC to prepare an international convention or a non-binding legal instrument on the independence of international secretariats and civil servants. In 1971, a proposal was made by a scholar for a 'universal statute' regulating the privileges and immunities of international organisations and staff.[57] However, such a statute alone is insufficient to achieve the independence of international secretariats and civil servants successfully. Although privileges and immunities are essential, they are not the only components of independence. A legal instrument dealing exclusively with privileges and immunities would likely contain obligations for member states only. It would, therefore, be insufficient to guarantee the independence of international secretariats and staff. As stated above, the independence of international secretariats and staff can be effectively protected only if all three actors comply with their respective obligations. Like a Rubik's Cube that cannot be solved one side at a time, the independence of international secretariats cannot be guaranteed by one actor alone. All three actors need to do their part to foster the independence of the international civil service. Therefore, this work proposes a much broader legal instrument, encompassing more elements than merely privileges and immunities. An international legal

57 Michaels, *supra* note 9.

instrument must regulate all aspects of the independence canvassed in previous chapters to be effective.

If the document developed by the ILC is an international convention, it will pose practical difficulties because only states would be parties to it. The other two actors – IGOs and international civil servants – would not become parties to this agreement or convention. It would not be feasible to compel all IGOs to become signatory parties to this instrument for several reasons. First, it would be difficult to determine which entity can be regarded as an IGO. Second, there are so many IGOs that negotiating a legal instrument acceptable to all member states and IGOs is not practical or feasible. Third, even if we assume that all IGOs can meaningfully participate in the negotiations and agree on a text, this agreement would be inapplicable to future IGOs. To be effective, the agreement must cover not only existing IGOs but also IGOs that might be established in the future.

Therefore, a non-binding legal instrument would be more effective as it would not exclude international organisations and international civil servants. This legal instrument would guide policies and institutional setups required to achieve independence of the international civil service.

States play a crucial role in shaping the independence of international secretariats and their staff at four different moments in an organisation's life. First, they play an important role in negotiating and drafting constitutive instruments and agreements pertaining to an IGO's mandate, funding, status, privileges and immunities. This occurs typically immediately before the establishment of the IGO. Second, states play a key role in adapting their domestic legislation and regulations to give full effect to international agreements that establish IGOs. This part is imperative for ascertaining that international obligations can be meaningfully implemented in the legal order of each member state. Third, member states play an important role in shaping the independence of international secretariats and civil servants when they negotiate seat agreements or host-country agreements. Each nation that intends to host an international organisation must be prepared to make significant concessions to ensure the independence of the IGO's secretariat and civil service. Finally, states play an important role in fashioning the internal regulations and institutional structure of IGOs through their voting and decision-making powers in governing bodies. If these powers are exercised judiciously, the organisation will be compelled to issue rules, regulations, and operating procedures designed to protect the independence of international secretariats and officials.

2.1 *Obligations for Member States*

"States, as founding fathers of international organisations, are in the best position to steer their governance in a responsible manner".[58] They can play a crucial role in strengthening the independence of international secretariats and civil servants by making difficult concessions essential to effective international cooperation.

2.1.1 Funding Mechanisms

As pointed out above, an organisation's ability to shield its secretariat and personnel from improper interferences by governments of member states depends on funding arrangements. When an organisation relies mainly on voluntary contributions instead of predetermined appropriations, it is necessarily more vulnerable to the political pressure of its member states, particularly the most significant contributors and donors. Hence, the organisation may feel compelled to tolerate a higher degree of external interference by interpreting and applying loosely or liberally the independence of its secretariat and staff. Voluntary contributions are not conducive to protecting the independence of international secretariats and civil servants. To ensure that the organisation's survival and ability to deliver its mandate are not at risk as soon as a significant donor decides not to contribute funds to bully the organisation into submission, member states should establish a scale of assessment to apportion the organisation's essential expenses. Voluntary contributions should fund exclusively optional or additional activities of the organisation and not the essential ones. The proposed legal instrument could specify that,

> Essential activities set out in the programme of work of international organisations shall be financed by appropriations. Optional activities funded through voluntary and discretionary contributions shall carry no conditions or restrictions that could require international organisations to seek or obtain instructions from any government.

2.1.2 Recognition of Legal Personality

Typically, international agreements in which founding member states confer legal personality to IGOs provide that the organisation "shall possess juridical

58 Martina Buscemi, "The Duty of States to Ensure Respect of the Duty of Care through Their Membership in International Organizations" in Andrea de Guttry et al, eds, *Duty of Care of International Organizations towards Their Civilian Personnel* (Berlin: Asser Press, 2018) at 128.

personality".[59] The main problem with such wording is that the provisions confer rights on the IGOs but place no corresponding obligations on signatory states to ensure these rights are respected. In other words, governments of member states are not required to take any concrete steps to ensure that their governmental agencies recognise the IGOs' legal personality. Nor do these provisions specify the courses of action available to the IGO whose rights are breached by governments of signatory states.

The provision's ambiguity effectively enables each government to interpret and implement it as it sees fit, giving rise to inconsistent application of the same rule by different member states. The proposed legal instrument must depart from the style of existing agreements by imposing explicit obligations on member states to take concrete actions and by giving corresponding rights to IGOs. For instance, it could provide as follows:

> Each Member State shall endow intergovernmental organisations with juridical personality. It shall ensure that intergovernmental organisations have under its domestic legislation the capacity to exercise all rights enjoyed by legal and natural persons, adapted as required, including the capacity to perform all forms of juridical acts.

2.1.3 Recognition of Jurisdictional Immunity

Chapters 2 and 3 described inconsistent interpretations and applications of jurisdictional immunity of IGOs by member states. In some countries, international organisations enjoy absolute jurisdictional immunity, while in others, they only enjoy restrictive or functional immunity.

Founding member states of some international organisations perpetuate and exacerbate the problem by including ambiguous provisions in legal agreements governing their privileges and immunities. The Agreement for the Establishment of the International Development Law Organisation[60] is a case in point. Article VIII of this agreement provides that IDLO and its staff

---

59 Convention on the Privileges and Immunities of the United Nations, 1 U.N.T.S. 15; Agreement on the status of the North Atlantic Treaty Organisation, National Representatives and International Staff signed in Ottawa, 20 September 1951, 200 U.N.T.S. 3; Agreement on the Privileges and Immunities of the International Criminal Court, 9 September 2002, 2271 U.N.T.S. 3; Convention on the Organisation for Economic Co-operation and Development (with Supplementary Protocols Nos. 1 and 2), 14 December 1960, 888 U.N.T.S. 179.

60 Agreement for the Establishment of the International Development Law Organisation of February 5, 1988, as amended on June 30, 2002, November 30, 2002, March 28, 2008, December 13, 2012, and November 28, 2017.

shall enjoy in the country of its headquarters (Italy) such rights, privileges and immunities as shall be stipulated in a headquarters agreement and that member states shall endeavour to grant comparable rights, privileges, and immunities in support of the Organisation's activities in such countries. This provision gives absolute discretion to member states in deciding whether the organisation and its staff will be given privileges and immunities on their territory. However, as already examined in this work, privileges and immunities are inseparable from the independence of the organisation's secretariat and staff, which is intrinsically linked to the organisation's success. Such important matters cannot be left to the discretion of individual member states.

To minimise the risk of inconsistent or contradictory interpretations of the same agreement by national courts of different member states, legal instruments relating to privileges and immunities must always opt for absolute jurisdictional immunities subject to waiver by the executive head or the governing body of the organisation. The instrument must expressly exclude the theory of restrictive or functional jurisdictional immunity, which, due to its vague nature, inevitably leads to inconsistent interpretations by domestic courts. It could contain an obligation on member states to enact domestic legislation making suits against international organisations not receivable before national courts. The instrument should also compel member states to take concrete steps to recognise the legal personality, privileges, and immunities of IGOs and to ensure that all branches of their governments (legislative, executive, and judicial) respect them. This could be in the form of an obligation for member states to enact legislation compelling governmental entities and organs to respect the legal personality, privileges, and immunities of the organisation and its staff. For instance, the relevant provision could read as follows:

> Intergovernmental organisations, their property, and assets shall enjoy absolute immunity from every form of legal process except in so far as, in any particular case, an authorised official acting on behalf of an organisation may expressly authorise the waiver of this immunity. No waiver of immunity shall extend to any measure of execution or detention of property.
>
> Each Member State shall take the necessary steps, in accordance with its constitutional processes, to adopt such legislative measures as may be necessary to give effect to the absolute jurisdictional immunity of intergovernmental organisations of which it is a member.

It may be prudent to include in the ILC instrument a provision compelling governments of member states to assert and defend the privileges and immunities of international organisations before their national courts. Indeed, on more than one occasion, ministries of Foreign Affairs of member states refused to represent the interests of international organisations before their national courts under the pretext that the rules of civil procedure of their country do not authorise the executive branch of the government to intervene in judicial proceedings of their national courts and to assert the IGO's jurisdictional immunity from all forms of legal process. This is an implied admission by member states that due to procedural limitations of their domestic legislation, their government is unable to give effect to its international obligation, requiring it to respect the organisation's jurisdictional immunity. This lacuna exposes organisations to the risk of having national courts disregard their jurisdictional immunity and make rulings prejudicial to their interests, thereby making the IGOs' jurisdictional immunity devoid of its meaning. To avoid such eventuality, the relevant provision of the proposed legal instrument could require as follows:

> Each Member State shall take the necessary steps, in accordance with its constitutional processes, to adopt such legislative measures as may be necessary to allow its ministry of foreign or external affairs to assert before its courts and tribunals the jurisdictional immunity of intergovernmental organisations of which it is a member.

2.1.4 Recognition of Privileges and Immunities

Often, national law enforcement authorities and domestic courts unilaterally determine that the actions of an international civil servant are unrelated to their official functions and, therefore, not covered by their functional immunities. However, international civil servants have very diverse roles and responsibilities. National authorities are not well-placed to determine whether certain acts were performed as part of an official's functions. Governments of some states have sometimes taken the view that, in certain instances, there can be no doubt that functional immunities do not cover some acts. Indeed, it would be unreasonable to argue that drug trafficking, driving under the influence of alcohol, domestic abuse, physical altercations, or theft are related to an international civil servant's official functions. Hence, it is tempting to consider that in these circumstances, national authorities should have no obligation to seek a determination from the international organisation that the acts were not performed as part of the international official's functions. Although this argument has some merit, it is based on two erroneous assumptions.

First, an act that constitutes a serious criminal offence in a particular nation and shocks the consciousness of its population may not be an offence in many other countries. Homosexuality and polygamy are two such examples. Homosexual staff members may expose themselves to prosecution in some countries by their mere presence. A staff member's sexual orientation is not related to their official functions; however, their physical presence in a country that criminalises homosexuality may be related to their functions.

Second, this argument also assumes that national authorities always act in good faith and prosecute international civil servants to enforce national laws. However, the UN Juridical Yearbook is rife with incidents of abusive attempts by certain governments to influence UN staff members through law enforcement agencies or judicial institutions. International officials have often been arrested and detained in relation to official acts performed on behalf of the organisation.[61] If national authorities had the discretion to determine what constitutes an act in performing an international official's functions, they could easily make functional immunities nugatory. For this reason, the International Court of Justice opined that the chief administrative officer of an IGO should be responsible for assessing whether the organisation's agents acted within the scope of their functions.[62] The Court did, however, point out that the determination by the chief administrative officer creates a strong presumption but an irrefutable one. This presumption "can only be set aside for the most compelling reasons and is thus to be given the greatest weight by national courts."[63] The ICJ's ruling implies that where national courts believe that the IGO's chief administrative officer is abusing their power by refusing to waive functional immunities of staff members who commit wrongful acts unrelated to their functions, they can set aside this determination and exercise their jurisdiction.

Multilateral agreements conferring functional immunities typically do not specify who determines whether international civil servants were acting within the scope of their functions or how this determination is made. To avoid unnecessary tensions between member states and international organisations, the proposed legal instrument should expressly recognise that only the organisation can determine whether a staff member's alleged wrongful act was performed as part of their official functions. It would be judicious to require the IGO to make that determination within a prescribed time limit. For example, the relevant provision could provide:

61 *Immunity from Legal Process of a Special Rapporteur*, *supra* note 26; *Applicability of Article VI, Section 22, of the Convention on the Privileges and Immunities of the United Nations*, Advisory Opinion, [1989] ICJ Rep 177 at para 47. See also *In re Stulz*, [1993] Judgement No. 1232 (ILOAT).

62 *Immunity from Legal Process of a Special Rapporteur*, supra note 26 at para 60.

63 *Ibid* at 61.

> To facilitate the proper administration of justice, a Member State may request the chief administrative officer of the organisation to waive the immunity or privilege accorded to an official who has, in its view, abused such immunity or privilege.
>
> The chief administrative officer shall reply to the request referred to in the paragraph above within 60 days of receiving it, failing which the immunity or privilege shall be deemed waived.

Another important element on which agreements regulating the status, privileges, and immunities of international organisations are often unclear is the fiscal privileges of the international organisation itself. International organisations are typically exempt from all forms of direct taxes. Regarding indirect taxes, such as value-added taxes, they usually have a right to remission or return under certain conditions, namely that the purchase is made 'for official use'.

As pointed out in Chapter 3, it is unclear whether purchases for official use relate to goods and services procured by the organisation for its own usage (such as furniture, IT equipment, and office supplies) or may also include purchases made in the furtherance of the organisation's mandate and mission. It is also unclear whether the determination of what constitutes 'official use' must be made by the IGO itself or by fiscal authorities of the state. This question is not merely theoretical; it has been a source of disagreement between member states and international organisations on several occasions.[64] Most recently, NATO was confronted with this problem when fiscal authorities of some Allies expressed the view that not all purchases made by NATO were exempt from value-added taxes, while others insisted on preserving the VAT-exempt nature of all purchases made by NATO. It took nations several years and dozens of sessions to agree on a common interpretation of Article X of the Ottawa Agreement, which regulates exemptions from indirect taxes.[65] The provision of the proposed legal instrument could specify as follows:

> Intergovernmental organisations, their assets, income, property, and purchases shall be exempt from all direct and indirect taxes, customs duties,

64 See, for instance, Rutsel Silvestre Martha, "Exemptions from Taxes and Customs Duties (Article III Sections 9–10 Specialized Agencies Convention)" in August Reinisch, ed, *Convention on the Privileges and Immunities of UN and Its Specialized Agencies* (Oxford: Oxford University Press, 2016) 235 at 238–239.

65 Agreement on the status of the North Atlantic Treaty Organisation, National Representatives and International Staff signed in Ottawa, 20 September 1951, 200 U.N.T.S. 3.

> and quantitative restrictions on imports and exports. This exemption shall not apply to purchases made by the intergovernmental organisation as an agent acting on behalf of a state or any third party.

2.1.5 Immigration Status and Other Forms of Restrictions

As described in Chapter 3, some member states, especially those hosting peace operations, often oppose the appointment of international civil servants who hold critical views of their governments or are nationals of a state that they consider unfriendly. The most frequent ways of opposing appointments or employment of such individuals by international organisations are refusals to grant credentials or *agrément*, declarations of *persona non grata*, or refusals to issue immigration papers. To not jeopardise its mission to maintain peace and stability in the country and to continue providing humanitarian assistance, international organisations succumb to pressure and comply with unlawful and unreasonable requests from harassing states. One way of preventing such conduct is to have all member states police each other. When one state harasses international civil servants, others must know it. Unfortunately, in most cases, the secretariats of the organisations themselves are responsible for the inaction of other member states. Not to embarrass the non-compliant member state, secretariats often negotiate bilaterally with the government of the concerned state without informing other member states of the problem. Since the bargaining power of the host state is usually greater, international organisations often capitulate by accepting terms and conditions that erode the independence of their secretariats and civil servants. However, the independence of international secretariats and civil servants does not only concern the IGO and the host state; it affects all member states. Hence, an organisation's chief administrative officer is obligated to bring to the attention of the governing body all attempts by a member state to encroach on the independence of international civil servants.

Another way of mitigating the risk of facing such actions by rogue governments is to include in the proposed legal instrument an obligation prohibiting states from requiring *agréments* for international civil servants or expelling them for reasons other than unlawful conduct. For instance, the relevant provision could state:

> Each Member State shall exempt officials of intergovernmental organizations, their spouses and dependents from immigration restrictions and registration. For greater clarity, no Member State may require agréments from or expel officials of intergovernmental organisations without first

providing written reasons in support of its decision and consulting with the chief administrative officer of the organisation.

2.1.6 Applicability of Domestic Law

Member states where international organisations establish their seat or headquarters normally conclude a 'seat agreement' or 'host country agreement'. Arguably, one of the most controversial issues in interpreting and applying these agreements is the applicability or inapplicability of national laws to international organisations.[66] There appears to be a consensus that in certain fields – such as employment law – the applicable regime is the IGO's internal law; thus, the legislation of the host nation is inapplicable. Similarly, there is little doubt that certain categories of local laws, including those regulating health and safety, transport, and environment, apply to IGOs irrespective of their immunity from jurisdiction. However, practitioners struggle to determine the applicability of a wide range of other important areas of law. For instance, legal advisors of international organisations do not have a unified position on whether the EU General Data Protection Regulation[67] (commonly known as the 'GDPR') should apply to international organisations headquartered or operating in EU member states (even if the GDPR expressly exempts IGOs). The answer to this question is important because if an IGO decides to comply voluntarily with the regulation, national authorities responsible for monitoring compliance with the GDPR may have the power to entertain complaints lodged against the organisation. Thus, it is essential to specify in the host country agreement categories of national laws from which the organisation is or is not exempt. The provision dealing with the applicability of national legislation to international organisations could read as follows:

> Rules of public order of a Member State hosting an intergovernmental organisation shall apply to it. Where an intergovernmental organisation does not have an internal policy regulating a specific field or activity, the legislation of the host nation shall normally apply to it mutatis mutandis. The applicability of national laws shall in no case authorise any fine or enforcement measure against intergovernmental organisations in cases of non-compliance.

---

66 See Finn Seyersted, *Common Law of International Organizations* (Leiden: Brill, 2008) at 525.

67 Regulation of the European Parliament and the Council on the protection of natural persons with regard to the processing of personal data and on the free movement of such data *O.J. L 119, 4.5.2016, p. 1–88.*

2.2 *Obligations for Intergovernmental Organisations*

Chapter 4 explored acts and omissions of international organisations that affect the independence of their secretariats and officials. One of the most perilous omissions is the organisation's failure to set up mechanisms for settling disputes with its personnel, external candidates for vacant posts, contractors, and bidders who are unsuccessful in securing contracts.

As mentioned in Chapter 1, the exact number of international organisations is unknown and depends on how they are defined. Many estimate the number of intergovernmental organisations to be between 500 and 700,[68] while the Union of International Associations lists approximately 300 traditional intergovernmental organisations.[69] Even by retaining the most conservative figure of 300 IGOs, only one-third of IGOs offer an acceptable legal recourse to their staff. At least two-thirds of international organisations do not have independent and impartial mechanisms for resolving employment disputes with their personnel.[70] An even smaller number of international organisations offer legal recourses to all categories of personnel, including consultants and individual contractors. Only two international organisations allow unsuccessful candidates for vacant posts to challenge decisions not to select or recruit them.[71] Similarly, international organisations normally do not allow unsuccessful bidders to challenge decisions to award contracts to competitors. As pointed out in Chapter 4, the absence of legal recourse exposes the IGOs to the jurisdiction of national courts.

---

68 Gerhard Ullrich, *The Law of the International Civil Service: Institutional Law and Practice in International Organisations* (Berlin: Duncker and Hublot, 2018) at 37.

69 Statistics published by the Union of International Associations (UIA) in the Yearbook of International Organisations, Number of IGOs by type.

70 Approximately 60 international organisations recognise the jurisdiction of the ILOAT. Three international organisations recognise the jurisdiction of the Administrative Tribunal of the Council of Europe. Approximately 15 UN entities – primarily UN Funds and Programmes – are subject to the jurisdiction of the UN Dispute Tribunal. Between 35 and 40 international organisations have their own administrative tribunals or appeals boards. Half a dozen organisations allow for some form of arbitration by an impartial and independent panel. In total, between 100 and 115 international organisations seem to offer adequate dispute resolution mechanisms to their staff.

71 Article 14.10.1 of the Staff Regulations of the Council of Europe of January 2023 provides that "In addition to staff members, the complaints and appeals procedure shall be open *mutatis mutandis* to [...] job candidates, insofar as their complaint or appeal concerns irregularities of the selection process directly affecting them". Article 1(c) of the Statute and Operation of the Administrative Tribunal of the OECD (adopted in December 1991) states that the Tribunal shall have jurisdiction over applications filed by persons who are not members of staff of the Organisation, challenging the refusal of their application for appointment where it is alleged that such refusal was the result of discrimination.

In employment law, it is paramount for all IGOs to either accept the jurisdiction of another international administrative tribunal, set up their own administrative tribunal, or establish procedures allowing for affordable arbitration. It is equally vital for international organisations to extend the jurisdiction of existing dispute resolution mechanisms to unsuccessful applicants for vacant posts with whom the organisation does not have a contractual relationship. This will not only give external candidates a legal recourse but also ensure that selection and recruitment decisions are subject to some oversight. Such oversight will discourage decisions based on favouritism, nepotism, or cronyism and will, in the long run, foster fairer and more transparent recruitment decisions. The main reason for not offering external candidates legal recourse is the fear of exorbitant costs triggered by a barrage of challenges. This fear is vastly exaggerated.

First, establishing dispute resolution mechanisms for external candidates can be relatively inexpensive. To limit its exposure to financial hardship, an IGO may require external applicants wishing to challenge an administrative decision to advance a deposit that would be reimbursed only if the appellant prevails. This will dissuade frivolous and abusive legal challenges by external candidates who are not confident they will succeed. Of course, imposing an obligation to pay a deposit may dissuade even strong cases; nevertheless, a restrictive legal recourse is infinitely better than no legal recourse.

Second, it is very likely that the IGOs will initially face many legal challenges from external candidates. However, these challenges will compel organisations to improve their policies and to perfect their decision-making processes. As a result, the number of appeals will gradually drop because administrative decisions made by international organisations will withstand much better judicial scrutiny.

Third, not all proceedings need to be equally complex; summary proceedings may suffice to adjudicate disputes with third parties with whom the organisation does not have an employment contract.

In contract law, international organisations should set up impartial and independent mechanisms allowing unsuccessful bidders to challenge decisions not to award them commercial contracts. Enabling bidders to challenge contract awards through impartial and independent mechanisms will improve the organisations' procurement processes and decisions. It will also curb fraud and corruption because contract awards would be constantly monitored by commercial entities and subjected to legal scrutiny by external experts. Most importantly, however, it will shield the organisation against challenges brought before national courts for want of alternative mechanisms.

The most economical and efficient way of establishing such a mechanism is to select impartial and independent experts through a competitive process who can be convened when needed to adjudicate complaints from unsuccessful bidders. To limit the organisation's expenses, the bidder may be asked to advance a deposit of arbitration fees reimbursable only if the bidder prevails. To compel international organisations to establish adequate dispute resolution mechanisms, the legal instrument could require the following:

> Intergovernmental organisations shall propose establishing an independent and impartial dispute resolution mechanism for resolving disputes arising out of contracts or other disputes of a private character to which the Organisation is a party.

Another area where international organisations can play an important role in protecting the independence of their secretariats and staff is personnel administration. Specifically, every organisation must promulgate detailed procedures for making administrative decisions in a way that leaves no room for any external actor to intervene. For instance, all members of personnel, irrespective of their grade, level, or rank, must be recruited and promoted through competitive selection processes. The initial shortlisting of candidates must be carried out by human resources officials who are not involved in any other stage of the selection process. Policies must expressly prohibit any third party, governmental official, or international civil servant from interfering in the shortlisting process. Subsequent steps must also be based on objective criteria such as anonymised written tests and psychometric assessments administered by external firms. Recruitment and promotion policies should expressly prohibit officials responsible for making the final selection decision to consider factors unrelated to the performance of candidates, including recommendations from governments of member states. Furthermore, staff rules and regulations of international organisations should expressly specify that favouring candidates in selection processes is a prohibited conduct that may result in disciplinary sanctions. The relevant paragraph of the proposed legal instrument could read as follows:

> Intergovernmental organisations shall promulgate regulations and procedures that require recruitment and selection decisions to be based on merit. Such regulations shall provide severe disciplinary sanctions for recruitment and selection decisions based on extraneous considerations, including nepotism and cronyism.

Policies governing the selection and recruitment of personnel must be accessible to the public. Yet, staff rules, regulations, and other internal policies of most IGOs are not available to the public. Websites of many international organisations restrict access to their internal policies to serving staff members and delegates of member states. In some cases, the heads of several international organisations even refused to disclose their staff rules and regulations to the author under the pretext that they were confidential. Public institutions that conceal their legal instruments exhibit short-sightedness. The accessibility of legal rules enhances transparency, which in turn helps to strengthen the independence of international secretariats and civil servants. For instance, the knowledge of rules and procedures can be a significant advantage in recruitment processes. If external candidates cannot easily find rules that an organisation applies to its recruitment processes and decisions, they might be tempted to seek alternative means of obtaining such information, which may often consist of lobbying national delegates, thus indebting themselves before even becoming international civil servants. Hence, by publishing their rules, IGOs create a level playing field for all candidates and remove the incentive to look for underhanded ways of obtaining information that should be public in the first place. The legal instrument could require the following:

> Intergovernmental organisations shall publish their policies relating to personnel administration.

Personnel administration policies should also leave no room for governmental officials to participate in decisions that may lead to a staff member's separation from service. Policies should enumerate grounds on which a manager may decide not to recommend the renewal of a staff member's contract. Of course, such grounds may include poor performance, lack of funding, abolition of the post, credible allegations of misconduct, etc. However, under no circumstances can a decision not to extend a staff member's contract be based on complaints or demands made by governmental officials of member states. For this reason, the practice of secondments from national public service and arrangements permitting staff to keep liens on posts in governments of member states must be discontinued. In their policies, international organisations must signal to all their member states that attempts by governmental officials to interfere in personnel administration are unwelcome and that all such attempts will be recorded and reported periodically to their governing bodies. If nations know that attempts to influence decisions relating to personnel administration might become public, they will be less tempted to interfere. To prevent such problems, the legal instrument could propose as follows:

> International organisations shall promulgate personnel administration rules that prohibit the appointment of seconded civil servants of Member States.
>
> The chief administrative officer of international organisations shall report periodically to the governing body any attempt by a government official of a Member State to interfere in an internal decision pertaining to personnel administration.

International organisations are also obligated to ensure that their personnel's behaviour is always appropriate so that governments of member states do not feel compelled to intervene to prevent or punish wrongful conduct. In most situations, interventions of this nature are incompatible with the privileges and immunities of IGOs and their staff. Many international organisations are not equipped to prevent, detect, investigate, and prosecute wrongful behaviour. IGOs must promulgate detailed codes of conduct defining acts and omissions that they consider reprehensible or unethical. They must also issue procedures for investigating and disciplining allegations of misconduct. To implement these policies, IGOs must develop in-house investigative capabilities by recruiting professional investigators or, for smaller organisations with limited financial resources, by training serving staff members to conduct investigations. In addition, victims of wrongful conduct by international civil servants should have a forum for lodging complaints and the right to receive regular updates on actions taken to investigate their complaints. If an organisation fails to investigate a complaint or to sanction reprehensible conduct within a reasonable time frame, the organisation's policies should empower the complainant to challenge its failure and to seek redress before the organisation's independent and impartial dispute resolution mechanism, such as an international administrative tribunal. International organisations should endeavour to have an ethics function for providing confidential advice on conflicts of interest and a robust whistle-blower protection system. The obligations of member states contained in the legal instrument can be formulated as follows:

> Intergovernmental organisations shall adopt a code of conduct containing obligations at least as exacting as those set out in the Report on Standards of Conduct in International Civil Service 1954 of the International Civil Service Advisory Board.
>
> Intergovernmental organisations shall establish internal organisational units to prevent, detect, investigate, and sanction all forms of misconduct by members of personnel and contractors of international organisations.

2.3 *Obligations for International Civil Servants*

Chapter 5 listed four fundamental values that all international civil servants must uphold: integrity, loyalty, impartiality, and independence. Like all public servants, international civil servants are vulnerable to ethics lapses.[72] Staff members may fail to uphold these values either intentionally or inadvertently.

Developing and maintaining the highest standards of integrity requires unwavering commitment and effort. Some believe that integrity and ethics are acquired at a young age; therefore, any effort to teach or learn about ethics in adulthood is fruitless. Other myths about integrity are that ethical people always act with integrity or that issuing a code of conduct is sufficient to eliminate transgressions of integrity. A corollary of these assumptions is that one can learn integrity and ethics only through the ordeal of personal experiences.

These views do not promote ethical and honest behaviour and discourage supervisors, managers, and senior leaders from building ethics and integrity into their organisational culture. Integrity is not genetic and is not acquired only at an early age. It is a learned behaviour that can be relearned and modified if needed. Therefore, mature organisations typically have ethics management strategies, which often involve mandatory staff training, the use of ethics as a criterion in performance appraisals, and the adoption of organisational rules that promote an ethical climate, such as requiring financial disclosure and approval of outside activities.[73] The most critical component of the strategy is a continuous and ongoing ethics training program, which amplifies the message that integrity and ethics matter.[74]

Nevertheless, no measure can be effective unless staff members willingly and actively participate in ethics management strategies. An ethics program imposed on staff will likely be ineffective. Hence, international civil servants must find internal motivation to periodically take integrity and ethics refresher training, irrespective of whether their organisation mandates or offers such training programs. Completing training sessions on integrity and ethics must become part of international civil servants' culture. International officials must also familiarise themselves with their organisation's code of conduct and procedures for seeking confidential advice from competent authorities if they have doubts about the appropriateness of certain acts or omissions, mainly when they believe a conflict of interests may exist. If their organisation does

72 GB Brumback, "Institutionalizing Ethics in Government" in Evan M Berman, Jonathan West and Stephen J Bonczek, eds, *Ethics Edge* (Washington DC: ICMA, 1998) at 66–69.

73 Donald C Menzel, *Ethics Management for Public Administrators: Building Organizations of Integrity* (Armonk: M.E. Sharpe, 2006) at 14.

74 *Ibid.* at 22.

not provide mechanisms for seeking and obtaining confidential advice, staff members should err on the side of caution and disclose any information that may raise an actual or perceived conflict of interest. This requires the establishment and funding of an independent Ethics Office. The legal instrument could require IGOs to take the following action:

> Intergovernmental organisations shall establish a functionally independent ethics office responsible for providing training and advice to their members of personnel. The ethics office shall propose a comprehensive ethics programme, which shall include mandatory annual training sessions for all members of personnel.

Staff members should also avoid soliciting the assistance and support of their national delegations in relation to decisions made by their organisation that may affect their terms of employment or conditions of service. Such decisions may include recruitment, promotions, performance appraisals, investigations into misconduct allegations, disciplinary proceedings, or non-renewal of contracts. All questions revolving around their employment rights and obligations must be dealt with internally and in accordance with the organisation's policies. Staff members dissatisfied with administrative decisions affecting them usually have an opportunity to challenge such decisions through internal dispute resolution mechanisms. Decisions or judgments of these mechanisms must be accepted as final. Where international organisations repetitively mishandle complaints or make arbitrary decisions, member states may intervene through the governing body to raise awareness among other nations and find a solution to a problem that may be systemic. Member states should not intervene on behalf of individual staff members by engaging directly with the members of the organisation's leadership team. The proposed instrument could state as follows:

> Each Member State undertakes not to intervene on behalf of individual members of personnel in any decision relating to personnel administration.
>
> The regulations of intergovernmental organisations shall expressly prohibit staff members from seeking support from their government in relation to any personnel administration matter.

Finally, international civil servants must remain neutral and anonymous. They should not take a stance on conflicts between two more member states, get involved in debates on controversial issues, or release statements and publications without first seeking authorisation from their employer. Staff should avoid political activities or retain formal ties to national administrations, including secondments or liens. The proposed legal instrument may oblige states to deny requests for liens to their public servants intending to accept an appointment with international organisations.

> Each Member State undertakes not to grant a lien or another form of right of return to any governmental official intending to accept an appointment with an international organisation.
>
> Intergovernmental organisations shall not appoint to a vacant post any governmental official who has kept a lien or another form of right of return.

In conclusion, the independence of the international civil service is at the core of international cooperation. It is a broad and elusive principle that continues to evolve organically and unsystematically. Given its importance, it is high time for states to agree on its definition, characteristics, and parameters and regulate it through concrete rules. If they do not circumscribe and regulate this principle, international organisations will continue interpreting and applying it as they see fit. This will further exacerbate divergencies and erode the principle of independence.

Bibliography

Books

Ahluwalia, Kuljit, *The Legal Status, Privileges and Immunities of the Specialized Agencies of the United Nations and Certain Other International Organizations* (The Hague: Martinus Nijhoff, 1964).

Amerasinghe, CF, *Principles of the Institutional Law of International Organization*, 2nd ed (New York: Cambridge University Press, 2005).

Amerasinghe, CF, *The Law of the International Civil Service: As Applied by International Administrative Tribunals*, 2nd ed (Oxford: Clarendon Press, 1994).

Barnett, Michael and Martha Finnemore, *Rules for the World: International Organizations in Global Politics* (Ithaca: Cornell University Press, 2012).

Barros, James, *Betrayal from Within – Joseph Avenol, Secretary-General of the League 1933–1940* (New Haven, Conn: Yale University Press, 1969).

Bastid, Suzanne, *Les Fonctionnaires internationaux* (Paris: Gidel, 1931).

Boutros-Ghali, Boutros, *Unvanquished* (London: I.B. Tauris, 1999).

Brown, Andrew D, *Organizational Culture*, 2d ed (London: FT Publishing International, 1998).

Brownlie, Ian, *Principles of Public International Law*, 7th ed (Oxford: Oxford University Press, 2008).

Cecil of Chelwood, Robert, *All the Way* (London: Hodder and Stoughton, 1949).

Chesterman, Simon, *Secretary or General? The UN Secretary-General in World Politics* (New York: Cambridge University Press, 2007).

Chukwuemeke Okeke, Edward, *Jurisdictional Immunities of States and International Organizations* (Oxford: Oxford University Press, 2018).

Cialdini, Robert B, *Influence: The Psychology of Persuasion* (New York: Harper, 2007).

Claude, Inis L Jr, *Swords into Plow Shares: The Problems and Progress of International Organization*, 4th ed. (New York: Random House, 1984).

Crawford, James, *State Responsibility: The General Part* (Cambridge: Cambridge University Press, 2013).

David, Éric, *Droit des Organisations Internationales* (Bruxelles: Bruylant, 2016).

Dzhirkelov, Ilya, *Secret Servant: My Life with the KGB and the Soviet Elite* (New York: Harper Collins, 1987).

Eagleton, Clyde, *International Government* (New York: Ronald Press, 1948).

Ellis, Charles Howard, *The Origin, Structure and Working of the League of Nations* (London: George Allen and Unwin, 1928).

Fox, Hazel and Philippa Webb, *The Law of State Immunity*, 3d ed (Oxford: Oxford University Press, 2013).

Garner, Bryan A, ed, *Black's Law Dictionary*, deluxe ninth ed (St Paul, MN: West, 2009).

Gordenker, Leon, *The UN Secretary-General and Secretariat*, 2nd ed (New York: Routledge, 2010).

Graham, Norman A and Robert S Jordan, *The International Civil Service: Changing Role and Concepts* (New York: Pergamon Press, 1980).

Grey, Earl, *Parliamentary Government*, 2d ed (London: John Murray, 1864).

Guttry, Andrea de et al., eds, *The Duty of Care of International Organizations Towards Their Civilian Personnel: Legal Obligations and Implementation Challenges* (The Hague: T.M.C. Asser Press, 2018).

Hammarskjöld, Dag, *The International Civil Servant in Law and in Fact: A Lecture Delivered to Congregation on 30 May 1961* (Uppsala: Dag Hammarskjöld Foundation, 2021).

Higgins, Rosalyn et al., *Oppenheim's International Law: United Nations* (Oxford: Oxford University Press, 2017).

Hill, Norman L, *The Public International Conference: Its Function, Organization and Procedure* (Stanford University: Stanford University Press, 1929).

Hobson, Asher, *The International Institute of Agriculture: An Historical and Critical Analysis of Its Organization, Activities and Policies of Administration* (Berkeley: University of California Press, 1931).

Howard-Ellis, Charles, *The Origin, Structure and Working of the League of Nations* (London: George Allen and Unwin, 1928).

Keohane, Robert O, *After hegemony : cooperation and discord in the world political economy* (Princeton, N.J.: Princeton University Press).

Klabbers, Jan, *An Introduction to International Institutional Law*, 4th ed (New York: Cambridge University Press, 2022).

Langrod, Georges, *La fonction publique internationale* (Leiden: Sythoff, 1963).

Lemoine, Jacques, *The International Civil Servant: An Endangered Species* (The Hague: Martinus Nijhoff Publishers, 1995).

Lie, Trygve, *In the Cause of Peace: Seven Years at the United Nations* (New York: Macmillan, 1954).

Lowe, Rodney, *The Official History of the British Civil Service: Reforming the Civil Service, Volume I: The Fulton Years, 1966–81* (London: Routledge, 2011).

Luard, Evan, *A History of the United Nations* (London: Palgrave Macmillan UK, 1982).

Macfadyen, David et al., *Eric Drummond and his Legacies: The League of Nations and the Beginnings of Global Governance* (Cham: Palgrave Macmillan, 2019).

Massey, Andrew, *International Handbook on Civil Service Systems* (Cheltenham: Edward Elgar, 2011).

Mathiason, John, *Invisible Governance: International Secretariats in Global Politics* (Bloomfield, CT: Kumarian Press, 2007).

Mboulé, Franck Elong, *Le régime juridique des biens des organisations internationales* (Geneva: Schulthess Médias Juridiques, 2022).

Menzel, Donald C, *Ethics Management for Public Administrators: Building Organizations of Integrity* (Armonk: M.E. Sharpe, 2006).

Meyer, Erin, *The Culture Map: Decoding How People Think, Lead, and Get Things Done Across Cultures* (New York: Public Affairs, 2014).

Michaels, David B., *International Privileges and Immunities A Case for a Universal Statute* (The Hague: Martinus Nijhoff, 1971).

Morlino, Elisabetta, *Procurement by International Organizations* (Cambridge University Press, 2019).

Muldoon, James P, Jr et al, *Multilateral Diplomacy and the United Nations Today*, 2d ed (New York: Routledge, 2005).

Pellet, Alain and David Ruzié, *Les fonctionnaires internationaux* (Paris: Presses Universitaires de France, 1993).

Plantey, Alain and François Loriot, *Fonction Publique Internationales*, 2d ed (Paris: CNRS Éditions, 2005).

Reinalda, Bob, *International Secretariats: Two Centuries of International Civil Servants and Secretariats* (Routledge, 2020).

Reinisch, August, *International Courts Before National Courts* (Cambridge: Cambridge University Press, 2000).

Reinisch, August, *The Privileges and Immunities of International Organizations in Domestic Courts* (Oxford: Oxford University Press, 2013).

Rovine, Arthur W, *The First Fifty Years: The Secretary-General in World Politics 1920–1970* (Leiden: Sijthoff, 1970).

Russell, Ruth B, *A History of The United Nations Charter: The Role of the United States 1940–1945* (Menasha, Wisconsin: The Brookings Institution, 1958).

Satow, Ernest, *International Congresses* (London: H.M. Stationary Office, 1920).

Saunders, Imogen, *General Principles as a Source of International Law: Art. 38(1)(c) of the Statute of the International Court of Justice* (Oxford: Hart Publishing, 2020).

Schelling, Thomas, *The Strategy of Conflict* (Cambridge, MA: Harvard University Press, 1980).

Schermers, Henry G and Niels M Blokker, *International Institutional Law: Unity within Diversity*, 6th ed (Leiden: Martinus Nijhoff Publishers, 2018).

Seyersted, Finn, *Common Law of International Organizations* (Leiden: Brill, 2008).

Shaw, Malcolm N, *International Law*, eighth ed (Cambridge: Cambridge University Press, 2017).

Shevchenko, Arkady N, *Breaking with Moscow* (New York: Ballantine Books, 1985).

Siotis, Jean, *Essai sur le Secrétariat International* (Geneva: Librairie Droz, 1963).

Spencer, David and Michael Brogan, *Mediation Law and Practice* (Cambridge: Cambridge University Press, 2006).

Suvorov, Viktor, *Inside the Aquarium: The Making of a Top Soviet Spy* (New York: Macmillan, 1986).

Tavadian, Alexandre, *United Nations Law, Politics, and Practice* (Toronto: Irwin Law, 2021).

Thant, U, *View from the UN* (London: David and Charles Publishing, 1978).

Ullrich, Gerhard, *The Law of the International Civil Service: Institutional Law and Practice in International Organisations* (Berlin: Duncker and Hublot, 2018).

Urquhart, Brian, *A Life in Peace and War* (New York: Harper and Row Publishers, 1987).

Urquhart, Brian, *Hammarskjöld* (New York: Harper and Row, 1972).

Van Ginneken, Anique HM, *Historical Dictionary of the League of Nations* (Lanham, Maryland: The Scarecrow Press, 2006).

Walters, FP, *A History of the League of Nations* (New York: Oxford University Press, 1952).

Wolton, Thierry, *Le KGB en France* (Paris: Grasset, 1986).

Book Chapters

Barros, James, "The Importance of Secretaries-General of the United Nations" in Robert S Jordan, ed, *ag Hammarskjöld Revisited: The United Nations Secretary-General as a Force in World Politics* (Durham: Carolina Academic Press, 1983).

Brumback, GB, "Institutionalizing Ethics in Government" in Evan M Berman, Jonathan West and Stephen J Bonczek, eds, *Ethics Edge* (Washington DC: ICMA, 1998).

Buscemi, Martina, "The Duty of States to Ensure Respect of the Duty of Care through Their Membership in International Organizations" in Andrea de Guttry et al., eds, *The Duty of Care of International Organizations Towards Their Civilian Personnel* (Berlin: Asser Press, 2018) 127.

Chukwuemeke Okeke, Edward, "The Tension between the Jurisdictional Immunity of International Organizations and the Right of Access to Court" in Peter Quayle, ed, *The Role of International Administrative Law at International Organizations* (Leiden: Brill Nijhoff, 2020) 25.

Gulati, Rishi and Thomas John, "Arbitrating Employment Disputes Involving International Organizations" in Peter Quayle, ed, *The Role of International Administrative Law at International Organizations* (Leiden: Brill, 2021).

Jonah, James OC and Amy S Hill, "The Secretariat: Independence and Reform" in *The Oxford Handbook on the United Nations*, 2nd ed (New York: Oxford University Press, 2018).

Jones, Dorothy V, "Seeking Balance: The Secretary-General as Normative Negotiator" in *The UN Secretary-General and Moral Authority* (Washington D.C.: Georgetown University Press, 2007).

Laurenti, Jeffrey, "Financing" in Thomas G Weiss and Sam Daws, eds, *The Oxford Handbook on the United Nations*, 2nd ed (New York: Oxford University Press, 2018).

Martha, Rutsel Silvestre, "Exemptions from Taxes and Customs Duties (Article III Sections 9–10 Specialized Agencies Convention)" in August Reinisch, ed, *The Conventions on the Privileges and Immunities of the United Nations and Its Specialized Agencies* (Oxford: Oxford University Press, 2016).

Martha, Rutsel Silvestre, "Exemptions from Taxes, Customs Duties, and Prohibitions on Imports and Exports" in August Reinisch, ed, *The Conventions on the Privileges and Immunities of the United Nations and Its Specialized Agencies* (Oxford: Oxford University Press, 2016).

Novak, Gregor and August Reinisch, "Austria" in August Reinisch, ed, *The Privileges and Immunities of International Organizations in Domestic Courts* (Oxford: Oxford University Press, 2013).

Pingel, Isabelle, "Article 105" in Jean-Pierre Cot, Alain Pellet and Mathias Forteau, eds, *La Charte des Nations Unies: Commentaire article par article*, 3d ed (Paris: Economica, 2005).

Reinisch, August, "Immunity of Property, Funds and Assets (Article II Section 2 General Convention)" in August Reinisch, ed, *The Conventions on the Privileges and Immunities of the United Nations and Its Specialized Agencies: A Commentary* (Oxford: Oxford University Press, 2016) 63.

Reinisch, August, "Privileges and Immunities" in Jacob Katz Cogan, Ian Hurd and Ian Johnstone, eds, *The Oxford Handbook on the United Nations* (Oxford: Oxford University Press, 2016).

Schachter, Oscar, "The International Civil Servant: Neutrality and Responsibility" in Robert S Jordan, ed, *Dag Hammarskjold Revisted: The UN Secretary-General as a Force in World Politics* (Durham: Carolina Academic Press, 1983).

Villalpando, Santiago, "International Administrative Tribunals" in Jacob Katz Cogan, Ian Hurd and Ian Johnstone, eds, *The Oxford Handbook of International Organizations* (Oxford: Oxford University Press, 2016).

Vinuesa, Raùl E, "Argentina" in August Reinisch, ed, *The Privileges and Immunities of International Organizations in Domestic Courts* (Oxford: Oxford University Press, 2013).

Ziegler, Andreas R, "Article 104" in Bruno Simma et al., eds, *The Charter of the United Nations: A Commentary*, 3d ed (Oxford: Oxford University Press, 2012).

Journal Articles

Abbott, Kenneth W and Duncan Snidal, "Why States Act through Formal International Organizations" (1998) 42:1 Journal of Conflict Resolution 3.

Baldwin, Simeon E, "International Congresses and Conferences of the Last Century as Forces Working Toward the Solidarity of the World" (1907) 1:3 American Journal of International Law 565.

Berenson, William M, "Squaring the Concept of Immunity with the Fundamental Right to a Fair Trial" (2012) 3 World Bank Legal Review 133.

Birch, AH, "Economic Models in Political Science: The Case of 'Exit, Voice, and Loyalty'" (1975) 5:1 British Journal of Political Science 69.

Blokker, Niels, "International Organizations: The Untouchables" (2014) 10:2 International Organizations Law Review 259.

Bonafe, Beatrice I, "Italian Courts and the Immunity of International Organizations" (2014) 10:2 International Organizations Law Review 505.

Bowett, Derek W, "Tenure, Fixed Term, Secondment from Governments: The United Nations Civil Service and the European Civil Service Compared" (1982) 14:4 N.Y.U. Journal of International Law and Politics 799.

Bradlow, Daniel D, "Using a Shield as a Sword: Are International Organizations Abusing Their Immunity" (2017) 31:1 Temple International & Comparative Law Journal 45.

Burns, C Delisle, "International Administration" (1926) 7 British Yearbook of International Law 54.

Caflisch, Lucius, "La Pratique Suisse en Matiere de Droit International Public 1992" (1993) 3:5 Swiss Review of International and European Law 669.

Carlston, Kenneth S, "International Administrative Law: A Venture in Legal Theory" (1959) 8:2 Journal of Public Law 329.

Carroz, JE and AG Roche, "Proposed International Commission for the Conservation of Atlantic Tunas, The." (1967) 61:3 American Journal of International Law 673.

Chandrasekhar, Sandhya, "Cartel in a Can: The Financial Collapse of the International Tin Council" (1989) 10:2 Northwestern Journal of International Law & Business 309.

Chukwuemeke Okeke, Edward, "Jurisdictional Immunity of International Organizations in the United States in the Wake of the Supreme Court Decision in Jam v. IFC" (2020) Intergovernmental Organisations In-house Counsel Journal J 1.

Clark, G Kitson, "'Statesmen in Disguise': Reflections on the History of the Neutrality of the Civil Service" (1959) 2:1 The Historical Journal 19.

Claude, Inis L Jr, "Peace and Security: Prospective Roles for the Two United Nations" (1996) 2:3 Global Governance 289.

Cohen, Maxwell, "The United Nations Secretariat – Some Constitutional and Administrative Developments" (1955) 49:3 American Journal of International Law 295.

Cohen, Maxwell, "The United States and the United Nations Secretariat: A Preliminary Appraisal" (1953) 1:3 McGill Law Journal 169.

Daugirdas, Kristina, "Reputation as a Disciplinarian of International Organizations" (2019) 113:2 American Journal of International Law 221.

David, Meryll, "Les stratégies d'influence des Etats membres sur le processus de recrutement des organisations internationales : le cas de la France" (2008) 2:126 Revue française d'administration publique 263.

De Brabandere, Eric, "Belgian Courts and the Immunity of International Organizations" (2014) 10:2 International Organizations Law Review 464.

De Brabandere, Eric, "Immunity of International Organizations in Post-Conflict International Administrations" (2010) 7:1 International Organizations Law Review 79.

Defeis, Elizabeth F, "U.N. Peacekeepers and Sexual Abuse and Exploitation: An End to Impunity" (2008) 7:2 Washington University Global Studies Law Review 185.

Dhinakaran, Renuka, "Law of the International Civil Service: A Venture into Legal Theory" (2011) 8:1 International Organizations Law Review 137.

Drummond, Eric, "The Secretariat of the League of Nations" (1931) 9:2 Public Administration 228.

Eeek, Hilding, "The Secretariat as a Principal Organ of the United Nations" (1953) 23 Nordisk Tidsskrift for International Ret 3.

Ewin, RE, "Loyalty and Virtues" (1992) 42:169 The Philosophical Quarterly 403.

Fedder, Edwin H, "The Functional Basis of International Privileges and Immunities: A New Concept in International Law and Organization" (1960) 9:1 American University Law Review 60.

Finer, SE, "The Individual Responsibility of Ministers" (1956) 34:4 Public Administration 377.

Fiti Sinclair, Guy, "The International Civil Servant in Theory and Practice: Law, Morality, and Expertise" (2015) 26:3 European Journal of International Law 747.

Ford, Christopher A, "Judicial Discretion in International Jurisprudence: Article 38(1)(c) and 'General Principles of Law'" (1994) 5 Duke Journal of Comparative & International Law 35.

Friedmann, Wolfgang and Arghyrios A Fatouros, "The United Nations Administrative Tribunal" (1957) 11:1 International Organization 13.

Graaf, Gjalt de, "The Loyalties of Top Public Administrators" (2011) 21:2 Journal of Public Administration Research and Theory 285.

Grabowska, Genowefa, "Independence of the International Civil Servants" (1988) 17 Polish Yearbook of International Law 61.

Grady, Kate, "Sex, Statistics, Peacekeepers and Power: UN Data on Sexual Exploitation and Abuse and the Quest for Legal Reform" (2016) 79:6 Modern Law Review 931.

Graham, Jill W and Michael Keeley, "Hirschman's Loyalty Construct Research on Hirschman's Exit, Voice, and Loyalty Model" (1992) 5:3 Employee Responsibilities and Rights Journal 191.

Haftel, Yoram Z and Alexander Thompson, "The Independence of International Organizations: Concept and Applications" (2006) 50:2 The Journal of Conflict Resolution 253.

Hoffmann, Elizabeth A, "Exit and Voice: Organizational Loyalty and Dispute Resolution Strategies" (2005) 84:4 Social Forces 2313.

Honig, F, "The International Civil Service: Basic Problems and Contemporary Difficulties" (1954) 30:2 International Affairs 175.

Inman, Samuel Guy, "Pan-American Conferences and Their Results" (1923) 4:3 The Southwestern Political and Social Science Quarterly 238.

Jalet, Frances T Freeman, "The Quest for the General Principles of Law Recognized by Civilized Nations – A Study" (1963) 10:5 UCLA Law Review 1041.

Johnstone, Ian, "Do International Organizations Have Reputations Editorial" (2010) 7:2 International Organizations Law Review 235.

Jonah, James OC, "Independence and Integrity of the International Civil Service: The Role of Executive Heads and the Role of States" (1982) 14:4 New York University Journal of International Law and Politics 841.

Kerr, Philip, "The Practical Organisation of Peace" (1919) 9:34 The Round Table Journal 217.

Kihara-Hunt, Ai, "Addressing Sexual Exploitation and Abuse" (2017) 21:1–2 Journal of International Peacekeeping 62.

Kunz, Josef L, "Privileges and Immunities of International Organizations" (1947) 41:4 American Journal of International Law 828.

Levitan, David M, "The Neutrality of the Public Service" (1942) 2:4 Public Administration Review 317.

Majone, Giandomenico, "Two Logics of Delegation: Agency and Fiduciary Relations in EU Governance" (2001) 2:1 European Union Politics 103.

Manulak, Michael W, "Leading by design: Informal influence and international secretariats" (2017) 12:4 The Review of International Organizations 497.

Mayr, Teresa F, "Where Do We Stand and Where Do We Go: The Fine Balance between Independence and Accountability of United Nations Experts on Mission", (2018) 15:1 International Organizations Law Review 130.

Meighan, Katherine and Gabriel Rodriguez-Rico, "To Join or Not to Join: A Comparative Analysis of Joining or Creating an International Administrative Tribunal" in The Role of International Administrative Law at International Organizations (2020) AIIB Yearbook of International Law 119.

Mele, Valentina, Simon Anderfuhren-Biget and Frédéric Varone, "Conflicts of Interest in International Organizations: Evidence from Two United Nations Humanitarian Agencies" (2016) 94:2 Public Administration 490.

Meron, Theodor, "Staff of the United Nations Secretariat: Problems and Directions" (1976) 70:4 American Journal of International Law 659.

Meron, Theodor, "Status and Independence of the International Civil Service" (1980) 167 Recueil des Cours de l'Académie de Droit International 289.

Mihajlov, Dobromir, "The Origin and the Early Development of International Civil Service" (2004) 1 Miskolc Journal of International Law 79.

Miller, Anthony J, "Legal Aspects of Stopping Sexual Exploitation and Abuse in U.N. Peacekeeping Operations Perspective" (2006) 39:1 Cornell International Law Journal 71.

Miller, Anthony J, "Privileges and Immunities of United Nations Officials" (2007) 4:2 International Organizations Law Review 169.

Muller, Sam, "International Organizations and Their Officials: To Tax or Not to Tax?" (1993) 6:1 Leiden Journal of International Law 47.

Papayannis, Diego M, "Independence, Impartiality and Neutrality in Legal Adjudication" (2016) 28 Revus: Journal for Constitutional Theory and Philosophy of Law 33.

Parker, Donald W, "The Value-Added Tax in the European Economic Community" (1988) 11 Boston College International and Comparative Law Review 155.

Pasquet, Luca, "Litigating the Immunities of International Organizations in Europe: The 'Alternative-Remedy' Approach and its 'Humanizing' Function" (2021) 36:2 Utrecht Journal of International and European Law 192.

Politis, N, "L'organisation de l'Union internationale des sucres" (1904) 2 Revue de science et de législation financières 1.

Preuss, Lawrence, "Immunity of Officers and Employees of the United Nations for Official Acts: The Ranallo Case" (1947) 41:3 American Journal of International Law 555.

Puig, Gonzalo Villalta, "Unethical Conduct in the Performance of International Government Contracts: AWB Ltd. and the United Nations Oil-for-Food Programme" (2007) 37:1 Public Contract Law Journal 59.

Ranshofen-Wertheimer, Egon F, "The International Civil Service of the Future" (1946) 24 International Conciliation 60.

Rappard, William E, "The Evolution of the League of Nations" (1927) 21:4 American Political Science Review 792.

Rathbun, Brian C, "Before Hegemony: Generalized Trust and the Creation and Design of International Security Organizations" (2011) 65:2 International Organization 243.

Reinalda, Bob, "Institutional Development of the United Nations Secretariat" (2020) 26 Global Governance 325.

Reinisch, August and Ulf Andreas Weber, "In the Shadow of Waite and Kennedy – The Jurisdictional Immunity of International Organizations, the Individual's Right of Access to the Courts and Administrative Tribunals as Alternative Means of Dispute Settlement" (2004) 1 International Organizations Law Review 59.

Reinisch, August, "To What Extent Can and Should National Courts Fill the Accountability Gap" (2014) 10:2 International Organizations Law Review 572.

Reinsch, Paul S, "International Unions and Their Administration" (1907) 1:3 American Journal of International Law 579.

Reuter, Paul, "Le droit au secret et les institutions internationales" (1956) 2 Annuaire français de droit international 46.

Ruzié, David, "Le non-renouvellement des contrats à durée déterminée et l'ingérence des Etats. A propos de l'Affaire Ballo" (1972) 18 Annuaire français de droit international 378.

Ryngaert, Cedric, "The Immunity of International Organizations before Domestic Courts: Recent Trends" (2010) 7:1 International Organizations Law Review 121.

Schwebel, SM, "The International Character of the Secretariat of the United Nations" (1953) 30 British Yearbook of International Law 71.

Shotton, Anna, "A Strategy to Address Sexual Exploitation and Abuse by United Nations Peacekeeping Personnel Perspective" (2006) 39:1 Cornell International Law Journal 97.

Sly, John F, "The Genesis of the Universal Postal Union: A Study in the Beginnings of International Organization Document No. 233" (1926) 11 International Conciliation 395.

Thanassis, Aghnides HE, "Standards of Conduct of the International Civil Servant" (1953) 19:1 International Review of Administrative Sciences 179.

Treichl, Clemens and August Reinisch, "Domestic Jurisdiction over International Financial Institutions for Injuries to Project-Affected Individuals: The Case of Jam v International Finance Corporation" (2019) 16:1 International Organization Law Review 105.

Tuyama Sollero, Barbara, "The Jurisdictional Immunity of International Organizations before the Brazilian Supreme Federal Court" (2021) 18:1 Brazilian Journal of International Law 45.

Vaubel, Roland, "Bureaucracy at the IMF and the World Bank: A Comparison of the Evidence" (1996) 19:2 The World Economy 195.

Veyne, Paul, "Naïvetés et noblesse de la trahison" (1985) 81 L'Histoire.

Wilcox, Francis O, "The United Nations in the Mainstream of History" (1956) 50 American Society of International Law Proceedings 187.

Wood, Michael, "Do International Organizations Enjoy Immunity under Customary International Law" (2014) 10:2 International Organizations Law Review 287.

Yi-Chong, Xu and Patrick Weller, "To Be, But Not To Be Seen: Exploring the Impact of International Civil Servants" (2008) 86:1 Public Administration 35.

News Articles

Al Shalchi, Hadeel, "Libya frees detained ICC staff after apology", *Reuters* (2 July 2012).

Applebaum, Anne, "How China Outsmarted the Trump Administration", *The Atlantic* (11 October 2020).

Babcock, Charles R, "FBI Arrests Two Soviets in Spying Case" *The Washington Post* (21 May 1978).

Babcock, Charles R, "Two Russians Are Indicted in Espionage" *The Washington Post* (31 May 1978).

Boone, Jon, "One in five Afghan ballots may be illegal, UN warns" The Guardian (24 August 2009).

Carrington, Damian, "UN environment chief resigns after frequent flying revelations" *The Guardian* (20 November 2018).

Chambers, Madeline, "U.S. spy agency bugged U.N. headquarters: Germany's Spiegel", *Reuters* (25 August 2013).

"Child Refugee Sex Scandal", *BBC News* (29 February 2002).

Corera, Gordon, "Russian GRU spy tried to infiltrate International Criminal Court", *BBC* (16 June 2022).

Emmott, Robin, "Turkey's purged NATO staff not coup plotters: alliance commander", *Reuters* (7 December 2016).

Fahrenthold, David A and Farnaz Fassihi, "A Pot of U.N. Money. Risk-Taking Officials. A Sea of Questions." *New York Times* (7 May 2022).

Fassihi, Farnaz, "Reforms Are Imposed on U.N. Agency That Made Questionable Investments" *New York Times* (10 June 2022).

Feltman, Jeffrey, "Restoring (some) impartiality to UN senior appointments" (2020) *Cairo Rev Glob Aff.*

Fick, Maggie, "U.N. officials recalled from Ethiopia over audio recordings" *The Reuters* (13 October 2021).

Flummerfelt, Robert and Ange Kasongo, "New Sex Abuse Claims Ebola Aid Workers Exposed in Congo", *Thomson Reuters Foundation* (12 May 2021).

Forbes, Mark, "Australia 'party' to bugging of UN", *The Age* (19 June 2004).

"French NATO Aide Jailed for Espionage", The New York Times (3 January 1994).

Gebremeskel, Gebrekirstos, "Ethiopian Regime Rewards Maureen Aching an IGAD Job for her anti-Tigrayan work at UN Ethiopia" *Tghat* (28 November 2022).

Hall, Allan, "German spy caught selling top secret U.S. battle plans while working for NATO is jailed for seven years" *Daily Mail* (20 November 2013).

Harding, Luke, "'Will they forgive me? No': ex-Soviet spy Viktor Suvorov speaks out" *The Guardian* (29 December 2018).

Hauswedell, Charlotte, "unhcr Probing Corruption in Resettlement Cases in Uganda, Kenya", *Info Migrants* (10 January 2020).

Hincks, Joseph, "Here is a Time Line of the Insane Number of People Turkey's President Has Fired Since July 15", *Time* (23 November 2016).

Holt, Kate, "DR Congo's Shameful Sex Secret", *BBC News* (3 June 2004).

"In the UN, China uses threats and cajolery to promote its worldview", *The Economist*, (7 December 2019).

Kersten, Mark, "Tinker, Tailor, Lawyer: ICC Staff Arrested in Libya", *Justice in Conflict* (12 June 2012).

Kingsley, Patrick, "Turkey sacks 15000 education workers in purge after failed coup", *The Guardian* (20 July 2016).

Kotecha, Sima and Sarah Bell, "UN sexual abuse claims 'must be investigated'" *BBC News* (21 June 2022).

Lyall, Sarah, "Aid Workers Are Said to Abuse Girls", *The New York Times* (9 May 2006).

Lynch, Colum, "Aid Donors Blast UNDP for Resisting Appeals to Fight Corruption" *Foreign Policy* (7 December 2020).

Lynch, Colum, "U.S. Once Jailed Uighurs, Now Defends Them at U.N.: China tries to silence the group and lashes out at a U.S. diplomat" *Foreign Policy* (25 May 2018).

Lynch, Colum, "UN Finds Fraud, Mismanagement in Peacekeeping", *The Washington Post* (18 December 2007).

MacAskill, Ewen, "Oil-for-Food Report Condemns Corrupt UN", *The Guardian* (7 September 2005).

Magid, Jacob, "Senior UN official loses her post after tweet condemning PIL rocket fire at Israel", *The Times of Israel* (13 August 2022).

Monaghan, John, "MEPs to probe EU auditors' expenses after media allegations", *Luxembourg Times* (1 December 2021).

Nichols, Michelle, "U.S. expels Russian Spy Working for United Nations – Spokesperson" *Reuters* (1 March 2022).

Parsons, Claudia, "US Urges Probe into UN Peacekeeping Fraud Report", *Reuters* (18 December 2007).

Price, Susannah, "New Sex Misconduct Claims Hit UN", *BBC News* (17 December 2004).

Quatremer, Jean, "Fraudes à la tête de la Cour des comptes européenne", *Libération* (26 November 2021).

Schultz, Teri, "Purged by Turkey, An Ex-NATO Officer Speaks Out about Detention under Erdogan", *NPR* (15 August 2018).

Shalal, Andrea, and David Lawder, "Analysis: World Bank, IMF face long-term damage after data rigging scandal", *Reuters* (4 October 2021).

Sieff, Kevin, "Members of a U.N. peacekeeping force in the Central African Republic allegedly turned to sexual predation, betraying their duty to protect", The *Washington Post* (27 February 2016).

Smith-Meyer, Bjarke, "IMF chief Kristalina Georgieva survives China scandal: What you need to know", *Politico* (12 October 2021).

"Trump envoy blocks ex-Palestinian PM from UN job 'to support Israel'", *The Guardian* (11 February 2017).

"Turkey's failed coup attempt: All you need to know", *Al Jazeera* (15 July 2017).

"UN recalls Ethiopia migration head over Tigray war remarks", *France24* (11 October 2021).
"UNRWA boss resigns amid probe into misconduct claims", *Al Jazeera* (6 November 2019).
Walton, Calder, "Soviet Espionage Under the Cover of Diplomacy" *The Cipher Brief* (16 March 2022).
Whitaker, Brian, "Bugging device found at UN offices", *The Guardian* (18 December 2004).
"Why the Head of IMF Should Resign", *The Economist* (25 September 2021).
Zabatta, Jeremy, "Luxembourg EU Court of Auditors member under scrutiny", *Delano* (9 February 2022).

United Nations Juridical Yearbooks

[1964] "Aide-Mémoire to the Permanent Representatives of various Member States" p. 261.
[1964] "Letter to the Minister of Foreign Affairs and International Cooperation of a Member State" p. 221.
[1968] "Scope and effect of the privileges and immunities required under the 1946 Convention on the privileges and immunities of the United Nations for locally recruited staff" p. 212.
[1972] "Privileges and immunities of locally recruited staff members of the United Nations – Obligation of Member States under Article 105 of the Charter to accord all staff members whether internationally or locally recruited such privileges and immunities as are necessary for the independent exercise of their functions" p. 191.
[1977] "Case brought against an international organization coming under the International Organizations Immunities Act" in Decisions of National Tribunals p. 260.
[1984] "Memorandum to the Legal Adviser, United Nations Relief and Works Agency for Palestine Refugees in the Near East" p. 188.
[1987] "Status of United Nations Correspondence Dispatched in Bags" p. 208.
[1994] "Letter to the Minister of Foreign Affairs and International Cooperation of a Member State" p. 452.
[1995] "Memorandum to the Chief of Protocol, Executive Office of the Secretary-General" p. 403.
[2000] "Illegal seizure of UNICEF property to satisfy court order" p. 346.
[2000] "Meaning of 'officials' of Economic and Social Commission for Western Asia" p. 364.
[2004] "Note verbale to a Permanent Representative of a Member State to the United Nations regarding the freezing of bank accounts of the World Food Programme" p. 326.

[2006] "Interoffice memorandum to the Deputy of the Under-Secretary-General for Safety and Security on the search of United Nations laptop computers by Host Country customs" p. 455.

[2008] "Interoffice memorandum to the Secretary to the Commission and Officer-in-Charge of the General Services Section, Economic Commission for Africa (ECA), regarding new Directive on Value Added Tax in Member State" p. 408.

[2010] "Note Verbale to the Permanent Representative of [State] concerning the privileges and immunities of [a United Nations entity]" p. 501.

[2011] "Note to the Permanent Representative of [State] concerning the non-reimbursement of certain amounts of Value-Added Tax paid by the United Nations Development Programme (UNDP)" p. 487.

[2012] United Nations Office of Legal Affairs, "Note to the Ministry of Foreign Affairs of [State A] concerning a request to [State B] staff members of the United Nations to leave the country or face possible detention" p. 457.

[2013] "Note to the Ministry of Foreign Affairs of [State], concerning privileges and immunities enjoyed by certain categories of United Nations personnel in [State]" p. 371.

[2013] "Note to the Ministry of Foreign Affairs of [State], concerning the privileges and immunities of a [United Nations entity] and its officials from legal process initiated against it by a former service contractor" p. 377.

[2014] "Note to the Ministry of Foreign Affairs of [State] concerning the imposition of certain taxes in respect of fuel purchases on [a United Nations Mission]" p. 329.

[2015] "Note to the Permanent Mission of [State] concerning the privileges and immunities of United Nations officials performing functions in [State] and who are [State] nationals or permanent residents" p. 303.

[2015] "Note to the Ministry of Foreign Affairs of [State] concerning privileges and immunities of United Nations officials to be granted visas, and other travel documents, necessary to enter [State] on official United Nations business" p. 308.

[2015] "Note to [State] concerning the privileges and immunities enjoyed by United Nations officials from [State] taxation on the salaries and emoluments paid by the United Nations to its officials and from mandatory contributions to national social welfare schemes, which is also a form of taxation" p. 299.

[2016] "Note to [State] concerning privileges and immunities of United Nations staff members regarding the recruitment of nationals of [State] by the United Nations, its Funds and Programmes and other subsidiary bodies in [State]" p. 337.

[2016] "Note to [State] concerning privileges and immunities of United Nations staff members regarding a declaration of a United Nations country representative as persona non grata" p. 347.

Index